Colin Taylor, retired associate professor in the Department of Geographical Sciences and Planning at the University of Queensland, is a Fellow of the Chartered Institute of Logistics and Transport and of two professional Planning Institutes. He has held senior positions in town planning and transport in Victoria, Tasmania and Scotland, and writes regularly for the *Railway Gazette International*. He has given conference papers, talks and broadcasts on rail systems and the fascination of rail travel, both in Australia and overseas.

In the last 30 years he has taken around 7000 rail journeys, covering some 652,500km (over 400,000 miles). He is also the author of *Great Rail Non-Journeys of Australia*, *Steel Roads of Australia* and *Traincatcher*.

Australia by Rail
Fifth edition: 2005

Publisher
Trailblazer Publications
The Old Manse, Tower Rd, Hindhead, Surrey, GU26 6SU, UK
Fax (+44) 01428-607571, info@trailblazer-guides.com
www.trailblazer-guides.com

British Library Cataloguing in Publication Data
A catalogue record for this book is available from the British Library

ISBN 1-873756-81-X

Editor: Anna Jacomb-Hood
Series editor: Patricia Major
Layout: Anna Jacomb-Hood
Cartography: Nick Hill
Index: Anna Jacomb-Hood

Printed on chlorine-free paper from farmed forests by
D2Print (☎ +65-6295 5598), Singapore

AUSTRALIA BY RAIL

COLIN TAYLOR

TRAILBLAZER PUBLICATIONS

Acknowledgements

Marvin Saltzman of California, author of the famous Eurail Guide Annual, encouraged the first edition of this book. I am indebted also to Hilary Bradt, publisher of that and two subsequent editions. From the first I have had support and assistance from managements and staff of nearly all rail operators in Australia, and at most levels – from chief executives to passenger attendants, drivers, guards and platform attendants – and from individuals and travellers too numerous to mention even if I remembered all their names.

Special mention must be made of Mike Kent, long-time friend and travel companion now a Queensland engine driver, of Roger Lascelles, Bill Hart, Charlie Mercer, Claudette Duckworth, George Milaras, Keith Taylor, Bob Schroeder, John Morley, Chris Gregg, Roger Stanton, Lachlan Woodrow, Peter King, and also Tony Braxton-Smith, Alice Tolley and Tara Sullivan of GSR, and Allen Hall and John McMillan of the Victorian Dept of Infrastructure. My thanks also to Bryn Thomas for taking on the task of publishing this and the previous edition, and to Anna Jacomb-Hood for her painstaking and meticulous work in editing the text.

Finally, without the patient tolerance of my wife Barbara, the guide could never have been produced in the first place, let alone run to six editions (including one in German).

A request

The author and publisher have tried to ensure that this guide is as accurate and up to date as possible. Nevertheless things change. If you notice any changes or omissions that should be included in the next edition of this book, please write to Colin Taylor at Trailblazer (address on p2) or email him at colin.taylor@trailblazer-guides.com. A free copy of the next edition will be sent to persons making a significant contribution.

Updated information is available on the Internet at
www.trailblazer-guides.com

Front cover: The Ghan © Great Southern Railway

CONTENTS

INTRODUCTION

By the scale of European countries, Australia is vast. Imagine the whole northern half of Africa, a great desert with population centres mostly on the edges. That is something like Australia. And travel in much of Australia is not unlike a journey on the African continent – the same timeless bush, the same enervating heat. In a car the distances and glare of the sky induce drowsiness. The unsealed gravel roads of the outback are like the laterite roads of the African savannah, slippery when wet, loose when dry, ridged like corrugated iron and infested with road trains – thundering great lorries hauling multiple trailers at breakneck speed. These are frightening to meet and more lethal than the snakes and crocodiles you will rarely see. Travelling by road you may reach your destination hot, tired and thirsty, hating both the bush and the concrete jungles of the city. Visitors can find Australia's road rules confusing and the unwary motorist can easily fall foul of the law. If a sign says 'Next Petrol 300km' you can be sure that when you run out of fuel and wander into the bush you will easily get lost.

It is better to see Australia by rail. Australia's railways offer a unique way of travelling round the country. You may not always get there more quickly but you will get there more safely and have time to relax, enjoy the scenery, and converse with Australians and tourists from all over the world, while sitting in comfort without the constraining bonds of a seat belt. Overseas visitors can make use of the excellent-value Austrail Flexipass and other passes and fare concessions offered by the country's railway systems, some of which residents can also benefit from to explore the country.

And Australia is worth exploring because it is a land of contrasts. Not only is there a world of difference between the wheat fields of Victoria and the sugar plantations of Queensland, or the dry red desert of the interior and the torrential downpours of the coastal ranges; there is a great contrast between the fastest and newest trains and some you may find on the lesser-known branch lines.

You can penetrate the remote outback in air-conditioned comfort on trains such as The Ghan or Spirit of the Outback and travel through Crocodile Dundee country on the Gulflander or Savannahlander. The world's fastest rack railway, the Perisher Skitube, will take you to the slopes of Mt Blue Cow in the Snowy Mountains or you can cross the famous Harbour Bridge by train in the heart of Sydney. By train you can also see examples of almost every type of Australian landscape – from the dense rainforests of tropical Queensland to the unbelievable emptiness of the Nullarbor Plain, the deep canyons of the Blue Mountains and the rocky crags of the outback ranges.

Options range from planned itineraries through package tours to doing it your own way. As well as giving essential details about the principal and other popular train services, *Australia by Rail* offers ideas not found in official publications or ordinary travel literature. This should assist both those who stick to the main lines and those who like to wander off the beaten track. And you can!

IMPORTANT NOTES

Train schedules

As with all guide books it is necessary to explain some general principles and issue a few words of caution to the intending traveller. First of all, before commencing any journey, double check the departure and arrival times given in this book or in any timetable, as they are subject to change without prior notice. Changes will usually be minor and have little effect on most of the trips described in this book but Australia is not as well served by rail networks as Europe, for example, and you would not want to miss the only train of the day. Most interstate and long-distance trains run regularly, though not necessarily every day of the week, but other trains may not operate on public holidays such as Christmas Day, Good Friday and Anzac Day (25 April). Train schedules are particularly liable to change at weekends and during holiday periods (see p101), eg the Gulflander and Savannahlander do not usually run between mid-December and early March, whilst additional trains may operate on other routes in December and January. Schedules should also be checked during Australian long weekend holidays, which vary from state to state.

Eastern Summer Time applies between late October and March in Victoria, New South Wales and South Australia. This affects the times of trains to or from the other states, eg interstate trains will arrive in or leave Queensland one hour earlier. Schedules to and from Western Australia are less likely to be altered but arrivals at and departures from Adelaide to and from the west should always be checked. There is a 30-minute time-zone change between the Eastern states and South Australia, and one of 90 minutes out in the Nullarbor. Usually the train conductor will tell you when to alter your watch.

No publication which includes railway (or any other) timetables can hope to remain up to date. Not even those published by the railways themselves! As an official in one major railway booking office said to me 'We'd be the last to know!' There are regular travellers who will swear that railway timetables should properly be classed as works of fiction; that their main use is 'to show how late the train is' is a well-known saying. The fact of life is that trains can be and often need to be rescheduled for all sorts of reasons which might or might not be understood if explained at the time to the unfortunate travellers. This is not peculiar to the railways of Australia; it is a worldwide phenomenon.

Most Australian rail services as well as bus and ferry schedules are summarized in the Thomas Cook *Overseas Timetable*; this is published bi-monthly. Timetables given in this book are extracts only and do not show complete schedules on most lines. In particular, the times given for any round trips may not reflect all the departure times from either the base city or the destination city. On a particular route there may be later departure times from the base city and earlier departure times from the destination city than are shown, none of which would be applicable to a one-day round trip, but which might be useful if an overnight stay were contemplated. Where it is stated that services are frequent, this usually means at least once an hour during normal daylight hours or between the time limits indicated.

Up-to-date information on changes and local timetables can usually be obtained free of charge at major railway stations and rail travel centres. A small charge may sometimes be made. Timetable information is increasingly becoming available on the Internet (see p24) but it is best to double check.

Timetables

All departure, arrival or other times in this book are based on the 24-hour clock. A departure at 1.10pm is shown as 13.10; midnight is 00.00. Time between midnight and 1am is shown as 00.01 to 00.59. This corresponds to the practice used in most railway timetables (eg in Europe) and in the timetables published by Thomas Cook, though some railways in Australia tend to use 'am' and 'pm'.

The numbers appearing at the start of each timetable (other than itineraries) are the relevant Thomas Cook numbers (*Overseas Timetable*) and are prefixed by a 'C'. This enables the traveller to make a preliminary check before making a booking. It does not obviate the need for a final check before actually going to the station. Where Cook's tables do not cover all the places or trains referred to, the word 'local' is used instead of, or additional to, table numbers. There are also some references to Cook's tables in the text using the same format.

Where arrival or departure times vary on some days by less than five minutes from the normal, the differences are not always shown in the tables so as to save space and simplify the presentation. In such cases the departure times given will always be the earliest, so that you do not miss your train.

Bus and coach services

Details of bus and coach services are given only where they connect otherwise isolated railheads or provide the only service to destinations of interest which are within reasonable distance of a railway. The Thomas Cook timetable gives details of bus and ferry services.

General

This book does not attempt to be a comprehensive guide to Australia. This would merely duplicate information available in more general guides, such as the Lonely Planet series. Lonely Planet's *Australia* is an extremely comprehensive volume and well worth the price. Another good buy is Thomas Cook's *Australia* in the Independent Traveller's series.

This book, however, provides enough information to keep the average visitor from going wrong, as well as offering a few tips on where to stay or eat. These are restricted to such establishments as are handy to railway stations or which have been personally sampled by the writer or recommended by others. This is no guarantee that things will not have changed or that other establishments might not better suit the traveller.

Fares

Fares quoted in this guide are correct to the time of going to press. Rail Australia warns that 'all fares as well as timetables are subject to alteration without notice'. This is, of course, also true for all other prices in this book.

PART 1: PLANNING YOUR TRIP

Getting to Australia

It is assumed you will be coming to Australia the most likely way: by air. Flights may be booked direct with the airline, on the Internet, or through a travel agent – the latter two are usually able to offer the best discounted fares.

Special package deals and inclusive tours abound and prices vary according to season, route taken and demand. Travellers should beware of bogus tour operators: stick to known firms with a sound reputation or ones recommended by other travellers, and **always** take out travel insurance.

It is often possible to arrange to fly into Australia at one place and leave from another: this is called an open-jaw ticket. This extends the range of options for working out a rail itinerary within Australia. Travellers from Western Europe have another option in that air fares via Asia and ones via America are not greatly different so that round-the-world fares or packages are available often at little more than the price of an ordinary return. From some countries, especially Britain, there are as many ways of flying to Australia as there are of skinning the proverbial cat. Often an indirect and seemingly expensive route can prove the best bargain.

MAKING A BOOKING IN THE UK AND IRELAND

From London, flights to Australia are offered by many airlines, for example: Air New Zealand via Los Angeles (LA) and Auckland; Cathay Pacific via Hong Kong; Emirates via Dubai and Singapore; Japan Air Lines via Tokyo or Osaka; Korean Air Lines via Seoul; Malaysia Airlines via Kuala Lumpur; Royal Brunei via Dubai or Abu Dhabi and Bandar Seri Begawan; Singapore Airlines; Thai via Bangkok; and United via LA or San Francisco, apart from the direct flights by the obvious airlines of Qantas and British Airways. Virgin, already well established within Australia, has also entered the London–Sydney market; the service goes daily via Hong Kong.

• **Austravel** (🖳 www.austravel.com) has several branches in the UK including: **London** (☎ 0870-166 2120, 🖳 westend@austravel.com, 61 Conduit St, London W1); **Bristol** (☎ 0870-166 2110; 🖳 bristol@austravel.com), **Edinburgh** (☎ 0870-166 2190, 🖳 edinburgh@austravel.com), **Leeds** (☎ 0870-166 2180, 🖳 leeds@austravel.com) and **Manchester** (☎ 0870-166 2170, 🖳 man chester@austravel.com). They can book flights, tours and accommodation.

• **Bridge the World** (☎ 0870-814 4400, 🖳 www.bridgetheworld.com), 45-7 Chalk Farm Rd, Camden Town, London NW1 8AJ, offers flights including round-the-world fares, a visa/ETA service and can arrange tailor-made packages on the main rail services.

• **Flight Centre** (☎ 0870-499 0040; 🖳 www.flightcentre.co.uk), a Queensland-based firm, has offices in and around London as well as in several other towns and cities; see their website for a full list. Staff can book flights, hotels, car hire and rail travel and arrange visas/ETAs.
• **Great Rail Journeys Ltd** (☎ 01904-521900, 🖳 www.greatrail.com), Saviour House, 9 St Saviourgate, York YO1 8NL. This excellent rail-holiday specialist will be offering tours on The Ghan from 2006.
• **Kuoni Travel** (☎ 01306-741111, 🖳 www.kuoni.co.uk), Kuoni House, Dorking, Surrey RH5 4AZ, offers packages on Great Southern trains.
• **Qantas Holidays** (☎ 020-8222 9125, 🖳 www.qantashols.co.uk), Sovereign House, 361 King St, Hammersmith, London W6 9NA. Books flights, accommodation etc and has tours on Great Southern and Queensland Rail trains. Visas/ETAs are arranged free of charge for people booking tours.
• **Rail Choice** (☎ 0870-165 7300, 🖳 www.railchoice.co.uk), 15 Colman House, Empire Square, High St, London SE20, can book rail passes and arrange a visa/ETA over the phone or online but they do not book flights.
• **STA Travel** (national telesales ☎ 0870-160 6070, 🖳 www.statravel.co.uk) has branches throughout Britain (check their website for the full list). They also have regional telesales numbers for: **Bristol** (☎ 0870-167 6777), **Cambridge** (☎ 01223-366966), **Edinburgh** (☎ 0131-226 7747), **Leeds** (☎ 0870-168 6878), **Manchester** (☎ 0161-834 0668) and **Oxford** (☎ 0870-163 6373). STA specializes in travel arrangements for student and independent travellers.
• **Trailfinders** (🖳 www.trailfinders.com) has branches in **London** at 194/215 Kensington High St, W8 (☎ 020-7938 3939), Waterstone's Piccadilly (☎ 020-7292 1888) and 1 Threadneedle St, EC2R (☎ 020-7628 7628). Other branches are in: **Birmingham** (☎ 0121-236 1234, 22-24 The Priory, Queensway, B4); **Bristol** (☎ 0117-929 9000, 48 Corn St, BS1); **Cambridge** (☎ 01223-461600, Waterstone's, 22 Sidney St, CB2); **Glasgow** (☎ 0141-353 2224, 254-84 Sauchiehall St, G2); **Leeds** (☎ 0113-246 2200, 77 Vicar Lane, LS1); **Manchester** (☎ 0161-839 6969, 58 Deansgate, M3); **Newcastle-upon-Tyne** (☎ 0191-261 2345, 7-9 Ridley Place, NE1); Oxford (☎ 01865-261000, 105-6 St Aldate's, OX1). Trailfinders offers flights including round-the-world fares, accommodation and a visa/ETA (☎ 0845-050 5905) service.

Rail Australia agent

• **International Rail** (☎ 0870-751 5000, 🖳 www.internationalrail.com), Chase House, Gilbert St, Ropley, Hants, SO24) can issue all the rail passes and also book Trainways, Traveltrain and Countrylink packages.

From Northern Ireland/Republic of Ireland

• **Australia Travel Centre** (☎ 01-804 7188, 🖳 australia@abbeytravel.ie), 43 Middle Abbey St, Dublin 1. Books flights and arranges ETAs.
• **Trailfinders** (🖳 www.trailfinders.com) has branches in **Dublin** (☎ 01-677 7888, 4/5 Dawson St, Dublin 2) and in **Belfast** (☎ 028-9027 1888, 47-9 Fountain St, BT1. For details of services see Trailfinders above.
• **Usit** (🖳 www.usit.ie) has several branches including: **Dublin** (☎ 01-602

1600, 19-21 Aston Quay, O'Connell Bridge, Dublin 2), **Cork** (☎ 021-427 0900, 66 Oliver Plunkett St); **Galway** (☎ 091-565 177, 16 Mary St); **Limerick** (☎ 061-415064, Central Buildings, O'Connell St), and also a few in Northern Ireland (💻 www.usitnow.com) including **Belfast** (☎ 90-327111, Fountain Centre, College St, BT1). Books flights and arranges visas/ETAs.

MAKING A BOOKING IN CONTINENTAL EUROPE

From Austria See Germany, below.

From Belgium

See The Netherlands, below.

- **Boundless Adventures** (☎ 02-426 40 30, 💻 boundless.adventures @joker.be), ave Verdilaan 23/15, 1083 Ganshoren, Brussels; can book flights.

From Denmark

- **My Planet** (💻 www.myplanet.com) has branches in **Copenhagen** (☎ 3355 7511, 💻 cph@myplanet.com, Frederiksberg Alle 18-20, 1820 Frederiksberg C) and **Holstebro** (☎ 9742 5011, 💻 hol@myplanet.com), Nørregade 51). Books flights and is a Rail Australia agent.

From Finland

- **AKTIV Resor** (☎ 09-602 900, 💻 www.aktiv-resor.fi), Lonnrotinkatu 35, 00180 Helsinki. Specializes in travel to Australia.

From France

- **Australie Tours** (☎ 01 53 70 23 45, 💻 infos@australietour.com), 129 rue Lauriston, Paris 75116. Rail Australia agent.

From Germany

- **hm-touristik Grafrath** (☎ 08144 7700, 💻 rail@hm-touristik.com), Hauptstrasse 61, Grafrath, Munich 82284. Rail Australia agent – also for Austria and Italy. See also The Netherlands below.

From Italy See Germany above.

From the Netherlands

- **Incento BV** (☎ 035-695 5111, 💻 www.incento.nl), Stationsweg 40, 1404 Ap Bussum (PO Box 1067, 1400 BB Bussum). Rail Australia agent – also for Belgium and Germany.

From Norway

- **My Planet** (☎ 023-326630, 💻 osl@myplanet.com, www.myplanet.com), Wergelandsveien 7, Postboks 7144, Majorstua 0307, Oslo. Rail Australia agent.

From Sweden

- **My Planet** (💻 www.myplanet.com) has branches in **Göteburg** (☎ 031-774 0075, 💻 got@myplanet.com, Kastellgatan 17, S-402-33) and **Stockholm** (☎ 08-442 9880, 💻 sto@myplanet.com, Roslagsgatan 35-37, S-113 54). Books flights and is a Rail Australia agent.

From Switzerland

• **Nova Tours** (🖳 www.novatours.ch) has branches in **Aarau** (☎ 62-823 3323 🖳 info@novatours.ch, Schoenenwerdenstr.35b, Ch-5001) and **Lausanne** (☎ 21-311 5040, 🖳 lausanne@novatours.ch, Rue de Valentin 34, CP 656, Ch-1004. Rail Australia agent.

MAKING A BOOKING IN NORTH AMERICA

From the USA

• **ATS Tours** (☎ 310-643-0044 ext 426, tollfree ☎ 800-423-2880, 🖳 info@ats-tours.com), Suite 325, 2381 Rosecrans Ave, El Segundo, California 90245. Rail Australia agent and arranges all aspects of travel to Australia.
• **Flight Centre** (☎ 1-866-WORLD-51, 🖳 www.flightcentre.us) has branches throughout the States (see the website for the one nearest to you) and can book flights and accommodation.
• **Goway Travel** (☎ 800-387-8850, 🖳 www.goway.com), 8651 Lincoln Blvd, Los Angeles, CA 90045. See Goway, Canada below.
• **Society of International Railway Travelers** (☎ 502-454-0277 or 800-IRT-4881, 🖳 www.irtsociety.com), 1810 Sils Ave 306B, Louisville, Kentucky 40205, runs occasional rail-based tours to Australia.
• **STA** (national telesales ☎ 1-800-781-4040, 🖳 www.statravel.com) has branches in most states – for details of branch locations call the telesales number or check their website. STA books discount flights and accommodation and arranges visas/ETAs for students and young people.

From Canada

• **Flight Centre** (☎ 1-888-96753-55, 🖳 www.flightcentre.ca) can book flights and accommodation and has branches in most cities; see their website for the most convenient branch.
• **Goway Travel** (🖳 www.goway.com) has branches in **Toronto** (☎ 416-322-1034; Suite 300, Airport Sq, 3284 Yonge St, M4N 3M7) and in **Vancouver** (☎ 604-264-8088; Suite 1050, 1200 West 73rd Avenue, BC V6P 6G5. Rail Australia agent and arranges all aspects of travel to Australia as well as fully-escorted tours.

MAKING A BOOKING IN AUSTRALASIA

From Australia

See pp22-3.

From New Zealand

• **Flight Centre** (☎ 0800-243544; 🖳 www.flightcentre.nz) can book flights as well as hotels, and has offices throughout New Zealand; check their website for the complete list.
• **Tranz Scenic** (☎ 03-339 3809 🖳 oz.rail@tranzscenic.co.nz), Troup Drive, Addington Station, Christchurch. Rail Australia agent.

• **Rail Plus Australasia** (☎ 09 375 9023 inside Auckland area, ☎ 0800-801 060 outside Auckland, 💻 info@ozrail.co.nz, 💻 www.railplus.co.nz), Level 1, 149-155 Parnell Rd, Parnell, Auckland, is a Rail Australia agent and operates a variety of rail tours.

MAKING A BOOKING IN SOUTH AFRICA

• **Flight Centre** (☎ 0860 400 727; 💻 www.flightcentre.za) has offices throughout South Africa (check their website for the full list) and can book flights and accommodation, and arrange visas.
• **Holiday Tours/Go Australia** (💻 www.go-australia.co.za) has branches in **Cape Town** (☎ 21-419 9382, 💻 capetown@holidayholdings.co.za), 3rd Fl Sanclare Bldg, Dreyer St, Claremont 7708), **Durban** (☎ 31-201 6061, 💻 durban@holidayholdings.co.za), Suite 810 Musgrave Centre, 901 Musgrave Rd Durban 4062, and **Johannesburg** (☎ 011-289 8160, 💻 info@holidaytours.co.za, Holiday House, 158-160 Hendrik Verwoerd Drive, Randburg 2125 (PO Box 2140). Rail Australia agent and can book flights, accommodation etc.

MAKING A BOOKING IN ASIA

From Japan

• **Japan Travel Bureau** (JTB; ☎ 03-3818 5671, 💻 www.jtb.co.jp), Hakusan NT Bldg, 4th Floor, 1-33-18, Bunkyo-ku, Tokyo 113-0001. Rail Australia agent and books flights, accommodation etc.
• **Travel Plaza International** (☎ 03-3820 8011, 💻 tpifit-rail@msd.biglobe.ne.jp), NV Tomioka Bldg 6F, 2-1-9 Tomioka, Koto-ku, **Tokyo** 135-8531; and Jutakukinyukoko-Sumitomoseimei Bldg, 4-5-20 Minamihonmachi, Chuo-ku, **Osaka** 541-0054 (☎ 06-6251 6804). Rail Australia agent and books flights.

From Hong Kong

• **Westminster Travel** (☎ 2369 5051, 💻 www.westminstertravel.com), 22nd Fl, One Peking Rd, Tsimshatsui, Kowloon. Rail Australia agent; books flights/tours.

From Korea

• **Seoul Travel** (☎ 2-755 1144, 💻 www.seoultravel.co.kr), 5th Fl, Jaenung Bldg, 1-KA Ulchi-Ro, 192-11 Chung-ku, Seoul. Rail Australia agent, books flights.

Before you leave

WHEN TO GO

Choose to come whatever time of year suits you! Compared with much of Europe and North America, Australia is warm.

In spring and autumn (seasons which are not as clearly distinguished as in much of Europe and North America), the climate is equable and there are no special problems of transport, holidays, or anything else to cause unusual difficulties for the visitor. But if you are from a really cold climate, you will find Australian summers (November to March) rather hot, especially in the north. Conversely if used to warmer climes you may find Tasmania and the south of Victoria rather cool in the winter (June to August).

PASSPORTS AND VISAS

All visitors need a passport which should be valid for at least the proposed period of stay but preferably longer in case of any emergencies.

Visitors from everywhere except New Zealand also need a visa/Electronic Travel Authority (ETA). A Tourist ETA is valid for 12 months (as long as your passport is valid for that period of time) and permits multiple entry with stays of up to three months at a time. Tourists with ETA-eligible passports (including citizens from the UK, most European countries, Japan, Canada and the USA) will be granted an ETA instantly on application via the internet (💻 www.eta.immi.gov.au), most airlines, travel agents or tour operators. The ETA itself is free but in most cases a service charge is made (A$20 or UK£17), even if applying online. A business ETA is also available.

Working holiday visas can be obtained by people aged between 18 and 30 years old from the UK, and several other countries, who hold a valid passport. Applications must be made in your home country and a charge is made.

ALICE SPRINGS

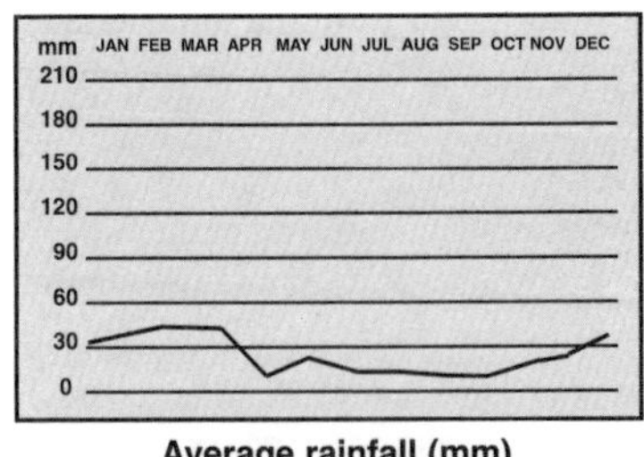

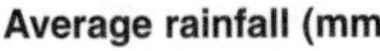
Average rainfall (mm)

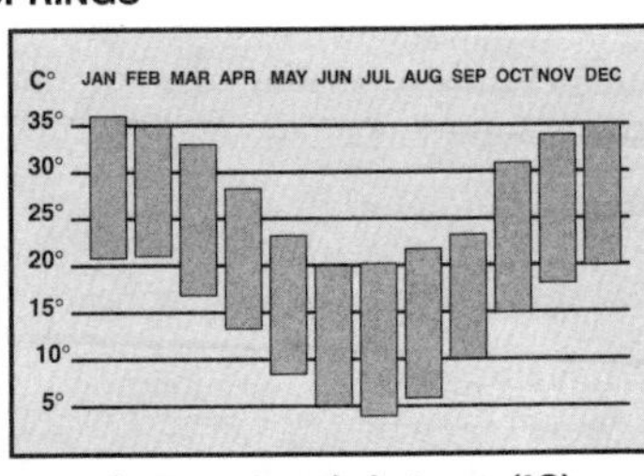

Average max/min temp (°C)

BRISBANE

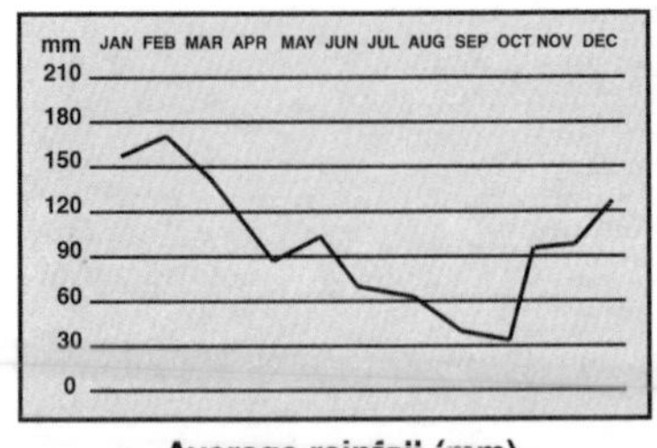

Average rainfall (mm)

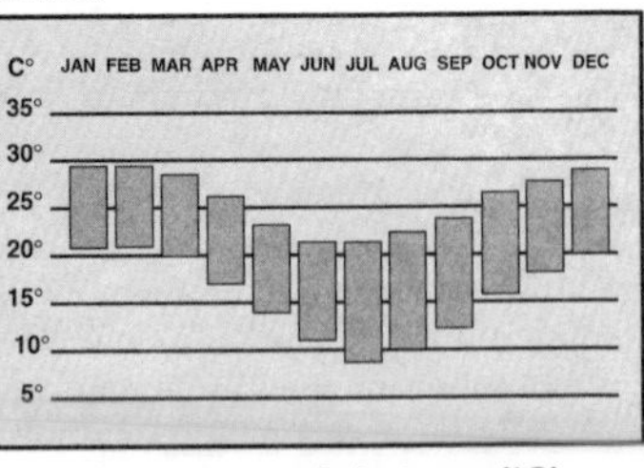

Average max/min temp (°C)

DARWIN

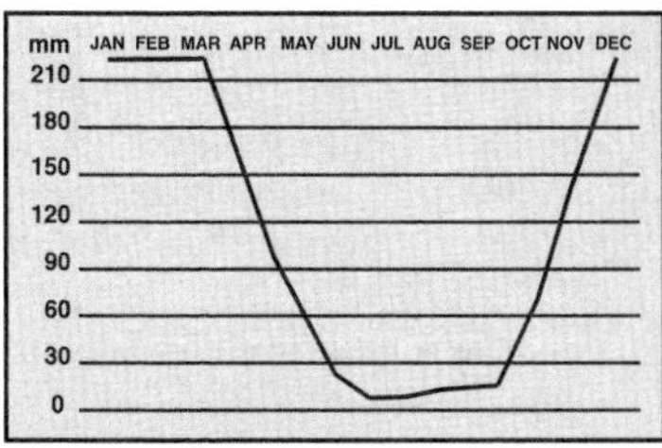

Average rainfall (mm)

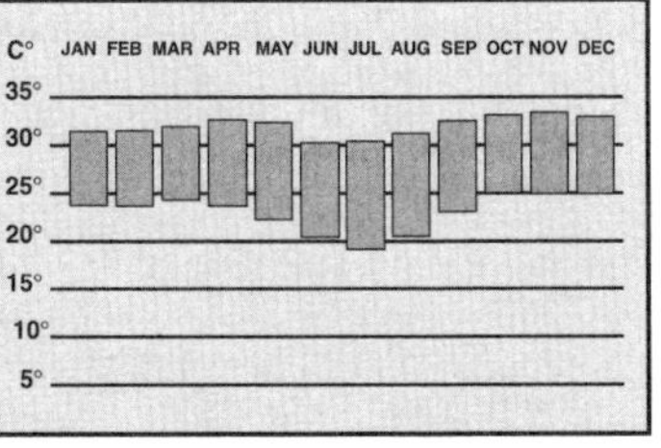

Average max/min temp (°C)

MELBOURNE

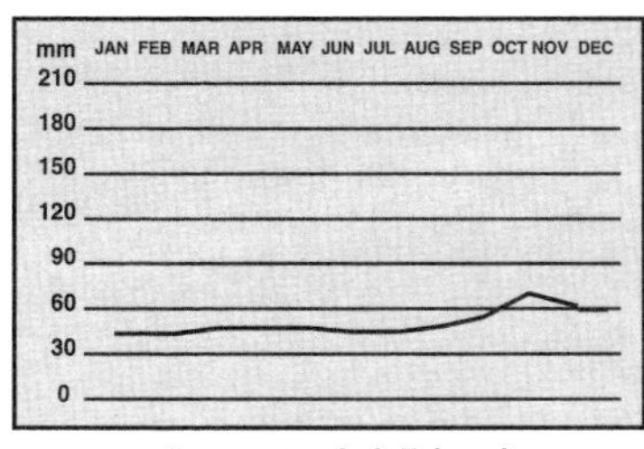

Average rainfall (mm)

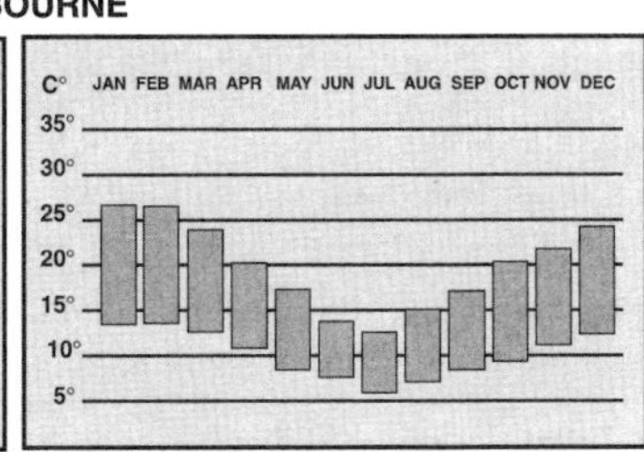

Average max/min temp (°C)

PERTH

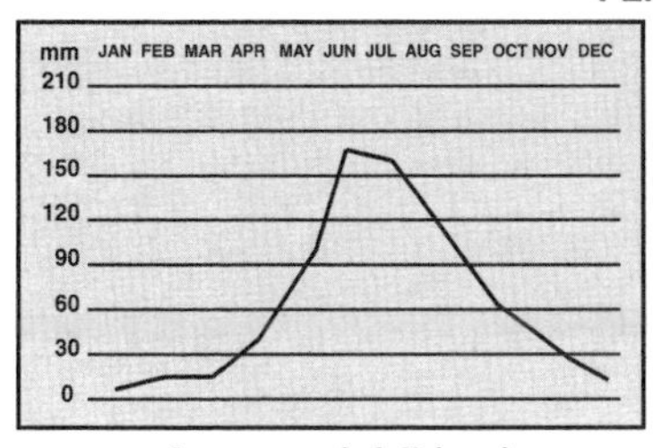

Average rainfall (mm)

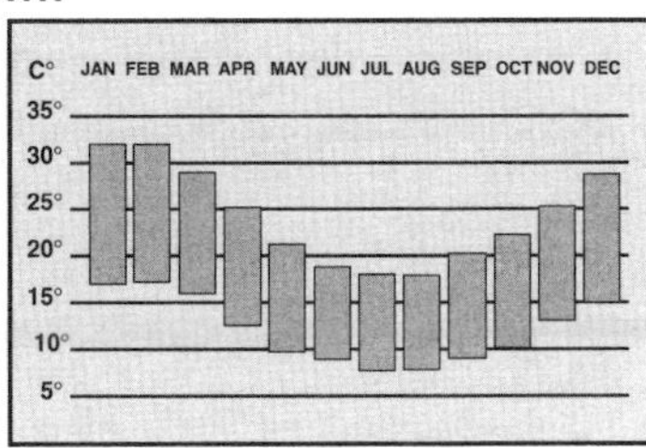

Average max/min temp (°C)

SYDNEY

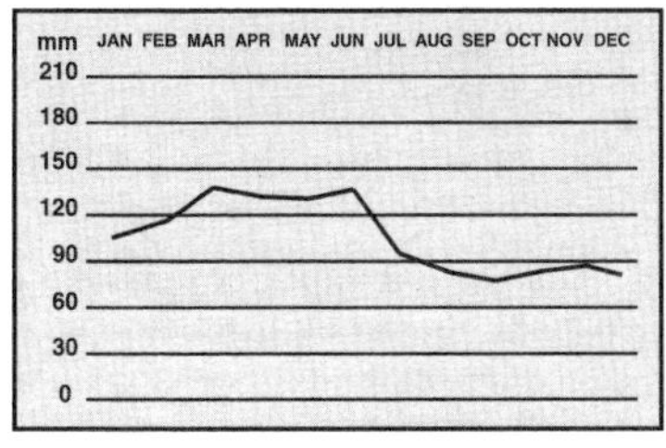

Average rainfall (mm)

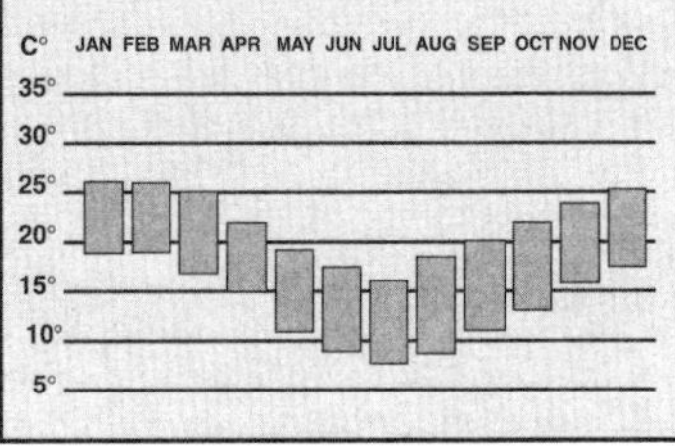

Average max/min temp (°C)

EMBASSIES AND CONSULATES

Details of some of Australia's embassies and consulates around the world are given below. For a full list visit 💻 www.dfat.gov.au/missions.

Belgium
Australian Embassy, Guimard Centre, rue Guimard 6-8, 1040 Brussels
☎ 02-286 0500, 💻 www.austemb.be

Canada
Australian High Commission
Suite 710, 50 O'Connor St
Ottawa, Ontario K1P 6L2
☎ 613-236-0841, 💻 www.ahc-ottawa.org
(Consulate offices: Toronto ☎ 416-323-1155; Vancouver ☎ 604-684-1177)

China – Hong Kong
Australian Consulate-General
23/F Harbour Centre,
25 Harbour Rd, Wanchai
☎ 2827 8881, 💻 www.australia.org.hk

France
Australian Embassy
4 rue Jean Rey, 75724 Paris, Cedex 15
☎ 01 40 59 33 00, 💻 www.austgov.fr

Germany
Australian Embassy
Wallstrasse 76-9, 10179 Berlin
☎ 30-8800 880, (Consulate office: Frankfurt/Main ☎ 69-905580)
💻 www.australianembassy.de

Ireland
Australian Embassy, 7th Floor, Fitzwilton House, Wilton Terrace, Dublin 2
☎ 01-664 5300, 📠 01-678 5185
💻 www.australianembassy.ie

Italy
Australian Embassy
Via Alessandria 215, Rome 00198
☎ 06-852721, 💻 www.italy.embassy.gov.au
(Consulate office in Milan ☎ 02-777041)

Japan
Australian Embassy
2-1-14 Mita, Minato-ku, Tokyo 108-8361
☎ 03-5232 4111, 📠 03-5232 4149

(Japan cont'd)
💻 www.australia.or.jp
(Consulate offices in Osaka, Nagoya, Sapporo, Sendai and Fukuoka)

The Netherlands
Australian Embassy
Carnegielaan 4, 2517 KH The Hague
☎ 070-310 8200, 📠 070-365 2350
💻 www.australian-embassy.nl

New Zealand
Australian High Commission
72-8 Hobson St, Thorndon, Wellington
☎ 04-473 6411, 📠 04-498 7103
💻 www.australia.org.nz
(Consulate office in Auckland ☎ 09-921 8800)

South Africa
Australian High Commission
292 Orient St (corner of Schoeman St), Arcadia, Pretoria 0083
☎ 12-342 3781, 💻 www.australia.co.za
(Consulate office in Durban ☎ 031-208 4163 and Johannesburg ☎ 011-784 0620)

UK
Australian High Commission
Australia House, The Strand
London WC2B 4LA
☎ 0891-600 0333, info 10am-12 noon only
☎ 020-7379 4334, 💻 www.australia.org.uk
(Consulate offices: Manchester ☎ 0161-237 9440, Edinburgh ☎ 0131-624 3333)

USA
Australian Embassy
1601 Massachusetts Ave NW
Washington DC 20036-2273
☎ 202-797-3000, 💻 www.austemb.org
(Consulate offices in Atlanta, Chicago, Denver, Detroit, Houston, Honolulu, Los Angeles, Miami, New York and San Francisco)

For further details about all kinds of visas and ETAs contact the Australian embassy, high commission or consular office (see the list opposite) in your country or check 🖳 www.immi.gov.au. Alternatively ask your travel agent, tour operator or airline, though agents may charge a fee for the service.

WHAT TO BRING

For summer wear, open-neck shirts and shorts are comfortable and acceptable for all but formal occasions. In winter, overcoats, scarves or gloves are rarely seen but in all seasons a light mackintosh or folding umbrella is useful. Also you should always bring or obtain a hat as the Australian sun is strong: our skies are blue and skin cancer, not to mention sunburn, is something to be reckoned with. Ensure you have a tube of high-factor sun-blocking cream, particularly if you come in the summer months. A roll-on stick or small spray can of 'Rid', or similar insect repellent, is useful especially if getting off the train and staying in bush country. For anyone planning to travel overnight sitting up in a train, or for any long journey, it is wise to bring or acquire on arrival an inflatable neck pillow.

HEALTH

No special requirements for health apply. Injections and vaccinations are not required. Tap water is universally drinkable, usually even on the trains.

MONEY (see also p100)

Money can be carried as travellers' cheques but credit cards are acceptable nearly everywhere. Also, most banks have an ATM with 24-hr access.

Banknotes should be changed into Australian dollars as other currencies are acceptable only in banks, currency exchange agencies or the most expensive hotels.

TOURIST INFORMATION

Offices of the Australian Tourist Commission (🖳 www.atc.australia.com, see box p20) have a variety of brochures which provide general information, such as where to stay and what to see. Alternatively see 🖳 www.tourism.australia.com.

The respective states also have websites (see box p20) and some have tourism offices; check the websites for details. Australian Tourist Commission offices should also be able to provide contact details for these.

❑ Telephone and fax numbers

Within Australia, telephone and fax numbers begin with a zero, eg 02-1111 1111. When dialling from overseas, the zero must be replaced by the country code (61). This does not apply to numbers beginning 1800 or 13; the former are freecall numbers within Australia only and the latter are calls charged at local rates. Neither can be dialled from outside Australia.

AUSTRALIAN TOURIST COMMISSION OFFICES

Australia
Head Office, Level 4, 80 William St, Wooloomooloo, NSW 2011
☎ 02-9360 1111, 🖷 02-9361 1388
💻 www.atc.australia.com

China: Hong Kong
Suite 6706, 67th Floor Central Plaza, 18 Harbour Rd, Wanchai
☎ 2802 7700, 🖷 2802 8211

China: Shanghai
Level 21, HSBC Tower, 101 Yin Cheng East Rd, Pu Dong, Shanghai 200120
☎ 21-6307 7055, 🖷 21-6307 0069

Germany
Neue Mainzer Strasse 22, D 60311 Frankfurt/Main
☎ 069-2740 0622, 🖷 069-2740 0640

Japan
Australian Business Centre, 28th Fl, New Otani Garden Court Bldg, 4-1 Kioi-cho, Chiyoda-ku, Tokyo 102-0094
☎ 03-5214 0720, 🖷 03-5214 0719

Korea
20th Floor, Youngpoong Bldg, 33 Seorin-dong, Chongro-ku, Seoul 110-752
☎ 02-399 6500, 🖷 02-399 6507

Malaysia
Suite 12-1 Faber Imperial Court, Jalan Sultan Ismail 50250, Kuala Lumpur
☎ 03-2611 1148, 🖷 03-2070 4302

New Zealand
Level 3, 125 The Strand, Parnell, Auckland 1
☎ 09-915 2826, 🖷 09-307 3117

Singapore
101 Thomson Rd, United Square 08-03, Singapore 307591
☎ 6255 4555, 🖷 6253 8431

Taiwan
Suite 2208, Level 22, 333 Keelung Rd, Sec 1 Taipei
☎ 02-2757 7188, 🖷 02-2757 6483

Thailand
Unit 1614 16th Floor, River Wing East, Empire Tower
195 South Sathorn Rd, Yannawa, Sathorn, Bangkok 10120
☎ 02-670 0640, 🖷 02-670 0645

UK
Gemini House, 10-18 Putney Hill, London SW15 6AA
☎ 020-8780 2229 🖷 020-8780 1496
☎ 0906-863 3235 (for brochures)

USA
2049 Century Park East, Suite 1920, Los Angeles, CA 90067
☎ 310-229-4870, 🖷 310-552-1215

❑ Useful state websites

Tourism New South Wales	www.tourism.nsw.gov.au
Tourism Victoria	www.tourism.vic.gov.au
Tourism Queensland	www.queenslandholidays.co.uk
South Australian Tourist Commission	www.southaustralia.com
Western Australian Tourism Commission	www.westernaustralia.net
Tourism Tasmania	www.discovertasmania.com.au
Tourism Canberra	www.visitcanberra.com.au
Northern Territory Tourist Commission	www.ntholidays.com

Rail travel in Australia

OBTAINING INFORMATION

Before you arrive

Rail Australia, based in Adelaide, co-ordinates marketing the principal Australian interstate, New South Wales (NSW) and Queensland Rail services overseas; there are sales agents in Canada, China (Hong Kong), Denmark, France, Germany (also for Austria and Italy), Japan, Korea, the Netherlands (also for Belgium and Germany), New Zealand, Norway, South Africa, Sweden, Switzerland, the UK and the USA. Your travel agent should be able to obtain information from these agents or you can contact them direct; see pp11-15 in the Making a booking section.

A privately-published book *Train Times: Passenger Trains of Australia and New Zealand* gives details of all Australian train services, including suburban lines. It can be obtained at the Railfan Shop in Melbourne, and at the ARHS Shop in Sydney, for around $12, or direct from the publisher, Victor Isaacs (🖳 abvi@webone.com.au), at 43 Lowanna St, Braddon ACT 2612.

The Australian section of the Thomas Cook Overseas Timetable, obtainable from bookshops around the world or through the Internet (see below), provides the next closest thing to an up-to-date Australia-wide rail timetable. It also includes bus and local shipping services and is revised bi-monthly. Thomas Cook also publishes an Independent Travellers' guide, *Australia*, obtainable in the UK from bookshops, Thomas Cook shops or direct from Thomas Cook Publishing (🖳 www.thomascookpublishing.com), PO Box 227, Peterborough PE3 6PU.

In Australia

Few travel agencies in Australia have much information on rail travel and many are unenthusiastic about finding it for you unless a rail trip is part of a package tour they are promoting. State tourist offices sometimes have branches in the capital cities of the other states; these are useful places to obtain general information, particularly about accommodation and tours, but not details about rail services or fares as such.

The state rail authorities and the privately-owned railways publish their own timetables, usually in the form of individual leaflets or booklets covering particular regions; these are mostly free of charge. Suburban timetables are published separately, and leaflets or booklets for particular lines can be obtained at most railway stations on those routes. Queensland Rail (QR) publishes regularly-updated individual timetable and fare sheets for all interstate and other major long-distance services, as well as for their own trains. A composite Traveltrain services sheet gives summary timetables for Queensland coastal and major inland services showing connections. Copies of these publications can be obtained only at QR travel centres (see p23).

Residents of Australia should have little difficulty starting out on a tour by rail, since they will know, or can easily find out, where the railway station is and can telephone for information and to make bookings, provided, that is, they can get through in the first place.

Railway enquiry numbers, like so many other telephone enquiry services, tend increasingly to be engaged and to put the caller in a holding queue listening to music or advertising blurb until, frustrated, they give up. This is all part of the general trend to economize by cutting staff numbers which is endemic to societies that have allowed so-called economic rationalism to take the place of commonsense and until people rise up and complain forcefully about it, it is something we all just have to put up with. If at first you cannot get through, just try again.

Within Queensland and New South Wales, for rail bookings only, the telephone number ☎ 132 232 should put you through to the nearest rail travel centre for QR and NSW Railcorp services.

RAIL TRAVEL CENTRES AND BOOKING OFFICES

Each Australian mainland state capital has an information and reservation office at its main railway terminal. There are also rail travel centres in central city locations and at some suburban, metropolitan or provincial stations but they are mostly open only during normal weekday business hours (9am-5pm). These offices can book hotels, tours etc, as well of course as rail travel. The list which follows should cover most needs:

Australian Capital Territory

• **Countrylink Travel and Booking Centre** (☎ 02-6239 7039, ☎ 132 232), Railway Station, Wentworth Avenue, Kingston, and at Jolimont Centre (☎ 02-6257 1576), 65-7 Northbourne Avenue.

New South Wales

• **Countrylink Rail Travel Centre** (☎ 02-9379 3800), Platform 1, Sydney Central Station, Railway Square, Sydney 2000, and at the underground stations

Timetable warning

Railway timetables have long confused many people. Australia has a wonderful variety for the timetable collector, full of information of fascination to historians, geographers and students of language, law, or philosophy, but not necessarily giving easy, ready to read information about what people want to know – how to get from A to B.

Even knowing when the train may leave or reach your destination can also be a problem. Different systems have been known to quote different times for the same interstate train and even publish the different times in their timetables. Often the information is out of date or wrong. The computerized train information and booking systems of the different systems are largely incompatible, just like the track in days gone by.

In short, check carefully.

for Town Hall on George St, and Wynyard on York St. Also at major metropolitan and regional railway stations throughout New South Wales.

• **Great Southern Railway** (GSR) bookings can be made at Trainways' Booking Office, Shop 2, Eddy Avenue, Sydney Central station.

Northern Territory

• **Travelworld Centre** (☎ 132 147), Railway Station (off George Crescent), Alice Springs. (At the time of writing there was no booking office in Darwin.)

Queensland

• **Brisbane Travel Centre** (☎ 1800 627 655 or ☎ 07-3235 1323), 305 Edward St (at Central Station), GPO Box 1429, Brisbane.
• **Roma St Travel Centre** (☎ 07-3235 1331), Brisbane Transit Centre, Roma St.
• **Robina Travel Centre** (☎ 07-5562 0539) Gold Coast.
• **Cairns Railway Station** (☎ 07-4036 9249 or 1800 630 324), Bunda St.
• **Townsville** (☎ 07-4772 8358) at the old Railway Station on Flinders St.
• **Rockhampton Railway Station** (☎ 07-4932 0453).

South Australia

• **Great Southern Railway** (☎ 132 147 within Australia or ☎ 08-8213 4592), Keswick Rail passenger terminal, Richmond Rd, Keswick, or PO Box 445, Marleston Business Centre, SA 5033 (✉ salesagent@gsr.com.au).

Tasmania

• **Tasmanian Travel Centre** (☎ 03-6232 0211), 80 Elizabeth St, Hobart, Tas 7000. There are no mainline railways in Tasmania but bookings through Rail Australia can be made on ☎ 132 147.

Victoria

• **V/Line Information** (☎ 136 196), Spencer St station, or by post to National Express Group Australia (V/Line Passenger Pty Ltd), GPO Box 5343, Melbourne, Vic 3001.
• **Countrylink** (Melbourne–Sydney) (☎ 132 232).
• **Great Southern Railway** (bookings ☎ 132 147), GSR Booking Office, Spencer St station.

Western Australia

The main bus/rail terminal is at the Public Transport Authority Building, East Perth.
• For **Transwa** services phone ☎ 08-9326 2600 or 1300 662 205.
• For **TransPerth** suburban services phone ☎ 08-9326 2277 or 136 213.
• For **Great Southern** services contact Interstate Booking Office, East Perth station, phone ☎ 132 147.

RESERVATIONS

As far as possible, key bookings should be made before you leave home, through your travel agent or direct through one of the companies listed on pp11-15.

❑ Useful railway information and reservation websites

- **Connex**: 🖳 www.connexmelbourne.com.au – timetables and assistance with trip planning for Connex services.
- **Countrylink** 🖳 www.countrylink.info – everything you need to know about Countrylink's services in New South Wales.
- **Great Southern Railway**: 🖳 www.gsr.com.au – fare and timetable information for The Ghan, Indian Pacific and Overland trains as well as for Trainways holidays.
- **Ozback Explorer**: 🖳 www.ozbackexplorer.com – details about The Ozback Explorer; see p44.
- **Queensland Rail**: 🖳 http://qroti.bit.net.au (Queensland Rail on the internet) or 🖳 www.qr.com.au – a journey planner, timetable, fare and general information for rail travel in Queensland.
- **Queensland transport information**: 🖳 www.transinfo.qld.gov.au – all you need to know re Translinks' services in south-eastern Queensland.
- **Railcorp NSW**: 🖳 www.railcorp.nsw.gov.au – has CityRail and Countrylink timetables, information and services.
- **Railpage** 🖳 www.railpage.org.au/ – news about and links to railway lines throughout Australia.
- **The man in seat 61** 🖳 www.seat61.com – a useful site for Brits planning rail travel in Australia but also with a good selection of photographs.
- **Trainways**: 🖳 www.trainways.com.au – same website as Great Southern Railway above; see also p74.
- **Transwa, Western Australia country rail and coach**: 🖳 www.transwa.wa.gov.au – details about the Prospector, Australind and Avonlink as well as coach services in Western Australia.
- **Traveltrain Holidays**: 🖳 www.traveltrain.com.au – details about Queenslander Class, The Sunlander, Tilt Train, Spirit of the Outback, Westlander, Inlander, Kuranda Scenic Railway and Gulflander.
- **V/Line passenger (trains and coaches)**: 🖳 www.vline.vic.gov.au – timetables, fares and maps for V/Line's services in Victoria.

Knowing about alternative routes and services can, however, be fruitful for the tourist who has been unable, or chose not, to make prior reservations and arrives in Australia to find some of the popular 'named' trains are already fully booked. Sleeping accommodation is particularly hard to find on trains in the Eastern states at short notice during December and January, the Australian summer holiday months, but trains can be fully booked at other times such as the beginning and end of school holidays and just before holiday weekends (p101). September/October tends to be the busiest period on the TransAustralian route whilst the northbound Ghan and Queensland north coast services can be heavily booked in the southern winter months (June, July, August). In fact, at the time of writing, the Darwin Ghan had been heavily booked since its introduction in February 2004.

You may have heard the standard Aussie assurance that 'she'll be right, mate'. If you haven't, you will! The railways will try hard to help the visitor in difficulty but it is not sensible to leave everything to chance. Advance booking is essential on the main long-distance trains: passengers cannot simply walk up and expect to board as the train arrives as they might do in Europe and anyhow many stations no longer have booking offices. In fact, almost all Australian long-distance trains and all the railway-operated buses, require advance booking and **do not take standing passengers**. Also, long-distance trains will often not stop at an intermediate station unless a booking has been made and some will not accept unbooked passengers in any case. Reservation at least 10 days in advance is almost essential if you have a tight schedule and want to be sure of travelling on the best-known trains over the main routes. Three months in advance is a fairly safe bet for almost any booking, though not guaranteed.

It can, however, be difficult to book sometimes. There are also restrictions on booking; it can be anything from a year in advance to not more than a week or the day before and sometimes on the day of travel only. Restrictions particularly apply for journeys between intermediate stations or for short trips such as Brisbane to Nambour on the QR Tilt Train.

There are no seat reservation fees on Australian railways but fees are charged for late cancellations of paid-for bookings. In extreme cases, no fare refund may be made.

FARES

Rail fares in Australia are mostly based on single point-to-point journeys. Return tickets, where issued, are normally twice the single fare. Single and return tickets (where available) on long-distance trains are normally valid for up to 12 months.

Concessionary fares are usually available for Commonwealth Seniors Health Card holders and Australian pensioners with a PCC card, students and children, though the actual discounts vary between operators and even trains. Various discounted promotional fares are also offered and on some systems off-peak and weekend fares are available. However, the cheap day return and monthly return tickets familiar to rail passengers in the UK are not a common feature of the Australian rail fare structure.

Except for special tickets such as the Austrail Flexipass, children aged under 16 (under 15 in Victoria) are entitled to discounted fares, generally half the normal adult fare. Children aged under 4 travel free unless occupying a separate seat on interstate trains or occupying a sleeping berth. Tertiary students, pensioners and senior citizens who can produce evidence of their status, such as a pensioner or senior citizen card, can travel at reduced fares (50-60% of the normal fare in NSW and Queensland). Students wishing to benefit from the reduced fare must produce an International Student Identification Card (ISIC), especially for interstate travel. On Countrylink (NSW) services, tickets pur-

❑ Fares

Fares quoted in this guide are correct at the time of going to press. Rail Australia warns that 'all fares as well as timetables are subject to alteration without notice'.

chased 14 days in advance, subject to availability of seats or berths, attract a 50% discount. Other discounted fares are available on some routes and some trains at various times of the year: details on application to the relevant system.

There are restrictions on the length of time allowed for a break of journey on a through ticket; in New South Wales a break of more than 12 hours and in Queensland four hours involves the fare being the sum of the fares for each sector, which makes it more expensive.

On GSR trains (The Ghan, Indian Pacific and The Overland) breaks of journey are allowed any time within the 60-day validity of a ticket, provided the bookings are made in advance.

A surcharge per person per night is made for sleeping berths where it is not included in the fare.

You can obtain full information on ticket prices from most railway stations and from rail travel centres. Some specimen fares are given in the section describing the trains (pp35-59).

CLASSES

Most Australian trains, other than suburban and interurban services, have both first-class and economy seating, though it is sometimes hard to tell the difference, and the different railways use different names for the different classes.

For the budget-conscious traveller the economy seating in XPT and Explorer carriages (Sydney to northern NSW and Tablelands, Dubbo, Griffith, Broken Hill, Brisbane, Melbourne and Canberra) is not noticeably different from first class – seats in the latter recline further.

Western Australia's Australind and Prospector (Perth–Bunbury and Kalgoorlie) have one class only and there are no different classes if you travel on Queensland Rail's Cairns Tilt Train, or on the Gulflander, Savannahlander or Kuranda Scenic Railway.

There are no first-class seats as such on Great Southern or QR trains except on the latter's Tilt Trains (p51), where it is called 'business class' instead. First-class fares on QR and GSR are inclusive of berths and in some cases, meals.

The terms 'Gold Kangaroo' and 'Red Kangaroo' describe the different classes on Great Southern trains, though the accommodation on The Overland differs from that on The Ghan and the Indian Pacific.

All sleeping berths in New South Wales require a first-class ticket. Besides first-class sleeping berths, most Queensland long-distance trains have economy berths which are not unlike the first-class couchettes of some European trains, three to a cabin but all one sex except when occupied by a family.

On The Ghan (Adelaide–Alice Springs–Darwin) and the Indian Pacific (Sydney–Adelaide–Perth), Red Kangaroo class offers twinette berths similar to typical first class but more compact. Holders of economy-class tickets (called 'Daynighter' seating on GSR), including the Austrail Flexipass, can upgrade to this class or to Gold Kangaroo (first class) on payment of a fare adjustment.

These two trains, as well as The Overland (Melbourne–Adelaide), The Sunlander (Brisbane–Townsville and Cairns) and The Spirit of the Outback (Brisbane–Longreach) have very comfortable economy seating and carry shower compartments for sitting passengers.

Rail passes

THE AUSTRAIL FLEXIPASS

Since the original consecutive days' Austrail Pass was discontinued in 2003 the correct term for the pass now available is the Austrail Flexipass. This pass is available only to visitors from overseas (including Australian passport-holders living abroad and having a valid return air ticket to their country of residence). Formerly allowing unlimited economy-class travel on government-owned or franchised rail systems in Australia, it now allows travel only on the railways of New South Wales (Countrylink, CityRail, and railway-operated or railway-contracted coach services), Great Southern Railway, and Queensland Rail (Traveltrain services) but not on QR Citytrains except to or from a Traveltrain station at which a booking is held on the day.

The Austrail Flexipass can be purchased (as a voucher to be exchanged for the Pass after arrival in Australia) from Rail Australia agents (see pp11-15) around the world. In Australia the pass can be purchased from Great Southern Railway at Keswick terminal, Adelaide, and their office in Melbourne at Spencer St station, and from the main Countrylink and QR rail travel centres. It can be bought only by residents of countries where there is no Rail Australia agent or by visitors who have been unable to obtain one before arrival in Australia. The applicant must produce a passport and outbound flight tickets to receive the pass and it must be presented with passport at the departure station of the initial journey for validation, and when booking further journeys. The pass is valid for six months from the date of first use, which must be within twelve months of the issue date of the pass or voucher. No refund is payable after use commences.

The Austrail Flexipass enables the holder to travel on a set number of days within a period of six months. This is ideal for people wishing to visit Australia and travel between places by train but not every day or even couple of days. With the Flexipass a day is counted as a period of up to 24 hours from the scheduled departure time of the train on which that day's journey commences. For example, an overnight trip between Melbourne and Adelaide starting one evening and finishing the following morning would count as only one day of use – provided there was no other rail travel using the pass on either of the two days. This also applies to the last day of use, when, for example, the pass would be valid for a journey commencing in Longreach at 07.00 and finishing in Brisbane at 06.30 the next morning.

❑ The Austrail Flexipass

Prices for the Austrail Flexipass are as follows:

8 days $599.50 **15 days** $862.40 **22 days** $1210 **29 days** $1569.70

Notes

* Although the Flexipass is for economy travel only, upgrading (see below) at the discretion of the rail operators may be permitted for a surcharge.

• The 8-day Flexipass is **not valid** for travel west of Adelaide, ie between Adelaide and Perth, Alice Springs or Darwin. However, it is valid from Adelaide to Melbourne and from Adelaide to Sydney on GSR.

• The 8-day and 29-day pass will be discontinued from 1 April 2005. However, anyone who has bought a voucher for one before the end of March 2005 need not start using it till early 2006.

• These passes cover seat reservations but not ancillary charges such as sleeping berths and meals. There is no reduction in price for children, students or pensioners.

• The following **upgrade charges** (not total fares) apply to adult single journeys using the Austrail Flexipass, or the GSR Pass (see opposite) where applicable.

Sydney–Perth & vv:	Red Kangaroo Sleeper $737	Gold Kangaroo $1127[1]
Adelaide–Darwin & vv:	Red Kangaroo Sleeper $950	Gold Kangaroo $1390[2]
Melbourne–Adelaide:		Gold Kangaroo $116
Adelaide–Melbourne:		Gold Kangaroo $90
Brisbane–Cairns & vv:	Economy sleeper $56.10[3]	Business Class $99[5]
	1st class sleeper $201.30[4]	Queenslander class $543.40[6]
Sydney–Melbourne/: Brisbane and vv	1st class seat $48.40	1st class berth $129.80

Charges until 31 Mar 2004: [1] $1047 [2] $1300 [3] $52.80 [4] $176 [5] $92.40 [6] $518.10

• Upgrade costs for backpackers and students are different and vary considerably. For **backpackers** they are from 7% to 41% *higher* than the comparable adult upgrade; for **students** they range from 3% to 48% lower than for adults. Full details can be obtained from GSR or Rail Australia agents.

It is unfortunate that a policy change led to the First Class Austrailpass being discontinued. The Austrail Flexipass now covers economy travel only, and according to the wording on the pass itself, cannot be upgraded to first class except where no economy sleeping or sitting accommodation is available.

The rationale for this curious and seemingly counter-productive restriction is unclear but the non-availability of first-class seating (other than with a sleeping berth) on most long-distance trains (ie all GSR and most QR services), coupled with changed marketing philosophies may be among the reasons. The implications do not appear to have been fully considered and it is a hangover from the time when there was a clear choice between first-class and budget

❑ Prices in this book – Australian dollars

Note that all prices quoted in this book are given in Australian dollars unless otherwise indicated. The exchange rate at the time of writing was Australian $1 to US$0.78 or UK£0.41. For up-to-the-minute rates visit **www.xe.net/currency**.

❑ **Sample savings with an Austrail Flexipass**

An itinerary of 14 days travelling from Sydney to Cairns including Kuranda and back to Brisbane by the Tilt Train, then across to Perth and returning via Melbourne would, by paying normal fares, cost $1745 as against $955 with a Flexipass.

Upgrading to economy sleeper for Brisbane to Cairns, plus 'Red Kangaroo' sleepers for the Sydney–Perth–Adelaide sectors the total would be $3185 as against $2395 with the Pass.

Full first-class sleeper where available on overnight sectors and Gold Kangaroo service inclusive of meals on Great Southern would add up to $3979 or $3189 with the Austrail Flexipass, which is still a 20% saving on the cost for the full itinerary.

passes. If rigidly applied, visitors wishing to follow a pre-planned itinerary might have to be content with economy travel throughout or pay a full first-class fare for any sector where the extra comfort and amenities of first class are desired, since economy berths and seats are usually among the last to be filled. In practice it is likely that, despite the stated restriction, upgrading to first class would not be refused on any train if berths are available and booking is sought a few days before travel. The best advice is, ask. Few railway systems in the world turn down the chance to take in more money when they can, and recent publicity leaflets and website information from Rail Australia in fact contain lists of surcharges for upgrading journeys on GSR, Countrylink and QR trains, so it appears the former policy is now honoured only in the breach. Examples of these upgrade charges, which for some single journeys can be as much as the cost of the Pass itself, are given in the box opposite.

The Austrail Flexipass is still a bargain compared to paying normal fares. It allows a fairly concentrated to extremely leisurely exploration of at least the main Australian rail routes, and enables the visitor to pack in a tremendous variety if full advantage is taken of overnight journeys. Much greater savings were possible with the first-class Austrailpass even though, as with all such passes worldwide, berth charges and meals were and are additional. However, the example in the box above (which is based on Itinerary 1, pp65-7) is sufficient to show that substantial savings are possible; in this simple case up to 45%.

OTHER PASSES

Expressed in terms of the amount of rail travel possible in one day of validity, some more recent passes, though covering more limited areas, offer better value than the Austrail Flexipass. Among these are the Great Southern Railway Pass and NSW Backtracker Pass described below:

The Great Southern Railway (GSR) Pass

Covers Great Southern trains only (The Ghan, Indian Pacific and Overland), but is valid for six months unlimited travel in Red Kangaroo (economy) Daynighter seating. Available for international visitors only at $590 for adults, $450 for students/backpackers (students must have a valid ISIC card and backpackers must be members of a major recognized Backpacker organization) and for children aged under 16. May be upgraded for specific journeys with the same surcharges as for the Austrail Flexipass.

New South Wales

Countrylink offers a **Backtracker Rail Pass** for overseas visitors holding valid passports. This is available from the rail travel centres and Countrylink's central reservation office in Sydney and from other main stations in New South Wales (NSW). The pass covers all trains and state-rail-operated buses in NSW including the Sydney to Brisbane and the Gold Coast routes, Sydney to Armidale, Moree, Griffith, Broken Hill, Canberra and Melbourne, and coach routes to Bourke, Lightning Ridge, Cobar, Hay, Mildura, Echuca, Gundagai, Cooma, Eden, and many smaller centres shown on maps included in free Countrylink timetables or other leaflets. It also allows a limited amount of travel on Sydney suburban trains, but not those in Brisbane or Melbourne.

The Backtracker Pass is available for 14 days, or one, three or six months; prices range from $217.80 (14 days) to $382.80 (6 months). Although covering economy travel only, upgrading is permitted. A Sydney–Melbourne or Brisbane upgrade to 1st class seating costs $48.40 extra, with a sleeping berth a further $129.80.

There is another special kind of ticket, rather misleadingly called a pass. This is the **East Coast Discovery Pass**. It is simply a one-way economy-class ticket at a special fare which can be used at any time over a period of up to six months (subject to the usual reservation restrictions) once only between the chosen stations, but allowing breaks of journey. Journeys may also be upgraded at the same rates as for the passes already described.

This ticket is available for travel between Sydney and Brisbane or Surfers Paradise, or Sydney and Melbourne ($93.50), Melbourne and Brisbane or Surfers Paradise ($176), Sydney and Cairns via Murwillumbah or direct ($312.40), Melbourne and Cairns, again by either of the two routes ($393.80) and Brisbane and Cairns ($224.40). 'Backtracking' is not allowed. Therefore if, for example, a visitor wishes to visit Surfers Paradise on a Discovery Pass between Melbourne or Sydney and Cairns, this can only be covered by paying an additional return fare between Lismore and Surfers (two hours by coach each way with a 90-minute wait at Lismore) or by paying a single fare on the QR Citytrain service between Surfers and Brisbane (but see box opposite for details of the Translink fare zone ticketing system).

Except for the Brisbane–Cairns version, the East Coast Discovery Pass is for overseas visitors only. However, Australian residents should note that for less than $25 more than the price of a Melbourne–Cairns Discovery Pass they can cover the same route with up to five breaks of journey on normal tickets.

CityRail in Sydney offers numerous passes and special tickets within the Sydney and Newcastle areas. For details contact CityRail on ☎ 131 500 or call at any major CityRail station.

Victoria

The **V/Line Victoria Pass** is a first-class pass which costs $180 for 14 days; half price for persons aged under 15, Australian pensioners, or holders of an ISIC. It can be purchased by both visitors and Australians.

A seven-day version ($115) is also available but only to holders of overseas passports and with no concessions. This pass is not valid on peak-hour services, ie trains arriving in Melbourne before 09.30, or leaving Melbourne between 16.00 and 18.00.

Passes are obtainable from V/Line (see p23), YHA Travel (205 King St) and at Spencer St and Flinders St stations in Melbourne; also at Geelong, Ballarat and Bendigo railway stations.

The pass covers all rail and coach services operated by V/Line Passenger within Victoria (Melbourne to Shepparton, Sale, Bairnsdale, Geelong, Warrnambool, Ballarat, Bendigo, Echuca, Cobram, Mildura, Swan Hill and many smaller towns). It also covers V/Line services to Albury but is not valid on Countrylink or Great Southern Railway trains or on Melbourne metropolitan train, bus or tram systems, for which separate daily and other passes at very reasonable rates are available.

Queensland

The **Sunshine Rail Pass** is available in either 1st class or economy, for 14, 21 or 30 days' travel throughout the Queensland Rail system, ie Traveltrain, Citytrain, Tourist train and coach services operated by or on behalf of QR (Charleville to Cunnamulla and Quilpie, Longreach to Winton, and some short-

Translink

Translink, the marketing name adopted by Queensland Dept of Transport, Brisbane City Council, and various private transport operators in south-east Queensland, offers, among other tickets, a series of **all-day unlimited journey tickets** covering different combinations of travel 'zones', served by train, bus or ferry, including BCC's Citycats. They are obtainable at railway stations and from ticket-vending machines and bus drivers.

Prices depend on the number of **zones** covered. One zone would cover, for example, the Brisbane or Ipswich central city area, costing $4 for the day (against a single ticket within the same area at $2). Five zones, costing $7.20, would cover from the CBD (Roma St or Central) to Redbank, Ferny Grove, Lawnton, Pinkenba, Wellington Point, Capalaba, Springwood bus station, and Kingston, whilst a 15-zone ticket at $20 would cover the whole suburban rail system for a day as far north as Eudlo (a 90-minute journey, situated beyond Landsborough) plus coach connections to or from Bribie Island, Surfers Paradise, Robina town centre, Toogoolawah and Grantham (almost as far west as Helidon at the foot of the Great Dividing Range). For $32.80, a day ticket covers all zones, from number 1, Central Brisbane, to number 23, Gympie North. Children and pensioner tickets are half price and there are also off-peak and season-ticket versions. Note: Translink tickets are not valid on Brisbane Airtrain or on QR Traveltrain services.

er runs), but not for the standard-gauge trains to the NSW border operated by Countrylink or for Trainlink buses such as those to Noosa or Airlie Beach. Like all passes it is subject to accommodation being available and does not guarantee a seat on a particular train.

The economy pass may be upgraded to first or business class and both passes may be used for sleeping-berth accommodation on payment of berth fees. The pass is not restricted to overseas visitors and may be obtained from QR travel centres and other main railway stations in Queensland. In 1999 it was proposed to replace this pass with a Flexipass, but this has not happened up to the time of writing.

Charges at the time of writing ranged from $335.50 Economy 14 days to $487.30 Economy 30 days, or 1st class 14 days to $731.50 1st class 30 days. Children aged under 16 and students are half price.

Western Australia

At the time of writing a kilometre-based pass was about to be introduced in Western Australia by Transwa, covering the whole rail and rail-operated coach system. This would supersede the **Southern Discovery Pass** described in earlier editions. However, it will not be valid for the special Wildflower coach tours, for the Transperth suburban rail system, or on the Indian Pacific operated by GSR. For further details phone Transwa (see p23).

Major routes and services

TRAVELLING THE NETWORK

Australia's vastness and diversity cannot be covered in just a few days. Be prepared for long distances from one major city to another – in fact from almost anywhere to anywhere else. From Brisbane northwards up the Queensland coast to Cairns is as far as from Paris to Naples; from Melbourne to Perth is further than from London to Moscow, while a rail journey from Brisbane to Perth is further and takes longer than one from New York to Los Angeles.

To explore the whole rail network of Australia – or rather those parts of it served by regular passenger trains – would take a minimum of 50 days' almost non-stop travel. Even then you would not cover the privately-operated preserved and narrow-gauge lines either on the mainland or in Tasmania, or the Normanton railway in the Crocodile Dundee gulf country of the far north.

The main routes join the cities of Sydney, Melbourne, Brisbane, Adelaide, Perth and Darwin. As far as passenger trains are concerned there is only one route between Brisbane and Sydney, two between Sydney and Adelaide, one of which is via Melbourne, and one between Adelaide and Perth or Darwin.

The only other line which can reasonably be classified as a main route is the North Coast line from Brisbane up to Cairns. On only two of these complete routes is there a train service every day of the week, those between Brisbane, Sydney and Melbourne. The major services comprise the following:

- The Brisbane XPT between Brisbane and Sydney
- The Olympic Spirit and Southern Cross XPTs between Sydney and Melbourne
- The Indian Pacific between Sydney, Adelaide and Perth
- The Ghan between Adelaide, Alice Springs and Darwin
- The Overland between Melbourne and Adelaide
- The Sunlander and Tilt Train between Brisbane, Townsville and Cairns
- The Spirit of the Outback between Brisbane and Longreach

These trains, along with others are described on pp35-59.
In Part 5 the various routes are described as the traveller might see them.

SCENIC ROUTES

In Thomas Cook's *European Timetable* a list is given of the most scenic rail journeys in Europe, based largely on research by the late John Price, former managing editor of Cook's Timetables. Scenic appreciation is partly an individual matter but not entirely so; there is a consensus about what is attractive, as evidenced by calendars, picture postcards, colour slide sales and the facts of where people go, where they stay and what they gasp about and take photographs of. My own list (pp34-5) of the most scenically-interesting or unusual routes served by regular or occasional (eg special excursion) passenger trains may help tourists plan an itinerary if scenery is what they most seek.

Timetable changes and bus substitutions in recent years in nearly all states have deprived rail travellers of much potentially attractive or dramatic scenery or confined it to periods of travelling in darkness, but sometimes because of late running, diversions or special excursions, there is a chance to discover and enjoy otherwise hidden panoramas.

The Thomas Cook European scenic rail list includes information on the type of scenery found on each route, ie coastal, forest, gorge, lake, mountain or river, or a combination of any or all of these. This has not been attempted for Australia because the scenery is in many ways so different. The sheer overwhelming nothingness of the Nullarbor, for example, does not fall into any of the foregoing categories, yet it cannot by any criterion be omitted. It has its own unique attraction.

Coastal scenery is rare on the railways of Australia. In terms of conventional scenic values, it might be said that the routes through the Great Dividing Range, combining mountain, forest, gorge and sometimes river scenery are the most attractive but how do you classify the wonderful sedgeland around Cromarty in Queensland with its teeming flocks of Burdekin ducks, brolgas and other birdlife?

The eye of the beholder will determine what appeals. The suggested list can only offer ideas. Some scenic areas are hard to access, involving long journeys away from population centres, but others are virtually on the doorstep of a city. It should be noted that the scenic sections in suburban Sydney – North Sydney to Wynyard, the Illawarra route south of Waterfall, and the Blue Mountains (Penrith–Lithgow) – are readily accessible and can easily be included in almost any itinerary focused on or including the Greater Sydney area.

An asterisk (*) indicates a route on which no scheduled services operate but for which special excursions might be advertised. For further details of routes with no page reference contact ARHS, see p254.

Scenic sections	Rail route	Page
New South Wales		
Penrith–Lithgow	Blue Mountains	p170
Lithgow–Mudgee	Mudgee line*	p171
Manildra–Parkes	Main Western	p173
Bungendore–Queanbeyan	Canberra branch	p216
Queanbeyan–Cooma	Michelago tourist railway*	p259
Sutherland–Cronulla	Illawarra line	p128
Waterfall–Wollongong	CityRail south coast line	p128
Unanderra–Bomaderry (Nowra)	CityRail south coast line	p128
Unanderra–Robertson	Cockatoo Run (3801 Ltd)	p255
Wynyard–North Sydney	NSW North Shore	p125
Cowan–Gosford	Central Coast	p218
Muswellbrook–Willow Tree	Main North line	p220
Tamworth–Armidale	Main North line	p221
Gloucester–Taree	North Coast line	p223
Nambucca Heads–Glenreagh	North Coast line	p224
Glenreagh–Dorrigo	Preserved railway*	p256
Lismore–Murwillumbah	Murwillumbah branch*	p225
Kyogle–Tamrookum (Qld)	North Coast line	p226
Victoria		
Ballan–Bacchus Marsh	Western line (Ballarat)	p200
Gisborne–Malmsbury	Bendigo line	p203
Ringwood–Belgrave	Connex (Met)	p140
Belgrave–Gembrook	Emerald Railway Tourist Board	p140
South Australia		
Coonamia–Port Augusta	Main east–west line	p179
Woolshed Flat–Quorn	Pichi Richi railway	p271
Adelaide–Bridgewater	Belair and Overland line	p196
Mt Barker Jctn–Victor Harbor	SteamRanger line	p271
West and Central Australia		
Kulgera–Alice Springs	Central Australia Railway	p181
Nullarbor Plain	TransAustralia Railway	p188
Northam–Perth	Kalgoorlie–Perth	p194

Queensland

Rosewood–Laidley	Western line	p238
Helidon–Toowoomba	Western line	p238
Warwick–Stanthorpe	Southwestern line*	p238
Caboolture–Gympie North	North Coast line	p227
Kilkivan–Murgon	Kingaroy branch*	–
Gladstone–Monto	Monto branch*	–
Gladstone–Mt Rainbow	Moura Short Line*	–
Gladstone–Mount Larcom	North Coast line	p229
Sarina–Bloomsbury	North Coast line	p231
Anakie–Alpha	Midland line	p244
Home Hill–Townsville	North Coast line	p232
Stuart–Charters Towers	Northern Railway (Mount Isa)	p247
Cloncurry–Mount Isa	Northern Railway (Mount Isa)	p249
Ingham–Tully	North Coast line	p234
Innisfail–Cairns	North Coast line	p235
Cairns–Kuranda	Kuranda Scenic Railway	p256
Atherton–Ravenshoe	Atherton Railway*	p267
Dimbulah–Lappa	Forsayth branch	p252
Almaden–Forsayth	Forsayth branch	p252

The trains

INTRODUCTION

There is great variety in Australia's passenger trains: the Tangara and Millennium suburban trains of Sydney are among the most modern in the world and the Great South Pacific Express (unfortunately currently withdrawn for an indefinite period) ranked with the Venice-Simplon-Orient-Express as the epitome of luxury travel.

Some other long-distance passenger trains are among the world's finest, with accommodation and service unmatched almost anywhere by normal scheduled services; air conditioned, with quality catering, lounge bars, entertainment and staff whose function is to make your journey not only enjoyable but memorable. The best have luxurious twinette sleeping compartments with showers – they even have doonas (duvets) on the bed. Some also carry motor cars; see p36 and pp39-44 for details.

By contrast, there are a few almost forgotten branch lines where the traveller can share the dust-laden breeze and searing afternoon heat with flies and nameless biting insects as the train rolls uncertainly along what railwaymen call 'two wires in the grass'. Up and down the railway goes, winding among the

Luggage

The passenger luggage allowance on Australian trains is 50kg (40kg on GSR), not counting hand luggage, with a maximum of two bags per person, neither over 25kg (20kg on GSR). A heavy tag may be required on some trains for items over 20kg.

Luggage may be checked in at major railway stations usually not less than half an hour before train departure. Such luggage will be placed in the baggage car and is not accessible during the journey, nor may it be possible to retrieve at small intermediate stations. It will also be difficult or impossible to retrieve should you decide to change your destination en route.

Sitting and sleeping cars on long-distance trains have ample space for luggage at the end of the carriage or in the compartments. Luggage may be left at many stations, either in lockers or depositories. Charges for this may vary from $4 or more to nothing at smaller stations where you can arrange it with the station master (if you can find one).

rocks of dry creek beds, into gorges, across trestle bridges, through timeless country that could have been the film-set for *Crocodile Dundee* and where nothing ever hurries except the occasional kangaroo or galah disturbed by the passing train, finally to reach some outback one-horse one-pub town. Such is a trip on the Savannahlander (Cairns to Forsayth) which takes four days there and back, including night stops.

All interstate trains require seat or berth reservations; see also box below.

As a general principle it can be expected that a long-distance train will not take passengers from its city of origin to somewhere in the suburbs, but may well pick passengers up from suburban stations to go a longer distance, or set them down there on a return journey.

All interstate and most other long-distance trains have catering of some sort, though not always for the entire journey; with a few exceptions non-smoking is the rule (as it is on all coaches and internal airline services and in most public buildings). Credit cards are usually accepted for meal payments exceeding $10.

Motor vehicles may be carried on the Cairns Sunlander (Brisbane–Townsville and Cairns), the Spirit of the Outback (Brisbane–Longreach), the

Warning – conditional or restricted stopping services (†)

Most interstate trains as well as many long-distance intrastate trains do not carry passengers between, or may not stop at, all intermediate stations for which times are given in the timetable. Many are conditional stops, where the train stops only on prior request and confirmed bookings. Some are restricted stops, either for picking up only or setting down only; yet others may be both conditional and restricted. Where '(†)' follows the name of a stopping place in this guide, it means there are some restrictions of this kind. These are mostly explained but conditions may vary and intending passengers should always enquire before attempting to travel to or from these places.

Gulflander (Normanton–Croydon), and trains between Adelaide and Melbourne, Sydney and Perth, and Adelaide, Alice Springs and Darwin.

Guide dogs for the blind may be carried on all services. Facilities for the disabled otherwise vary and should be checked before starting a journey.

INTERSTATE TRAINS

The Indian Pacific – Cruise Ship of the Desert

• **Introduction** 'Cruise Ship of the Desert' well describes this train. Affectionately known to railwaymen as simply 'The Indian' or even just 'IP' (with the Australian tendency to shorten names), the Indian Pacific runs between Sydney, Adelaide and Perth, departing Sydney westbound on Wednesdays and Saturdays at 14.55 and Adelaide a day later at 18.40; it departs East Perth eastbound on Wednesdays and Sundays at 11.55 and Adelaide two days later at 10.00. The journey – a three-day 4348km transcontinental trip, the longest in Australia with three nights on the train – is advertised as 'The adventure that spans Australia'.

• **Stops** Although the Indian may stop or is scheduled to stop at Lithgow (†), Bathurst (†), Blayney (†), Orange East Fork (†), Parkes, Condobolin (†), Ivanhoe (†), Menindee (†), Broken Hill, Peterborough (†), Gladstone (†), Adelaide, Coonamia (†), Port Augusta, Pimba (†), Kingoonya (†), Tarcoola, Cook, Loongana (†), Rawlinna (†), Kalgoorlie, Southern Cross (†), Merredin (†), and Northam (†), all except the major towns of Broken Hill, Adelaide, and Kalgoorlie, plus Cook, are subject to specific request on booking. Travel just between Sydney and Lithgow, or between Northam and Perth, in either direction is not permitted.

• **Accommodation** The train has premium level ('**Gold Kangaroo**') roomettes (single sleeping cabins); twinette cabins with upper and lower berths, en suite toilet and shower and a suite; and the Pullmans cabin, for disabled passengers. Gold Kangaroo Twin cabins have a three-seat sofa with armrests converting to upper and lower sleeping berths at night. Single cabins have an armchair converting to a sleeping berth. An on-board magazine and complimentary toiletry packs are provided. Cabins have a 3-pin/240-volt power point, wash basin, wardrobe, mirror and reading lights. There is a conductor call button and a wake-up cup of tea or coffee is brought to your cabin in the morning. You are treated royally. Great Southern like to refer to their passengers as guests and attend to their needs accordingly. Gold Kangaroo service includes a reception

Civilized travel

There is no better way to experience the diversity and the great size of this stunning country, than first-hand on the Indian Pacific. There's something particularly civilized and comforting about this form of travel. The sound of the wheels on the rails, with the train's gentle rocking never fails to send me to sleep. And the ability to meet other travellers over an afternoon gin and tonic – and dining – this has an appeal all of its own. **Natasha Genat**

Train names

It has long been a practice for railways to give their best trains individual names. Many started as nicknames: Britain's Flying Scotsman being one of the first and most famous. Thus it is not surprising that railways in Australia have their share of these too.

The legendary Ghan is Australia's oldest named train. It is now very different from the old narrow-gauge train which first acquired the appellation Afghan Express and which took 33½ hours – when it was on time – to cover the 869km from Marree near Lake Eyre to Alice Springs at 26km/h overall with 20 intermediate stops, some of nearly an hour. The Ghan derives its name from the Afghan drivers of the camel trains who pioneered this south–north trade route.

Visitors may well wonder when they hear about the Fish and Chips. These are two separate trains, the Fish named after John Heron, a driver they called The Big Fish when the business commuter train he drove down from the Blue Mountains in the 1860s was hauled by a single driving wheel Beyer Peacock steam locomotive. A semi-fast train which followed later naturally became The Chips and both names have been officially recognized and survive to this day in the timetable. At one stage these trains even had a headboard. Later another train on the same line, calling at the smaller stations they missed, was called the Heron, and yet another in the Sydney area, the Gull.

The famous Tea and Sugar (just The Sugar to rail workers) served the isolated camps on the TransNullarbor route from when the line was under construction until the late 1990s. This unique travelling supermarket was open at each major stop – a major stop in this context being a railway settlement of perhaps no more than half a dozen houses. It included a butcher's shop and a community-services car which at Christmas brought Santa Claus himself.

Leaping Lena or The Tin Hare are unofficial names for the Normanton–Croydon Gulflander, which itself was originally a nickname to match Queensland's other 'lander' trains: Inlander, Sunlander, Westlander and Midlander.

A contest was held to find names for the Brisbane and Murwillumbah XPT trains when these replaced the popular overnight dining and sleeping-car trains north from Sydney, but nobody won and nothing better than Brisbane XPT and Murwillumbah XPT has emerged. Some disrespectful names such as The Masochist for the overnight version were frivolously suggested but understandably not taken up by State Rail. At least the message was brought home that the new trains had to have sleeping cars; this amenity was restored a few years later.

The Melbourne XPTs which replaced the Intercapital Daylight and overnight Southern Aurora have been named the Olympic Spirit and Southern Cross but the names appear neither in the public timetables nor on the trains themselves. Like the TGV of France, an XPT is an XPT is an XPT. Individuality is not evident.

with champagne cocktails, when travellers are introduced by the Train Manager. There is also an information session and regular newsletters about the journey and the day's events. A commentary, as well as music, can be listened to in the cabins. Although the lounge car has a video, it is rarely used – travellers instead enjoying the company, making new friends and viewing the passing scenery.

Whilst even the best in first-class service on a train can hardly match the luxury of a five-star hotel, it is these sorts of features that make travel on the great trains of the world more memorable that sitting in a lonely hotel room.

'**Red Kangaroo**' service offers sleeper cabins featuring two facing lounge chairs converting to upper and lower sleeping berths at night, while 'Red Kangaroo' sitting cars have reclining 'Daynighter' seats. These cars and all sleeping cars have showers and toilets at the end of each carriage.

• **Eating and entertainment** **Gold Kangaroo** service on The Indian includes meals in a 48-seat restaurant car, the Queen Adelaide, and there is a lounge bar car with 24-hour complimentary tea and coffee service. An effort is made to incorporate some Australian native bush foods in the menus. A substantial cooked breakfast is normal, but breakfast packs may be delivered to cabins on some Indian Pacific and Ghan services to allow for early morning arrivals or off-train touring. Lunch may include dishes such as pumpkin and bush honey yoghurt soup, whilst a typical dinner menu might offer main courses like grilled snapper or Tasmanian salmon. More familiar dishes like lamb cutlets are not without that special touch. The first sitting is called the Sunset Dinner, whilst the second, preceded by canapés, is the Moonlight Dinner. Local fine quality wines are available for purchase, as well as beer, spirits and soft drinks.

Bar and buffet service is available in the separate **Red Kangaroo** lounge and diner (subject to a dress code). There is video entertainment in the Red Kangaroo Daynighter Seat section and in the Red Kangaroo lounge, and there are separate areas set aside for smokers.

Merchandise of various kinds including CDs and audio cassettes of the journey and souvenirs such as polo shirts with the train's motif (the wedge-tailed eagle) are available for purchase on board and in Adelaide at the Train Shop.

Optional off-train tours at modest cost are available while the train is at Broken Hill, at Adelaide, and on arriving at Perth from the east. There is also time to explore the surroundings while the train is watered at Cook in the middle of the Nullarbor.

• **Fares** see box p43.

• **Motorail services** The Indian carries motor vehicles between Sydney, Adelaide and Perth. Charges vary from $340 (Perth–Adelaide) to $705 (Sydney–Perth) for an accompanied vehicle up to 5.5m long. Charges for unaccompanied or longer vehicles are higher. The prices westbound are dearer than eastbound except between Sydney and Adelaide where the charge is $359 either way. Where two people travel together with Gold Kangaroo service, there is a special rate of $99 offered, subject to conditions. For details, check with Great Southern when enquiring about booking.

The Ghan

• **Introduction** On Sunday 4 August 1929 the first steam-hauled Ghan passenger train pulled out of Adelaide for the town of Stuart in the Red Centre (now Alice Springs). The old Ghan (the name itself being a contraction of 'Afghan Express') was notorious for being held up by flooding in the many creeks but a new line, branching at Tarcoola, was opened in 1980. Since then a new Ghan has followed a more western route after leaving Port Augusta which, though not immune from flooding, ensures a faster journey and greater reliability. The Ghan is an Australian legend and in 1991 won the Australian Tourist Industry

For that special occasion

For travellers really wishing to indulge themselves or for that special occasion, Great Southern Railway has a private carriage, the **Chairman's Car,** which can be attached to the Indian Pacific, The Ghan or The Overland. This has two double bedrooms and two twin cabins, a lounge area with CD player and video entertainment, private dining room and self-contained kitchen, though occupants are served meals in the Gold Kangaroo diner at no extra cost. One-way hire costs vary with the sector travelled: Melbourne–Adelaide $2920, Sydney–Adelaide $4920, Adelaide–Alice Springs $6800, Adelaide–Perth $9520, Sydney–Perth $12,840 and Adelaide–Darwin $13,920. A two-way (return) booking costs proportionately less – on average about 50% on top of the one-way charge if returning within three days; beyond this a surcharge applies. With a full party of eight people the cost per person can compare quite favourably with normal Gold Kangaroo fares.

There are also: the **Prince of Wales carriage**, which sleeps up to ten people and can be attached to The Ghan and IP on certain routes; the **Sir John Forrest carriage** and the **Sir Hans Heysen carriage**, sleeping six and four people respectively. These cars can be attached to any of the GSR great trains. For further information on each of these special carriages contact GSR or a Rail Australia agent.

Association's award for the Best Tourist Transportation service. The year 2004 has seen the ultimate development in the route extension to Darwin, bisecting the continent south to north and fulfilling a hundred-year-old dream.

So popular has the route extension to Darwin been that, since the first public run on 8th February 2004 the standard train consist of 15 coaches plus loco and motorail totalling 403 metres in length has been augmented by additional sets of Gold Kangaroo carriages (normally 5, each with separate lounge and dining cars) to make a train total of over 30 carriages (on one occasion 47) with a length of nearly a kilometre.

• **Stops** The Ghan (see table below) now runs twice-weekly year-round between Adelaide and Alice Springs, extending once weekly to and from Darwin with two nights on board for the whole trip each way. Journey time Adelaide–Alice Springs is 18 hours northbound, 19 hours southbound. From Alice Springs to or from Darwin takes a further day but there is a break in Alice Springs which allows a leisurely exploration of the city itself.

❑ The Ghan timetable

Adelaide to Darwin

Adelaide	d	Sun 17.15	Fri 17.15
Alice Springs	a	Mon 11.55	Sat 11.55
Alice Springs	d	Mon 16.10	
Tennant Creek	a	Mon 22.34	
Tennant Creek	d	Mon 23.21	
Katherine	a	Tue 08.00	
Katherine	d	Tue 12.10	
Darwin	a	Tue 16.30	

Darwin to Adelaide

Darwin	d	Wed 10.00	
Katherine	a	Wed 13.40	
Katherine	d	Wed 18.20	
Tennant Creek	a	Thur 02.23	
Tennant Creek	d	Thur 04.27	
Alice Springs	a	Thur 09.20	
Alice Springs	d	Thur 12.45	Sat 14.00
Adelaide	a	Fri 09.00	Sun 09.00

Notes: d = depart a = arrive

'The Alice to Wonderland'

In 1983 a different train, named The Alice, with its headboard 'The Alice to Wonderland' ran from Sydney via Broken Hill and Port Pirie to Alice Springs to let people explore the scenic wonderland of central Australia. For various reasons, including disagreement between rival managements and lack of vigorous promotion it was withdrawn at the end of 1988. The Alice took 45 hours from Sydney, a journey which after its withdrawal took over 50 hours with train changes in Melbourne and Adelaide. The journey time for today's Ghan, with connection on the Indian Pacific from Sydney, is practically the same as the Alice, but includes the 400km diversion to Adelaide and back.

Off-train touring options are available both at 'The Alice' and at Katherine (for Katherine Gorge), offering the chance to explore these outback towns and their surroundings and encounter some of the unique desert wildlife and flora. Other intermediate stops, such as Port Augusta and Tennant Creek, may be made and requests for embarking or disembarking must be made at the time of booking.

• **Accommodation** The Ghan today is a far cry from the primitive travel standards of the pioneer days. As on the Indian Pacific, it offers the choice of stylish 'Gold Kangaroo Service' twin and single sleeper cabins, or 'Red Kangaroo Service' with the choice of sleeper cabin or 'Daynighter' seat. These last could well be called first class on other railway systems, being of ample width, with generous leg room and comfortably reclining for night-time slumber. Showers and toilet facilities are at the end of each carriage and in the bathrooms of Gold Kangaroo twin cabins. The Ghan also has a de luxe cabin with double bed and a fold-down single bed and its own lounge area; the supplement for this is $395 per cabin per night.

• **Eating and entertainment** **Gold Kangaroo** dining is in an attractive restaurant car with silver service and tantalizing dishes served to the table, such as Northern Territory Salt Water Barramundi, Prime Australian Beef Fillet with grilled Swiss Brown Mushrooms and Native Pepper Hollandaise, or Sage and Pancetta wrapped Supreme of Chicken. Meals are included in the fare, while quality wines and other drinks are available for purchase. After dinner, travellers can relax over a drink in the Lounge Car or settle in their private sleeper cabin, where complimentary toiletries and an on-board magazine are provided. Guests are welcomed and introduced as on the Indian Pacific, yet it somehow seems different. There is a special atmosphere to The Ghan, travellers sensing they are part of history, being on a new transcontinental journey on a train with a name that has become a living legend. The Ghan, the Indian and all great named trains everywhere – each somehow has its own character.

Travellers in Gold Kangaroo service who are continuing by the same train are taken on a locally-guided tour of Alice Springs during the break here; the tour includes the award-winning Desert Park. Off-train touring options are available to all passengers at Katherine (see p185).

Red Kangaroo service offers a separate Lounge and Diner offering light meals, snacks and drinks for purchase at reasonable prices.

Separate smoking compartments are provided in the Gold Kangaroo lounge and adjacent to the Daynighter section of the train. Souvenirs featuring The Ghan motif, a camel (in recognition of the Afghan camel drivers who pioneered the route), as well as CDs/audio cassettes of the journey can be purchased from the bar.

• **Fares** (see box opposite) Gold Kangaroo service includes complimentary transfer to and from hotels in Darwin whilst Red Kangaroo passengers have the option of finding their own way or taking a coach to the city centre, about 18km distant at a fare of around $9.

• **Motorail services** Accompanied motor vehicles may be carried between Adelaide, Alice Springs and Darwin, prices varying from $389 to $899.

The Overland

• **Introduction** This service had just celebrated its 100th anniversary when the first edition of *Australia by Rail* was published in 1988. Although The Overland had a variety of names in its early years and followed a different route for most of the 20th century, it has remained an overnight service noted for its comfort.

The Overland connects in Adelaide on Fridays with The Ghan to Alice Springs and on Sundays with both the Darwin Ghan and the Indian Pacific to

The Great South Pacific Express

Newly introduced in 1999, the Great South Pacific Express (GSPE; Australia's Orient-Express) was a joint venture between the Orient-Express Trains and Cruises company and Queensland Rail (QR). Built at QR's Townsville workshops, the train recreated the opulence and charm of the luxury trains of the 19th century while taking full advantage of the technical achievements appropriate to the 21st century. Both internally and externally it displayed richness in design, quality in construction, attentiveness to detail and perfection in finish.

Although not a heritage train in the true sense, it had the feel of one. Its striking external appearance, based on a 1903 Queensland Rail carriage, more than matched that of its sister trains the Venice Simplon-Orient-Express and the Eastern and Oriental Express of South-East Asia. This, together with features such as leadlight clerestory windows, quality wood panelling, marble bar top, custom-made brass fittings and general interior decor, realized QR's then Chief Executive Vince O'Rourke's vision of 'the world's most beautiful train'.

The GSPE (as it was known), like the Indian Pacific and the Ghan, had features associated more with a holiday cruise than a 'here to there' train journey, with off-train excursions included in the fare or as optional extras. It followed a leisurely schedule and passengers were pampered from the moment of boarding. In the words of the promotional literature the train laid 'every claim to being the most unashamedly romantic hotel on wheels in the Southern hemisphere'; it was also the most expensive. It was altogether an experience of a lifetime for all who could afford it – and a surprising number did. The reasons leading to its withdrawal in mid-2002 were complex, but the train is being kept in storage and could yet return. For up-to-date information contact Orient-Express Trains and Cruises (☎ freecall 1800 000 395, 🖳 www.orient-express.com).

❑ Fares for The Ghan, Indian Pacific and The Overland

	Gold Kangaroo	Red Kangaroo Twin sleeper	Red Kangaroo Daynighter
Adelaide–Darwin (The Ghan)	$1830 ($1244)	$1390 ($834)	$440 ($198)
Adelaide–Alice Springs (The Ghan)	$890 ($605)	$680 ($408)	$215 ($97/$105)
Sydney–Perth (The Indian Pacific)	$1640 ($1178)	$1250 ($805)	$513 ($240/$252)
Adelaide–Perth (The Indian Pacific)	$1250 ($850)	$960 ($576)	$309 ($139/$155)
Sydney–Adelaide (The Indian Pacific)	$590 ($465)	$450 ($325)	$223 ($109)
Adelaide–Melbourne* (The Overland)	$149 ($94)	–	$59 ($34/$42)
Melbourne–Adelaide* (The Overland)*	$175 ($146)	–	$59 ($34/$42)
Return fare (A-M/M-A)	$245 ($233)	–	$118 ($68/$84)

Notes: * no Red Kangaroo sleeper
• All fares (other than the special return fare offered on The Overland) are per person one way and apply whichever direction the journey is done.
• Gold Kangaroo fares include berth (in a single or twin sleeper cabin) and meals.
• Concessionary fares (child, pensioner, CSHC and student) are shown in brackets; where two concessionary fares are shown the second one is for students).

Perth. Eastbound, The Overland has connections from Darwin and Perth in Adelaide on Fridays and from Alice Springs only on Sundays.

• **Stops** Now running four days a week between Adelaide and Melbourne on the standard-gauge line opened in 1995, The Overland covers the 834km in an average of 10 hours 15 mins. The eastbound run is in daytime, leaving Adelaide at 08.30 (CST) on Thursday, 10.00 on Fridays, Saturdays and Sundays, returning overnight the same days at 21.10 and 22.10 (EST) from Melbourne. Travel to or from intermediate stations, which include Geelong North Shore (†), Ararat (†), Dimboola (†) and Murray Bridge (†) is by prior booking only.

• **Accommodation** The train carries Gold Kangaroo roomette and twinette sleepers. Twinettes have en suite shower and toilet, roomettes have washbasin with showers and toilet at the end of the carriage. Red Kangaroo Daynighter seats recline, have individual footrests, reading lights and video entertainment. They are two abreast and can swivel to make a foursome. There are no Red Kangaroo sleeping berths.

❑ Prices in this book – Australian dollars

Note that all prices quoted in this book are given in Australian dollars unless otherwise indicated. The exchange rate at the time of writing was Australian $1 to US$0.78 or UK£0.41. For up-to-the-minute rates visit **www.xe.net/currency**.

• **Eating and entertainment** Covering a shorter journey than other GSR trains, service on The Overland is slightly less elaborate; the meals for example offering less choice. Nevertheless, Gold Kangaroo service includes a complimentary glass of champagne or orange juice on departure, full breakfast on the westbound train, lunch and light dinner on the day service from Adelaide, and a lounge car for the purchase of additional snacks and drinks. Meals and drinks are also available in a separate Red Kangaroo lounge car.

• **Fares** See box p43.

• **Motorail services** Owing to the redevelopment of Melbourne's Spencer Street station, Motorail service will not be available in Melbourne until mid-2005. For an update and further details contact GSR.

The Ozback Explorer

• **Introduction** August 2004 saw the introduction of a new train, the Ozback Explorer, which further develops the concept of 'Rail Cruising' without quite the opulent luxury offered by Orient Express, but with more excursions en route. A unique feature of this train is that it carries a small fleet of mini-buses for its local excursions.

Rail passes are not valid. For further information and bookings contact Head Office, Ozback Explorer (☎ 02-9498 3124, 🖳 info@ozbackexplorer.com, www.ozbackexplorer.com), 6 Roper Place, East Killara, Sydney 2001.

• **Route and itineraries** Based in Lithgow, the Ozback Explorer travels between the Sydney area and the Northern Territory via Sydney's outer suburbs or Bathurst and Forbes to the main south line to Victoria. From Melbourne it follows the routes of The Overland and then The Ghan through Adelaide and Port Augusta to Alice Springs. Intermediate stops are at Yass Junction, Melbourne, Ararat, Adelaide, Port Augusta, Mangouri, and Kulgera, from where local tours are made by bus; these include Sydney and the Blue Mountains, Canberra, Melbourne, the Great Ocean Road, Adelaide, Kangaroo Island, Flinders Ranges, Uluru (Ayers Rock), and Alice Springs.

From Alice Springs in the 2005 programme there are two options: by The Ghan to Darwin, or by coach to Tennant Creek, Katherine and the Top End (Kakadu). Extension of the Explorer train to Darwin was being sought at the time of writing but had not been finalized due to technical difficulties; contact Ozback Explorer for further details.

Itineraries in 2005 include the following package tours: Four Cities Explored, a 7-day Sydney to Adelaide or vice versa (vv) rail cruise; Outback Discovered, 8 days Adelaide to Alice or vv; Passage to Beyond, 11 days Melbourne to Alice or vv, and Splendours of Australia, 14 days Sydney to Alice or vv. There is limited space on the Four Cities and Outback tours.

All the tours that include Alice Springs can be extended in one of two ways as an additional package; either by Red Kangaroo sleeper on The Ghan to or from Darwin (subject to availability) or by a 5-day 'Top End' bus tour covering Tennant Creek, Katherine and Kakadu. Tours operate approximately monthly.

- **Accommodation** There are different classes of accommodation, from Pelican Plus double or twin suites to Rosella cabins (single or twin) with shared facilities. Most nights are spent on the train but in some places hotels are used instead.
- **Eating and entertainment** The dining car has a self-service buffet for a full cooked breakfast, while dinner features special menus each day. Lunch is at the discretion of travellers during the various tours. There are two lounge cars, one with a bar and the other with a souvenir shop and a piano. Nightly entertainment varies depending on the time and place.
- **Costs** Prices range from $2995 (Rosella twin/double cabins on The Four Cities Explored tour to Pelican Class on The Splendours of Australia with Top End bus tour at $8590. Whilst all packages include all accommodation, train transportation, all breakfasts and daily touring (in some places with a choice of options) there are supplements for single accommodation on the Top End tour and for Pelican Plus accommodation.

This train is a bold and unique innovation, which deserves to flourish.

Melbourne XPTs

Olympic Spirit This was the name given to the Melbourne XPT but it is no longer publicized. This XPT service (Melbourne–Sydney and vice versa) replaced the Intercapital Daylight Express which was withdrawn in 1991. The 962km are covered in just over 11 hours, departing Melbourne 08.30 and Sydney 07.43, calling at Benalla, Wangaratta, Albury, Culcairn (†), Henty (†), The Rock (†), Wagga Wagga, Junee, Cootamundra, Harden, Yass Junction, Gunning (†), Goulburn, Moss Vale, Campbelltown (†) and Strathfield (†), connecting southbound with the Overland to Adelaide.

The XPT is a sleek, modern diesel train based on the British InterCity 125 HST. It carries a take-away buffet including bar. A payphone is available (phonecard or credit card).

Countrylink coach connections from Albury, Wagga Wagga and Cootamundra serve places in northern Victoria and southern New South Wales formerly connected by train.

The normal Melbourne–Sydney first-class fare is $161.70, economy $115.50; concessionary fares are roughly 50% of these.

The Southern Cross (see box p46) Also now just referred to as another Melbourne XPT, this is the night-time counterpart of the Olympic Spirit; it offers limited first-class sleeping accommodation (18 berths in twinette compartments) as well as first-class and economy seating. There is a take-away buffet with a restricted bar service.

The service operates Melbourne–Sydney and vice versa daily, departing Melbourne at 19.55 and Sydney at 20.43, with stops as for the daylight service except that Harden and Yass are conditional and there is no stop at Gunning.

The normal fares are the same as for the Olympic Spirit; a first-class berth costs $81.40 extra.

The land of the Southern Cross

Mariners of old navigated by the stars. Visitors from the Northern hemisphere will not see familiar constellations such as the Great Bear, or Plough as it was generally known in England, in Australian skies. You may discern Orion's belt pointing to Sirius low down on the horizon as in the north, but in Australia look out instead for the Southern Cross. It is identified by the Pointers, two 1st magnitude stars, Alpha and Beta Centauri, in the constellation Centaurus. If you take an imaginary line at 90° to a line joining the Pointers and another line projected from the longest axis of the Southern Cross, where these lines meet is the South Celestial Pole, due south. Taking your direction from the Southern Cross you may find your way and perhaps feel something of the spirit of Australia.

The Southern Cross is an Australian icon. From the Eureka Stockade of 1854, the adoption of the Australian Flag in 1903, the Antarctic exploration ship of 1898 to the aeroplane in which Charles Kingsford Smith crossed the Pacific in 1928 and the Atlantic in 1930; it has symbolized Australia. It has even given its name to a place in Western Australia and to the XPT night train between Sydney and Melbourne.

XPT services on the NSW North Coast Line

Brisbane XPT A daily overnight Sydney–Brisbane service departing at 16.24, with a daylight return from Brisbane departing at 07.30 (06:30 in Eastern Summer Time); 990km in 14½ hours.

The service calls at Strathfield (†), Hornsby (†), Gosford (†), Wyong (†), Broadmeadow, Maitland, Dungog, Taree, Kendall (†), Wauchope, Kempsey, Macksville (†), Nambucca Heads (†), Urunga (†), Sawtell (†), Coffs Harbour, Grafton, Casino and Kyogle (†). The day train (southbound) calls unconditionally at Kyogle and Macksville and additionally at Wingham and Gloucester. Countrylink coach connections operate to NSW North Coast centres and the Gold Coast.

The night service carries one 18-berth sleeping car consisting of first-class twinette compartments with a bathroom (toilet and shower) cubicle for each two twinettes. On the day service this car is available as first-class three-seat compartment stock. There is first-class and economy seating with a take-away buffet (at-seat refreshments are available for the aged or infirm) and limited bar service (light beer only and no spirits). A breakfast voucher for sleeping-car passengers gives a choice of juice or yoghurt plus muffin or croissant and tea or coffee. A payphone is available as on all XPT trains. The seating, in common with all XPT services, is in 2+2 formation in both first-class and economy and although Countrylink boasts that it is based on top European designs some passengers find it uncomfortable on long journeys such as this.

The normal fares (Sydney–Brisbane) are the same as for the Melbourne–Sydney XPTs.

Murwillumbah XPT The former Murwillumbah XPT, which itself replaced the earlier Gold Coast Motorail Express, was identical to the Brisbane XPT, running Sydney–Murwillumbah, wholly within NSW but with coach connections to Queensland.

This train, so far not re-named, now departs Sydney daily at 07.15 for Casino, returning from there at 19.25. It covers the 805km in 11 hours 20 mins northbound and just less than 12 hours southbound, calling at Strathfield (†), Hornsby (†), Gosford (†), Wyong (†), Broadmeadow, Maitland, Dungog, Gloucester, Wingham, Taree, Kendall (†), Wauchope, Kempsey, Macksville, Nambucca Heads (†), Urunga (†), Sawtell (†), Coffs Harbour and Grafton. The southbound (night service) calls only conditionally at Macksville and Gloucester and does not serve Wingham.

Countrylink coach connections serve Lismore, Byron Bay, Murwillumbah, Tweed Heads, Surfers Paradise, Robina, Beenleigh and Brisbane to and from Casino, the Brisbane coach connection taking over three hours.

Fares from Sydney to Brisbane by this route in economy class are the same as via Kyogle, but in first class are $154 (concessions $77).

Grafton XPT The third daily XPT train on the NSW North Coast Line, with similar facilities, leaves Sydney at 11.35 and Grafton at 06.30, 695km in 10½ hours northbound, 10 southbound. The service calls at all the above stations plus Eungai. The normal first-class fare (Sydney–Grafton) is $125.40, economy $90.20. Concessionary fares are roughly 50% of these.

OTHER LONG-DISTANCE TRAINS

Except where stated, the following trains are air conditioned and require seat reservations. Concessionary fares are roughly 50% of the fares quoted below.

New South Wales

The Armidale Xplorer/Moree Xplorer (Formerly jointly called the Northern Tablelands Xplorer) These services go daily from Sydney to Armidale (579km) and vice versa and Sydney to Moree (666km) and vice versa.

The combined train departs Sydney at 10.05, Moree at 08.20 and Armidale at 09.00, with journey times varying from eight to nine hours. Intermediate stops are at Strathfield (†), Hornsby (†), Gosford (†), Wyong (†), Fassifern (†), Broadmeadow, Maitland, Singleton, Muswellbrook, Aberdeen (†), Scone, Murrurundi (†), Willow Tree (†), Quirindi and Werris Creek, where the train divides. The Armidale portion then calls at all stations to Armidale (Tamworth, Kootingal, Walcha Road and Uralla), while the Moree portion calls at Gunnedah, Boggabri, Narrabri, and Bellata (†). Countrylink has bus connections to Walcha, Burren Junction, Warialda, Inverell, Glen Innes and Tenterfield.

The Xplorer is somewhat similar to the XPT and is well suited to the shorter runs to which it is assigned. It offers first-class and economy seating with a buffet bar. The normal first-class fare (Sydney–Armidale) is $116.60, to Moree $125.40, economy to Armidale is $83.60, to Moree $90.20.

❑ **Conditional or restricted stopping services**
See box p36 for an explanation of this symbol (†) after the name of a stopping place.

The Dubbo XPT (formerly named Central West XPT) This is a daily express linking Sydney with Katoomba, Bathurst, Blayney, Orange, Stuart Town, Wellington, Geurie and Dubbo (462km), with conditional stops at Strathfield, Parramatta, Blacktown, Penrith, Lithgow, Rydal and Tarana. The service departs Sydney at 07.10 and Dubbo at 14.10; the journey time is 6½ hours. There are numerous coach connections for this route, including Mudgee, Cowra, Bourke, Lightning Ridge, Cobar, and even to Broken Hill, although an 8½-hour bus ride after 6½ hours on the train is unlikely to appeal to anyone other than masochists. The train has first and economy-class seating as well as a buffet bar. The normal first-class fare (Sydney–Dubbo) is $95.70, economy $69.30.

Regional train services to Griffith and Broken Hill have changed considerably over the last two decades, since the demise of the former Riverina Express and the famous Silver City Comet, Australia's first air-conditioned train. Services were virtually nil in the early 1990s but to fulfil an election promise two new loco-hauled weekly trains were introduced in 1996. A further period of uncertainty followed, but July 2002 saw the introduction of Xplorer services once-weekly to both destinations. Xplorers are diesel trainsets with first-class and economy seating and a takeaway buffet/bar.

The Griffith Xplorer The Griffith Xplorer leaves Sydney at 07.05 on Saturday, an 8½-hour journey of 657km, returning from Griffith at 07.40 on Sunday, calling regularly at Moss Vale, Goulburn, Yass Junction, Cootamundra, Junee, Coolamon, Narrandera and Leeton. Conditional stops are at Strathfield, Campbelltown, Mittagong, Bowral, Bundanoon and on the return journey only, at Harden. On board the train is sometimes still referred to as the Riverina Express.

The first-class fare (Sydney–Griffith) is $125.40, economy $90.20.

The Broken Hill Xplorer This leaves Sydney on Mondays at 06.20, calling at Strathfield (†), Parramatta (†), Penrith (†), Katoomba, Lithgow (†), Bathurst, Blayney, Orange, Parkes, Condobolin, Eubalong West, Ivanhoe, Darnick (†), and Menindee, 1125km in 13 hours. The return journey, leaving Broken Hill at 07.45 on Tuesday, calling at the same stations, takes an hour longer.

The fare between Broken Hill and Sydney is $170.50 first class and $122.10 economy.

The Canberra Xplorer This service (Sydney to Goulburn and Canberra) has been reduced to a twice-daily return service and with a rather complicated timetable. The Xplorer departs Sydney at 07.05 and Canberra at 06.37 daily except Sunday. On Tuesday, Thursday, Saturday and Sunday another service leaves Sydney at 12.14, returning from Canberra at 17.07, whilst on Sunday, Monday, Wednesday and Friday a service leaves Canberra at 12.05 (10 minutes earlier on Sunday), returning from Sydney at 18.14. The 327km journey takes just over 4¼ hours. All trains call regularly at Moss Vale, Goulburn, Tarago,

(Opposite) Stopping for a break on the Savannahlander (see p53).

FORSAYTH

2815

Bungendore and Queanbeyan and conditionally at Strathfield, Campbelltown, Mittagong, Bowral and Bundanoon. There are connections with railway-contracted bus services from and to Cooma, Bega, and Eden in the southern highlands and south coast of New South Wales, but not to or from every train. Connections can also be made on some days to and from Bombola and Jindabyne.

The first-class fare (Sydney–Canberra) is $70.40, economy $49.50.

Endeavour Endeavour is a generic name given to the newest diesel railcar sets operating on the outer urban sections of the Sydney CityRail network; Dapto–Nowra, Campbelltown–Goulburn, and Newcastle to Maitland, Dungog, Scone and Muswellbrook.

Economy class has surprisingly comfortable air-conditioned carriages with 3+2 seating and schedules connect with CityRail electric trains to and from Sydney. Seat reservations are not required and there is no catering.

The Fish, The Chips, The Heron, and The River These are names (see box p38) given to some Sydney outer-urban Inter-City commuter trains which have no special distinguishing characteristics (not even a nameboard) but have either a special history, express timing, or follow a special route, or a combination of such features. Details are given in the local Blue Mountains and Newcastle Area timetables.

Queensland

The Sunlander This service, which replaced the former Sunshine Express as the QR flagship in June 1953, follows the Queensland north-coast route from Brisbane through Rockhampton to Townsville and Cairns. It runs four days a week; Tuesday and Saturday to Townsville, Thursday and Sunday to Cairns, returning from Cairns on Tuesday and Saturday and from Townsville additionally on Monday and Thursday. The full journey of around 1660km takes just over 31 hours northbound and a little longer southbound. Continual track realignments over the last 25 years have shortened this former 1681km main line and accurate figures are currently unavailable.

The service departs at 08.55 from Brisbane, 08.35 from Cairns and 15.55 from Townsville, calling at Caboolture (†), Nambour (†), Cooroy (†), Gympie North, Maryborough West, Bundaberg, Miriam Vale, Gladstone, Mount Larcom, Rockhampton, St Lawrence, Carmila, Sarina, Mackay, Proserpine, Bowen, Home Hill, Ayr, Giru, Townsville, Ingham, Cardwell, Tully, Innisfail, Babinda and Gordonvale, but stops may be omitted when there are no bookings. Connecting Trainlink buses (additional fare) serve Hervey Bay, Yeppoon (Saturday only) and Airlie Beach/Shute Harbour.

Accommodation includes first-class twinette and some roomette sleepers, plus triple-berth economy sleeping as well as economy sitting cars. See the box p50 for details about Queenslander class.

(Opposite) Top: The chef prepares dinner for Queenslander Class passengers in the kitchen of The Sunlander's Coral Cay Restaurant. **Bottom:** The Sunlander (see above) crossing one of the many creeks on Queensland's North Coast line.

Queenslander Class

Queenslander Class (www.queenslanderclass.com.au) is offered on the Cairns Sunlander. The Queenslander, as a separate train, ousted the Sunlander as the QR flagship from its inception in 1986 until its withdrawal in 1992. QR was the only rail system in the world to have received the Royal Doulton Award for excellence in service and cuisine, in recognition of the standards achieved on the original Queenslander, which had a piano lounge, the Daintree (named after the World Heritage Greater Daintree National Park), featuring a regular entertainer, special cocktails, and a 'happy hour'. There was also an all-night disco available to economy as well as first-class passengers.

Queenslander Class accommodation comprises twinette sleepers with wash basin, mirror, wardrobe and complimentary stationery packs, dressing gowns and slippers. Showers and toilets are at the end of each sleeping car and passengers have their own cabin key. Special fares (first class plus a supplement which is payable by all passengers including passholders) include berths, meals, complimentary tea and coffee and an information brochure about the train and the places through which it passes.

The Queenslander-class dining car offers superior at-table service with a high-quality menu. Favourite main dishes include a seafood platter of crab or Moreton Bay Bug, banana prawns, oysters and smoked salmon, also fillet of beef or rack of lamb, followed by a choice of attractive desserts. The bar serves cocktails and quality vintage wines or wines by the glass as well as the usual range of drinks, and entertainment or games are a feature of the lounge car.

The Queenslander-class inclusive fare (Brisbane–Cairns) is $690.80, with an additional 20% for passengers wishing sole occupancy of a twinette compartment. Fares between intermediate stations are available on request. There are some concessionary fares; contact QR (see p24) for details.

Queenslander Class is a travel experience not to be missed, even though the supplementary fare costs over half as much as a 15-day Flexipass. After all, even going by ordinary train you would still need to eat and sleep, and you could spend almost as much money sitting in a lonely motel room for the day and a half it takes you to travel through entrancing scenery in comfort and style!

There is a buffet restaurant car and club lounge car, offering a wide range of meals and refreshments, from snacks and fork-type dishes such as spaghetti bolognaise and chicken curry, meat pies, sausage rolls and sandwiches for $10 or less in the club cars to substantial meals in the buffet. Drinks including beer, wine in mini-bottles, and spirits, are available for consumption in the buffet and club cars. If the train is full, and to avoid lengthy queues, it is advisable to go to the buffet promptly when service is announced. The catering services are not available during periods of night travel. Video films are screened at set times in the club car and a public telephone is available.

There is a car-carrying facility on the Cairns Sunlanders only. Accompanied vehicles are charged $187 between Brisbane and Cairns, $165 to or from Townsville.

The first-class fare which includes sleeping berth, is $338.80 to Townsville, $377.30 to Cairns. Economy seats are $162 and $187 respectively, with couchette-type berths $52.80 extra.

The Cairns Tilt Train A seven-coach diesel set, which was introduced in June 2003 and runs three times weekly between Brisbane and Cairns. Services on the 25-hour journey call at Caboolture (†), Nambour (†), Cooroy (†), Gympie North, Maryborough West, Bundaberg, Gladstone, Rockhampton, St Lawrence, Carmila, Sarina, Mackay, Proserpine, Bowen, Home Hill, Ayr, Giru, Townsville, Ingham, Cardwell (†), Tully, Innisfail, Babinda (†), and Gordonvale (†), with connecting Trainlink bus (extra fare) between Proserpine and Airlie Beach/Shute Harbour.

Though without sleeping berths, the Cairns Tilt 'business class' offers comfortable reclining seats with a pillow and footrest. Seats have a fold-out personal audio-video entertainment system, a special feature of which is the 'driver cam' view of the track ahead. Information on train speed, distance to the next station, and the outside weather are other unusual and interesting features. Toilets, showers (BYO towel!), baby change and disabled passenger facilities are available and there is a small buffet bar as well as at-seat delivery of meals ordered in advance from passing attendants.

The Brisbane–Cairns fare is $280.50 each way. A special break of journey fare is permitted, allowing one, two or three intermediate stopovers at $28 to $60 above the through fare – but substantially less than the sum of point-to-point fares for the different sectors.

The Rockhampton Tilt Train An air-conditioned all-electric express service between Brisbane and Rockhampton covering 639km in 7¼ hours, which is among Australia's fastest services (and holder of the world speed record for narrow-gauge trains). It departs Brisbane at 11.00 daily except Saturdays, (07.15 daily from Rockhampton) and calls at Caboolture (†), Landsborough (†), Nambour, Cooroy, Gympie North, Maryborough West, Howard (†), Bundaberg, Miriam Vale (†), Gladstone and Mount Larcom (†), with connecting coach to Gympie, Maryborough and Hervey Bay.

The train has first-class and economy seating with a take-away buffet and an at-seat service. Baby change, wheelchair, phone and fax facilities are available; video and audio entertainment with headphones, as on an airline, are also provided. First class (called business class) is airline style with complimentary newspaper and orange juice on joining.

On Mondays to Fridays there is an additional service from Bundaberg, departing at 05.30, with a return service from Brisbane at 17.00. The return service also runs on Sundays and continues to Rockhampton on Sundays and Fridays. The normal business-class fare (Brisbane–Rockhampton) is $140.80, economy $93.50.

The Spirit of the Outback A loco-hauled through-train which travels twice weekly between Brisbane and Longreach, 'Gateway to the Outback', in central Queensland. It departs Brisbane (Roma St) at 18.25 on Tuesdays and Saturdays and Longreach at 08.00 on Thursdays and Mondays; a 1325km journey in 23½ hours outward and 23 hours homeward. The train carries first (single/twin berth) and economy (triple-berth) sleepers and economy sitting cars, with the

High tea on The Spirit of the Outback

Between Barcaldine and Longreach high tea is served in the Tuckerbox Restaurant of The Spirit of the Outback, the arrival time in Longreach being rather early for dinner. This is rare in railway catering nowadays, but is reminiscent of pre-war days in the north of England where dinner was the midday meal, followed later by high tea and then supper. The Spirit of the Outback high tea, however, is unlikely to include succulent York Ham or other typical English tucker. The menu instead offers snacks such as 'chicken ding wings' with jasmine rice or 'beer-battered potato wedges', albeit with hot scones, jam and cream as afters – the typical Devonshire (cream) tea known all over Britain and Australia.

Tucker Box restaurant-car, the Stockman's Bar (for sleeping-car passengers only) and the Captain Starlight club car for all passengers. A public telephone is available.

The service calls at Caboolture (†), Nambour (†), Cooroy (†), Gympie North (†), Maryborough West, Bundaberg, Miriam Vale, Gladstone, Rockhampton and 15 other stations, some only on request, between there and Longreach, the major stops being at Blackwater, Emerald, Alpha, Jericho, Barcaldine and Ilfracombe. A QR-contracted road coach connects at Longreach for Winton (a two-hour trip).

The normal first-class fare (Brisbane–Longreach), including berth, is $338.80, economy $162.80, with berth $52.80 extra. Meals can be included for passengers travelling between Brisbane and Longreach at $64.90 Brisbane to Longreach, $59.40 Longreach to Brisbane. Accompanied motor vehicles are carried between Brisbane and Longreach for $165.

The Inlander This goes from Townsville to Mount Isa and vice versa; 977km in 21 hours outbound, 20 hours 40 mins return. The service runs on Sundays and Wednesdays from Townsville, departing at 15.30, returning on Mondays and Fridays from Mount Isa, departing at 16.30, serving Charters Towers, Pentland, Torrens Creek, Hughenden, Richmond, Julia Creek, Cloncurry and Duchess, as well as several smaller intermediate stations on request. The train has first and economy sleepers, economy coach cars and a buffet/lounge with snacks/light meals and other refreshments ordered from the counter.

The normal first-class fare (Townsville–Mount Isa) is $254.10 including berth, economy $110, with berth $52.80 extra.

The Westlander A similar train, linking Brisbane with Charleville in western Queensland, from where QR coach connections serve Cooladdi, Cheepie, Quilpie, Wyandra and Cunnamulla. The service operates on Tuesdays and Thursdays leaving Brisbane at 19.20, returning from the west on Wednesdays and Fridays at 18.15; the 777km overnight journey takes 16½ hours outward, 17 hours return. Intermediate stations are Corinda (†), Ipswich (†), Rosewood (†), Toowoomba, Dalby, Chinchilla, Roma, Mitchell, Morven and numerous smaller places west of the Citytrain terminus of Rosewood, on request. The train has

The Yaraka Mixed and Hughenden–Winton goods trains
These two trains are the remnants of a dwindling number of unofficially named non-air-conditioned long-distance Queensland trains with a passenger van attached. These trains are discussed on p270 but, along with the Gulflander and Savannahlander, are ones which should be experienced rather than described, provided you can persuade Queensland Rail to let you travel on them. They are not for the faint-hearted but a journey on any of them will, as Scottish poet McGonagall would have said, 'be remembered for a very long time'!

first twinette and economy three-berth sleepers plus economy-class seating, with a buffet/lounge car similar to that on the Inlander.

The normal first-class fare (Brisbane–Charleville) is $221.10 including berth, economy $110 or 162.80 with sleeping berth.

The **Gulflander** A unique rail-motor service on the remote Normanton Railway in North Queensland's Gulf Country; details are given on p87.

The **Savannahlander** A two-car rail-motor set linking Cairns, Mareeba, Mount Surprise and Forsayth in the rangeland country of north Queensland. Introduced first in 1995 running only between Mount Surprise and Forsayth, it replaced the former 'last great train ride', the Forsayth 'mixed', train 7A90, which ran all the way (see pp86-7). Trains run every Wednesday from Cairns at 06.30, returning from Forsayth on Friday at 08.45, calling at Freshwater (†), Redlynch (†), Stoney Creek (†), Barron Falls (†), Kuranda (†), Koah, Mareeba, Dimbulah, Lappa, Almaden, Mount Surprise and Einasleigh. There are overnight stops outbound at Almaden with a bus to Chillagoe and inbound at Mount Surprise, for which hotel accommodation must be booked.

The service includes commentary, wayside stops at places of interest and limited on-board refreshments. The single fare (Cairns–Forsayth) is $175 or $290 return. The Austrail Flexipass is currently honoured. There is a supplementary return coach fare for the Chillagoe diversion, if required.

Victoria

In Victoria the appellation InterCity was adopted by V/Line for its principal country expresses which are air-conditioned, usually of three or more coaches and diesel hauled, with first- and economy-class seats.

There have been changes in the last two decades when trains on some former inter-city routes have been replaced by buses and others have been privatized. Services between Melbourne and the regional destinations of Shepparton, Swan Hill, Bendigo, Sale and Warrnambool have in fact increased and improved in recent years. On the Bendigo route former loco-hauled trains have mostly been replaced by Sprinter diesel rail-cars which can operate singly or in multiple-unit formation. These are economy class only but the major intercity loco-hauled services have first-class seating as well and most carry a buffet. New self-powered diesel units are currently being tested for the introduction of faster trains on V/Line routes, so timetable alterations can be expected in the near future. Although not specifically referred to now as InterCity the trains listed below are the remaining services outside the metropolitan area. Special off-peak as well as weekend fares offer discounts on normal first or economy.

The Northerner This is the name attached to V/Line intercity trains between Melbourne and Swan Hill, the timetable for which varies with the day of the week (C 9032). The train runs daily and takes an average of four hours to cover the 345km route. On Sundays it leaves Swan Hill at 16.40 and on other days at 07.25, whilst from Melbourne the departure times are 16.32 on Fridays, 17.57 Saturdays and 17.33 other days. There are coach connections with Melbourne–Bendigo trains at other times. This is probably the most complicated train service in Australia for the number of trains involved.

All Northerner trains require reservation and call at Kyneton, Castlemaine, Bendigo, Eaglehawk, Dingee, Pyramid and Kerang. Weekday northbound trains also call at North Melbourne to take up, while on Fridays and Sundays there are additional stops, some conditional, between Melbourne and Bendigo (except southbound on Fridays). These variously include Footscray (†), Sunshine (†), St Albans (†), Watergardens (†), Sunbury (†), Gisborne and Woodend. Reference to local timetables is recommended! V/Line coaches connect with trains to serve Mildura, a 2 hour 40 minute journey from Swan Hill (but see below).

The first-class single fare (Melbourne–Swan Hill) is $73, with return double the single fare. The train carries first-class and economy seats and a licensed buffet; if you want an egg and bacon roll for breakfast go to the buffet soon after leaving Swan Hill!

The Vinelander This popular overnight sleeping-car train between Melbourne and Mildura in north-western Victoria was withdrawn in 1993, and replaced only by a bus via Robinvale. The railway follows a quite different route, from Ballarat through Maryborough, St Arnaud and Ouyen. (It is currently being standardized and trains are expected to resume running in 2005 or later).

The Goulburn Valley Limited train This links Shepparton with Melbourne, leaving Shepparton at 07.15, arriving Melbourne 09.28, returning at 18.15, arriving 20.35, Mondays to Fridays. This is matched by a Melbourne-based service leaving at 09.50 and returning from Shepparton at 15.10. Times differ at weekends, particularly on Sunday when there is only one Shepparton–Melbourne train at 17.40, with its northbound counterpart leaving Melbourne at 18.30.

The trains call at Broadmeadows (†), Seymour, Nagambie, Murchison East and Mooroopna. Accommodation and facilities are similar to other V/Line intercity trains, but the buffet at last reports was unlicensed. The economy single fare (Melbourne–Shepparton) is $25.70. Conductors will arrange taxis to

❑ Conditional or restricted stopping services

See box p36 for an explanation of this symbol **(†)** after the name of a stopping place.

> **❑ Prices in this book – Australian dollars**
> Note that all prices quoted in this book are given in Australian dollars unless otherwise indicated. The exchange rate at the time of writing was Australian $1 to US$0.78 or UK£0.41. For up-to-the-minute rates visit **www.xe.net/currency**.

meet trains on request. Coach connections serve Cobram and Griffith from Shepparton and Echuca from Murchison East.

Echuca is also served by direct train via Bendigo on Fridays and Sundays (not at the same times), calling at various stations up to Bendigo, then Elmore and Rochester. A useful summary of V/Line rail and coach services between Melbourne and Echuca is given in the V/Line North timetable booklet, but the number of direct train services may improve so enquiry is recommended. The first-class fare (Melbourne–Echuca) is $42.40 (if available), economy $32.30.

The Gippslander The principal day service linking Melbourne (Spencer St) and eastern Victoria. In the mid-1990s it was withdrawn beyond Sale, then a dead-end terminus, but 2004 saw a restoration of the service over a further 70km to Bairnsdale, with a relocation of track and a new station at Sale to eliminate the need for reversal. The trains now depart Melbourne on weekdays at 07.47 and 18.26, with return services at 06.10 and 12.40. Saturday times are a little later in each direction and Sunday times later still. There are additional services to Sale at 13.25, except Sunday, and daily from there to Melbourne at 16.45, again slightly later at weekends (C 9030).

The trains cover 274km in an average of just under 3¾ hours, calling at Flinders St (†), Caulfield (†), Dandenong (†), Pakenham, Warragul, Moe, Morwell, Traralgon, Rosedale, Sale and Stratford. The trains are air-conditioned with first-class (2+2 layout) and economy (2+3) seating and a buffet service (except the 08.20 from Bairnsdale on Sunday and the Sale services on Saturday). V/Line coaches connect to Lakes Entrance and other places in East Gippsland and over the border into New South Wales. There are additional trains at other times, up to nine a day between Melbourne and Traralgon, but not with the same facilities. The first-class fare (Melbourne–Bairnsdale) is $45.20, $32.30 economy; concessions $27.00 and $20.50.

Twin City Limited This is the name of the morning V/Line Albury to Melbourne train which returns in the evening, but there is little to distinguish it from other trains on this run. There are three weekday intercity trains each way between Melbourne and Albury, two on Saturdays and Sundays, all with first and economy seating and a buffet.

The 307km journey takes an average of 3¾ hours, calling at Broadmeadows (†), Seymour and various stations between Seymour and Albury always including Euroa, Benalla and Wangaratta. The first- and economy-class seating is similar to the Gippslander and there is a buffet; the buffet has traditionally been dry since the days of the Albury Express, sometimes

Victorian attitudes to alcohol

The provision of alcohol on trains has a curious history in Victoria; for several years the intercity trains served only light beer and cooler, a local effervescent wine/cordial mix popular with some young people. Even the Vinelander served no wine in the days before its withdrawal but the last decade has seen an improvement, the wowser influence has declined, wine as well as beer are once more available to thirsty travellers on V/Line passenger's main intercity trains, including what was once the Albury Express.

'Wowser' attitudes to grog are not confined to Victoria. Though Australians may have a reputation as hard drinkers there is an underlying puritanism which rears its head from time to time with restrictions like 'alcohol only with meals', 'light beer only'. In September 2004, Countrylink placed new restrictions on the hours of service: rumours that alcohol will be banned completely have so far not been confirmed.

dubbed the travelling 'pub with no beer', and V/Line in recent years made the unusual boast in their promotional literature that 'Most services are alcohol free' – happily no longer true!

The first-class fare (Melbourne–Albury) is $65.40, $46.70 economy. Countrylink XPT trains also serve Benalla, Wangaratta and Albury, adding two more daily trains each way, but V/Line tickets are not accepted.

West Coaster The former name used by West Coast Railway (WCR) for trains between Melbourne and Warrnambool on Victoria's south-west coast, a service now operated by V/Line. The timetable is, at the time of writing, subject to alteration, and some services have been temporarily replaced by buses. As with most country trains in Victoria, the service at weekends differs markedly from that on normal weekdays (a Victorian Sunday has long perpetuated some of the characteristics of the era so named in Britain). The new timetable has trains leaving both Melbourne Spencer St and Warrnambool early in the morning, around mid-day and in the evening, except on Sundays when there are only evening departures.

The 267km journey normally takes just over three hours, calling at Geelong, Winchelsea, Colac, Camperdown and Terang. Some trains call additionally at Birregurra. The Sunday evening train from Melbourne calls at Werribee to take up only, while the evening train from Warrnambool calls there daily to set down only. The last weekday return train from Warrnambool calls additionally at North Geelong, Corio, Lara and conditionally at Footscray.

Connecting coaches at Warrnambool serve Port Fairy, Portland and other places on the Victorian west coast, and Mount Gambier in South Australia. The trains have comfortable and roomy first-class plus economy seating and a buffet car. The first-class single fare (Melbourne–Warrnambool) is $57.60 (concessions $28.80), economy $41 (concessions $20.50. There are also off-peak return fares of $86.20 1st class, $57.40 economy.

South Australia

Regional services in South Australia, comprising the Silver City Limited (Adelaide–Broken Hill and vice versa), the Iron Triangle Limited (Adelaide–Whyalla and vice versa) and the Blue Lake (Adelaide–Mount Gambier and vice versa) were all suspended in 1991 and, despite much local agitation, independent inquiry, solemn agreement and careful estimates of replacement costs, they remain victims of misplaced government economic policy. With the standardization of the Adelaide–Melbourne route, Mount Gambier in particular, on the 1600mm broad-gauge system, has been isolated. For the foreseeable future, buses may be the only option for regional centres in South Australia other than Port Augusta, a conditional stop for interstate trains of Great Southern.

An exception recently introduced is a privately-run tour train which has brought back a rail service by refurbished Bluebird rail-cars to the famous Barossa Valley north-east of Adelaide. This is the **Barossa Wine Train**, which operates a day tour to Tanunda leaving Adelaide four times weekly (Tuesday, Thursday, Saturday and Sunday) at 08.50, arriving at 18.50 on the return. The 70.5km journey takes 1½ hours each way, with seven hours at Tanunda. A coach tour of famous wineries and a lunch is included at a total cost of $139. The Austrail Flexipass is not valid on the Barossa Wine Train. For further details and bookings contact ☎ 08-8212 7888, or 💻 info@barossawinetrain.com.au.

Western Australia

The new **Prospector** goes from Perth to Kalgoorlie and vice versa; 655km normally in 6 to 6½ hours. The schedules differ almost every day and the timetable at the time of writing was provisional (C 9033). It runs daily in both directions with an extra run each way on Mondays and Fridays. Apart from Sunday there is a daily departure from Perth at 07.10 (07.25 on Sats) and from Kalgoorlie at 07.05, with up to 13 intermediate stops, usually including Midland, Northam and Merredin. There are afternoon departures in each direction on Sunday, also

---

Meals on wheels

A word about railway catering, especially eating on trains. Sometimes you will have to indulge; there is nowhere else to find sustenance without taking your own (which though not exactly prohibited is frowned upon). Generally Australian railway food is good, some of it excellent. You can get tasty hot snacks reasonably cheaply on trains like the XPT or Xplorer, and on all Queensland Rail's long-distance trains. V/Line's Intercity trains have rather more limited fare but there is no need to starve. Main meals in buffet cars cost no more, often less, than they would in a comparable restaurant (one with sit-down service, not a pub counter lunch). Dining cars are becoming scarce, except where premium fares are paid and meals are included in the fare. On trains such as The Ghan, the Indian Pacific, and Queenslander Class on the Sunlander, these may border on gourmet style. Less extravagant is the humble Railway Pie (meat and gravy, served piping hot with or without tomato sauce), which has recently made a comeback, and is a very tasty, inexpensive form of sustenance for the hungry, even if a trifle messy to consume even if you are provided with a knife and fork – the railways usually offer plastic ones.

---

on Monday and Friday at different times. The service connects at Kalgoorlie with Westrail buses to and from Esperance.

The standard adult fare (Perth–Kalgoorlie or vv) is $68.40, but 'Gold Service' with meals, coffee, tea, fruit juice, personal service and specially-contoured seats is available at $124.50.

There is also the **Avon Link**, a commuter version of the Prospector which runs between Northam and Midland on weekdays and from Perth to Merredin and back on Mondays, Wednesdays and Fridays.

Transwa also operates the sleek, modern little **Australind**. This narrow-gauge train zips along at a steady 80km/h through the wild flowers of the Western Australian coastal plain from Perth to the historic little town of Bunbury. It leaves Perth City main station at 09.30 and 17.55, Bunbury at 06.00 and 14.45; the journey time averages 2½ hours and trains call at up to 10 intermediate stations provided bookings have been made. A buffet service is available on the train, and a courtesy bus from the rail terminal to the city centre in Bunbury is provided except on Sundays and public holidays. The fare (Perth–Bunbury) is $21.70.

SUBURBAN AND INTERURBAN TRAINS

Tedious though many suburban rail journeys can be, the train is clearly superior to driving a car or riding a bus in the rush hour. Within all the state capitals there are suburban rail services giving access to the city centre and other points of interest.

By tram, on the oldest passenger rail line in Australia, you can go down to Port Melbourne where the ships used to bring the migrants under the Assisted Passage Scheme. You can go across Sydney Harbour bridge by train and look out at the hot, congested streams of frustrated motorists on the adjoining road; they also have to pay a toll that is more than your train fare and will take longer to reach their city destinations than you will on the state-of-the-art double-deck trains of Sydney's CityRail network. You can go by rail to the Olympic Stadium, up into the Blue Mountains, down to the beach at Cronulla or to the Royal National Park at Sutherland just south of Botany Bay.

Suburban and interurban trains in Australia vary tremendously. **Sydney** has modern suburban trains (eg the Tangara and Millennium), continuing the pioneering spirit which gave it the honour of being the first city in the world to have double-deck suburban electric multiple-unit (EMU) trains. CityRail's Interurban EMU trains are also double deck, air conditioned and have toilets. The network extends as far north as the Hunter Valley, providing a commuter service for the city of Newcastle.

In **Melbourne** some modern suburban sets have been introduced. The Melbourne Met system has been privatized but under very strict operating conditions, which apply also to Victoria's privatized intercity network.

Melbourne's suburban trains are now operated by Connex, while all trams are run by Yarra Trams. The rail services cover the former Hillside routes of Epping, Hurstbridge, Lilydale, Belgrave, Alamein and Glen Waverley as well as the former Bayside routes to Upfield, Broadmeadows, St Albans, Williamstown, Werribee, Frankston, Cranbourne and Pakenham. Trams serve a multitude of routes including some former rail lines. Detailed timetables are issued by Yarra Trams, and details are obtainable by phone from Metlink on ☎ 131 638 or 🖳 www.metlinkmelbourne.com.au.

The Melbourne Metcard, issued by Metlink, covers train, tram and Met bus services throughout the metropolitan area, and is also valid on some outer urban V/Line routes. The City Circle tram, recently extended, is free.

A Passengers' Charter ensures that service levels will be maintained, fares will not increase above the rate of inflation, concessions will continue, tickets will be valid on all modes and performance and punctuality will be monitored, with incentives and penalties applied. And more! In some circumstances passengers can actually be compensated, eg by ticket extension following bad punctuality. Australia has not yet adopted the Japanese practice of refunding fares when express trains are late. This would be an expensive matter in some parts of Australia in the wet season, when lateness may be measured in hours or even days rather than minutes. But the Victorian idea may be a start in the right direction. The signs are that it is working well.

Brisbane's Interurban (IMU) sets serving the Gold Coast hinterland boast toilet and rest-room accommodation, as well as luggage racks, not normally found on suburban trains, and are capable of speeds up to 140km/h.

Most **Perth** suburban services run every 15 minutes even at weekends. **Canberra** and **Darwin** have very good bus services but no suburban rail.

No Australian suburban trains, so far, have any first-class accommodation or buffet service as you might find in European cities such as Frankfurt or Bonn or in Greater London.

Suburban rail services operate usually at least every half-hour during daytime and at least hourly in the late evening and on Sundays but this varies between cities; between central city stations in Sydney the frequency is often every few minutes. Some ideas and itinerary suggestions are given in Part 4 to help the visitor make the most of even one day in each capital. They assume a start from the main station, but remember that suburban locations are often very convenient to reach and often offer cheaper accommodation.

Tour and itinerary options

INTRODUCTION

Before considering how to make the most effective use of whatever passes or tickets you have, it would be helpful to read the preceding section on the trains (pp35-59), if you have not already done so.

If your journeys have to be fitted into a limited period much of your time may be spent on quality trains, which will become your travelling hotel. You

The bell tolls for the one-month Austrailpass

An itinerary for the one-month Austrailpass has been a feature of this guidebook since the first edition in 1988, and was almost its raison d'être, being developed from a chapter in an earlier book *Great Rail Non-Journeys of Australia*. This pass has now been discontinued. The 8- and 29-day Flexipasses also go in March 2005, leaving only the 15- and 22-day versions – see box p71 for ideas for the latter.

will need to take enough clean clothes and money to last, because there will be limited time for shopping or bank transactions after leaving your starting point.

With a Flexipass you can have more time to look around at places you reach, you will be able to do your banking and have your laundry attended to. You can plan your own excursions from selected bases, leaving your heavy luggage at a hotel to be called for later. You need not always rent a hotel room for this: it is usually possible to come to some arrangement with the management. Luggage can also be left at railway station depositories (though these can be expensive) and laundry can be left at laundries where it belongs. Remember to keep a note of where you've left everything: it is annoying to have to make a special trip back somewhere just to collect a suitcase or a couple of shirts you had forgotten about.

Whatever you do, watch the days of the week! Saturday afternoons and Sundays must be counted as dead periods for attending to these necessities. Even in Sydney on a Sunday it is almost impossible to obtain cash unless you have a card with a pin number and can find the right autobank (cash machine). American Express and Thomas Cook offices are useful in an emergency but you will find them only in the larger cities. It is easy to forget the day of the week when travelling on long-distance trains such as the Indian Pacific. Time-zone changes are enough to contend with as it is.

The additional comfort of a sleeping berth (not covered by rail passes) is not prohibitively expensive. A twin-berth sleeper on an interstate train costs up to 30% less than the price of a double room in a first-class (four-star) hotel in a city such as Melbourne. For the single traveller the difference is even greater. Although the train cannot offer quite the luxury or spaciousness of the hotel it is still, with air-conditioning, privacy, handy toilet and shower, an attractive proposition for the traveller wishing to use limited time to the best advantage.

By spending some of your nights sleeping comfortably on a train you can wake up in a new place every day with new things to see and do. You will not only save money and cover more of the country, but have opportunities to meet, talk and relax with people far more than in a lonely suite in a big city hotel. Depending on where you want to start and finish your tour, you can visit all the mainland state capitals of Australia; Perth, Adelaide, Melbourne, Sydney and Brisbane in less than a month and you can include a side trip to Cairns, Alice Springs or even Darwin as well.

Getting to Alice Springs by train is simple, thanks to the twice-weekly Ghan service from Adelaide, with connections from Melbourne and Sydney (C 9034, 9035). However, travelling to Alice or Darwin by train from the west involves

❑ Table 1: Perth–Alice Springs–Darwin and vice versa (C 9033, 9034)

Perth–Alice Springs–Darwin

Perth	dep	Wed 11.55		
Port Augusta	arr	Fri 03.15		
Port Augusta	dep	Fri 21.20	Sun 21.15	
Alice Springs	arr	Sat 11.55	Mon 11.55	
Alice Springs	dep		Mon 16.10	
Darwin	arr		Tue 16.30	

Darwin–Alice Springs–Perth

Darwin	dep	Wed 10.00	Wed 10.00	
Alice Springs	arr	Thu 09.20	Thu 09.20	
Alice Springs	dep	Sat 14.00	Thu 14.00	Thu 14.00
Tarcoola	arr		Thu 23.10	
Port Augusta	arr	Sun 04.45		Fri 04.50
Port Augusta	dep	Sun 23.00		Sun 23.00
Tarcoola	dep		Fri 04.21	
Perth	arr	Tue 09.10	Sat 09.10	Tue 09.10

Notes: The five-hour wait at Tarcoola would attract only the most dedicated rail traveller and is not encouraged, probably not even allowed by GSR. Passengers instead must continue at least to Port Augusta, adding three days to a Darwin–Perth journey. There are hotels and other facilities at Port Augusta but changing there involves late night or early morning arrival or departure in either direction. It is probably more sensible and convenient to continue on to Adelaide to transfer there, but this adds to the distance (and to the fare if you have no Pass).

either changing at Port Augusta at inconvenient times and with no sensible connections or diverting to Adelaide and back en route. Table 1 opposite shows how inconvenient such a journey can be.

PLANNING A 15-DAY ITINERARY

Yes! Despite some time-consuming non-connections (see Table 1 opposite), you can actually travel round most of the country by train in only two weeks. But if you want to make the most of any Australian railpass in a limited time it is imperative that you make advance reservations for all the trains on which you will need them. Your first decision must therefore be the cities at which your rail tour will begin and end.

In planning your itinerary it is important to realize that Australia is nearly as big as the United States of America and three-quarters the size of Europe. Texas would fit into a corner of Queensland – and does! It is in fact the name of a little town on a former freight branch (the trains used to carry a passenger van) in Queensland's south-west.

In the old days a trans-Australian journey by rail was not for the faint-hearted. Breaks of gauge, changes of train, intense heat, dust and flies made it something to be contemplated with misgiving and remembered with mingled horror and amazement. Many are the tales that have been told and the books that have been written. As recently as 1970 it was still not possible to go from Sydney to Perth without four changes of train – at Melbourne, Adelaide, Port Pirie and Kalgoorlie.

It still takes three days to cross the whole continent. The return trip takes six days if you start from Perth, seven if you start from Sydney, and this without spending much more time at the other end than it takes for the train to be turned around, cleaned and reprovisioned (5 hours in Sydney, just over 24 in Perth). It is therefore sensible, if you want to avoid going backwards and forwards over the same route and cover as much of the country as possible in a limited time, to plan your arrival at one port and your departure from another. This can often be arranged easily when making your airline bookings. Many international flights regularly serve Perth, Sydney, Melbourne and Brisbane. Cairns and Darwin are also on several regular international routes. Sydney is the base with the greatest concentration of rail as well as external air routes, but starting your rail trip in Perth and finishing in the east or starting in Queensland or Darwin and finishing in the west can give better options for the holder of a short-term Austrail Flexipass. Also, many airline package deals to and from Australia allow one or more internal flights without extra charge. This sort of concession could be useful for bridging some of the gaps in the rail network such as Perth–Darwin–Cairns or for travelling direct between Canberra and Melbourne without having either to change trains at Goulburn or use the bus between Canberra and Cootamundra.

The Austrail Flexipass, which has now entirely replaced the former consecutive-day pass is a real boon to travellers who wish to spin out a tour by spending several days, perhaps a week or more, in one place before going on to another. Journeys can be spun out over a six-month period, or if wished concentrated into a selected number of days one after the other or nearly so. But see the warning on p64.

The basic triangle

With almost any itinerary at all, some retracing of route is necessary because there is no real rail network in the sense of a web of intersecting routes as in Europe. Basically, Australia has a fundamental triangle of passenger main lines – Adelaide, Sydney, Melbourne. Every other route, however long or short, is a dead-end system branching from this triangle, with here and there a minor loop on one of the branches.

To give some idea of the time-scale of things, the basic south-eastern capital-city triangle takes a minimum of 2 days 2½ hours (clockwise from Sydney starting on a Thursday) to 3 days 65 minutes (anti-clockwise from Melbourne starting on a Tuesday). This is shown in Table 2 opposite; the summary table of interstate trains on the basic south-eastern triangle.

Alice Springs is a three-day round trip from Adelaide and Darwin (more from Sydney or Melbourne) whilst Cairns is a five-day round trip from Sydney. You can just go from Perth to Cairns and back, or vice versa in 13 days, but you would not have much more than a night there or anywhere in between.

❑ Table 2: The basic triangle
Sydney–Melbourne–Adelaide–Sydney & vv (C 9020, 9026 & 9035)

	Daily	Daily		Wed and Sat	
Sydney	07.43	20.43	Sydney	14.55	
				Thur and Sun	
Melbourne	18.55	07.35	Adelaide	15.15	
	Thur	Fri/Sa/Su		Fri/Sa/Su	Thur
Melbourne	21.10	22.10	Adelaide	10.00	08.30
	Fri	Sa/Su/Mo		Fri	Sa/Su/Mo
Adelaide	07.10	08.00	Melbourne	21.00	19.15
	Fri	Tues		Daily	Daily
Adelaide	10.00	10.00	Melbourne	08.30	19.55
	Sat	Wed			
Sydney	10.15	10.15	Sydney	19.53	06.53

Note: All trains have refreshments, must be booked, and have sleeping accommodation on overnight journeys. Daily except as stated.

On many interstate trips you will cross time zones, which may vary with the season. Summer time operates in the eastern states except Queensland. As a general rule, travelling west between the eastern states and South Australia, you put watches back 30 minutes and between South and Western Australia back 90 minutes; forward in the other direction. Be careful at Broken Hill, which is in New South Wales but observes South Australian time. The train conductor will clear up any doubts for you and in fact west of Adelaide the train operates on its own sweet time, so you need not worry unless you need to telephone somebody.

SOME 15-DAY ITINERARIES WITH A FLEXIPASS

This book offers some ideas on how to make good use of the Austrail Flexipass if you are staying for a month or more, but if you are limited to an ultra-short stay the most you can pack into it in the way of rail travel is set out in the following five itineraries. These packages are essentially quick reconnaissance tours – seeing on the move. Using only the 15-day Flexipass any of them can be achieved in less than a month. Most visitors would probably prefer to spread these itineraries over a longer period. This can now readily be done since the Flexipass covering 15 or 22 days of travel can be spread over six months, but if you are really pushed you can see an astonishing amount of the country in a very short time – and at little cost.

It is possible even in 15 consecutive days to visit **all** the mainland state capital cities as well as the national capital of Canberra as Itinerary 2 (p68) shows. But be warned. Fifteen-day 'maximum mileage' itineraries are not for geriatrics or the faint-hearted, though if you 'boldly go' you will have something to talk about for years afterwards – and few people will believe you did it all by train!

These itineraries cover mainly capital cities, but capital cities are not what everyone wants to see. To many visitors, an Australian trip would not be ful-

Flexipass warning

The definition of a travel 'day' on the Flexipass may seem rather confusing (it **IS** confusing!) so you have to be very careful in varying any itinerary you plan to follow. A 'day' is defined as up to 24 hours from the commencement of a journey. Over 24 hours but not more than 48 hours counts as two days. An overnight journey will not necessarily involve more than one day's use of the Pass. The following examples illustrate this principle:

1. Journey starting at Brisbane at 18.25 on one day, reaching Longreach at 18.00 next day. Travel time 23 hours 35 minutes equals one day's pass use. If, however, there is an earlier journey to Brisbane on the first day in the above example, that would make two days' use of the Pass.
2. Journey starting in Sydney at 16.24 on one day, reaching Brisbane 06.35 next day, changing to Tilt Train leaving Brisbane at 11.00 the same day, and again at Rockhampton to the Sunlander that evening, to reach Cairns at 16.00 two days after leaving Sydney. Travel time 47 hours and 25 minutes equals two days' use of the Pass, but **only** if the bookings through to Cairns were made before leaving Sydney. Otherwise three flexidays would be used up, the same as if a break were made for a night in Brisbane; the Sydney–Brisbane sector would be one day's use of the pass, but the Brisbane–Cairns journey would be two days' use (29 hours), making a total of three. This is where you need to be very careful if breaking journeys on a pre-planned itinerary.

Note that where there is more than one train journey shown within the same 'flexiday', but not completed within the same calendar day it will be necessary to book those journeys in advance. For example, in Itinerary 1, the Sydney–Taree and Taree–Brisbane sectors must be booked together to avoid possible argument. Another trap for the unwary is if a stopover is introduced where not included in a pre-planned itinerary. The following examples from the specimen itineraries illustrate the danger of introducing unplanned breaks.

To help travellers avoid getting caught somewhere away from a capital city with a Pass having not enough days of use left in which to travel back, a table on pp277-80 of the Appendix shows the time you need to allow to get back to base within the period of validity of your Pass.

filled without seeing romantic places like the 'Town called Alice' or the railway station at Kuranda. Itineraries can easily fit in trips either to the 'red centre' or to tropical north Queensland, or both. Caution! If you insist on staying for a night in the middle of the Nullarbor, climbing to the top of Ayers Rock or scuba-diving off the Barrier Reef, you are not going to manage it in 15 days – even though a day away from trains does not count as a day off your Pass. But you can come close to such achievements if you plan your itinerary carefully, following the advice given in this book.

Note that the Flexipass and other rail passes do **not** cover air or boat trips, nor are discounts offered on other transport as, for example, with the Eurailpass.

(Opposite) The Spirit of the Outback (see pp51-2) winds its way through the Drummond Range in the outback of central Queensland.

Whilst the first two 15-day itineraries are based on Sydney, more economic and interesting use can be made of an Austrail Flexipass if you start your journey on one side of Australia and finish it on the other. After all, you may feel that one crossing of the Nullarbor in 15 days of travel is sufficient (though many travellers find it draws them back again and again – the writer is one). Further sample itineraries therefore allow such variation.

Whilst the itineraries featured in the book are almost exclusively limited to rail travel, making the journey between Perth and Darwin by air would enable the holder of an Austrail Flexipass or Great Southern Railway Pass to avoid retracing some routes. This would allow more time for side trips and variations in an itinerary. For example, in Itinerary 3 (p69) Flexiday 3 is spent returning to Adelaide from Alice Springs, followed by a two-night stopover before travelling on to Perth in flexidays 4 and 5. The next two flexidays are spent returning from Perth across the Nullarbor to Adelaide. By that time you will have traversed the line between Adelaide and Tarcoola (the junction between Trans-Australian and Darwin routes) no less than four times. It was explained (see p68) that although the time in Alice Springs would allow continuation to and from Darwin this would add two flexidays of travel. If instead of returning south from Darwin you flew from there to Perth, only one flexiday, number 3, would be used up before the start of the eastbound trip across the Nullarbor. This would provide two spare flexidays for some side trip or other variation later on, and the airfare might be no more than the surcharge you might otherwise consider justified if deciding to upgrade to sleeper or Gold Kangaroo on the two-night stint across the Nullarbor.

Itinerary 1 (see p66)

Itinerary 1 shows how it is possible to spend a day or more in each of the mainland state capital cities, as well as time in north Queensland in less than a month, using a 15-day Austrail Flexipass. Travelling to the NSW coast, north Queensland, South Australia, Western Australia and Victoria, this itinerary based on Sydney allows stopovers in Brisbane, Cairns, Perth, Adelaide and Melbourne with seven nights on trains and a return to Sydney half-way through. Sleeping berths are available (at extra cost) on overnight trains. This itinerary allows one day in hand (Flexiday 15), which might be used for a day trip from Sydney eg to the Blue Mountains or down the Illawarra coast. See the section 'Longer day trips from Sydney' (p128).

Even this simple itinerary is capable of variation and extension. For example, since the Cairns–Brisbane direct journey uses two flexidays (the quickest by Tilt Train taking just less than 25 hours), there are some attractive options of breaking the journey without using any more flexidays. A break can be made at Townsville or further south as far as Mackay at reasonable hours of the day. the table on p67 shows these options. If the pass is used consecutively with

(Opposite) Top: Interior of the Red Kangaroo Daynighter coach on The Ghan.
Bottom: Fork-lift help for needy passengers on The Ghan.

❑ Itinerary 1: Sydney–Cairns–Brisbane–Sydney–Perth–Adelaide–Melbourne–Sydney

Flexiday	Day	Place	Time	Remarks
Day 1	Any day	dep Sydney	11.35	Grafton XPT
		arr Taree	17.11	4½ hours free
		dep Taree	21.42	Brisbane XPT
		arr Brisbane	06.35#	three hours free or stopover
Day 2	Thur, Sun	dep Brisbane	09.55a	Sunlander
Day 3	Fri, Mon	arr Cairns	16.00	stopover
Day 4	Any day	dep Cairns	08.30b	Kuranda Scenic Railway
		arr Kuranda	10.15b	over three hours free
		dep Kuranda	14.00b	Kuranda Scenic Railway
		arr Cairns	15.45b	stopover
Day 5	Sun, Wed, Fri	dep Cairns	08.15	Tilt Train (c)
Day 6	Mon, Thur, Sat	arr Brisbane	09.10	Stopover
Day 7	Any day	dep Brisbane #	07.30	Brisbane XPT
		arr Sydney	21.51	stopover
Day 8	Wed, Sat	dep Sydney	14.55	Indian Pacific
Day 9	Thur, Sun	en route: Broken Hill to Spencer Gulf		
Day 10	Fri, Mon	en route: Nullarbor plain and Kalgoorlie		
	Sat, Tue	arr Perth	09.10	stopover
Day 11	Sun, Wed	dep Perth	11.55	Indian Pacific
Day 12	Mon, Thur	en route: the Nullarbor Plain		
	Tue, Fri	arr Adelaide	07.20	stopover
Day 13	Fri, Sat, Sun	dep Adelaide	10.00d	The Overland
		arr Melbourne	21.00	stopover
Day 14	Any day	dep Melbourne	08.30	Olympic Spirit
		arr Sydney	19.53	
Day 15	Any day	Optional day return trip from Sydney		

Notes

One hour earlier during Eastern Summer Time.

a An alternative is to depart Brisbane at 11.00 on the Tilt Train, changing to the Sunlander at a pre-selected (and booked) station, either Bundaberg (a few minutes' wait), Gladstone (1 hour) or Rockhampton (100 mins). There is also the option, at extra cost, of travelling Queenslander Class on the Sunlander. On Monday, Wednesday or Friday another option is the Cairns Tilt Train (extra fare) dep Brisbane 18.25 arr Cairns 19.20 next day.

b Additional services as follows: Cairns 09.30 except Saturdays, arr Kuranda 11.15, dep 15.30, arr Cairns 17.15

c Involves additional fare. Alternative dep Cairns Tue or Sat 08.35 on the Sunlander, arriving Brisbane 15.55 next day, but this adds to the minimum number of **calendar** days required.

d Alternative Adelaide–Melbourne service on Thursday dep 08.30 arr 19.15.

stopovers lasting one night only, a minimum of 16 calendar days is needed, but it should be noted that not all the trains run every day of the week so that if you decided to spend an extra day or two in some place, you might not find a train on the day you are ready to leave. For example, if you miss the Indian Pacific

❑ Itinerary 1 (Table): Flexipass 2-day options for break of journey between Cairns and Brisbane

Place	Flexiday	Day	Time	Day	Time
Cairns dep	1	Tuesday (a)	08.35	Wednesday (b)	08.15
THEN					
Townsville arr	1	Tuesday (a)	15.30	Wednesday (b)	14.20
Townsville dep	2	Wednesday (b)	14.35	Thursday (c)	15.55
OR					
Giru arr	1	Tuesday (a)	17.01	Wednesday (b)	15.25
Giru dep	2	Wednesday (b)	15.25	Thursday (c)	17.01
OR					
Ayr arr	1	Tuesday (a)	17.27	Wednesday (b)	15.50
Ayr dep	2	Wednesday (b)	15.53	Thursday (c)	17.32
OR					
Home Hill arr	1	Tuesday (a)	17.45	Wednesday (b)	16.06
Home Hill dep	2	Wednesday (b)	16.09	Thursday (c)	17.48
OR					
Bowen arr	1	Tuesday (a)	19.13	Wednesday (b)	17.16
Bowen dep	2	Wednesday (b)	17.19	Thursday (c)	19.18
OR					
Proserpine arr	1	Tuesday (a)	20.05	Wednesday (b)	18.05
Proserpine dep	2	Wednesday (b)	18.10	Thursday (c)	20.10
OR					
Mackay arr	1	Tuesday (a)	22.34	Wednesday (b)	20.00
Mackay dep	2	Wednesday (b)	20.20	Thursday (b)	22.44
THEN					
Brisbane arr	2	Thursday (d)	09.10	Friday (e)	15.55

Notes

(a) also Saturday
(b) also Sunday and Friday
(c) also Monday, Tuesday and Saturday
(d) also Monday and Saturday
(e) also Tuesday, Wednesday and Sunday

from Sydney on a Saturday, the next one would not be until the following Wednesday. Although the tour can be started on any day as the Sydney–Taree–Brisbane trains run daily, different days of starting mean different numbers of consecutive calendar days used to complete the tour. As another example, if the tour starts on a Friday, with the trains to Taree and Brisbane, 19 consecutive days would be the minimum, since a stopover from Tuesday to Friday would be required in Adelaide. On the other hand, if a Brisbane stopover were taken at the end of the first flexiday this would not add to the number of flexidays used, but would add to the total calendar days. Stopovers can be any number of days within the six-month validity of your Pass.

This itinerary can equally be based on other capital cities (Melbourne, Brisbane, Perth or Adelaide), or on Cairns. For example, if based in Melbourne, Flexiday 1 would be as Day 14 below, Flexiday 2 would allow a Sydney-based day trip, Flexiday 3 would be as Day 1 in the example, Flexiday 4 as Day 2 and so on, with Flexiday 15 as Day 13.

❑ **Itinerary 2: Sydney–Perth–Adelaide–Melbourne–Canberra–Sydney–Brisbane–Sydney**

Flexiday	Day	Place	Time	Remarks
Day 1	Saturday	dep Sydney	15.55	Indian Pacific
Day 2	Sunday	en route: Western NSW and Spencer Gulf		
Day 3	Monday	en route: the Nullarbor Plain		
	Tuesday	arr Perth	09.10	stopover
Day 4	Wednesday	dep Perth	11.55	Indian Pacific
Day 5	Thursday	en route: the Nullarbor Plain		
	Friday	arr Adelaide	07.20	stopover
Day 6	Saturday	dep Adelaide	10.00	The Overland
		arr Melbourne	21.00	stopover
Day 7	Sunday	dep Melbourne	19.55	Southern Cross XPT
	Monday	arr Sydney	06.53	stopover
Day 8	Tuesday	dep Sydney	07.05	Canberra Xplorer
		arr Canberra	11.23	stopover
Day 9	Wednesday	dep Canberra	12.05	Canberra Xplorer
		arr Sydney	16.24	stopover
Day 10	Thursday	dep Sydney	11.35	Grafton XPT
		arr Taree	17.11	4½ hours free
		dep Taree	21.42	Brisbane XPT
	Friday	arr Brisbane	06.35#	stopover
Day 12	Saturday	dep Brisbane	07.30#	Brisbane XPT
		arr Sydney	21.51	

Notes # One hour earlier during Eastern Summer Time.

Itinerary 2 (see above)

To show more clearly how a round tour can be made in only 15 days, this itinerary is set out in consecutive day order. Most trains run on other days, but travellers are warned that introducing one or more overnight stops in any of the places not shown with such a stop in the specimen itinerary would exceed the 15-days of the Flexipass. Based on Sydney, it allows a visit to each mainland State capital, Perth, Adelaide, Melbourne and Brisbane, with a full day or more in each, a full day in Canberra and seven nights on trains. It uses only 12 flexidays, leaving three days which can be used for other trips afterwards or by varying the itinerary, in either case extending the travel period beyond 15 **calendar** days.

Possible variations might be to take an out-and-back two-day trip from Brisbane to Charleville in south-west Queensland or to further north like Bundaberg or Rockhampton before returning to Sydney, or to break the final return journey at Maitland and make a two-day trip up the Hunter Valley to Tamworth or Armidale.

Itinerary 3 (see opposite)

This itinerary shows how a 15-day Flexipass can economically be extended over a full month, with useful two- or three-night stopovers in different places.

Itinerary 3: Sydney–Alice Springs–Adelaide–Perth–Melbourne–Cairns –Brisbane–Sydney

Travel day	Flexi day	Day	Place	Time	Remarks
1	1	Saturday	dep Sydney	14.55	Indian Pacific
2	2	Sunday	arr Adelaide	15.05	Change trains
			dep Adelaide	17.15	The Ghan
3	2	Monday	arr Alice Springs	11.55	three-night stopover
6	3	Thursday	dep Alice Springs	14.00	The Ghan
7	3	Friday	arr Adelaide	09.00	two-night stopover
9	4	Sunday	dep Adelaide	18.40	Indian Pacific
11	5	Tuesday	arr Perth	09.10	night-stop
12	6	Wednesday	dep Perth	11.55	Indian Pacific
14	7	Friday	arr Adelaide	07.20	night-stop
15	8	Saturday	dep Adelaide	10.00	The Overland
	8		arr Melbourne	21.00	three-night stopover
18	9	Tuesday	dep Melbourne	08.30	Olympic Spirit XPT
	9		arr Sydney	19.53	night-stop
19	10	Wednesday	dep Sydney	16.24	Brisbane XPT
20	10	Thursday	arr Brisbane	06.35#	Change trains
	10		dep Brisbane	08.55	Sunlander (a)
21	11	Friday	arr Cairns	16.00	two-night stopover
23	12	Sunday	dep Cairns	08.30b	Kuranda Scenic Rly
	12		arr Kuranda	10.15b	over three hours free
	12		dep Kuranda	14.00b	Kuranda Scenic Rly
	12		arr Cairns	15.45b	two-night stopover (c)
25	13	Tuesday	dep Cairns	08.35	Sunlander (c)
26	14	Wednesday	arr Brisbane	15.55	three-night stopover (c)
29	15	Saturday	dep Brisbane	07.30#	Brisbane XPT
	15		arr Sydney	21.51	

Notes

One hour earlier during Eastern Summer Time.

a An alternative is to depart Brisbane at 11.00 on the Tilt Train, changing to the Sunlander at a pre-selected (and booked) station, either Bundaberg (a few minutes' wait), Gladstone (60 mins) or Rockhampton (100 mins). There is also the option, at extra cost, of travelling Queenslander Class on the Sunlander. On Monday, Wednesday or Friday another option is the Cairns Tilt Train (extra fare) dep Brisbane 18.25 arr Cairns 19.20 the next day.

b Additional services as follows: Cairns 09.30 except Saturdays, arr Kuranda 11.15, dep 15.30, arr Cairns 17.15

c An option is for a three-night stopover in Cairns, leaving by Tilt Train at 8.15 on Wednesday (extra fare), arr Brisbane 09.10 Thursday, extending the calendar period by one day.

Based on Sydney, with a return to base half-way through, it allows visits to Alice Springs, with ample time to visit Uluru (Ayers Rock) or even enjoy a night-stop there, Adelaide, Perth, Melbourne, Cairns, plus the Kuranda Scenic Railway, and Brisbane. Ten nights are on trains with sleeping berths available

❑ Itinerary 4: Darwin–Alice Springs–Adelaide–Melbourne–Sydney–Cairns–Brisbane–Perth

Flexiday	Day	Place	Time	Remarks
Day 1	Wednesday	dep Darwin	10.00	The Ghan
	Thursday	arr Alice Springs	09.20	stopover or 4½ hours free
Day 2	Thur, Sat	dep Alice Springs	14.00	The Ghan
	Fri, Sun	arr Adelaide	09.00	
Day 3	Th, Fr, Sa, Su	dep Adelaide	10.10	(08.30 on Thur) The Overland
		arr Melbourne	21.00	(19.15 on Thur) stopover
Day 4	Any day	dep Melbourne	08.30	Olympic Spirit
		arr Cootamundra	14.37	change to bus
		dep Cootamundra	14.50	Countrylink bus
		arr Canberra	17.40	stopover
Day 5	Most days	dep Canberra	06.37c	Canberra Xplorer
		arr Sydney	10.55c	stopover
Day 6	Any day	dep Sydney	11.35	Grafton XPT
		arr Taree	17.11	4½ hours free
		dep Taree	21.42	Brisbane XPT
		arr Brisbane	06.35#	stopover or two hours free
Day 7	Thur, Sun	dep Brisbane (Roma)	08.55	Sunlander (a)
Day 8	Fri, Mon	arr Cairns	16.00	stopover
Day 9	Any day	dep Cairns	08.30b	Kuranda Scenic Railway
		arr Kuranda	10.15b	over three hours free
		dep Kuranda	14.00b	Kuranda Scenic Railway
		arr Cairns	15.45b	stopover
Day 10	Tue, Sat	dep Cairns	08.35	Sunlander (d)
Day 11	Wed, Sun	arr Brisbane	15.55	stopover
Day 12	Any day	dep Brisbane #	07.30	Brisbane XPT
		arr Sydney	21.51	stopover
Day 13	Wed, Sat	dep Sydney	14.55	Indian Pacific
Day 14	Thur, Sun	en route: Broken Hill to Spencer Gulf		
Day 15	Fri, Mon	en route: Nullarbor plain and Kalgoorlie		
	Sat, Tue	arr Perth	09.10	

Notes

One hour earlier during Eastern Summer Time.

a An alternative is to depart Brisbane at 11.00 on the Tilt Train, changing to the Sunlander at a pre-selected (and booked) station, either Bundaberg (a few minutes' wait), Gladstone (60 mins) or Rockhampton (100 mins). There is also the option, at extra cost, of travelling Queenslander Class on the Sunlander. On Mon, Wed or Fri another option is the Cairns Tilt Train (extra fare) dep Brisbane 18.25 arr Cairns 19.20 next day.

b Also: Cairns 09.30 except Sat, arr Kuranda 11.15, dep 15.30, arr Cairns 17.15.

c Leaving Canberra on this train (runs Mon–Sat) allows the option of a break en route at Goulburn, Moss Vale or Bowral; see 'Longer day trips from Sydney' p128. On Sundays dep Canberra 11.55, arr Sydney 16.24. There are alternative departures from Canberra at 12.05 on Mondays, Wednesdays and Fridays and at 17.07 on all other days, arriving Sydney 16.24 and 21.53 respectively.

d This schedule offers the opportunity to travel Queenslander Class (at a substantial additional fare). An alternative, also with an additional but lower fare, is the Tilt Train dep Cairns on Wed, Fri or Sun at 08.15, arriving Brisbane 09.10 the next day.

at extra cost. Note that on Travel day 19, the Sydney–Brisbane–Cairns journey covering Flexidays 10 and 11, must be booked through from Sydney.

Important: Although the time in Alice Springs would allow continuation to and from Darwin with a nightstop there, this would add two flexidays travel, which would mean either finishing the trip in Cairns or obtaining a 22-day instead of a 15-day Flexipass.

Note that in this itinerary travel day numbers are in two columns, showing Travel day ie consecutive days in a month of travel, and Flexiday ie the 15 Flexipass days.

Itinerary 4 (see opposite)

Starting in Darwin and ending in Perth, this itinerary includes visits to all mainland state capital cities plus Canberra, Alice Springs and Cairns (including the Kuranda Scenic Railway). It offers the opportunity to travel on Australia's three top trains ie The Ghan, Queenslander Class on the Sunlander, and the Indian Pacific. There are eight nights on trains, with night-stops where indicated. A minimum of 18 calendar days are needed if used consecutively with stopovers for one night only.

Itinerary 5 (see p72)

Starting in Perth on a Wednesday or Sunday and ending in Cairns, north Queensland with eight nights on trains and visiting all the other mainland capital cities including Canberra and Darwin, plus the Blue Mountains, Hunter

Ideas for a 22-day Flexipass

For visitors wishing to make the most of a 22-day pass, there should be enough useful suggestions in the section 'Itinerary Variations and Side Trips' (pp76-88) to extend one of the 15-day itineraries over a further six days. To whet the appetite, here are a few ideas:

From Sydney, two flexidays would cover an excursion to Broken Hill, allowing a full day there, going by Countrylink's Xplorer on a Monday, returning by the Indian Pacific. But the Xplorer leaves rather early in the day, so try exploring Sydney by rail first, ending the day at Katoomba or Lithgow in the Blue Mountains, then take the XPT after breakfast another day (08.51 from Katoomba, 09.31 from Lithgow) up to Dubbo for a night or two. When tired of Dubbo, return south to Orange from where, after a suitable break, you can catch the Broken Hill Xplorer the following Monday. That adds three flexidays, leaving another flexiday to see parts of the Sydney area you may have missed at first.

If you prefer to explore **more of Queensland** instead two days are all that is needed for an out-and-back trip to Charleville from Brisbane, two days Flexipass use for a similar trip to Longreach from Brisbane or Rockhampton, and the same from Townsville to visit Mount Isa. So with six flexidays to spare, you can enjoy all the main Queensland outback trips. Remember, you don't have to do all these in just six days: the Flexipass allows them to be spread out over whatever time your stay in Australia lasts within the six-month validity of the Pass. You can spend a week in Broken Hill, two or three days in Charleville, or a week in each of the outback Queensland centres if you wish. The choice is yours.

❑ Itinerary 5: Perth–Darwin–Alice Springs–Adelaide–Melbourne–Canberra–Sydney–Brisbane–Cairns

Flexiday	Day	Place	Time	Remarks
Day 1	Wed, Sun	dep Perth	11.55	Indian Pacific
Day 2	Thur, Mon	en route: the Nullarbor plain		
	Fri, Tue	arr Adelaide	07.20	stopover if desired
Day 3	Fri, Sun	dep Adelaide	17.15	The Ghan
	Sat, Mon	arr Alice Springs	11.55	stopover or four hours free
Day 4	Monday	dep Alice Springs	16.10	The Ghan
	Tuesday	arr Darwin	16.00	stopover
Day 5	Wednesday	dep Darwin	10.00	The Ghan
	Thursday	arr Alice Springs	09.20	4½ hours free or stopover
Day 6	Th, Sa	dep Alice Springs	14.00	The Ghan
	Fr, Su	arr Adelaide	09.00	(09.10 on Sun)
Day 7	Th, Fr, Sa, Su	dep Adelaide	10.00	(08.30 Thur) The Overland
		arr Melbourne	21.00	(19.15 Thur) stopover
Day 8	Any day	dep Melbourne	08.30	Olympic Spirit
		arr Cootamundra	14.37	change to bus
		dep Cootamundra	14.50	Countrylink bus
		arr Canberra	17.40	stopover
Day 9	Most days	dep Canberra	06.37c	Canberra Xplorer
		arr Sydney	10.55c	stopover
Day 10	Any day	dep Sydney	09.02d	Citytrain
		arr Katoomba (e)	10.58d	
		dep Katoomba (e)	17.26d	Citytrain
		arr Sydney	19.23d	
Day 11	Any day	dep Sydney	10.05	Armidale Xplorer
		arr Muswellbrook	13.52	five hours free
		dep Muswellbrook	18.51f	Local Endeavour service
		arr Maitland	20.03f	stopover
Day 12	Any day	dep Maitland	09.58	XPT train
		arr Taree	12.35	nine hours free
		dep Taree	21.42	Brisbane XPT
		arr Brisbane	06.35#	stopover or two hours free
Day 13	Th, Su	dep Brisbane	08.55a	Sunlander
Day 14	Fr,Mo	arr Cairns	16.00	
Day 15	Any day	dep Cairns	08.30b	Kuranda Scenic Railway
		arr Kuranda	10.15b	Over three hours free
		dep Kuranda	14.00b	
		arr Cairns	15.45b	

Notes: see box opposite

Valley and holiday coast of New South Wales. Night-stops include Alice Springs and Maitland in the Hunter Valley. Taking a minimum of 18 calendar days starting Wednesday, with stopovers one night only except where more than one are needed between trains, eg at Adelaide (Friday and Saturday nights) or Alice Springs (Saturday and Sunday nights if arriving there on a Friday): 21 calendar days would be the minimum required for a Sunday start in Perth.

❑ Notes for Itinerary 5 (see box opposite)

One hour earlier during Eastern Summer Time.

a An alternative is to depart Brisbane at 11.00 on the Tilt Train, changing to the Sunlander at a pre-selected (and booked) station, either Bundaberg (a few minutes' wait), Gladstone (60 mins) or Rockhampton (100 mins). There is also the option, at extra cost, of travelling Queenslander Class on the Sunlander. On Mon, Wed or Fri another option is the Cairns Tilt Train (extra fare) dep Brisbane 18.25 arr Cairns 19.20 the next day.

b Additional services as follows: Cairns 09.30 except Saturdays, arr Kuranda 11.15, dep 15.30, arr Cairns 17.15.

c Leaving Canberra on this train (runs Mon–Sat) allows the option of a break en route at Goulburn, Moss Vale or Bowral; see 'Longer day trips from Sydney' p128. On Sundays dep Canberra 11.55, arr Sydney 16.24. There are alternative departures from Canberra at 12.05 on Mondays, Wednesdays and Fridays and at 17.07 on all other days, arriving Sydney 16.24 and 21.53 respectively.

d Other trains approx every hour; see local timetables.

e Option of stopping or calling en route at other Blue Mountains resorts; see 'Longer day trips from Sydney' p128.

f Dep 21.00 Sat and Sun, arr Maitland 22.12.

ITINERARIES FOR OTHER RAIL PASSES

The Great Southern Railway Pass

This pass covers only the trains of Great Southern. Its base is Adelaide, from where GSR services extend east to Sydney and Melbourne, west to Perth and north to Darwin. Any journeys therefore are out-and-back from Adelaide. There are no cross-route connections and the routes themselves intersect only at Crystal Brook and Tarcoola. Neither of these is a suitable transfer station although both the Indian Pacific and The Ghan pass through.

Services between Adelaide and Sydney, Melbourne, Perth and Darwin are included in the listed Inter-capital Connections in Part 4 of this book (pp116-19). Those to or from Adelaide are covered by a GSR Pass, except Melbourne via Sydney and Sydney via Melbourne. Brisbane is not covered by this Pass.

The NSW Backtracker Pass

As with the GSR Pass, the NSW Backtracker essentially covers out-and-back routes from Sydney, although thanks to connecting coach services, some cross-country travel is possible, albeit usually involving overnight stops. The publisher Lonely Planet has a brochure of suggested itineraries, available free of charge from Countrylink and associated outlets, offering a variety of suggestions that need not be repeated here.

PRE-PLANNED PACKAGES

Most of the railway systems offer pre-planned package tours. These all-inclusive packages should particularly interest visitors not using one of the rail passes. They vary from half-day trips to excursions lasting anything up to a fortnight. Some are on offer regularly; others on selected dates, and all are subject to advance booking. One thing to watch if planning to use such packages is whether the rail fare is included. Many do not include the fare to the place on which the tour is based, or where it begins or ends. This assumes you make your own way to the tour starting point, whether by rail using a pass you hold or by some method of your own devising. But there is no point in taking a trip that includes the train fare if you already have a pass or ticket covering that part of the journey. You would simply be paying twice.

There is a vast range of such tours, from two-night packages at moderate cost to 'see it all' tours lasting a fortnight or more with costs well into four figures. They may include rail travel, coach tours, boat cruises, air connections, hotel accommodation and/or transfers – you will need to check.

To list all possible tours would be beyond the scope of this or almost any guidebook. Places and itineraries vary from time to time. It is best to ask at the travel centres in the main railway stations. A few specific examples illustrate the range. These tours effectively start and finish at railway stations, from which you are picked up and to which you are returned when the tour ends. The prices quoted are per person for twin-share accommodation.

Some Inter-state tours

- **Trainways Ultimate Rail Adventure** A 16-day tour starting in Sydney, crossing the continent to Perth by the Indian Pacific (Gold Kangaroo class), four nights in Perth with local tours followed by a flight to Darwin for a tour of Kakadu National Park including Nourlangie Rock and Yellow Waters. Then by The Ghan back to Adelaide, with tours of Katherine Gorge and Uluru en route. Return to Sydney by air or rail is not included in the package price of $5050 twin share. Neither does this include the airfare Perth to Darwin (a few hundred dollars depending on the season), optional tours of Adelaide and Kalgoorlie, an optional scenic flight in Kakadu area, or most hotel meals.
- **Kevin Pearce Tours** Kevin has been running rail tours of Australia for over 20 years and has tours on many routes, mostly using regular services such as the Australind, Indian Pacific, The Ghan, and outback trains of Queensland, but he offers also a unique Goldfields–Esperance tour from time to time which covers the West Australian lines running north from Kalgoorlie to Leonora (259km) and south past Norseman to Esperance (383km) on the coast near Cape Le Grand and the Archipelago of the Recherche, routes which have not seen regular passenger trains for many, many years. For details of running dates, costs, etc contact Kevin Pearce (☎ 08-9316 6153, 💻 www.users.bigpond.com/rail tour/), PO Box 201, Applecross, Western Australia 6153.
- **Great Southern** offer numerous outback excursions based on their rail services; Broken Hill, Kalgoorlie, Coober Pedy, Uluru and the Olgas, Kings Canyon, Katherine Gorge, Darwin attractions, and Kakadu being among them. None is cheap, but by combining rail travel with special hotel deals probably work out cheaper than doing it on your own. Also, an organized tour avoids the hassles of making a succession of bookings. Against that is the loss of individual freedom,

the ability to change plans at short notice, and the fact that such tours usually include upper-range motel-style accommodation, when the independent traveller can often find a cheaper 'pubstay' type hotel near the station or town centre.

Queensland

In Queensland such tours cover the Gold Coast, Sunshine Coast, Capricorn Coast, the Barrier Reef, Fraser Island, Yeppoon, Daintree rainforest and the outback. A series of Tilt Train short breaks are offered based on Rockhampton, ranging from afternoon tours to nearby heritage features, caves and sanctuaries to four-night packages visiting Great Keppell Island. Prices are based on hotel accommodation and transfers, not including rail fare ex-Brisbane.

• **Queensland Rail Reef 'N' Outback Tour No 2 'Spirit of Queensland'** An escorted 15-day tour covering places of interest in outback Queensland including Barcaldine, Longreach (Stockman's Hall of Fame), Winton, Walkabout Creek Hotel ('Crocodile Dundee' fame), Cloncurry, Undara Lava Tubes and Cairns, including rail travel on the Spirit of the Outback, the Gulflander, Kuranda Scenic Railway and 'Queenslander' class on the Sunlander. Book through a licensed travel agent or QR Travel Centre; $3275 per person twin share.
• **Sunlover Holidays Outback Rail Adventure** A 9-day tour covering much of the above except the Gulf country, Cairns and Kuranda but including the Capricorn coast at Rockhampton. Rail travel on the Spirit of the Outback and returning to Brisbane on the Rockhampton Tilt Train; $2229 twin share or $2529 sole use.
• **Sunlover Tropical Rail Adventure** A 12-day tour covering Hervey Bay, Fraser Island, Rockhampton, Daydream and the Whitsundays, Airlie Beach, Cairns and Port Douglas, ending in Cairns. Rail travel includes the Rockhampton and Cairns Tilt trains and the Kuranda Scenic Railway, with the return to Brisbane on the Sunlander (Queenslander Class) as an optional extra costing from $691; Tour price $2699 twin share, $3499 sole occupancy.

New South Wales

Currently CityRail in Sydney offers an attractive Blue Mountains Explorer Link ticket, which covers rail to Katoomba and back with unlimited travel on an Explorer bus stopping at 27 locations around the Blue Mountains. Useful if a visit to the Katoomba Scenic Railway (see p258) is among your plans. Other tours in New South Wales may include parts of the South Coast, the Hunter Valley, Hawkesbury River, and Old Sydney Town, a recreated historic settlement near Gosford. Local enquiry is necessary, at CityRail and Countrylink centres.

Victoria

In Victoria, tours based on Melbourne may or may not include rail fares, accommodation and guided sightseeing. These may include places such as Ballarat, Bendigo, Castlemaine, Daylesford, Echuca, the Goulburn Valley area, featuring attractions such as old gold-mining sites, the Murray riverboats, a yabby (fresh-water crayfish) farm, WWII camps, and Shepparton Equestrian Centre with its Andalusian horses.

Western Australia

For tourists with a week or more to spend in Western Australia, Transwa's famous wildflower tours are a good way to see the amazing colours of the desert flora. Tours are usually held between August and October and last a week, but rail passes are not valid. Details from Transwa (see pp23-4) or East Perth Terminal station.

PLANNING YOUR OWN ITINERARY

Although this guide suggests several pre-planned itineraries many people prefer to plan their own. But even the most detailed, such as some in this guide, can be varied to get the utmost value from the Austrail Flexipass or other passes. However, a few comments may help if you decide to work out your own salvation, plus a word or two of warning where appropriate.

Your starting point will be where you intend to land in Australia (or where you live if already here), and your finishing point will be determined likewise. Most probably you will have already decided where you want to go and what you want to see. If your aim is to cover as much of the country as you can by train an Austrail Flexipass is the best basis if you are eligible for it.

You have already seen something of what you can do in as little as 15 days (see Itineraries pp63-73) and been warned about what is and is not possible within a limited time. Before planning your itinerary you might find it useful to look at Parts 4, 5 and 6: Part 4 deals with getting between the capital cities and suggests things to do and see in each of them, especially using the local rail services. It also describes various day trips and other excursions you can make from these major centres, including important advice on how to make sure of getting back when you have intercity or interstate trains to catch, or when your ticket is about to expire. The routes are described in detail in Part 5. Part 6 gives details about private and preserved railways.

Itinerary variations and side trips (see below) highlights some of the other possible options. Although there are not too many ways you can go between the major cities – in fact keeping exclusively to trains there is usually only one – there are still branch routes which you can follow by breaking a journey some place en route and making that a temporary base for an excursion. The possibilities are many. Subject to the kind of ticket you have and the time of day or night you are willing to embark or disembark, there is a great variety of places you can visit.

ITINERARY VARIATIONS AND SIDE TRIPS

From Sydney

In the section on Sydney (see pp120-31) various day or two-day trips from Sydney are outlined: the South Coast, Southern Highlands including Canberra, Blue Mountains, Central West, Central Coast and Newcastle and its hinterland. Longer excursions or diversions from an itinerary which includes a break in Sydney might be to the Riverina area based on Griffith, to the Western Plains (Dubbo or Broken Hill) or to the Northern Tablelands and New England (Tamworth, Armidale and Moree). Route maps and descriptions are given later.

Neither Griffith, Broken Hill or the Tablelands can be covered in a day excursion. Not only is a night-stop required; a base nearer to the area is a sensible starting point. For Griffith, where there is only one train a week, Junee on the main Sydney–Melbourne route or Cootamundra would be good bases. For access to the Tablelands, Hamilton near Newcastle, or Maitland would be a good base. The trains run daily.

• **Sydney westwards** The Indian Pacific interstate train on the western route from Sydney starts in the afternoon and returns in the morning. This allows an optional morning start or evening finish to an interstate journey by using one of the reasonably frequent interurban trains to break the journey at Lithgow in the Blue Mountains, where there are convenient pub hotels near the station (but often fully booked – see p260 for details). Going west on the Indian Pacific there is also the option of taking the XPT to break the journey for several hours further west, at Bathurst, Blayney or Orange, but prior booking is essential.

Note that to join the Indian Pacific to continue west it is necessary to go to Orange East Fork, 1.8km from Orange main station, from where it leaves at 21.30.

• **Broken Hill night-stop options** The full range of options for a break of journey in Broken Hill are set out in Table 3, below. They involve either waiting between two successive calls of the Indian Pacific (three or four days for trains going in the same direction, two days if you are taking a there and back trip from Adelaide, or at least one day if going there and back from Sydney). Countrylink's Outback service allows an overnight stop but if combined with a return by the Indian Pacific allows most of the following day there – a two-day return trip. The Countrylink coach via Dubbo runs daily.

❑ Table 3: Sydney–Broken Hill–Adelaide (C 9020)

All services below are air-conditioned, have refreshment facilities and require reservations. The Adelaide services also have sleeping accommodation. Times are Eastern Standard Time except where noted.

Sydney to Adelaide		**Mon**	**Daily**	**Wed/Sat**
dep	Sydney	06.20	07.10	14.55
arr	Dubbo	–	13.40	–
dep	Dubbo	–	14.15b	–
arr	Broken Hill	19.10a	22.45a	06.45c
dep	Broken Hill–	–	–	08.20a
arr	Adelaide Keswick	–	–	15.15a
Adelaide to Sydney		**Daily**	**Tue**	**Tue/Fri**
dep	Adelaide Keswick	–	–	10.00a
arr	Broken Hill-	–	–	16.30a
dep	Broken Hill	04.00ab	07.45a	18.30a
arr	Dubbo	13.25	–	–
dep	Dubbo	14.10	–	–
arr	Sydney	20.48	21.48	10.15c

Notes: a Central Standard Time b Bus connection c Next day

• **West of Broken Hill** Beyond Broken Hill there are no opportunities for side trips or substantial variations to an itinerary since there is only the twice-weekly Indian Pacific or The Ghan between Adelaide and Port Augusta (or possibly Tarcoola, see p180) to choose from. Even west of Kalgoorlie the addition of the Prospector adds nothing to the prospects of a deviation, only to the number of trains available and the places one can stop at. Side trips from Adelaide and Perth are discussed on p156 and p160 respectively.

The only other deviations possible anywhere west of Broken Hill are private and preserved railways such as the Pichi Richi which are described in Part 6 (pp254-75).

• **Between Adelaide and Melbourne** It is sensible to arrange your itinerary so that whichever route you take between Sydney and Adelaide you come back by a different one. The choice, apart from coach links, is via Broken Hill on the Indian or via Melbourne on The Overland. The latter offers only overnight travel westbound but a daylight run from Adelaide.

Ararat is a centre from which to explore Victoria's Grampians, Pyrenees and Central Highlands. It is reached in late afternoon on the eastbound Overland. The only other option for travelling to or from Ararat with a Flexipass is via the westbound train calling (by prior booking only) around one o'clock in the morning. Tourists wishing to see this part of Victoria, with its many attractions, might therefore consider the V/Line bus, there being three services a day (two on Saturdays and Sundays), all connecting with V/Line trains at Ballarat, or using the recently reinstated V/Line Inter-city train service (see p200). The V/Line coaches also serve Great Western, Stawell, Murtoa, Horsham and Dimboola, most of which are also served, with prior booking, by The Overland (C 9035, 9401).

From Melbourne

Since the Flexipass no longer covers V/Line or other Victorian services apart from Countrylink, a Victoria Pass or local tickets are necessary for the one- or two-day trips based on Melbourne outlined on pp139-41, which include Port Phillip Bay, Gippsland area, Warrnambool and the south-west coast, Ballarat, Bendigo, Swan Hill and Echuca.

A diversion of two days or more to the Gippsland area could include a trip to **Bairnsdale** by train or connecting V/Line bus from Sale (C 9030). Bairnsdale is the main gateway to the coastal lakes of eastern Victoria. Paynesville on Lake Victoria (10km from Bairnsdale) and Lakes Entrance (35km) are specially popular resorts, the latter adjoining Victoria's Ninety Mile Beach. At **Nowa Nowa**, north of Lakes Entrance is the largest timber trestle bridge in the Southern hemisphere, on the freight-only Orbost branch of the railway, now closed to traffic altogether.

Ballarat, a historic mining centre 119km west of Melbourne, is a convenient day trip from Melbourne and also worth an overnight stay (see p200). Ballarat trains (C 9024) take on average 90 minutes, running approximately every two hours. The single (economy class) fare to Ballarat is $16.50; first class may be available on one or two trains.

Swan Hill, north of Bendigo at the confluence of the Marraboor river and the Murray, is worth a visit but cannot be reached by train on a day trip. For details of the train service see Table 10 (p141); features of the route are described on pp203-6.

If you have time to spare in Victoria it would be a pity to miss a trip to **Mildura**, a city of flowers and vines on the banks of the Murray near historic Wentworth where the Murray and the Darling meet. Mildura is capital of Sunraysia district, noted for its wide streets with a profusion of flowers in the centre strips, its wineries and dried fruits, Hattah Lakes National Park, and the ***Mildura Workingmen's Club*** which in the 1970s boasted the longest bar in the world. For several years the only regular train to Mildura was the Vinelander, a pleasant sleeping and sitting-car train with buffet, which left Melbourne's Spencer St nightly, Saturdays excepted, to arrive in Sunraysia's capital at breakfast next day. The trains on that line now go only as far as Ballarat; there is a daily bus connection from the train at Swan Hill but restoration of a train service is still under consideration.

An interesting variation on any itinerary is to take a Junction Tours coach from Mildura to Broken Hill, a useful shortcut if five hours on a bus does not appal you, especially if having to reach Mildura by bus in the first place. A unique geological feature, the Walls of China, at the ancient bed of Lake Mungo, is accessible by day coach tour from Mildura.

You can still enjoy a night and most of a weekend in Mildura if you leave Melbourne on a Friday at 16.32, returning to Swan Hill by bus leaving at 13.45 on Sunday. Otherwise, a Mildura trip on current schedules, with any useful time there at all, means going all the way from Bendigo by bus or arriving and leaving there between midnight and 04.40 in the morning (C 9110). Mildura is the kind of place where you will want to linger.

Melbourne to Sydney

If it is fruit harvest time you might like a diversion to **Shepparton** in Victoria's fertile **Goulburn Valley** to try their luscious pears. There are direct trains from Melbourne but you will need to change train at Seymour if travelling on a Melbourne–Albury train or at Benalla, then Seymour, if on the XPT from interstate. You will have time to spare at Seymour before going on to Shepparton.

If continuing north the same day a trip to the Goulburn Valley will still bring you back to Melbourne in time for the Southern Cross XPT for Sydney, but you can change instead at Seymour and take the intercity north to Benalla, Wangaratta, or Albury. Stop for dinner, then join the train for Sydney afterwards.

Assuming you have appropriate tickets, such as an Austrail Flexipass plus a V/Line Victoria Pass, an itinerary which includes a day or more in either capital city could allow the option of a break of journey in north-east Victoria or southern New South Wales, since between Melbourne and Sydney there is a choice between day and night trains, both running daily. If leaving Sydney on the daylight train, for example, you could break your journey at Cootamundra,

Junee, or Wagga Wagga. Or, if you prefer, carry on to Albury and stay there beside the River Murray for the night. In the morning you could then, if a compulsive early riser, board the V/Line intercity at 06.35 (07.55 on Sundays) or wait for the 12.25 (weekdays only). You can break the journey again at Chiltern, Wangaratta or Benalla but watch your times if intending to catch The Overland to Adelaide that same night. The last connection from Chiltern is at 16.35; from Wangaratta and Benalla at 17.02 and 17.25 respectively; five minutes or half an hour later from all three on Saturday and Sunday (C 9029 and local).

Northbound, a Melbourne departure at 08.30 on the XPT would allow a break at Benalla or Wangaratta or both, with plenty of time to reach Albury for a night-stop or in time to catch the XPT sleeper to Sydney from there at 23.15. In either direction the timetables favour journey breaks for periods of a few hours in places between Melbourne and Albury. Between Albury and Sydney the scheduling and less frequent service necessitate a 24-hour break unless you like catching or leaving trains in the middle of the night.

• **A Riverina diversion to Griffith** Junee has been suggested as a base for an excursion to Griffith (see p214) in the Riverina district of NSW. Table 4

❑ **Table 4: Riverina Links from Main South Line (C 9027, 9111, 9112)**

		Daily	**Daily**	**Daily**	**Saturday**
Melbourne	dep	08.30	–	08.30	–
Wagga Wagga	arr	13.09	–	13.09a	–
Junee	arr	13.50	–	–	–
Cootamundra	arr	14.37a	–	–	–
Sydney	dep-	–	07.43	–	07.05
Cootamundra	arr	–	12.47	–	12.28
Junee	arr	–	13.27	–	13.08
Wagga Wagga	arr	–	13.54a	–	–
Wagga Wagga	dep	–	14.15b	14.15b	–
Junee	dep	–	–	–	13.08
Cootamundra	dep	14.55b	–	–	–
Griffith	arr	17.31b	16.53b	16.53b	15.41
		Sunday	**Sunday**	**Daily**	**Daily**
Griffith	dep	07.40	07.40	09.46b	09.46b
Junee	arr	10.11	10.11	–	13.27ce
Cootamundra	arr	10.57	10.57d	12.26c	12.26c
Junee	dep	10.11	–	–	13.52
Cootamundra	dep	10.57	–	–	14.37
Sydney	arr	16.24	–	–	19.53
Cootamundra	dep	–	12.47	12.47	–
Junee	dep	–	13.27	13.27	–
Melbourne	arr	–	18.55	18.55	–

Notes: All trains have first class and economy seating, with buffet service.
a Change to bus **b** By bus **c** Change to train **d** Change trains
e Change at Cootamundra

below shows the train service options (C 9027). The weekly Countrylink Griffith Xplorer allows the option of either an overnight or full week stay in Griffith, but Countrylink coaches serve Griffith daily from Wagga Wagga and Cootamundra. V/Line coaches of Victoria connect with trains at Shepparton but the times of these are unattractive and are not shown in the table: nor are some middle of the night connections at Wagga with overnight Sydney and Melbourne trains.

Sydney to Brisbane

Assuming a daylight start from Sydney refreshed and ready for the road (the railroad of course) you have the opportunity of starting north much earlier than the 16.24 departure time of the Brisbane XPT suggested in Itinerary 1 (see p66). The Tablelands Xplorer at 10.05 or the morning Grafton XPT at 11.35, or one of the numerous, fast, double-deck, air-conditioned electric interurban trains north from Sydney will give you time to visit all sorts of places en route.

If you are exploring the area north of Sydney, up as far as Newcastle or even Maitland and you are going further north overnight the same day, there is no need to go back to Sydney because the Brisbane XPT calls at Hornsby at 16.56, Gosford at 17.41, Broadmeadow at 18.45 and Maitland at 19.09. There are later trains from Sydney to the Central Coast and Newcastle if you intend a longer break by staying overnight.

If intending to travel south from Sydney the day you are exploring the NSW Central Coast (as the area up to Newcastle is called) your deadline times to return for the Southern Cross Melbourne XPT on weekdays are 18.02 from Newcastle, 18.11 from Broadmeadow, 19.01 from Wyong, 19.17 from Gosford and 19.41 from Hawkesbury River. Weekend and holiday times are earlier, by up to 35 minutes from north of Wyong. These connections all involve changing at Strathfield to the Melbourne train. If you have left your luggage at Sydney and not booked it on the XPT you will have to leave the Central Coast earlier but times vary at weekends so local enquiry is recommended.

Another option for the northbound traveller is to take the Casino or Grafton XPT during the daytime to Dungog, Gloucester or even Taree. From there a seat or berth on the Brisbane XPT can be taken overnight; the overnight train must be picked up at Dungog at 19.55. From Gloucester it is necessary to leave at 17.40, returning south to pick up the northbound XPT at Dungog. For the overnight Melbourne XPT departure deadline you must return to Sydney by local connecting trains from Dungog at 15.05 Mondays to Fridays or at 15.17 on Saturdays. On Sundays the XPT from Dungog at 13.18 or from Gloucester at 12.24 is the only return connection.

Options are also possible travelling south from Queensland if you have a day in hand. Break your journey at a northern NSW town such as Casino, Grafton or Coffs Harbour, and continue south the next day.

Byron Bay and the Gold Coast

Earlier versions of this guide suggested an overnight stop in Byron Bay on the NSW north coast and outlined how determined rail addicts could avoid the bus connection from there via the Gold Coast to Brisbane by returning on the XPT to Grafton, then taking the Brisbane XPT north. The withdrawal of trains serving the Northern Rivers district between Casino and Murwillumbah alters the situation drastically. To reach Byron Bay it is now necessary to take the Countrylink bus from Casino, an 80-minute journey. Murwillumbah, formerly the end of the line, takes a further 55 minutes. Coaches connect from the morning XPT from Sydney and the Brisbane XPT, the latter only by changing to the coach at 04:00. The morning XPT reaches Casino at 18.34 and there are coaches to Byron Bay at 18.50, 18.55 and 19.05. A nightstop at Casino offers another alternative, with a Byron Bay coach at 10.20 the next day.

Connections to the Gold Coast may also be made from Casino at similar times, the coach journey taking two hours and 40 minutes, reaching Surfers Paradise at 06.43 and 21.40.

Returning from Byron Bay there are several options. With an Austrail Flexipass or NSW Backtracker Pass you can take a return bus to Casino at 07.58, 16.58 or 18.03 for the morning or evening train back south. The 16.58 bus would allow a 45-minute break en route at Lismore for a quick drink or snack. Continuing further north from Byron Bay is far from straightforward, involving backtracking and changing from bus to train, bus to bus or even from one train to another, and taking considerable time. If you want to stick to train, take the southbound XPT from Casino at 19.25 to Macksville, arr 23.09. The northbound Brisbane XPT calls there at 00.08. Alternatively, from Lismore at 19.25 there is a Countrylink coach to Brisbane (three hours) or at 19.27 to Surfers Paradise on the Gold Coast (two hours ten minutes). From there, after a day, night and a day or more enjoying the attractions of the area, you could retrace your steps to Casino for a train back to Sydney or north to Brisbane.

A quicker and more straightforward option from Surfers Paradise, though incurring fares not covered by any rail pass, is to take the Trainlink bus from there to Nerang (25 mins). QR Gold Coast inter-urban electric trains operate a half-hourly service from there to Brisbane, taking just over an hour. It is also possible to take a Countrylink bus from Byron Bay at 20.00 direct to Robina, southern terminus of the QR Gold Coast line. But there are only two minutes for the bus/train transfer, so you should allow for an hour's wait at Robina and a Brisbane arrival near midnight.

In Queensland

Side trips and day excursions from Brisbane are discussed on pp145-51.

On a journey from New South Wales to north Queensland you do not need to spend a night in a Brisbane hotel. Budget-conscious travellers wishing to make the train their travelling hotel can leave Brisbane the day they arrive from the south, whether the Sunlander runs that day or not, by taking the Tilt Train up to **Bundaberg**, **Gladstone** or **Rockhampton** and spending a day or more there before continuing northwards. Alternatively, the Sunlander or other northbound train can be picked up there, if running that day. You can also break the journey at many other places north of Brisbane. Inland excursions are possible, offering a marked contrast to the scenery of the North Coast line.

There are several long rail trips in Queensland, taking at least two days out and back from the coastal centres of Brisbane, Rockhampton, Townsville or Cairns. To cover the whole system would need a long holiday. With a greater passenger route length than any other Australian state and sometimes only once-weekly trains several weeks of virtual non-stop travelling would have to be set aside to cover all possible QR routes where passenger trains or mixed freight and passenger trains still run.

• **The real outback** Whilst the experience of crossing the Nullarbor by train gives a vivid impression of the vast expanse of near nothingness that is a feature of inland Australia, and you can understand the remoteness and heat experienced by workers in the railway camps along the track, this is not really the true outback of the cattle and sheep stations, or of the tiny towns with their dusty roads and pubs with verandahs. To see these you have to leave the main routes (but not necessarily the air-conditioned trains) and you have to allow plenty of time. Most such journeys are in Queensland, the only state which still has rail services solely to small inland settlements. This is not to say there are not some delightful small towns to come upon in other states, but you will see these usually on your way through to somewhere else and if the place attracts your attention you can break your journey there, depending on the time. Rather than present an itinerary (which might well cover two months or more), the following is a summary of rail safaris from major Queensland centres, leaving the traveller to select one or more as time and inclination dictate.

The base cities for these outback safaris are Brisbane, Rockhampton, Townsville and Cairns. With all of them the climbing of the ranges – the northern spurs of the Great Dividing Range – is always of scenic interest, though unfortunately done at night by some of the main air-conditioned trains. Once beyond the ranges, the countryside becomes fairly flat, semi-bushland, brigalow scrub, with occasional hills and rocky outcrops, numerous small creeks, dry for most of the year, but with here and there a deep ravine and, on the Mount Isa line, a major bridge over the Burdekin River. Soil gives way to sand and the bush to flat plains the further you travel west. On some routes the rails may be very lightweight, reducing speed to 40km/h or less. The towns bask in the hot glare of the sun and the locals seek the cool shade of the verandah or bar. Some will sit on the station platform for hours and it is a good idea to wave to them. The arrival of the train, perhaps only once a week, is still something of an event.

Exploring Queensland by rail offers glimpses of the coast, of cities, canefields, rainforest, wetlands, mighty rivers, ranges and seemingly endless vistas of bush and the red dust of the outback. The adventurous could try the four-day round trip by The Savannahlander on the former Etheridge Railway to Forsayth and back.

Looking at the options in order from Brisbane, getting 'a little further north' if not 'each year', as the popular Queensland song has it, the first and nearest is out west from Brisbane up the ranges to Toowoomba, then across the Darling Downs through Dalby, Chinchilla, Miles and Roma **to Charleville**. The return trip takes 2½ days including two nights on the train and allows over six hours at Charleville, with the option of a there-and-back coach trip to the even more remote settlement of Cunnamulla or Quilpie instead of waiting in Charleville. The journey could alternatively be broken at Mitchell or Morven. Notes on these places are on p240. If a longer stay is desired, the next train back is either two or five days later than the one you came on.

The next major stop on the North Coast line from which outback excursions may be made is **Rockhampton**. A diversion from Rockhampton into central Queensland or from Townsville inland to Mount Isa (see below) will easily fill two days or more with experiences of the rural and outback Australia many tourists never see and which you are unlikely to forget quickly. From Rockhampton, The Spirit of the Outback, which starts its journey in Brisbane, follows the route of the old Midlander Mail as far as Longreach. Two full days from Rockhampton are needed, with a night-stop at Longreach or anywhere else en route that takes your fancy. Emerald, Barcaldine and Ilfracombe are places full of interest, the last named especially if the Wellshot Hotel, closed in 2004, has been reopened (see p246). The route description (pp242-7) will provide further suggestions. The journey in each direction is entirely in daylight. There is a coach connection to Winton but this is only a viable option if you wait for a later train back to Rockhampton, either three or four days depending which train you came on.

Townsville, headquarters of the former Great Northern Railway, is the home station for Queensland's oldest 'lander' train, the Inlander which, like its Charleville and Longreach cousins, runs twice weekly. As far as time to spend in the west is concerned there is a choice with this service: the Sunday train from Townsville returns the next day from Mount Isa, whereas the Wednesday train remains there a whole day, returning on the Friday.

Among places of interest en route are Charters Towers, Hughenden Richmond, Julia Creek and Cloncurry. See the route description and maps pp247-50. At **Hughenden** there is a connection of sorts by goods train with a carriage attached for passenger use (possibly), to Winton (see p270). Enquiry at QR Townsville station is essential before seriously considering undertaking this diversion.

❑ Table 5: Townsville–Ingham

		Mon/Fri	**Tue/Thu/Sat**
Townsville	dep	08.45	13.05
Ingham	arr	10.23	14.46
		Sun/Wed/Fri	**Tue/Sat**
Ingham	dep	12.41	13.28
Townsville	arr	14.20	15.30

Notes All trains have refreshment facilities. Advance booking is recommended.

• Between Townsville and Cairns A pleasant day or two-day trip from Townsville is possible to **Ingham**. Table 5 (p84) shows the times which allow just over two hours there (worth it – see p234) on Friday only, or a day or more with stopovers.

Approaching Cairns from the south there are opportunities for a break of journey at **Tully**, which lays claim to being Australia's wettest town, or further north at Innisfail, Babinda or Gordonvale, even though there are only five trains weekly each way.

The options comprise (a) breaking the journey north before reaching Cairns, (b) breaking the journey on the way back south or (c) making Cairns your base and doing an out-and-back trip, varying from a possible brief hour or so at Tully on a Friday to a couple of nights or as long as you wish. Table 6 (below) illustrates these options.

• From Cairns Even a brief night-stop in Cairns is enough to see the nightlife and experience the warm extrovert feeling of the tropics. But Cairns is a useful base for local trips, by train, coach, launch, or hired car. A day trip to one of the islands on the Great Barrier Reef is easily undertaken from Cairns if you have a whole day there. Full-day coach tours are available to Atherton Tableland with its crater lakes, orchid gardens and waterfalls; or to Cape Tribulation and Mossman gorge.

Best known of all outback trains is The Gulflander railcar on the still isolated **Normanton–Croydon** branch (see p87), the only difficulty being in finding a way to reach it in the first place. Cairns is the nearest mainline station and obvious starting point, although Townsville offers another possible entry to Gulf Country via Cloncurry or Mount Isa.

More accessible, and still unforgettable, is the now world-famous **Kuranda Scenic Railway** (see p250) based in Cairns. This has become one of Australia's

❑ Table 6: Cairns–Tully–Cairns Options

		Tuesday	Wednesday	Friday	Saturday	Sunday
Cairns	dep	08.35	08.15	08.15	08.35	08.15
Gordonvale	arr	09.02	08.47	08.47	09.02	08.47
Babinda	arr	09.39	09.28	09.28	09.39	09.28
Innisfail	arr	10.23	10.07	10.07	10.23	10.07
Tully	arr	11.39	11.06	11.06	11.39	11.06
		Tuesday	**Thursday**	**Friday**	**Saturday**	**Monday**
Tully	dep	16.31	16.31	12.32	16.31	12.32
Innisfail	dep	17.25	17.25	13.57	17.25	13.57
Babinda	dep	18.03	18.03	14.35	18.03	14.35
Gordonvale	dep	18.43	18.43	15.20	18.43	15.20
Cairns	arr	19.20	19.20	16.00	19.20	16.00

Notes All trains have refreshment facilities. Booking is recommended.

most popular train rides and not without reason. The line twists and turns through a series of five chain curves, through tunnels and across creeks, along the sides of gorges and almost under a waterfall, for its 33km ascent of the range to the plant-festooned station of the 'village in the rainforest', Kuranda in north Queensland.

• The Rainforest Skyrail Although there are daily trains (two daily except on Saturday) between Cairns and Kuranda (C 9000) there are also many private coach tours which allow outward or return travel by train. There is also the option of taking the 7.5km Skyrail Rainforest aerial cableway from the Caravonica Lakes terminal, two minutes from Smithfield shopping centre and 11km from Cairns city centre by bus. Winner in the Major Tourist Attractions category of the 1999 National Tourism Awards, the Skyrail is a breathtaking experience, with tremendous views over the rainforest of the ranges and over the Barron Gorge. Even in heavy rain you are among the clouds just above the tree canopy and you may see the Barron Falls in flood. There are two intermediate stations en route, Barron Falls and Red Peak, where passengers can leave their gondola car and follow a boardwalk in the rainforest. Rangers are on hand as guides.

The Skyrail fare is $25 single for an adult. Skyrail/Kuranda Scenic Railway combined return bookings may also be made for $70; children pay half fare. Note that only hand luggage similar to cabin baggage on an aircraft may be taken aboard Skyrail, so leave your heavy stuff at your hotel or the railway station in Cairns or Kuranda. Kuranda terminal adjoins the railway station. For more details and to make a booking phone ☎ 07-4038 1555. The local Sunbus (☎ 07-4057 7411) has a regular service past Caravonica terminal. While waiting for a return bus there is time to visit the adjoining Tjapukai Aboriginal centre and experience something of the culture of Australia's first custodians.

• Atherton Tableland An alternative to a night-stop in Cairns or Kuranda is to go up to the Atherton Tableland. Take the Kuranda Scenic Railway to have a quick look around Kuranda, then you might find a tour coach which could take you to Mareeba, Atherton, Herberton or even Ravenshoe, stay the night and be back in Cairns the next day.

Close to **Ravenshoe**, the former end of the Atherton railway (and where a private railway now operates – see p267), are Millstream Falls, the widest waterfall in Australia, and dense Eucalypt forests. The Atherton Tableland is one of the oldest land masses in the world. Its many attractions include a giant curtain fig tree and the tranquil crater lakes of Eacham and Barrine, all about 15km east of Atherton. Private coach tours visit these features. While in the area, do your best to urge restoration of full rail services to this scenic paradise!

• Gulf Country and the Etheridge Railway Probably the nearest places on the railway to the real Gulf Country of *Crocodile Dundee* fame are **Mount Surprise, Einasleigh** and **Forsayth** in Etheridgeshire, and **Croydon** and

Normanton in the shire of Carpentaria. The last two are isolated from the rest of the system, while the others are near the end of a long inland branch from Mareeba. This long journey is unique. Until early 1995 a weekly freight train carrying passenger cars, called 'The Last Great Train Ride', covered the whole route. When this was withdrawn a railcar operated a reduced service over the isolated section between Mount Surprise and Forsayth but a through service from Cairns was later reinstated as The Savannahlander. Up and down the line goes, here curving along the side of a gorge, there descending to the creek bed and meandering among the boulders. It passes through timeless country where you just let it all happen.

On this journey there is no dining car, but the co-driver has an Esky (portable ice box) loaded with limited supplies of essentials like drinking water, soft drinks, potato crisps and possibly even beer, available on request at moderate prices. There are also lengthy stops at places where pies, cake, sandwiches and other foodstuffs and drinks can be obtained. Operated by Queensland Rail until 2004, this service is now in the care of a private group that also runs a Cairns–Kuranda Steam Train (☎ 07-4053 6848, 🖳 ckst@iig.com.au).

• **Normanton–Croydon Railway: The Unforgettable Adventure** This completely isolated 152km branch of Queensland Rail is now well-known and frequented by many tourists other than rail enthusiasts. The once-weekly regular passenger service (sometimes with non-passenger wagons attached) is by The Gulflander railmotor. It also carries motor vehicles.

By the current timetable The Gulflander (C 9006) leaves Normanton on Wednesdays at 08.30, reaching Croydon at 13.00, with a half-hour refreshment break at Blackbull at the 56 milepost from Normanton – distance indicators on this line have never been changed to metric. The return trip is on Thursday with the same departure and arrival times. At the present time, however, there appears to be no public transport linking either Croydon or Normanton with anywhere else, except by air. Unless you can find a package tour, you might be able to fly to Normanton, take the train to Croydon and back, then fly back to Cairns. Hiring a car in Cairns is another option, but you could need the best part of a week. Croydon is over 563km from Cairns and much of the road is rough!

Those who venture this far into Gulf country know they are experiencing something unique as the elderly driving railcar with its little front bogie and large single rear axle rattles along with its trailer car over the kinky track, brush-

❑ **Table 7**

Normanton–Croydon and vice versa (The Gulflander C 9006)

	Wednesday		Thursday
dep Normanton	08.30	dep Croydon	08.30
arr Croydon	12.30	arr Normanton	12.30

ing aside grass (see photo opp p145) and small trees on its four-hour dash between Croydon, once a thriving gold-rush town with its own suburban rail service, and Normanton with its magnificent heritage railway station building.

No two trips on The Gulflander are ever the same. Blackbull is one regular stop, for refreshments, but the train may stop anywhere: just ask the driver if you see something interesting. The trip is one you will never forget. One tourist told the driver 'Thanks for the wonderful ride. It's taken all the kinks out of my back'.

Useful bus connections and extensions

Since the railways in Victoria and New South Wales operate or charter bus services covering some routes no longer served by rail and to other places worth visiting and within reasonable distance of a railway station, it may be useful to list some of these.

Road coaches owned or contracted by State Rail can extend the range of places you can visit in New South Wales (and some go into Victoria). Maps and timetables can be obtained at railway stations. The places listed in the Appendix (p283) are served by bus from the stations named.

Australia probably has the longest feeder bus connection in the world, according to Thomas Cook, the well-known timetable publishers and authorities on world rail. This was introduced when State Rail of NSW replaced the historic Silver City Comet (the first air-conditioned train in the Southern Hemisphere) by a bus. Leaving Broken Hill in the middle of the night, the bus offers a 9½-hour trip to connect with the Central West XPT at Dubbo which then takes only 6½ hours to reach Sydney (See Table 4 p80).

Although V/Line abandoned many of its former passenger rail routes, the V/Line Victoria Pass-holder may use the bus services listed in the Appendix (p283) which augment or extend the rail service on major routes.

Queensland Rail does not operate bus services to anything like the extent seen in New South Wales or Victoria. The few rail-contracted bus services that exist simply replace trains on some of the remote branch lines (Cunnamulla and Quilpie from Charleville, Winton from Longreach and Toogoolawah from Ipswich) or link new stations on the outskirts of some towns with the older stations in the central area (as at Gympie and Maryborough).

There are no railway bus services linking railheads, but private buses, particularly McCafferty's offer some useful cross-country connections. To list all these would be beyond the scope of this book. Many of them make poor connections or connections at unreasonable times of day. Those listed in the Appendix (p283) are those that might just prove useful to a traveller who is willing to endure some hours in a bus to go from one remote destination to somewhere equally obscure.

PART 2: AUSTRALIA

Facts about the country

GEOGRAPHY

Australia is the sixth largest country in the world and a continent in its own right. Approximately 4000km from east to west and 3200km north to south it has a total land area of 7.68 million square kilometres but a population density of less than three persons per square kilometre. Most of these live on or near the south and eastern seaboard from Cairns in north Queensland round to the Spencer Gulf in South Australia.

The continent is bounded on the west by the Indian Ocean, on the north by the Timor and Arafura seas and the Torres Strait, on the east by the Coral Sea and the Tasman Sea, both being part of the South Pacific Ocean, and on the south by the Southern Ocean.

The mainland comprises the states of New South Wales (NSW), Victoria, Queensland, South Australia (SA), Western Australia (WA), Northern Territory (NT) and Australian Capital Territory (ACT). Tasmania is the island state, separated from the south coast of Victoria by Bass Strait.

There are many other islands of which the most significant are Bathurst and Melville to the north, Groote Eylandt and Mornington Island in the Gulf of Carpentaria, Fraser Island on the east coast, King and Flinders islands in the Bass Strait and Kangaroo Island off the coast of South Australia. The coastline on the whole appears smooth on a map; only that of the Kimberley region in the north-west and Arnhem Land in the north show the kind of fractal pattern that might have been noted by Mandelbrot or other exponents of chaos theory. The main indentations in the coastline are the Great Australian Bight and Spencer Gulf in the south and the Gulf of Carpentaria in the north.

Mountainous areas are generally confined to the coastal regions. The Great Dividing Range extends 3500km from Cape York, at the tip of northern Queensland, down through the state (Queensland) and New South Wales to near Ballarat in Victoria, its highest point being Mt Kosciusko at 2228m. Other mountainous areas include Victoria's Grampians and Pyrenees, the Mt Lofty and Flinders ranges east of Adelaide, the extreme south-west, the Pilbara and Kimberley regions of the north-west and Kakadu and Arnhem Land in Northern Territory. Tasmania is almost wholly mountainous.

The interior of the continent is mostly low lying, broken only by a few ranges, such as the MacDonnell Ranges, and strange monoliths such as Uluru (Ayers Rock) in the Red Centre. The interior is also largely stony or sandy desert: the Simpson desert, Great Victoria desert (not in Victoria), the Great

Sandy desert and the Nullarbor Plain. Travelling in a straight line from Ceduna on the South Australian Bight to the coast at the Eighty Mile Beach near Broome on the north-west coast, if such a journey were possible, would be through nothing but desert for the whole 1900km, the only signs of human occupation being the TransAustralian Railway near Maralinga and a few barely motorable desert tracks.

There are many lakes but the largest, Lake Eyre, is rarely full of water. Rivers draining into this area tend to lose their waters in the sands of the desert, except at times of exceptional heavy rain and flood, and many inland lakes are usually seen as nothing more than salt pans. The extensive, many branched rivers of the 'Channel country', the Georgina, Diamantina, Thompson River and Cooper Creek which start in the north, never reach the sea.

The Murray is Australia's greatest river; with its tributaries the Darling, the Lachlan and the Murrumbidgee, its catchment extends through most of Victoria and NSW north and west of the Dividing Range, as well as most of western Queensland south of the Tropic of Capricorn. By comparison with the Murray, the famous Snowy River is a trickle, especially since much of its water has been diverted for hydro-electric power.

CLIMATE

Australia extends from latitude 10 to 44 south. The northern third of the country is therefore within the tropics. The hottest months are December and January, while winter is in July and August, but in the north the seasonal distinction is more between dry (winter) and wet seasons; Darwin is in the monsoon belt. Christmas dinner to many Australians is a barbecue in the garden beside the pool.

Although temperatures may fall below freezing point, snow is rare except in the Snowy Mountains of NSW and the High Country of Victoria where skiing is popular in season, yet snow is not unknown even in Queensland. It can be bitterly cold in Southern Tasmania or Canberra (normal range 1° to 28°C) or in the interior of the continent at night, but visitors from Europe tend to find Australia warm. It is not unknown for a newly-arrived migrant in Tasmania from northern Europe to go for a swim in August, something few Australians would contemplate other than in a heated pool.

The climate is usually not extreme in populated places. Sydney's temperature normally ranges between 8° and 26°C, Alice Springs between 4° and 37°C, while Cairns enjoys a fairly general warmth of 18° to 32°C and Darwin a couple of degrees higher. Cloncurry in Queensland holds the record for the hottest temperature in Australia of 53.1°C in January 1889. Marble Bar in WA holds the record for the hottest sustained temperature, over 37.8°C (100°F) for 160 days, while Wyndham, also in WA, sweltered for 333 consecutive days in 1946 with temperatures at or above 32.2°C (90°F). See pp16-17 for climate charts.

The Darwin area and north Queensland have the highest average rainfall. Tully (p234) has the reputation of being Australia's wettest city, while Mt

Bellenden Ker in the ranges south of Cairns, recorded over 11,000mm of rain in 1979, 960mm (38 inches) being in one period of 24 hours. By contrast, there is a country song of which the words assert that 'the rain never falls in the dusty Diamantina' and it must seem like that until it does, and then they complain of floods.

Cyclones are a fairly regular occurrence in the wet season. Cyclone Tracy devastated Darwin in 1974 and early in 2000 Cyclone Steve cost millions of dollars in damage by a most unusual circling of the north attacking Queensland, the Northern Territory and Western Australia in succession, each time retreating out to sea only to re-form. Tornados are comparatively rare but can occur with little or no warning. Severe winds during electrical storms are more frequent. In the dry season enervating heat can be experienced in the outback, but also in the cities and often quite unexpectedly. In a city such as Melbourne the temperature can rise quite a number of degrees in the middle of the night with a wind change from cool southerly to hot blasts from the interior. Bush fires in the dry season are a regular hazard. Timetables for steam trains usually show a footnote 'does not run on days of total fire ban' and on some lines special speed restrictions are imposed when temperatures are high.

Recounting that in the summer of 1939, 368 people died from a heatwave that hit the southern states, the Readers Digest *Book of Australian Facts* asserts that Australia is 'one of the least comfortable continents in the world' but most residents including Australians by adoption would tend to disagree.

However, visitors should beware of the sun. Queensland proudly boasts of being the 'Sunshine State': it is also the skin-cancer capital of the world. Always wear a hat outdoors, use sunscreen (locally bought) liberally on exposed flesh and you should have a good day.

THE ENVIRONMENT

Flora and fauna

Since the early observations of botanist Joseph Banks who accompanied Captain Cook, it has been well known that Australia has a rich, diverse and unusual range of plant and animal life. The gum tree and the kangaroo are now known worldwide but there are thousands more – the colourful and often noisy birds, the marine life and the unbelievable curiosities such as the duck-billed platypus, an egg-laying mammal.

Although a visitor can spend weeks in Australia without seeing a kangaroo, let alone a platypus, unless at a wildlife sanctuary, one would have to be both blind and deaf not to become aware that the flora and fauna are different from that found in most other countries.

A walk through a suburban park or down a street can be disturbed by a crowd of noisy galahs or the raucous laughter of a kookaburra, while underfoot the leaves scattered on the footpath are of unfamiliar shape and colour and apparently being shed from trees irrespective of the season; the distinction between deciduous and evergreen trees is blurred. Flowers seem to bloom throughout the year. These are among the differences a migrant notices in the first few months but a short-term visitor who spends time only between four-star hotels in the main cities will miss many of the natural wonders of Australia. Worth looking out for are the following:

• **Birds and beasts** The black and white **magpie** is widespread; its tuneful call is heard especially in the early morning but its habit of swooping down to attack people approaching too close to its nest in spring does not endear it to postmen.

The **kookaburra**'s call is unmistakable. Once known as the laughing jackass the kookie is a well-loved and easily-recognized member of the kingfisher family, at home in the suburbs as well as the bush.

The **parrot** family is widely represented. Flocks of pink and grey galahs swoop above suburban gardens, while screeching white cockatoos disturb the morning calm. Unbelievably colourful **lorikeets** (bright red, blue, green and yellow like something painted) and **rosellas** can be seen feeding on the blossoms which adorn many garden shrubs.

In the bush you may hear the curious call of the **whipbird** – a faint whimper followed by the sound of a lash but you would be hard put to see one, or to recognize it if you did. More likely sounds in the bush will be the shrill chorus of **cicadas** or the variety of barks, gulps, grunts and rattling sounds produced by the different species of **frogs**.

The **lyrebird** and the golden **bowerbird** are worth looking out for, the Dandenongs east of Melbourne being a favoured habitat of the former and Lamington National Park on the Queensland/NSW border of the latter. The less-colourful **satin bowerbird** with its nest strewn with blue lures to attract the female (anything from blue feathers to blue felt-pen tops) may well be among the bush features visible on a trip on Queensland's Savannahlander (see p53 and pp251-3 for the route description).

Larger birds such as the wedge-tailed **eagle** (the symbol of The Indian Pacific) can be seen on a trip across the Nullarbor, while on lines in western Queensland and NSW **emus** are a common sight, usually running away from the train. As the song says of Old Man Emu 'I can't fly, I'm telling you, but I'll run the pants off a kangaroo'. In similar places you should see mobs of roos, perhaps standing up looking towards the train, then bounding away when they conclude it not to be friendly. Travelling by road, **kangaroos** and their smaller cousin the **wallaby** are more often seen dead at the roadside than moving around. In zoos and managed sanctuaries you can feed roos and wallabies; you may be able to on the Savannahlander excursion too.

One of the smallest of the roo tribe is the little pademelon. These may be seen hopping around like rabbits up at O'Reilly's (see p150) in Lamington National Park, a day excursion by road from Brisbane.

Koalas are another distinctive Australian marsupial. Cuddly-looking like a teddy bear they are shy creatures whose environment is very much threatened. Koalas' diet is very limited since they can only eat the leaves of a few of the 700 species of Eucalypt.

• **Trees and flowers** **Eucalypts** vary tremendously, particularly in the bark. The visitor will soon discern the difference between a scribbly gum, a paperbark, a bloodwood and a ghost gum. Gum species often have confusing names, like peppermint (nothing to do with the herb) or mountain ash (as different from the rowan tree as can ever be imagined). Tasmanian blue gums rival the redwoods of North America for sheer size, as do the jarrah trees of south-west Australia.

The **coolabah**, famed in song, is a rather undistinguished tree common in the northern bush. Various species of **acacia**, known as wattles, are widespread, many being noted for their colourful blooms. In fact, most Australian trees at one time or another have noticeable blossoms. The colourful **jacaranda**, an attractive feature of many built-up environments, is, however, an introduced species.

Wild flowers also abound but, if wandering in the bush, beware of picking flowers; many are poisonous, like the snakes and spiders, and many have sharp prickles. Even the dead leaves of some plants can give a painful sting. Beware the **Gympie Tree**: it stings like a nettle only ten times worse.

But in spite of the dangers, you are safer in the bush than on the roads of the city.

Ecology

The word 'ecology' (the relationship between living organisms and their environment) first appeared in 1873 and it was perhaps not until then that people began to realize that their own activities could and did change the environment: changes were not due just to nature. Ecology and the environment are inextricably linked with the history of human settlement.

Arthur Holmes, in his classic *Principles of Physical Geology* (1944, pp15-16) asserts that, 'Man himself has been one of the most prodigal of the organic agents of destruction', citing experience in Africa and America as evidence. Recent controversy in Queensland over tree clearing shows that many are still unaware that 'Forests break the force of rain ... they regularise the actual rainfall' and that 'reckless removal of forests may imperil the prosperity of whole communities.'

The dangers are startlingly evident in Australia today, with fears of the whole Murray basin being ruined by increased salinity, one result of deforestation and overcultivation in areas of low annual rainfall. There is also no doubt that the environment has been substantially altered in many parts of Australia over the years of recorded human activity. The continuing process of degradation can be seen from the train on the plains of the outback, in the bush, among the ranges and even on the coast.

HISTORY

Without written records little is known about Australia's earliest inhabitants. Archaeological excavation, mainly by wind and rain, reveal that ritual burial was practised 15,000 years before the construction of the Egyptian Pyramids and that chipped stone implements were used to prepare food from animal carcasses. Rock paintings depict hunting and other scenes, including pictures of animals now extinct.

The Aborigines probably had a better understanding of ecology than modern Europeans. Their way of life involved moving from place to place, burning the bush in one area, taking its fruits, then moving on and allowing regeneration. The Aboriginal relationship to the land is something quite alien to societies brought up on the concept of private ownership. The principle that the land belongs to the tribe, however, is common to many cultures. The Aboriginal concept goes further – the land and the people are as one:

> 'Listen carefully this, you can hear me.
> I'm telling you because earth just like mother
> and father or brother of you.
> That tree same thing.'
> (*Story about Feeling*, Bill Neidje, Magabala Books 1989)

Another Aboriginal philosopher and writer, Kevin Gilbert, expressed the same theme. The first and last verses of his poem *Earth* read:

> 'Of the earth am I
> The breath that nurtured all the young
> Of earth; with earth to earth again I fly
> With every thought I thought and song I sung
> Was earth and earth in all its bounty
> Gave to me and mine a wise increase.'
>
> 'The learned came; and said gods had I none
> No politics nor sovereign embassy
> Their learned ignorance served as a pass
> For pioneers to kill the god in me.'
>
> (Race Memories, in *Because a White Man will Never Do it*, 1973
> Reprinted by permission of Harper Collins, Publishers)

Australian Aboriginal society has the world's longest continuous cultural history. Although a few European explorers saw and may have set foot on parts of the coast from the early 1600s, the year 1770 marked what must have been to the then inhabitants the beginning of the end of dreamtime and the start of nightmare time. Captain James Cook reported that the locals wanted nothing more than that the strangers go away.

But they did not, except temporarily. They came back and claimed the land for Britain: named it New South Wales and regarded the whole continent as Terra Nullius under British law (Land with No People). Aborigines did not count in any census until 1967: Section 127 of the Constitution of 1901 stipulated that 'Aboriginal natives shall not be counted'.

The history since European settlement has been well covered in many books and from different points of view. Several are suggested in the Appendix (p280). Following is a very brief outline:

The selection of Australia as a suitable place for convicts followed Britain's loss of the American colonies. The First Fleet which sailed into Botany Bay, Sydney, in 1788 carried 750 convicts, forerunners of over 168,000 before transportation was abolished 80 years later. Settlers including freed convicts, seeking a living out of the land, broke the delicate balance between the original people and nature. The invaders cut down trees and introduced feral and domestic animals which competed with the native fauna for food and water. Hungry Aborigines might spear cattle and sheep for food. This brought savage reprisals. It is now well known that Tasmanian aborigines were systematically wiped out through a series of punitive actions which culminated in an official drive to collect and resettle the remaining natives on an offshore island where they died. What is less well known is that it was official policy for many years after that to dilute the Aboriginal race by gradual assimilation into white society. A hundred years after the invasion, untainted Aboriginal society had become largely confined to Arnhem Land and small pockets in the interior.

Australia became a nation in the eyes of the rest of the world in 1901 with Federation. In an astonishing repudiation of its history, a bill was passed by the parliament restricting immigration of non-whites. Known as the White Australia Policy, this remained in force until 1972. The non-white Australians who had been custodians of the land for thousands of years were never consulted on the matter.

Land rights remain a contentious issue. The terra nullius legal fiction was finally laid to rest by the High Court Mabo decision of 1992. A Native Title Act was passed by the Federal Government in 1993, following Mabo, which recognized Aboriginal land rights to a very limited extent. Even this was bitterly opposed by vested interests, most notably the mining and farm lobbies. Some years later the High Court Wik decision confirmed that native title could exist even where pastoral leases had been granted. The Federal government responded by amending the Native Title Act so as to remove or water down the limited land rights already won by Aboriginal people.

Argument continues and until some of these questions are settled, true 'reconciliation' between Aboriginal people and later settlers may remain unresolved. Discussion continues on subjects such as the 'stolen generation' where, over several generations, children of Aboriginal mothers were taken to be brought up in what to them was an alien society. Though many still believe it to have been a well-intentioned policy at the time, documentary evidence shows it was far from benign, at best born of ignorance and now generally recognized as a tragic blunder. But even expressing sorrow for what happened in the past seems difficult for some today.

AUSTRALIAN SOCIETY TODAY

Australia is a multicultural society; ethnic groups abound. Melbourne is said to have a larger Greek population than Athens. Italian migrants are dominant in parts of the Riverina of NSW. In Brisbane's Fortitude Valley the street signs are in Chinese; Chinese were among the earliest settlers of the non-Aboriginal groups. More recently Vietnamese have formed communities of their own, though not in ghettos but mingling with their neighbours. Racism is evident but mainly subdued in spite of the degree of support in 1999 for the short-lived political party, One Nation, with its perceived racial policies, since denied.

The theme 'We are Australian' and the idea of mateship are what most Australians aspire to, but inequalities in the treatment of different groups continue and fuel the misunderstandings and ignorance which so often cloud issues.

All Australian residents aged over 18 are allowed a vote and voting is compulsory. Elections are held all too frequently in the view of some, since there are three levels of government, federal, state and local. The main political parties are (in alphabetical order) Labor, Liberal, and National. Minor parties include the Greens, the Democrats and the remnants of One Nation. Independents are significant in the political arena, sometimes holding the balance of power in a parliament.

There is a Senate as well as a House of Representatives, with the governor-general representing the queen. There is popular support for a republic but distrust of politicians, an Australian tradition, led to the failure of a 1999 referendum on the subject. Each state has its own government and a parliament, though not all have a senate. Local authorities generally devolve their power from state governments but are elected by the residents of their areas.

The distribution, and separation, of powers between federal, state and local governments, between government and judiciary, and the financial arrangements between them, while to some extent enshrined in the constitution, are matters of constant debate. Keen argument existed over the introduction of a new taxation system, ostensibly beneficial to the states but which included a Goods and Services Tax. Though welcomed by big business and the well-to-do, this has remained unpopular with the general public.

Practical information for the traveller

This section is not meant to be a comprehensive guide to Australia; providing general practical information would merely duplicate what is available in guides such as Lonely Planet's *Australia* which is an extremely comprehensive volume and well worth the price. Another good buy is Thomas Cook's *Australia* in the Independent Traveller series, whilst for details of accommodation you cannot do better than Jason's Guides which are obtainable free at Visitor Information Centres and many hotels. *Australia by Rail* does, however, provide enough essential information to keep the average visitor from going wrong, as well as offering tips on places to stay and eat.

ARRIVING IN AUSTRALIA

Most airports – certainly the main international ones – have bus services which convey passengers to city hotels and railway stations at fairly reasonable prices and usually with a fairly frequent service; buses conveniently wait outside the baggage collection areas at airports. There are always taxis as well; these offer a door-to-door service and are generally quicker but cost twice as much (or sometimes considerably more). Sydney and Brisbane are the only cities with an airport-to-city rail link. For details of services in the main cities see the box below.

❑ Airport links

The following is a summary of the airport links currently available:

• **Adelaide** Skybus every hour or half-hour to and from the city, the 7km journey calling at hotels as required and the Great Southern rail terminal at Keswick when trains are due. For further details phone ☎ 08-8332 0528.

• **Brisbane** Coachtrans buses (☎ 07-3238 4700) leave on the hour and half-hour from Brisbane Transit Centre, calling at hotels en route. The 'Airtrain' Airport rail link service (☎ 13 12 30 within south-east Queensland or ☎ 07-3215 5000) runs every half hour from 05.00 (05.40 on Sundays) to 18.45 daily from Robina via the city's stations. Extra services operate to and from Roma St except on Saturdays. The journey time between the city and international airport is 23 minutes; three minutes more to the domestic airport. One-way fares are $10 from the city (Roma St or Central), $20 from the Gold Coast (Robina). A special 'door to door' fare of $28 covers delivery or pick-up from Gold Coast hotels.

• **Cairns** Airport Shuttle Bus to the city (7km) departs following the arrival of flights, calling at hotels. The railway station is in the city centre. For further details phone ☎ 07-4048 8355.

• **Darwin** There is no regular public transport to or from the airport, but a shuttle bus serves arrivals and departures at the airport at Marrara. Fares to the city are $8, and between the airport and railway station at Berrimah $9. For further details phone Tourism Top End at ☎ 08-8936 2499 or Freephone ☎ 1300 138 886.

• **Melbourne** 'Skybus Express' services most flights, calling at Spencer Street Station and also at hotels on weekdays. Allow at least one hour for the 23km journey. Phone ☎ 03-9670 7992 for further details.

• **Perth** The 'Feature Tours' bus calls at hotels and East Perth station en route to the city centre; a 13km journey. Allow 45 minutes from boarding the bus which meets all arrivals. Phone ☎ 08-9475 2900 for fares and further information.

• **Sydney** The Airport Rail Link, with stations at the domestic and international terminals connects directly to Central, to the six City Circle stations and to the Campbelltown and Illawarra lines at Wolli Creek. Travel time from Central is 10 minutes and trains are very frequent, only minutes apart at peak times. The one-way fare is $10 with reductions for children, students and pensioners. Holders of rail passes valid on CityRail pay only an access fee of $6.20 to embark or disembark at either airport station.

Arrivals at Sydney are subject to a noise tax and various other taxes are payable at Australian airports. A departure tax is payable for all international flights. These taxes are added to the ticket prices quoted and not paid separately.

GETTING AROUND

Qantas and Virgin Blue operate regular **flights** between the major cities. Jetstar, a Qantas offshoot, was a newcomer in 2004, with cut-price fares and reduced amenities. Smaller operators serve regional routes, mostly based on services to the nearest state capital though with some useful interstate links, eg Broken Hill to Adelaide.

All major towns have **bus services**, though with development at a generally low density compared to European cities the coverage is not always good and large areas, particularly of newer suburbs may have no public transport.

Suburban **train services** operate in Sydney, Newcastle, Melbourne, Brisbane, Adelaide and Perth and **ferries** are an essential complement to other public transport in Sydney and Brisbane. **Taxis** are plentiful in all but the smaller towns and **car hire** is similarly available.

ACCOMMODATION AND EATING OUT

There are hotels, motels, hostels and camp/caravan sites almost everywhere, ranging from luxury (five-star) hotels in the major cities to the country pub, bed and breakfast and backpacker hostel; prices vary accordingly.

Tourist offices supply free brochures such as 'What's on in Our Town' with lists of hotels/restaurants. Railway travel centres provide similar information, and the Australian Hotels' Association (see box below) is another source. The NSW Hotels' Association (☎ 1800 807 772 or 🖳 www.pubstay.org.au) issues a leaflet *Pubstay* listing hotels (mostly budget ones) throughout NSW. The Yellow Pages telephone directories, which can be consulted at any post office and may still be found in some telephone boxes, list all the places to stay and eat, in whatever town you happen to be.

Some hostels are operated by the Youth Hostel Association (YHA) or are privately run. For details of YHA hostels in Australia contact the YHA/HI in your own country or the Australian YHA (☎ 02-9565 1699, 🖳 www.yha.com.au), PO Box 314, Camperdown, NSW 1450.

The two main chains of privately-owned hostels are VIP

❑ Australian Hotels' Association (AHA) head offices

AHA offices are combined with the relevant state organization, thus Queensland Hotels Association (QHA) is the same as AHA Queensland.

Australian Capital Territory	☎ 02-6273 4007
New South Wales	☎ 02-9281 6922
Victoria	☎ 03-9822 0900
Queensland	☎ 07-3221 6999
South Australia	☎ 08-8232 4525
Western Australia	☎ 08-9321 7701
Northern Territory	☎ 08-8981 3650
Tasmania	☎ 03-6278 1930

Backpackers Resorts of Australia (VIP-BRA; 💻 www.backpackers.com.au) and NOMADS Backpackers International (💻 www.nomads-backpackers.com).

Prices in backpacker-type hostels range from about $15 (dorm bed) to $70 or more (single, en suite). Rooms in budget hotels range from about $25 with shared facilities up to around $80 for en suite, air-conditioning, fridge and TV. Medium-range hotels and motels (one-star to three-star) may vary in price from $50 to over $120, some including breakfast, some not. Where actual prices are quoted in this guide, they are subject to alteration, and where not given, are likely to be within or close to the ranges outlined above.

Rooms in pubs and country hotels will nearly always have a washbasin but less likely en suite facilities. A motel in Australia almost invariably provides a fridge, tea-making facilities, en suite and TV. Motels with a three-star classification are also likely to have private (en suite) facilities; this is not necessarily so with hotels with a one- or two-star classification.

Suggestions for places to stay in the main cities, some of which were chosen because they are near railway stations, are listed in Part 4 under Where to Stay. Prices quoted are, unless specified, for a single room. Twin/double rooms generally cost the same or little more, unless breakfast is included.

Flag Choice has a wide range of accommodation throughout Australia and also operates a Flag Hotel Pass which must be bought before arrival in Australia. For further information ask your travel agent or visit Flag Choice's website 💻 www.flag choice.com.au. Flag Hotels are usually three or four star, in a slightly higher price range than the hotel prices quoted above. Four- and five-star hotels, such as the Hilton, range from $180 to $330 for a single room to over $1000 for an executive suite.

Note that the star rating awarded by motoring or government organizations is based on facilities and thus is not necessarily commensurate with quality. The absence of a rating in no way indicates a low standard of amenities or service. Surly or indifferent service can be encountered in a four-star hotel while friendly hosts may go out of their way to look after your needs in a country town pub with no classification at all.

Meal prices and the quality of food in restaurants also vary tremendously. Unlike hotels, capital city eateries are often no dearer than those in smaller towns. It is possible to obtain a satisfying counter meal in a pub for less than $10, some even less than half that, and main courses in restaurants range from about $16 to $35. A Townsville quayside open-air restaurant offers monster steaks and seafood platters for less than $20 and a dozen fresh oysters for less than $10 (p233). Even in a Queensland Rail buffet-diner a two-course meal may cost no more than $18;

❑ Prices in this book – Australian dollars

Note that all prices quoted in this book are given in Australian dollars unless otherwise indicated. The exchange rate at the time of writing was Australian $1 to US$0.78 or UK£0.41. For up-to-the-minute rates visit **www.xe.net/currency**.

there are separate courses and snack meals for less. If you pay twice that anywhere you are either exceedingly well-heeled or you have picked the wrong place. Always look out for a price list at the door before being committed.

TIME

Australia has three time zones; Western Standard Time (WST) in Western Australia is GMT +8; Central Standard Time (CST) in South Australia and Northern Territory is GMT +9½, and Eastern Standard Time (EST) in New South Wales, ACT, Victoria, Queensland and Tasmania is GMT +10.

Daylight saving operates in South Australia (CST +1), but not Northern Territory, and in the eastern states (EST +1) except Queensland, from the last Sunday in October (the first Sunday in Tasmania) to the last Sunday in March. Broken Hill, NSW, adopts South Australian time.

POST AND TELECOMMUNICATIONS

Post offices are generally open from 9am to 5pm, Monday to Friday, though some are open at the weekend, particularly Saturday mornings. Branches within major shopping complexes may also be open on Sundays. Local letters and cards cost 50c. Parcel, express post and other special services are available.

Poste restante services are available throughout Australia – mail can be sent c/o any post office. **Telephone kiosks** are found in most population centres. Some take coins (minimum 40c); others need phonecards which can be purchased locally. It is increasingly common to find coin-operated machines out of order so it is useful to carry a mobile phone. The **mobile phone network** is being converted to digital, but there is difficulty in some rural areas where the analogue system has still to be effectively replaced. **Internet centres**, many with cafés, are increasingly common in major cities and even small towns.

ELECTRICITY

Electricity supply is at 240v and three-pin plugs of an unusual design are used. Adaptors for British and North American plugs are available from most good hardware shops.

BANKS AND MONEY MATTERS

There are banking and exchange facilities at Thomas Cook and American Express offices in major cities, as well as at banks themselves. Banks are usually open from 09.30 to 16.00 Monday to Friday and most have an ATM with 24-hour access. There are autobanks (ATMs) at the main railway stations in most capital cities though they are not all easy to find; just ask. At all major stations there is a counter for enquiries about facilities needed by the traveller.

Most credit cards are acceptable for rail bookings at major stations, and for meals or other refreshments on most major train services, usually subject to a $10 minimum. Countrylink of NSW does not, however, accept Amex or Diners

Club cards. Taxis usually add a surcharge for credit card use.

The Australian currency is the Australian dollar, consisting of 100 cents. Notes are issued in $5, $10, $20, $50 and $100 denominations and coins are 5c, 10c, 20c and 50c. Prices in odd numbers of cents are rounded to the nearest 5.

❑ **Exchange rates**

USA	$1	A$1.30
Canada	$1	A$1.10
Europe	€1	A$1.72
UK	£1	A$2.47
New Zealand	$1	A$0.92
Japan	¥100	A$1.25
South Africa	R1	A$0.23

For up-to-the-minute exchange rates visit **www.xe.net/currency**.

TIPPING

Tipping in Australia is optional; it is occasionally practised in restaurants (and in dining cars), less often – if ever – in bars, rarely in sleeping cars, and hardly ever in taxi cabs – where it is customary to sit next to the driver and engage in friendly conversation. A genuine 'thanks, mate' will be more appreciated than a tip, which is regarded as patronizing or even insulting. Remember, the Australian ethic is that everyone is as good as you, and you as good as they provided you don't commit the unforgivable sin of comparing Australia unfavourably with your own country!

HOLIDAY PERIODS

Public holidays

Many firms close or operate with skeleton staff between Christmas and New Year, and January is a holiday month when some businesses are closed for two or more weeks. The following are Australia-wide public holidays:

- **1 January** New Year's Day
- **26 January** Australia Day (commemorating the 1st Fleet's arrival in 1788)
- **March/April** (dates vary) Good Friday, Easter Saturday, Sunday and Monday plus Easter Tuesday in Tasmania
- **25 April** Anzac Day (commemorates the troop landings at Gallipoli, Turkey, 1915)
- **25 and 26 December** Christmas Day and Boxing Day

Other public holidays vary from state to state as follows:

- **14 February** Regatta Day (Tasmania)
- **1st Monday in March** Labour Day (WA), Eight Hours' Day (Tasmania)
- **2nd Monday in March** Labour Day (Victoria)
- **1st Monday in May** May Day (NT), Labour Day (Queensland)
- **1st Monday in June** Foundation Day (WA)
- **2nd Monday in June** Queen's Birthday (all except Western Australia)
- **1st Monday in August** Bank Holiday (ACT, NSW), Picnic Day (NT)
- **Last Monday in September** Queen's Birthday (WA)
- **1st Monday in October** Labour Day (ACT, NSW, South Australia)
- **1st Tuesday in November** Melbourne Cup Day; this annual horse race is rec-

ognized and honoured throughout the country and watched on every available TV set. It is a public holiday in Melbourne.

- **Last Tuesday in December** Proclamation Day (South Australia)

There are numerous regional and local events which attract much attention and may affect transport or disrupt other normal activities. These include such varied events as the Sydney to Hobart Yacht Race (starts on Boxing Day), Sydney Gay & Lesbian Mardi Gras (February), Darwin Beer Can Regatta (August, see p165), Birdsville Races in Queensland (August/September, p241), Henley-on-Todd Regatta (p184) and the Australian Country Music Festival in Tamworth, New South Wales (p221).

School holidays

School holidays vary from state to state. Most schools have two weeks' holiday around Easter, two further weeks some time between the last week in June and the third week in July, two more between mid- and late September and the first week in October and the main summer holiday is from just after the middle of December to about the end of January. Private schools generally have up to an extra week in most holiday periods. University vacations are longer. Trains are more crowded at these times thus it is particularly important to book early.

CULTURE AND LEISURE ACTIVITIES

Despite a popular belief overseas that Australians spend most of their spare time in the pub playing 'two up' there is a wide variety of leisure activities to which Australians are devoted. **Cricket**, of course, is one of them, whether watching it on TV, going to see a match or participating as the legendary bloke who 'scored a hundred in the backyard at mum's'. **Football** is also a popular game, though not usually English soccer or American gridiron. Australia has its own strange Aussie rules football (a development of Gaelic football) while **rugby**, both Union and League, is almost sacred.

Swimming, surfing and other **water-based activities** are also popular: they even have a boat race at Alice Springs in the dry centre of the continent (see p184). When the Melbourne Cup **horse race** is on, almost everything else stops. In some places they even race cockroaches or cane toads (and bet on them – gambling is widespread).

Cinemas and **theatres** have many devotees. **Ballet** and **opera** are also popular; the Sydney Opera House is not just a monument and operas and concerts are even performed on occasion in the outback by visiting artistes. An evening spent drinking and socializing in the **pub** is still common but drink-driving laws have tended to dampen enthusiasm somewhat.

Watching television at home (and playing computer games) are popular with old and young alike. Many favourite British and American TV series are just as popular here. There are commercial and national channels to choose from. The ABC is Australia's free-from-advertising (except of their own programmes and products) radio and TV channel. Listen to Macca's Sunday Morning ABC broadcast *Australia All Over* for a potpourri of real Australiana.

PART 3: THE RAILWAY SYSTEM

The history of the railways

INTRODUCTION

One of the earliest of all Australian lines and the first to carry passengers was probably unique; with timber rails laid on the ground, the passengers in open trucks and the motive power supplied by unfortunate convicts spurred on by whips, the 8km (5-mile) Tasman Peninsula railway linked Taranna and Oakwood, carrying warders and visitors to the infamous prison of Port Arthur. Very little of this rail route can still be seen but other early lines remain, many of which are still in use. The horse-drawn service at Port Elliot, now part of the SteamRanger route (see p271), was the first public railway in 1854. The Melbourne and Hobson's Bay Railway, the first loco-hauled passenger railway, also started that year: running from Flinders St to Sandridge (as Port Melbourne was then known) it has after a gauge change become the Port Melbourne light rail branch of Melbourne's extensive tramway network.

The system has developed gradually since 1827 when the first coal wagonway was constructed near Newcastle – reminiscent of the early wagonways of England's Tyneside which had heralded the start of modern railways a century earlier. New lines are still being planned and constructed as older lines are abandoned, but there has never been a national plan. Most of the first railways were spur lines penetrating inland from the coast, tapping areas of primary produce – wheat, wool and minerals, but taking general freight and passengers too. Most were not connected and there was no uniform gauge.

THE PROBLEM OF DIFFERENT RAIL GAUGES

Rail gauge differences have plagued railways the world over but few countries have suffered more than Australia where, for most of its railway history, long-distance passengers had to transfer from one train to another, often in the middle of the night. Historians have described the rivalries and parochial mentalities which produced this proliferation of gauges. There were sound reasons for different states choosing the gauges they did but some decisions, in retrospect, were unforgivable.

Early days

The story of how they failed to cooperate reads like fiction. The seeds of confusion were sown in the early administration arrangements of the new colonies. Some rail routes began as private ventures, but it was not long before governments took over. The governments of New South Wales (NSW), Victoria and South Australia settled on a uniform gauge before construction commenced but the stubbornness of their engineers led them subsequently to disregard this arrangement.

Historian Geoffrey Blainey recounts the role of one of the key figures, an Irish engineer called Shields, who rejected advice that standard gauge should be adopted, maintaining that the Irish 1600mm-gauge was superior. So it was, in a way, but not enough to make much difference. When New South Wales, following Shields' advice, planned its first lines on the Irish gauge, Victoria decided to follow suit and so did South Australia. These Irishmen certainly have the gift of the blarney! They promptly went ahead. This was in the early 1850s. But by the time they had started Shields had resigned and another engineer took his place who made it his first duty to convince the NSW government that the original plan to build standard gauge was the right one. It should have been easy to resolve differences before things went too far but as politicians postured construction went on, and the longer it went on the less chance there was of putting it right.

Expansion

Things were further complicated from the 1860s when railway construction began in Western Australia and Queensland. It was popularly believed that narrow-gauge railways were cheaper to construct, so with vast distances to cover, these two colonial governments opted for the 1067mm (3ft 6in) narrow gauge. South Australia also opted for new lines on this gauge.

The first railway in Queensland opened in 1865. Extending 35km, it linked Ipswich to Grandchester (then Bigge's Camp). Ten years later another spur had commenced at Rockhampton. Railways gradually penetrated the interior, moving inland from the ports to tap the resources of the hinterland and by 1895 there were seven completely unconnected systems focusing on Brisbane, Rockhampton, Mackay, Townsville, Cairns, Normanton and Cooktown. By 1925 the east-coast branches were linked but the Normanton Railway is still isolated.

Differences remain

New South Wales, from Sydney west to Broken Hill, south to Albury and Canberra, north to the Tablelands and coast and up to Queensland, uses standard gauge (1435mm or 4ft 8½in). The systems in Victoria, radiating north, east and west from Melbourne, are mostly of the broader Irish gauge (1600mm or 5ft 3in) though some have been converted to standard gauge, leaving several branches quite isolated. Victoria had until recently the largest Irish-gauge system in the world.

The main passenger lines of South and central Australia are now all standard gauge but most of the rest of South Australia has different gauges. South Australia has almost the only world example of triple-gauge track; combined 1067, 1435 and 1600mm with four parallel rails. Much of this could still be seen at Gladstone where sidings of three gauges combined remained in use well into the 1980s but they were torn up in the 1990s. A small section still remains in the yard at nearby Peterborough.

Queensland, from Brisbane north and west retains the narrower 1067mm-gauge giving it the first and largest mainline network in the world at a narrower than standard (less than 1435mm) gauge. In international railway parlance this is sometimes called colonial gauge, a name best not used in Australia; 'Queensland gauge' is preferable. Queensland also has a sugar-cane rail network of 600mm gauge and the private Comalco line at Weipa in the far north is standard gauge. Western Australia has both narrow and standard gauge with some sections combined. Of its two main passenger trains one runs on 1435mm track between Perth and Kalgoorlie and the other on 1067mm track between Perth and Bunbury. Tasmania has 1067mm gauge.

Years of inconvenience

It is easy to picture the havoc this has caused for interstate trains. Before 1917 there was no Trans-Australia railway linking east and west. There was a great gap across the dry, sparsely populated semi-desert country between Port Augusta in South Australia and Kalgoorlie in the west. The missing link was completed on 17 October 1917 when construction teams, working simultaneously from each end as they did in the USA in 1869, met at Ooldea on the eastern edge of the Nullarbor. Even so, gauge differences in the state rail systems prevented through running.

In the early days gauge differences meant as many as four changes of train on a journey from Brisbane to Perth. Not until 1930 was a Brisbane to Sydney journey possible without a change of train. The older inland link where standard and Queensland gauge met at Wallangarra was eclipsed when the standard-gauge route from Kyogle in NSW crossed the ranges by the dramatic Border Loop spiral, an engineering feat which reveals the difficulties of the terrain.

The standard gauge was not extended to Melbourne until 1962 when a new single line was built alongside the Victorian broad-gauge line to Albury; Perth had to wait until 1970 and Adelaide until 1983. It was not until 23 February 1970 that a new train, appropriately named the Indian Pacific from the oceans bordering Australia on the west and east, and using the newly standardized Broken Hill to Port Pirie line, marked the end of the former train changes that had so inconvenienced long-distance passengers. The train was welcomed by a crowd of 10,000 as it burst through the welcoming banners at East Perth terminal four days later.

Standardization at last – in part

Since 1995 the gauge problem has been overcome on all the main interstate routes. Brisbane in Queensland, Sydney in NSW, Melbourne in Victoria, Adelaide in South Australia, Perth in Western Australia, and Alice Springs and Darwin in the Northern Territory are all now linked by the standard-gauge network, yet the Great South Pacific Express, formerly running between Cairns and Sydney, required a bogie exchange in Brisbane. Surprisingly, the Spanish Patentes Talgo wheelset-adjustment principle has never been adopted in Australia.

Ironically, the last of the interstate lines to be standardized was Australia's oldest – The Overland rail route from Adelaide to Melbourne. In 1887, 14 years before Federation, the first interstate train in Australia was introduced, appropriately named the Intercolonial Express. In 1901 the now despised adjective 'colonial' was dropped and the name was changed to Melbourne Express. This in turn gave way in 1936 to the present name The Overland.

Route changes

The route between Adelaide and Melbourne has changed in the last ten years. When it was decided to convert to standard gauge, a more level but longer route via North Geelong and Maroona was chosen in place of the old route between Melbourne and Ararat via Ballarat. There has never been a time without a passenger service between Melbourne and Adelaide since 1887 except for a short period in 1995 when the necessary changes to the various sections of track were made to achieve a complete standard-gauge link. Rumours about the future of The Overland have been rife since well before that time.

Following standardization, few trains were left serving the older route via Ballarat which, apart from its historical role as the interstate link was the main western line of Victoria, serving Ballarat and places west to Serviceton on the South Australian border. Since no thought was apparently given to retaining the broad gauge, combined or alongside the new track, except in the Adelaide and Melbourne suburban areas, Victorian intrastate passenger trains had to be withdrawn west of Ararat where the different gauges now meet. The line south from Ararat to Hamilton and Portland was converted to standard gauge as were some smaller branches, but the result has been the isolation of some sections of the broad-gauge networks in both Victoria and South Australia.

The Wimmera Ltd linking Melbourne and Dimboola through Ballarat and Ararat has been replaced by a bus. So also has The Vinelander night service between Melbourne and Mildura and all other passenger trains on the historic Geelong–Ballarat line have gone. On this route there used to be a delightful old stone station building at Lal Lal, halfway between Geelong and Ballarat. The standard-gauge route between Geelong and Ararat via Cressy has disused stations with equally quaint names – Nerrin Nerrin, Pura Pura and Vite Vite, the last two sounding like some sort of health drink. (Double-barrelled place names are of Aboriginal origin.)

The Geelong–Ballarat line was part of the route on which, in 1867, the then Duke of Edinburgh, Prince Alfred, travelled. He was particularly impressed with the train's speed: Bendigo to Ballarat via Melbourne and Geelong took just over four hours at an average of 75km/h. As an interesting indication of progress, the same trip would have taken about the same time in 1996 (before the Geelong–Ballarat trains were withdrawn) except that it would miss the connection in Melbourne by three minutes! Connectivity, not only in terms of track gauge but of timetabling, has never been a strong point with Australian railways but they are not alone in this.

The only V/Line train services west from Melbourne are now to Ararat (restored from Ballarat in 2004) though the south-west route to Warrnambool via Geelong remains.

RATIONALIZATION AND LINE CLOSURES

Failure to think nationally and develop a true railway network, acknowledged repeatedly throughout Australian railway history, has always been submerged under the stronger forces of state autonomy, interstate rivalry and the vested interests of competing modes.

The inability to think nationally

In spite of the vision of lateral thinkers such as Sir Harold Clapp, who reported on standardization in 1944 and stated that any effective national plan had to be 'accompanied by unification of railway thinking and planning', little has been done to follow his advice. Extension of the railway from Alice Springs to Darwin, enshrined in what was called the Northern Territory Acceptance Act of the Australian parliament in 1907, was not implemented until nearly a century later, with the first train in February 2004. Sir Harold envisioned a more rational connection from Bourke in the far west of NSW through western Queensland, tapping areas of primary produce and connecting Darwin more directly to the eastern seaboard at Sydney. More recently a Brisbane engineer, Dr Ken Davidson, conceived an inner circle route linking Melbourne to the Northern Territory through NSW and Queensland, affording closer links with the more developed areas of the east coast. A few years ago a grant for a pre-feasibility study was given by the federal government to a consortium led by entrepreneur Everald Compton interested in pursuing this as a high-speed route, but little has materialized so far. Meanwhile, governments are still allowing existing lines to deteriorate and services to dwindle through lack of funding.

Economic rationalism

Economic rationalism became a popular catchword among politicians in the 1970s when a spate of rail closures took place. Just as there was no national thinking or planning when the network was constructed there was no national thinking or logic to the process called rationalization. It ignored historical, social and other factors including future potential, instead adopting narrow financial criteria often based on the assumption that inefficient practices evident in some areas would continue. The policy of spending money on a route or service earmarked for closure, well known to observers of economic rationalism in railway and other fields the world over, was secretly pursued and is far from dead.

Line closures and service reductions

Extensive closures of secondary routes took place in the early 1970s and again in the early 1980s. Between 1970 and 1985 trains were withdrawn from over 50 branch lines and 15 cross-country links or potential links between main routes were severed. Further closures between 1988 and 1994 left a basic national network which was little more than one long curving spine with a series of dead-end branches. The only really significant positive development of the network since then has been the 1420km Alice Springs to Darwin line on which construction began in April 2002 and was completed in September 2003. The first passenger train ran on 1st February 2004, with weekly services commencing a week later.

Long-distance passenger train kilometres within the NSW system were reduced by 46% between September 1988 and May 1990, the number of actual trains being slashed from 207 to 98 per week, most being replaced by buses. This, however, was exceptional and some services (to the NSW Northern Tablelands, Broken Hill and the Riverina) have at least been partially restored, but some are again under threat, and the Northern Rivers branch through Lismore to Murwillumbah closed during the research for this edition. As some governments have opted out of rail management and operation, private enterprise has taken over with mixed results. There have been years of neglect to make up. Current evidence suggests that the tide is turning, but slowly.

ELECTRIFICATION AND MODERNIZATION

Pre-electrification

Steam traction reigned supreme on Australian railways until dieselization of all the major systems between 1950 and 1971, though coal trains in the Newcastle area used steam until 1973. The South Maitland Railway continued with it even longer but steam is now confined mainly to tourist specials and various private or preserved railways. In a category of its own the West Coast Railway of Victoria operated a regular Saturday mainline steam-hauled passenger service as late as 2002. As in other parts of the world, dieselization was rushed through when there were steam locomotives capable of many years of useful life. So good were some, such as the C38 class of New South Wales of which No 3801 has become an institution, that they remained in regular use up to 15 years after serious dieselization began.

The process starts

Electrification was for many years confined to metropolitan networks, such as that of Melbourne, where it began in 1919, and Sydney, from 1926. It spread to Victoria's Gippsland line east from Dandenong in 1954, when the new Gippslander train first ran, electrically hauled as far as Warragul. Electrification was extended to Moe in 1955 and Traralgon in 1956. In 1987, in contradiction of world trends, the line beyond Warragul was de-electrified, the reasons (excuses?) being a decline in non-passenger traffic, the closure of the line beyond Bairnsdale and the cost of replacing ageing electric locomotives.

In 1957 the New South Wales electrified suburban system was extended to the Blue Mountains, in 1960 north to Gosford, in 1986 south to Wollongong and in 1984 the interurban route to Newcastle was electrified. These developments resulted in a substantial saving in average journey times on all interurban routes.

Queensland joins the bandwagon

Although preliminary work was started in Brisbane in 1950, other priorities along with funding cutbacks and changes of government delayed electrification of Brisbane's suburban network until almost the end of 1979, after the Whitlam federal government for the first time offered states subsidies for approved public transport projects. The Brisbane suburban system was steadily electrified and extended and electrification of the North Coast mainline and coalfield routes soon followed.

Queensland's mainline electrification programme of the 1980s increased the proportion of routes electrified from less than one per cent (55km) in 1980 to nearly 17 per cent (1699km) of the QR system by 1990. Substantial speed up of trains resulted, with express freight schedules equalling former passenger speeds and passenger journeys being cut by several hours on North Coast services. The last diesel-hauled suburban service ran in Brisbane 20 years to the day after the first electric.

Perth is the most recent Australian capital to electrify its suburban network. In the 1970s one report recommended closing the system altogether (typical of similar reports of that time elsewhere) and in fact the Fremantle line was closed

Facts and figures

Australia's rail network totals over 40,000 kilometres, of which many lines are used only occasionally or even abandoned altogether. Whilst a decade ago most of the railways were owned by the various state governments or Australian National, the twin processes of part-privatization and separation of infrastructure from operations, coupled with 'open access' policies make it almost impossible to present accurate statistics today.

The main components however, excluding privately-run preserved railways such as the Emerald Tourist (Puffing Billy) Railway in Victoria, NSW's ZigZag, South Australia's SteamRanger and Pichi Pichi Railway, are Queensland Rail, controlling over 9000km, the Rail Infrastructure Corporation with nearly 9000km and the Australian Railroad Group with around 6000km. The State Rail Authority of NSW, formerly owning nearly 10,000km of route, controlled only a little over 2000km in 2003, and has since been merged into a new body, Railcorp.

There was an Australia-wide reduction of more than 10% between the end of 1980 and the end of the 1990s, all states except Queensland sharing this decrease. In 1980 Australia's total rail network consisted of some 45,455 route kilometres of six different gauges, owned and operated by six governments and nearly 50 private organizations. These ranged from giant industrial firms like Hammersley Iron and Broken Hill Proprietary Ltd to small preservation societies such as the Van Dieman Light Railway Society of Tasmania. Passenger services of some kind then operated regularly on 51.6% or 23,450 route kilometres and occasionally on a few other sections, serving 2335 stations, of which 676 were in the city and suburban areas of the mainland state capitals and almost half of all were in Queensland.

Now, over 20 years later, there are still almost as many owners and operators but some very significant changes, not all for the better. Many passenger services have been reduced or withdrawn completely. Some which were operated jointly by two or more railways are now run by a single entity. This has an obvious management benefit but there is a downside. For example, the Sydney–Melbourne trains were formerly managed jointly by NSW State Rail and Victorian Railways. Now under exclusive Countrylink management V/Line tickets are not accepted, even for journeys entirely within Victoria. Some of this may be remedied in time. Any major change in a long-established system is prone to teething problems and the Victorian government has gone to great lengths to ensure compatibility between privatized rail systems under its overall control.

in 1979, the trains being replaced by 'banana buses' as the articulated vehicles were called. A change of government responded to public pressure and trains were restored. Increased patronage led to electrification and the entire 65km network, plus a new 29km line to the northern suburbs, was served by frequent and interconnecting services by March 1993. A further line to Mandurah, south of Fremantle, is under construction with an expected opening date in 2006.

Modernization

Suburban and mainline trains in all states have been gradually modernized. Air conditioning has become almost universal. The Tangara electric cars of Sydney's CityRail, introduced in 1988, are among the most up-to-date in design and won the 1990 Engineering Excellence Award of Australia. Brisbane's IMU (Interurban Multiple Unit) trains on the Gold Coast line are a match for any in the world, while on the main line north to Rockhampton QR operates Australia's first tilting train sets which hold the world speed record for trains on narrow gauge. The later diesel Tilt Train to Cairns and the new Prospector in Western Australia are state-of-the-art in concept. So are Victoria's newest intercity and suburban trains.

The current management picture

The management picture is basically as follows but may well change during the life of this edition. In NSW, Countrylink and CityRail together form the passenger arm of Railcorp, formerly State Railways of NSW, while in Queensland, Queensland Rail (QR) operates all train services. The passenger group comprises Traveltrain and Citytrain, yet both operate under separate contracts. Currently, a new entity, Translink, is involved in Brisbane city and suburban rail and bus services and more changes are in the wind.

In Victoria, West Coast Railway took over Victoria's south-west route and Hoys Coaches Rail Division took over the Shepparton route in 1993, but both have since reverted to V/Line. The rest of V/Line passed into private hands in 1999, though the name V/Line passenger was retained. In the Melbourne metropolitan area, Hillside and Bayside trains have vanished, and since April 2004 Connex have become the Met's sole suburban train operator, with Yarra Trams operating the light rail system.

On 1 November 1997 Great Southern Railway, owned by Serco Asia Pacific Ltd, took over operation of the three passenger services then operated by Australian National, namely the Indian Pacific, The Overland and The Ghan. Before the takeover, service on all three had been gradually allowed to deteriorate through lack of government interest and funding, in spite of the efforts of management and a dedicated troop of railway workers. The Overland in particular had shrunk from one of Australia's longest trains to only a few carriages and had almost ceased running altogether.

Westrail formerly operated the mainline services and the Transperth suburban network in Western Australia. The mainline and coach services are now operated by Transwa, with Transperth responsible for Perth suburban services.

THE PUBLIC FACE OF THE SYSTEM TODAY

The Australian railway scene is one of contrasts, loved by many but hated by others. Much depends on which journey you undertake. Modern trains and advanced train control systems come side by side with quaint relics of the past, but the station master in a white pith helmet ringing a bell for the 'right away' at a country station has gone the way of the stagecoach. Station masters themselves are a threatened species, disappearing even from some major centres. Those who remain are called 'station managers' .

Most Australian trains and all interstate trains are air-conditioned. In fact, Australia had the first air-conditioned trains in the Southern hemisphere. It was also among the first with double-deck suburban electric trains and the first (if not the only) country to provide on-train shower cubicles as part of the facilities for economy-class passengers on long-distance trains.

Australia is also among the world leaders with solar-powered signalling, locotrol and electric traction. Heavy mineral trains rival any in the world while the best long-distance passenger trains offer a standard of service comparable to any except the really luxurious trains designed for the most affluent travellers.

Train speeds

Impressions and reputations do not always accord with facts. For years Spain had the reputation, at least in British eyes, of having the slowest trains in the world. In fact, since 1993 Spain has been way ahead of Britain in the speed league.

The first Australian trains were much faster, as well as more comfortable, than stagecoaches on the dusty corrugated roads, but there seemed to be a process of stagnation for much of the 20th century, so much so that one guidebook of the period described Australian passenger trains as 'lamentable'. It is true that as recently as 1980 one passenger train averaged 11.2km/h (seven miles an hour)! From Thangool where it started it took nearly 16 hours to cover 178km to its terminus at Rockhampton. Seven of those hours it spent at Biloela, the first stop on the line, where it shunted wagons or perhaps just rested to gain strength for the harrowing journey ahead. In reality of course it was a goods train with a passenger van.

Long waits, rather than slow running speed, still characterize much of Australian rail travel even on the main lines. Yet Australia is one of fewer than two dozen countries worldwide which ever earned a place in the *Railway Gazette* 'Roll of Honour' of trains with a start to stop speed between any two stations of over 120km/h. It also holds the world speed record for narrow gauge – rails less than 1430mm (4ft 8½in) apart – at 210km/h (130½mph) achieved by Queensland's electric Tilt Train on Sunday 23 May 1999.

No Australian trains travel as fast as British or European expresses, nor are the rail networks anything like the intricate pattern of routes found in Europe, where there can be many different ways of going between one place and another; Australian express trains are mostly only about half to two-thirds as fast as their counterparts in Europe. Sharp curves and stiff gradients on many routes contribute to Australia's generally slow average speeds. The vintage tourist train from

Records

Australian railways boast several records and near records, together with some world 'firsts'. Best known is the famous 'long straight', the longest straight line of railway in the world, 478 kilometres across the Nullarbor Plain between Ooldea, South Australia, and Nurina in Western Australia. Here passengers can cruise in air-conditioned comfort at a steady 100km/h all day, looking out at the brown circle of the far horizon all around.

Apart from the famous 'long straight' there are other sections of straight track rivalling the longest anywhere. Between Nyngan and Bourke in the far west of New South Wales is a straight of 187km, probably the third longest in the world. The new line to Darwin includes a straight section of 115km between 79 and 195km north from Alice Springs. By contrast, some of the most tortuous sections of track exist, such as in the Drummond Range west of Bogantungan in central Queensland where trains go into snake-like contortions to negotiate the succession of 80 to 120m (four to six chain) reverse curves by which the line overcomes the difficult terrain.

The widest passenger rail vehicles in the world are those operating on the Perisher Skitube railway (see p260), an incline rack system of eight kilometres, taking skiers and others up from Bullocks Flat in Perisher Valley to Blue Cow in the Snowy Mountains of New South Wales. This is the fastest rack railway in the world and one of only two funicular railways in Australia. The other, the Katoomba Scenic Railway (see p258) in the Blue Mountains west of Sydney, is of an unusual 1219mm (4ft) gauge, is cable operated, and has the steepest incline of any railway in the world, a gradient of 52 degrees – steeper than 1 in 1 – at its maximum. This excludes fairground roller-coaster type railways, enclosed mine railways and the unique enclosed capsule 'tramway' in Saarinen's famous Gateway Arch in St Louis, USA.

Cairns to Kuranda in the far north of Queensland takes 90 minutes to go 33km (20 miles) but when you see where and how it goes it is no more surprising than the fact that mountain railways in the world are even slower. For example, the Jungfrau railway in Switzerland takes almost an hour to go barely ten kilometres.

Slowness of travel, however, is not a problem with highly scenic routes, whilst longer journeys take on the nature of a cruise.

Frequency of service

Except in suburban, most outer-urban, and some interurban areas (such as Newcastle–Sydney–Wollongong and Melbourne–Geelong), Australian train services are nowhere near as frequent as would be expected in Britain, most countries of Europe, or Japan.

For almost all the long-distance routes, including some interstate routes, the frequency is less than one train a day in each direction. For many routes there are no more than two per day: exceptions are the routes from Rockhampton to Brisbane, Grafton to Sydney, Albury to Melbourne and the regional routes from Melbourne to Sale, Bendigo, Ballarat and Warrnambool. Between Junee and Griffith in NSW, Alice Springs and Darwin in the Northern Territory, Kuranda and Forsayth and Normanton and Croydon in Queensland the normal frequencies are one train a week in each direction. So it can become very important not to miss a train.

Trends and the future

FRAGMENTATION

Although it is now possible to travel on standard gauge from Brisbane to Perth or Darwin the same 'State Rights' mentality and inability to think in terms of the 'best interests of the railways or of Australia as a whole', so bemoaned by Sir Harold Clapp in 1945, persists, affecting train scheduling, wagon pooling, ticket validity, computerized booking, concession travel for pensioners and railway staff and many other things.

Even within individual states, railway functions are being increasingly divided, one body responsible for track, another for stations or signalling, and under a misguided National Competition Policy any number of players can be in the game of running trains, using the same track.

The potential for confusion and inefficiency is obvious, as any two young boys with a toy train set between them would know. In spite of this the best traditions of railways are largely maintained. There is still pride among rail workers: the philosophy of 'the mail must go through' tends to prevail even against strikes over genuine grievances and the fact that mail trains as such no longer exist.

TRAFFIC AND ATTITUDES

Traffic

Freight, or more accurately mineral traffic, is what brings the money in and passengers tend to take second place, except in urban areas. In describing the kind of traffic railways should seek, it has been said (and some Australian rail managements would endorse this view) that 'if it breathes, forget it'.

The potential for tourist traffic on cane railways in Queensland has recently been ignored by the sugar-mill owners, with the demise or near demise of exciting rail experiences such as the Mulgrave Rambler at Gordonvale and Ballyhooley Express at Mossman.

Attitudes

Attitudes change little. In the early days of railway development, revenue-minded managements shuddered with horror at the thought of wasting revenue space on things like toilets, let alone dining or sleeping cars! They still do. Many former dining cars have been replaced by take-away buffet services.

Although freight and minerals are the mainstay of most rail systems worldwide, and mineral traffic is the raison d'être of most Australian lines built in the last few decades the systems of most countries including Australia are continuing to provide high-quality passenger services and investing in new track and rolling stock. In the last 15 years around 2000km of new lines have been built in Australia, mostly in Queensland and the Northern Territory. New trains have been introduced on almost every system, though many other lines have been closed and services withdrawn.

Economics are not the only consideration. Throughout the whole history of Australian railway development, decisions have been made on political grounds, sometimes wrongly and unjustifiably to serve electoral purposes, but often rightly as representing the triumph of popular demand and genuine need over narrow accounting. The one time ‘common carrier’ principle has been replaced by ‘community service obligation’, recognized to some extent by all governments, however much they may require their railways to be commercially activated.

Apart from in Queensland, railways have abandoned stock trains and the carrying of small freight is now rare. Passengers may be considered a loss-making proposition yet some new lines have been built or former routes re-opened solely for this traffic. In the 1990s the Queensland government rebuilt the Beenleigh–Gold Coast line which had been closed in 1964. In 1998 the Emerald Railway Tourist Board restored the long-closed Emerald–Gembrook narrow-gauge line solely for use by the Puffing Billy tourist train in Victoria’s Dandenongs.

Railways in Australia still excite the imagination. In outback areas it often seems that half the population comes out to greet the once- or twice-weekly arrival. When new services have been introduced, such as the Cairns Tilt Train and the Darwin Ghan, local residents stand in their gardens to wave, schoolchildren come out of their classrooms in droves (presumably with official approval as an educational experience) and guards of honour, brass bands, or cocktail parties may bid farewell or greet the train at major stations.

When the famous LNER Flying Scotsman engine number 4472 visited Australia (August 1988 to October 1989) its route was lined by scores of photographers and train-gazers at every vantage point and its tour was extended to nearly a year so that it could be seen everywhere – from Brisbane to Perth, from Melbourne to Alice Springs. Similar enthusiasm greets veteran steam locomotive 3801 of New South Wales whenever it appears on a special excursion. Who does not thrill to the sight of a mighty iron beast pouring forth smoke and steam, hissing and pounding its way along the steel road, or to the rhythm of railway wheels and the exhilaration of speed in the safe cocoon of a railway carriage through cityscape and landscape, relaxed in a comfortable seat or sipping a cool drink?

Even the phenomenon of trains reclaiming passenger patronage from short-haul airlines, observable in Europe in the last two decades, was also noted in Australia with the advent of Queensland’s first Tilt Train.

THE FUTURE?

So what of the future for the railways of Australia? No-one knows. Considerations of energy, the environment and social need may well outweigh – and should outweigh – the dismal deliberations of the pseudo-economic rationalists who have so long been influencing government thinking, who would have most of the rail system shut down, who would replace most freight trains by thundering multi-trucks and all the non-urban passenger trains by buses or nothing at all.

They will tell you that most passengers on long-distance trains are pensioners and others heavily subsidized. Many are, but there are children too, mothers with young ones, tourists and even business travellers. What matters more is that people travel by rail because they want to. They like it. Aircraft may be quicker, bus travel cheaper, the car more convenient at the start and end of the journey but there is nothing else quite like the train where you eat, talk, stroll around, play cards, sleep and enjoy the travel experience so eloquently expressed by Ludovic Kennedy in his anthology *A Book of Railway Journeys* (see p281).

A 1991 Industry Commission report on the railways, if heeded, would have spelt the demise of all but suburban passenger trains. It offered little more than pious platitudes for the future of rail freight. But micro-economics and financial accountability, important in their place, do not determine events. There are other factors at work. Not only is public opinion a shaper of policy, there are intrinsic technical advantages in the rail mode. The railway is 'not bound for the museum for the same reason that the stage coach landed there', to quote the US Interstate Commerce Commission of 1970. Steel wheel on narrow rail has far less rolling friction than rubber on tarmac, takes less energy to move a given mass, can go faster and obtain its momentum from electricity. With no need for individual steering rail has an unquestionable advantage in safety.

Couple this inherent superiority with tradition and public concern, compare the trends worldwide, the swings back and forth, where Amtrak is renewing services on former abandoned routes and where even in car-oriented Los Angeles they have voted millions of dollars for railway development. 'Man has yet to invent an overland passenger mode of transport with the train's unique combination of speed, safety, comfort, dependability and economy' said the US Commission. They might well have added, 'or a more efficient mass mover of freight or produce'.

'Travelling by rail is relaxing, uncomplicated', said a Victorian railway advertisement, ironically just at the time they were substituting buses for trains on some of their routes.

Queensland Railways' promotion has included a television jingle 'Take it easy, take a train' and a clever billboard advertisement aimed at the motoring commuter: 'For relief of stress, take two a day', the illustration being not of pills but a Brisbane suburban electric train.

In *A Book of Railway Journeys*, Ludovic Kennedy praised rail travel even further, not specifically in Australia: 'One is transported in comfort, even style, to the wild places of the earth ... one can move around ... strike up a conversation, read, sleep, snore, make love'. The latter may not be easy nowadays with few compartment carriages and no sleeping cars on some overnight trains but there's no harm in trying.

❑ INTERCAPITAL CONNECTIONS

For those who wish to base their tour on the capital cities the following alphabetically-arranged list summarizes the train services between them. This section then tells you how to use the local trains and gives suggestions on what to see. This should enable visitors to devise itineraries to taste.

Notes

- Some connections to and from Brisbane and Canberra can be quicker using a Countrylink coach service for part of the journey. These are included in this table.
- Canberra arrivals and departures via coach to or from Cootamundra may be made by departing 16 minutes earlier from Queanbeyan or half an hour later from Canberra Jolimont, or arriving 20 minutes earlier at Jolimont or 15 minutes later at Queanbeyan (see p164).
- A change of train is required at the places named 'via' on each route.
- Where an overnight stop is required en route, the place name is followed by 'NS'
- Note that in summer time (October to March) times at Brisbane are an hour different and should be checked locally.

From Adelaide:

to **Brisbane** dep 08.30 Thursday via Melbourne and Sydney, arr 22.26 next day with coach connection from Casino, or 06.35 two days later direct from Sydney
dep 10.00 Tuesday and Friday via Sydney, arr 06.35 two day later
dep 10.00 Friday, Saturday and Sunday via Melbourne (NS) and Sydney; arr 06.35 three days later, or 22.26 two days later with coach connection from Casino

to **Canberra** dep 08.30 Thursday via Melbourne and Sydney, arr 11.23 next day
dep 10.00 Friday via Sydney, arr 16.30 next day
dep 10.00 Friday, Saturday and Sunday via Melbourne (NS) and Cootamundra, then coach arr 17.40 next day
dep 10.00 Tuesday via Sydney, arr 22.31 next day

to **Darwin** dep 17.15 Sunday arr 16.30 two days later

to **Melbourne** dep 08.30 Thursday, arr 19.15
dep 10.00 Friday, Saturday and Sunday arr 21.00

to **Perth** dep 18.40 Wednesday and Sunday, arr 09.10 two days later.

to **Sydney** dep 08.30 Thursday via Melbourne, arr 06.53 next day
dep 10.00 Tuesday and Friday, arr 10.15 next day.
dep 10.00 Friday, Saturday and Sunday via Melbourne (NS), arr 19.53 next day

From Brisbane:

to **Adelaide** dep 07.30 Wednesday via Sydney (NS) and Melbourne, arr 07.10 two days later
dep 07.30 Thursday, Friday and Saturday via Sydney (NS) and Melbourne, arr 08.00 two days later.
dep 15.10 Wednesday via coach to Casino, then via Strathfield and Melbourne, arr 07.10 two days later.
dep 15.10 Thursday, Friday and Saturday via coach to Casino, then via Strathfield and Melbourne, arr 08.00 two days later.
dep 15.10 Tuesday and Friday via coach to Casino, then via Sydney, arr 15.05 two days later

(cont'd opposite)

INTERCAPITAL CONNECTIONS (cont'd from p116)

From Brisbane (cont'd):

to **Canberra** dep 07.30 daily via Sydney (NS), arr 11.23 next day (arr 16.30 on Sunday)
dep 15.10 daily via coach to Casino, then Strathfield, arr 11.23 next day (arr 16.30 on Sunday)

to **Darwin** dep 07.30 Friday via Sydney (NS), Melbourne and Adelaide, arr 16.30 four days later
dep 15.10 Friday by coach to Casino, then via Sydney and Adelaide, arr 16.30 four days later

to **Melbourne** dep 07.30 daily via Sydney (NS), arr 18.55 next day
dep 15.10 daily via coach to Casino, then via Sydney, arr 07.35 two days later

to **Perth** dep 07.30 Tuesday and Friday via Sydney, arr 09.10 four days later
dep 15.10 Tuesday and Friday via coach to Casino, then via Sydney, arr 09.10 four days later

to **Sydney** dep 07.30 daily, arr 21.51
dep 15.10 daily via coach to Casino, arr 07.13 next day

From Canberra:

to **Adelaide** dep 06.37 on Thursday via Goulburn, then via Melbourne, arr 07.10 next day
dep 06.37 on Friday and Sunday via Goulburn, then via Melbourne, arr 08.00 next day
dep 06.37 on Wednesday and Saturday via Sydney, arr 15.15 next day
dep 09.32 on Thursday via coach to Cootamundra, then via Melbourne, arr 07.10 next day – see notes opposite
dep 09.32 on Friday, Saturday and Sunday via coach to Cootamundra, then via Melbourne, arr 08.00 next day – see notes opposite
dep 12.05 on Friday via Goulburn and Melbourne, arr two days later at 08.00
dep 17.07 on Thursday via Goulburn and Melbourne, arr two days later at 07.10
dep 17.07 on Saturday and Sunday via Goulburn and Melbourne, arr two days later at 08.00

to **Brisbane** dep 06.37 daily except Sunday via Sydney, arr 06.35 next day
dep 11.55 Sunday via Strathfield, arr 06.35 next day
dep 12.05 Monday, Wednesday and Friday via Strathfield, arr 06.35 next day
dep 17.15 on Tuesday, Thursday, Saturday and Sunday via Sydney (NS) and Casino, then by coach, arr 22.26 next day

to **Darwin** dep 06.37 on Saturday via Sydney and Adelaide arr 16.30 three days later
dep 09.32 on Saturday via Cootamundra (by coach), Melbourne and Adelaide, arr 16.30 three days later – see notes opposite

to **Melbourne** dep 06.37 daily except Sunday via Goulburn, arr 18.55
dep 09.32 daily via Cootamundra (by coach), arr 18.55 – see notes opposite
dep 12.05 on Monday, Wednesday and Friday via Goulburn, arr 07.35 next day
dep 17.07 on Tuesday, Thursday, Saturday and Sunday via Goulburn, arr 07.35 next day

(cont'd over)

INTERCAPITAL CONNECTIONS **(cont'd from p117)**

From Canberra (cont'd):

to **Perth** dep 06.37 Wednesday and Saturday via Sydney, arr 09.10 three days later
dep 09.32 on Saturday via Cootamundra (by coach), Melbourne and Adelaide, arr 09.10 three days later – see notes p116

to **Sydney** dep 06.37 daily except Sunday, arr 10.55
dep 11.55 Sunday, arr 16.12
dep 12.05 Monday, Wednesday and Friday, arr 16.24
dep 17.07 Tuesday, Thursday, Saturday and Sunday, arr 21.26

From Darwin:

to **Adelaide** dep 10.00 Wednesday, arr 09.00 two days later

to **Brisbane** dep 10.00 Wednesday via Adelaide and Sydney, arr 06.35 four days later

to **Canberra** dep 10.00 Wednesday via Adelaide and Sydney, arr 16.30 three days later

to **Melbourne** dep 10.00 Wednesday via Adelaide, arr 21.00 two days later

to **Perth** dep 10.00 Wednesday via Adelaide (2 NS), arr 09.10 six days later (see note below)

to **Sydney** dep 10.00 Wednesday via Adelaide, arr 10.15 three days later

Note: re Darwin–Perth journey The distance travelled, but not the time taken, can be shortened by changing at Port Augusta instead of Adelaide, but the times are unattractive: see table on p61.

From Melbourne:

to **Adelaide** dep 21.10 Thursday, arr 07.10 next day
dep 22.10 Friday, Saturday and Sunday, arr 08.00 next day.

to **Brisbane** dep 19.55 daily via Sydney, arr 22.26 next day by coach connection from Casino
dep 19.55 daily via Sydney arr 06.35 two days later

to **Canberra** dep 08.30 daily via Cootamundra, then coach arr 17.40
dep 19.55 daily except Saturday via Sydney, arr 11.23 next day
dep 19.55 Saturday via Sydney, arr 16.30 next day

to **Darwin** dep 22.10 Saturday via Adelaide, arr 16.30 three days later

to **Perth** dep 19.55 Tuesday via Sydney, arr 09.10 four days later
dep 22.10 Saturday via Adelaide, arr 09.10 three days later

to **Sydney** dep 08.30 daily, arr 19.53
dep 19.55 daily, arr 06.53 next day

From Perth:

to **Adelaide** dep 11.55 Wednesday and Sunday, arr 07.20 two days later

to **Brisbane** dep 11.55 Wednesday and Sunday via Sydney, arr 06.35 four days later

to **Canberra** dep 11.55 Wednesday via Sydney, arr 16.30 three days later
dep 11.55 Sunday via Sydney, arr 22.31 three days later

to **Darwin** dep 11.55 Wednesday via Adelaide (2NS), arr 16.30 six days later

to **Melbourne** dep 11.55 Wednesday via Adelaide, arr 21.00 two days later
dep 11.55 Sunday via Adelaide and Sydney, arr 07.35 four days later

to **Sydney** dep 11.55 Wednesday and Sunday, arr 10.15 three days later

(cont'd opposite)

INTERCAPITAL CONNECTIONS (cont'd from p118)

From Sydney:

to **Adelaide**	dep 07.43 Thursday via Melbourne, arr 07.10 next day
	dep 07.43 Fri, Sat and Sun via Melbourne, arr 08.00 next day
	dep 14.55 Wednesday and Saturday, arr 15.15 next day
to **Brisbane**	dep 07.15 daily via Casino, then by coach connection, arr 22.26
	dep 16.24 daily, arr 06.35 next day
to **Canberra**	dep 07.05 daily except Sunday, arr 11.23
	dep 12.14 Tuesday, Thursday, Saturday and Sunday, arr 16.30
	dep 18.14 Monday, Wednesday, Friday and Sunday, arr 22.31
to **Darwin**	dep 14.55 Saturday via Adelaide, arr 16.30 three days later
to **Melbourne**	dep 07.43 daily, arr 18.55
	dep 20.43 daily, arr 07.35 next day
to **Perth**	dep 14.55 Wednesday and Saturday, arr 09.10 three days later

❑ Station locations

In all Australian state capital cities there is more than one railway station. Unless otherwise stated in tables and itineraries in this book, trains arrive and depart from the main interstate stations, which are as follows:

Sydney: Central station (also called Sydney Terminal). **Melbourne**: Spencer Street station. **Brisbane**: Roma Street station (also called Brisbane Transit Centre) not to be confused with Brisbane Central station. The stations are about a kilometre walking distance apart but less by rail on which there are frequent local trains. **Adelaide**: GSR Terminal, Keswick, is 3.5km from the city centre and ten minutes' walk from a suburban station of the same name, from which there is a local service roughly every half-hour to the central city station in North Terrace. **Perth**: East Perth Terminal station, West Parade, East Perth, is just over 1.7km (one mile) from City station. Adjoins the suburban station of East Perth, from which there is a frequent service to City station in the town centre. **Canberra**: The railway station is at Kingston, about 5km from the city centre at Civic or the bus station at Jolimont. Local bus services and taxis are available, while Countrylink coaches to destinations such as Cooma connect with trains. **Darwin**: The new station is in the suburb of Berrimah, over 15km from the city centre. Coach connections are available.

At Port Pirie in South Australia, Bunbury in Western Australia, and Gympie, Maryborough, Mackay, Bowen and Townsville in Queensland, new stations have been built which are anything up to 8km out of town. At **Mackay** and **New Bowen** passengers are left to their own devices (taxi or a lift from someone with a private car), whilst at **Maryborough West** and **Gympie North** the railways provide a coach or taxi.

Orange East Fork station in NSW, used by the Indian Pacific, is 1.8km from the main Orange station in the town centre. There is no public transport between the two, so if descending at Orange East Fork from a Great Southern train it would be worth asking the Train Manager to arrange something for you (such as a taxi) before arrival (you might be offered a lift in a railway van).

Port Pirie (Coonamia) station is 3km from town, so there also you should ask the Train Manager for advice. At **Bunbury,** there is a connecting bus for most trains. **Townsville**'s new station, opened in 2003, is a good ten minutes' walk from the city centre, but there are local buses (normally every half-hour) from stops just over the road north-west of the rail tracks, and taxis are readily available.

PART 4: CITY GUIDES AND PLANS

Sydney

ORIENTATION

Australia's largest city has enough to keep you sightseeing for days. Sydney's extensive suburban railway system can take you to many of the principal attractions and right into the heart of the city. **St James**, **Town Hall** and **Wynyard** are the best stations for the central business district, but the main terminal (Central Station) itself is close to Chinatown.

Two useful places to obtain information are the Travellers Information Service (☎ 02-9281 9366) in Sydney Coach Terminal, outside Central station, and Sydney Visitor Information Centre (☎ 02-9669 5111, 💻 www.sydneyvisitorcentre.com), 106 George St, The Rocks (open 09.00-18.00). There are also information kiosks at Martin Place, Town Hall and Circular Quay, open daily 09.00-17.00.

WHAT TO SEE AND DO

Around St James and Circular Quay stations

You can enjoy panoramic 360° views of the city, the harbour and the Pacific Ocean from the top of the tallest building in Australia, the 305m-high **AMP Tower** at Centrepoint shopping centre opposite **Galeries Victoria** monorail station. The tower features a revolving restaurant, and access is available, for a modest fee, to the tower observation deck. **St James** station is close by on CityRail.

A fine collection of traditional and modern, Australian and European art may be seen at the **Art Gallery of New South Wales** (in The Domain), open daily, admission and tours free; take Art Gallery Rd from nearby St James station. You can carry on from there into the **Royal Botanic Gardens**, open daily until sunset, and see the lush tropical plants and exotic trees including cuttings from the world's oldest-known species, the Wollemi Pine, recently discovered in Wollemi National Park near the Blue Mountains.

North of the gardens at Bennelong Point is the famous **Opera House** (☎ 02-9250 7250); guided tours (60 mins, every half hour, $23 adult, $16 for concessionary tickets) are offered daily. **Circular Quay station** is nearby and is convenient for a walking tour around **The Rocks**, the oldest part of Sydney and well supplied with quality eating places.

The **Museum of Contemporary Art** (☎ 02-9241 5892, open daily, free), 140 George St, and the **Museum of Sydney** (☎ 02-9250 5988, open daily, $7), on the corner of Bridge St and Phillip St, are both within walking distance of Circular Quay station.

From here you can also take a **harbour cruise**, a ferry to one of the many coves or to Manly for **Oceanworld** (☎ 02-9949 2644), where you can see sharks being fed, or the beach; alternatively take a hydrofoil (depart every 30 minutes) to **Taronga Park Zoo**. Coach tours also depart from here: Sydney Buses run an Explorer bus to 20 places of interest; you can hop on and off where you like.

Around Museum and Martin Place stations

From **Museum** station it is easy to get to the **ANZAC War Memorial** in Hyde Park where they change the guard every Thursday at 13.30, and also to the **Australian Museum** (corner of William and College Sts, open daily, $8), for Australia's largest natural history collection and a display of Aboriginal artefacts and relics.

Should the revolving meal at the AMP Tower turn you 'crook', **Martin Place** station is near Sydney Hospital. It also adjoins the mall of that name, where you can listen to a free **lunchtime concert**, and is convenient for visiting the **NSW State Library** and seeing **Parliament House**.

Around Town Hall station

Town Hall station adjoins **Sydney Town Hall**, which features a magnificent pipe organ and rich internal decoration. Underground at Town Hall is also an extensive **shopping and restaurant area**. There are many hotels between here and Sydney Central. Town Hall is close to Pitt St Mall, many shops and the George St cinemas. It is also the best place to transfer to the Metro monorail circuit which is a must for every Sydney visitor. **Galeries Victoria** (formerly called City Centre) and **Park Plaza** monorail stations are one block east between Town Hall and the Mall.

The Metro Monorail and Metro Light Rail

The **monorail** will take you over Darling Harbour across Pyrmont Bridge to the **Australian National Maritime Museum** (Harbourside station) and the Convention Centre (Convention station).

At the city end of the bridge is the **Sydney Aquarium** (Darling Park station) where you can stroll through underwater tunnels past live sharks and other denizens of the sea.

The Metro Monorail (formerly Darling Harbour Monorail, see p259) is owned by Metro Transport Sydney and is operated by Connex Sydney. First commissioned in 1988, the Monorail is an elevated straddle-type system powered by sheathed conductor rails below the running plate. There are eight stations; the total circuit is 3.5km, the speed between stops is 33km/h, the service frequency is three to five minutes and it operates 364 days of the year (all except Christmas Day) mostly from 07.00 to 22.00

Rail tickets for the suburban area

Sydney offers a great range of rail and other tickets by which visitors as well as regular commuters can get around the city and outer suburbs. Various leaflets can be obtained at CityRail stations: these give details of routes, fares, bus connections, ferries and places of interest, together with maps, contact numbers and times.

The **Day-Tripper** ticket gives day-long train, bus and ferry travel within the Sydney suburban area, bounded by Cowan, Emu Plains, Richmond, Carlingford, Macarthur, Cronulla, Otford and Bondi Junction, for $15. It includes discounts for access to Taronga Zoo, various museums, Olympic Park and other attractions.

The **CityHopper** at $6.80, or $4.80 off-peak, gives one-day train travel in the central area between Redfern and North Sydney including the Central loop and the Bondi line as far as Kings Cross.

There are also **day tickets** for buses, ferries, the Light Rail and Metro Monorail. **Off-peak returns** are useful for getting beyond the suburban area, and there are other **special tickets** such as the Blue Mountains Explorer Link. Passes for longer periods are also available.

The CityRail website (□ www.cityrail.info) has timetables and fare information and there are information centres at Central, Town Hall and Circular Quay stations, open most days during normal working hours – the office at Central is open daily until 10pm.

Other useful websites include: □ www.131500.com.au – up-to-date information on train, bus and ferry travel in Sydney and to the north (Hunter Valley/Central coast), west (Blue Mountains) and south (Southern Highland and South Coast); □ www .metromonorail.com.au; and □ www.sydneybuses.nsw.gov.au.

(to midnight Thursdays to Saturdays). The adult fare is $4 but day passes and multi-trip Metrocards are also available.

One attractive feature of the Monorail, apart from seeing much of the city centre from treetop level, is that it connects with the **Metro Light Rail** at two places; Convention and Haymarket. The latter is the station for the **Powerhouse Museum** (see p260) arguably Sydney's best, the **Sydney Entertainment Centre** and **Paddy's Market** (open Saturday and Sunday). Haymarket is also next door to **Chinatown** and the Metro Light Rail goes from there along Hay St to the Capitol Square stop, handy for the **Capitol Theatre** and ***Bridie O'Reilly's Irish Pub*** (on Hay St just near the tram stop and a fine place to have a cool Guinness and watch the world, and the trams, go by, before returning to the bustle of Central station). Central station offers a perfect connection with CityRail and Countrylink trains.

In the other direction the Metro Light Rail serves **Star City casino** (Pyrmont), **Sydney Fish market** (Pyrmont, open from 7am) and **Wentworth Park**, home of the renowned greyhound races. The 3.7km Metro Light Rail was opened in 1997 and operates approximately every 10 minutes,

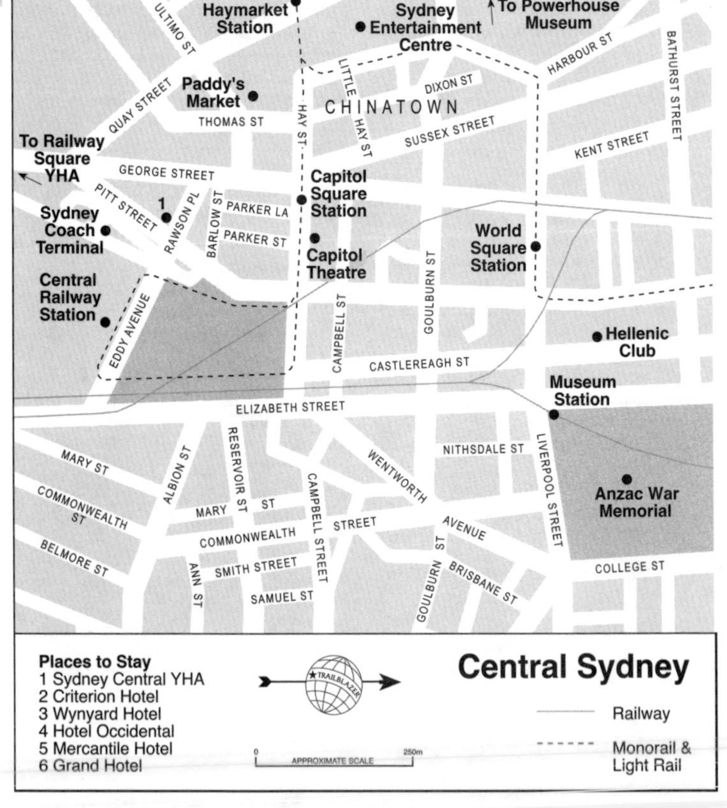

24 hours a day. A 3.1km extension to Glebe, Rozelle Bay and Lilyfield opened in August 2000 and future plans include a city centre loop and potentially a further westward extension. Current adult fares are $2.80 to $5.20 depending on the fare zones you travel through; various day and weekly passes are available.

Rail tours

With even half a day in Sydney, several interesting rail tours are possible – you can go:

- over the Sydney Harbour bridge and see the commuters on their daily rat race. Take the **round trip** via Hornsby and Strathfield (85 to 105 minutes, C 9014 and local timetables) but go first on the City railway to Circular Quay (eight minutes) to view Sydney Harbour and the Opera House.
- to **Bondi Junction** (ten minutes), though the junction might prove a disappointment if you are expecting Bondi beach. Bondi Junction has a mall, with plenty of interesting shops, market stalls and restaurants. Bondi beach, with many more restaurants, is but a short bus ride or a 20-minute walk from the station.
- all the way to **a beach in the Sydney area**: it you want to do this take the Cronulla service (47 minutes); you may

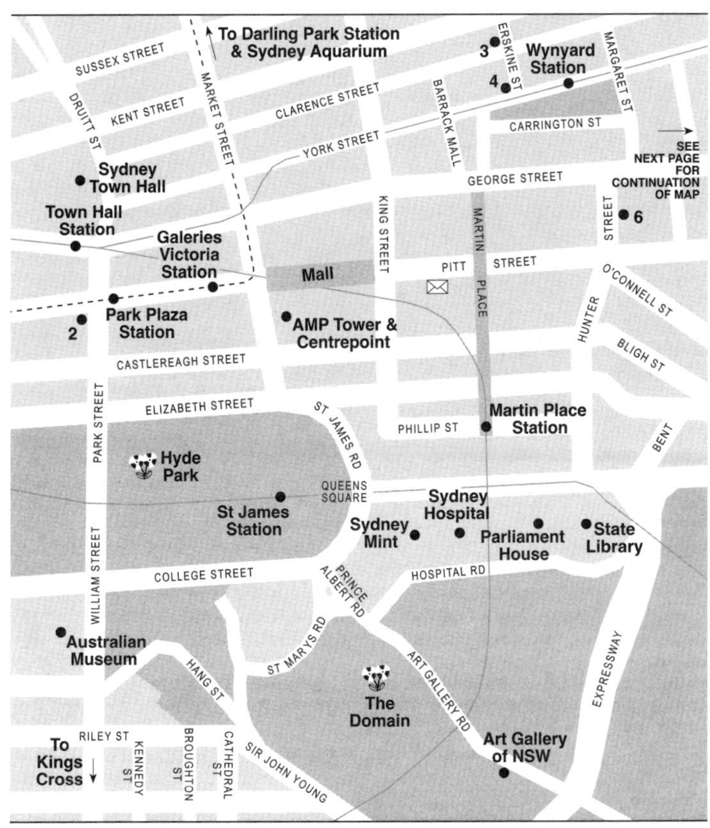

find it full of bronzed, golden-haired kids out for a day of sunshine and surf. En route to Cronulla, the Sydney–Wollongong rail route skirts Sydney airport at Sydenham and passes close to the famous Botany Bay. Rail buffs will note the XPT depot at Tempe.

The route then skirts the first of Australia's national parks, the Royal, just south of Sutherland (27 mins, C 9014). A branch to the park ranger's office, where the traveller is in the heart of the 'bush', has closed but has been reopened as a tramway (see p260). You can spend a whole day exploring the park's walking tracks and enjoying its excellent views.

• visit **Olympic Park**, which is just beyond Strathfield in Sydney's inner western suburbs. The junction station for the Olympic Sprint shuttle service is Lidcombe but there are direct services from Central for special events.

• see the **birthplace of Batman** at Parramatta. No, not the Gotham City 'caped crusader' but the surveyor who went over Bass Strait from Launceston in Tasmania (not accompanied by Robin), and on the banks of the River Yarra in Victoria

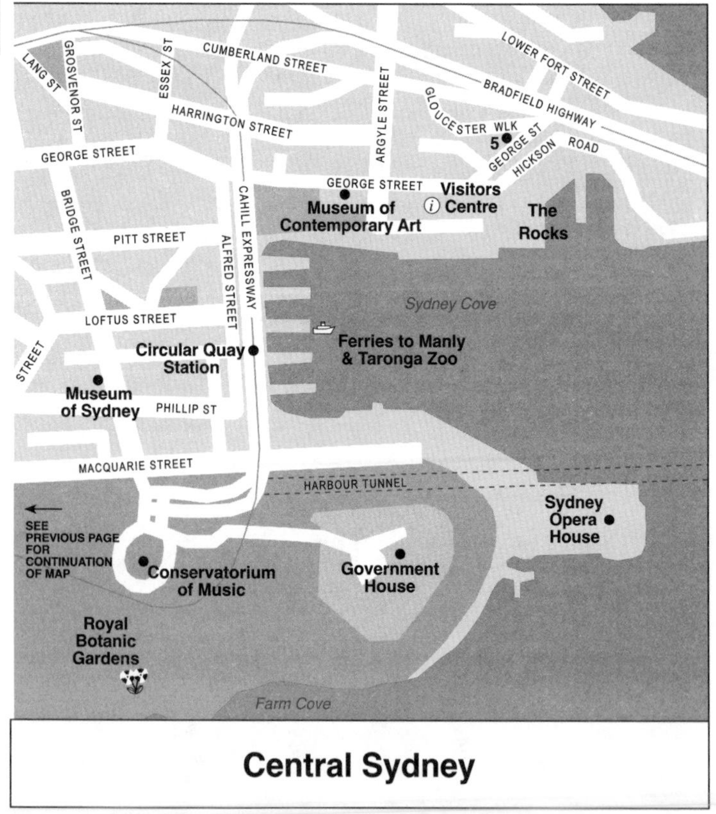

Central Sydney

said 'Here is the place for a city' and thus founded Melbourne. Within walking distance of Parramatta station (25 mins from Central) you can also find the **1802 Lennox bridge**, the **old Government House**, the remains of Australia's first **observatory** and other **historic buildings** maintained by the National Trust.

• or you could **go at night to Kings Cross**, noted for its colourful (some would say 'off-colour') goings on that might broadly be categorized as 'alternative lifestyles'. One guidebook described the Cross as 'a cocktail of strip joints, prostitution, crime and drugs, shaken and stirred with a handful of classy restaurants, designer cafes, international hotels and backpacker hostels'. If that is your scene you can certainly have a good time and find budget-priced accommodation but unless you are the partying type you may find it too noisy.

For a **day tour** of the Sydney area by rail you could:

• start at Central station, visit Town Hall or Wynyard for the shopping centre, then Circular Quay for the harbour and Opera House, go over Harbour bridge to Milsons Point (for Luna Park amusement centre) and North Sydney, then back to Central for the train to Cronulla for a spell at the beach before returning to the city centre for dinner.

• alternatively go to Campbelltown new town (49 mins via East Hills), Parramatta (23 to 30 mins) for its history, Richmond (80 mins) to see the air base or just for a quiet suburban retreat (a good place to stay), or to Warwick Farm (45 to 50 mins) for the races if they are on.

WHERE TO STAY

Budget/mid-range

Hostels worth trying are the 556-bed ***Sydney Central YHA*** (☎ 02-9281 9111, 🖳 sydcentral@yhansw.org.au), 11 Rawson Place (near Central station), and the ***Railway Square YHA*** (☎ 02-9281 9666, 🖳 railway@yhansw.org.au), 8A Lee St, which opened in June 2004. The ***Original Backpackers Lodge*** (☎ 02-9356 3232, 🖳 www.originalbackpackers.com.au), 162 Victoria St, is a short walk from Kings Cross station.

Being a capital city, hotels in Sydney are not cheap. Hotels where you should expect to pay roughly \$60 to \$80 include ***Criterion*** (☎ 02-9264 3093), corner of Pitt and Park Sts (Town Hall station) and ***Wynyard Hotel*** (☎ 02-9299 1330), which is near Wynyard station.

A little further out, ***Pymble Hotel*** (☎ 02-9144 1039), a Pubstay at 1134 Pacific Highway round the corner from Pymble station on the North Shore line, has single rooms including self-serve continental breakfast at \$60. ***O'Malley's*** (☎ 02-9357 2211, 🖳 www.omalleyshotel.com.au), 228 William St, near Kings Cross station, charges only \$66 for an en suite room including breakfast.

A particularly convenient base for exploring Sydney and the NSW rail system is ***Whelan's Strathfield Hotel*** (☎ 02-9747 4630), right opposite the station at Strathfield, where single rooms range from as little as \$50. Slightly further up the price range is ***Hotel Occidental*** (☎ 02-9299 2531), 43 York St, close to Wynyard station, with pub-style rooms for \$70. ***Grand Hotel*** (☎ 02-9232 3755), 30 Hunter St, near Wynyard station is a one-star Pubstay hotel where a single costs \$77. Another Pubstay one-star hotel is ***Mercantile Hotel*** (☎ 02-9247 3570, 🖳 merc@tpg.com.au), 25 George St, The Rocks, where the charge includes breakfast.

Up-market

Castlereagh Inn (☎ 02-9284 1000, 🖳 castlein@ozemail.com.au), 169 Castlereagh St, a three-star hotel near Town Hall station, charges \$125 to \$160 for a single room.

WHERE TO EAT

In Sydney you can enjoy Oriental cuisine equal to any in Hong Kong (and some pretty awful stuff as well). Quality does not always vary in proportion to price and since proprietors and menus frequently change it would be potentially misleading to suggest specific establishments in a book of this sort. Local advice is worth seeking.

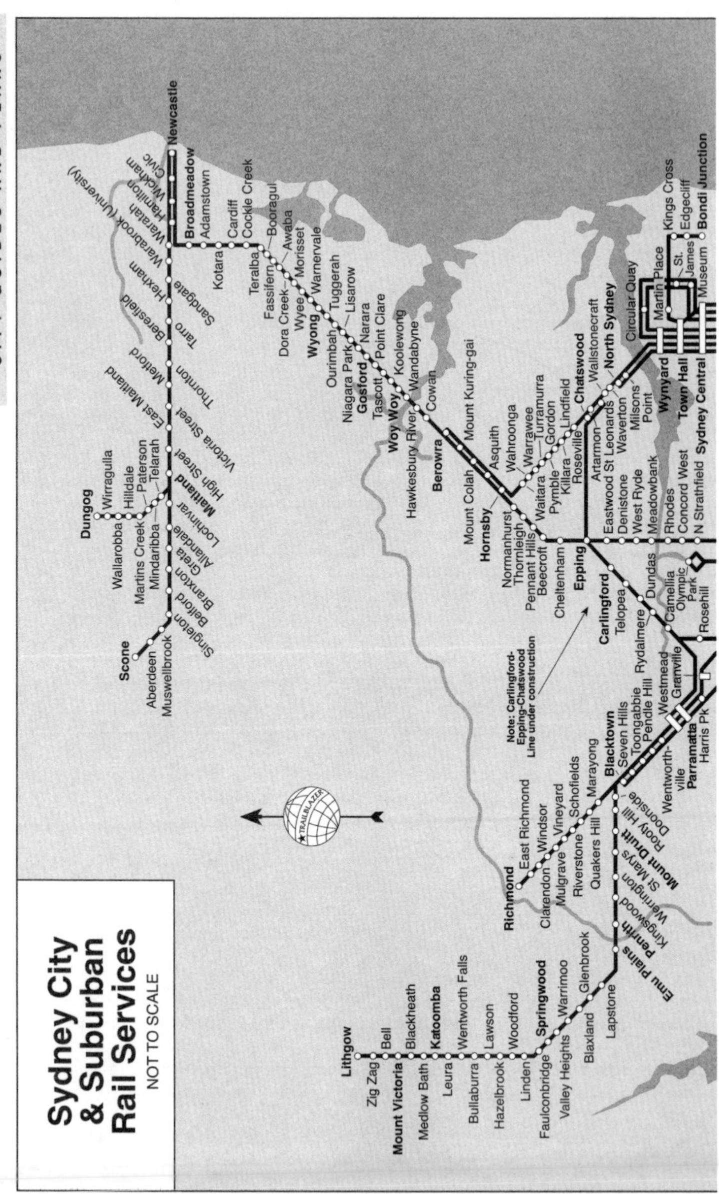
Sydney City
& Suburban
Rail Services
NOT TO SCALE
TRAILBLAZER
Lithgow
Zig Zag
Bell
Mount Victoria
Blackheath
Medlow Bath
Katoomba
Leura
Wentworth Falls
Bullaburra
Lawson
Hazelbrook
Woodford
Linden
Springwood
Faulconbridge
Valley Heights
Warrimoo
Blaxland
Glenbrook
Lapstone
Emu Plains
Penrith
Kingswood
Werrington
St Marys
Mount Druitt
Rooty Hill
Doonside
Blacktown
Richmond
East Richmond
Clarendon
Windsor
Mulgrave
Vineyard
Riverstone
Schofields
Quakers Hill
Marayong
Seven Hills
Toongabbie
Pendle Hill
Wentworth-
ville
Westmead
Parramatta
Harris Pk
Granville
Note: Carlingford-
Epping-Chatswood
Line under construction
Carlingford
Telopea
Dundas
Rydalmere
Camellia
Rosehill
Olympic
Park
Epping
Cheltenham
Beecroft
Pennant Hills
Thornleigh
Normanhurst
Hornsby
Mount Colah
Mount Kuring-gai
Asquith
Berowra
Wahroonga
Warrawee
Turramurra
Waitara
Gordon
Pymble
Killara
Lindfield
Roseville
Chatswood
Artarmon
St Leonards
Wollstonecraft
Waverton
North Sydney
Milsons
Point
Eastwood
Denistone
West Ryde
Meadowbank
Rhodes
Concord West
N Strathfield
Sydney Central
Town Hall
Wynyard
Circular Quay
Martin Place
St.
James
Museum
Kings Cross
Edgecliff
Bondi Junction
Cowan
Hawkesbury River
Wandabyne
Koolewong
Woy Woy
Tascott
Point Clare
Gosford
Narara
Niagara Park
Lisarow
Ourimbah
Tuggerah
Wyong
Warnervale
Wyee
Morisset
Dora Creek
Awaba
Fassifern
Booragul
Teralba
Cockle Creek
Cardiff
Kotara
Adamstown
Broadmeadow
Newcastle
Civic
Wickham
Hamilton
Waratah
Warabrook (University)
Sandgate
Hexham
Tarro
Beresfield
Thornton
Metford
Victoria Street
East Maitland
High Street
Maitland
Telarah
Paterson
Wirragulla
Hilldale
Dungog
Wallarobba
Martins Creek
Mindaribba
Lochinvar
Allandale
Greta
Branxton
Belford
Singleton
Muswellbrook
Aberdeen
Scone

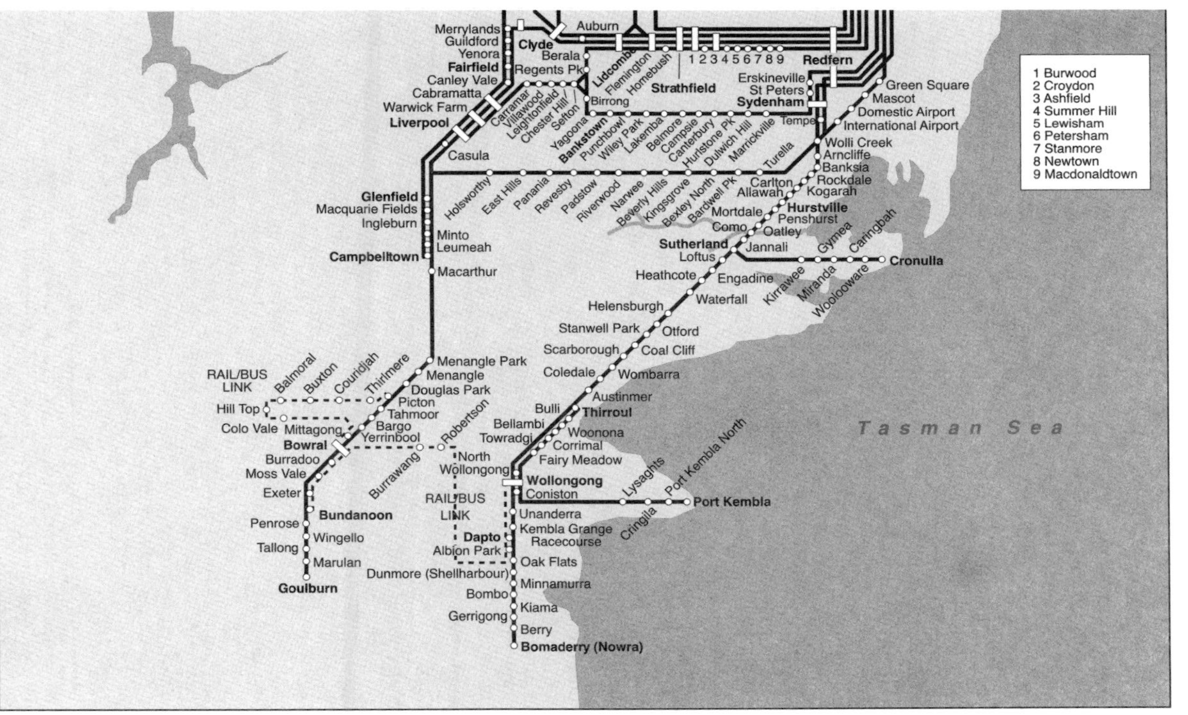
1 Burwood
2 Croydon
3 Ashfield
4 Summer Hill
5 Lewisham
6 Petersham
7 Stanmore
8 Newtown
9 Macdonaldtown
Tasman Sea
Merrylands
Guildford
Yenora
Fairfield
Canley Vale
Cabramatta
Warwick Farm
Liverpool
Casula
Clyde
Auburn
Berala
Regents Pk
Lidcombe
Flemington
Homebush
Strathfield
1 2 3 4 5 6 7 8 9
Redfern
Erskineville
St Peters
Sydenham
Tempe
Carramar
Villawood
Leightonfield
Chester Hill
Sefton
Birrong
Yagoona
Bankstown
Punchbowl
Wiley Park
Lakemba
Belmore
Campsie
Canterbury
Hurlstone Pk
Dulwich Hill
Marrickville
Turella
Green Square
Mascot
Domestic Airport
International Airport
Wolli Creek
Arncliffe
Banksia
Rockdale
Kogarah
Carlton
Allawah
Hurstville
Penshurst
Mortdale
Oatley
Como
Jannali
Sutherland
Loftus
Holsworthy
East Hills
Panania
Revesby
Padstow
Riverwood
Narwee
Beverly Hills
Kingsgrove
Bexley North
Bardwell Pk
Glenfield
Macquarie Fields
Ingleburn
Minto
Leumeah
Campbelltown
Macarthur
Gymea
Caringbah
Cronulla
Kirrawee
Miranda
Woolooware
Heathcote
Engadine
Waterfall
Helensburgh
Stanwell Park
Otford
Scarborough
Coal Cliff
Coledale
Wombarra
Austinmer
Bulli
Thirroul
Bellambi
Woonona
Towradgi
Corrimal
Fairy Meadow
North Wollongong
Wollongong
Coniston
Lysaghts
Port Kembla North
Port Kembla
Cringila
Unanderra
Kembla Grange
Racecourse
RAIL/BUS LINK
Dapto
Albion Park
Oak Flats
Dunmore (Shellharbour)
Minnamurra
Bombo
Kiama
Gerringong
Berry
Bomaderry (Nowra)
Menangle Park
Menangle
Douglas Park
Picton
Tahmoor
Bargo
Yerrinbool
Robertson
Burrawang
RAIL/BUS LINK
Balmoral
Buxton
Couridjah
Thirlmere
Hill Top
Colo Vale
Mittagong
Bowral
Burradoo
Moss Vale
Exeter
Bundanoon
Penrose
Wingello
Tallong
Marulan
Goulburn

Another good indicator is to note how well a restaurant is patronized. Plenty of Chinese people in a Chinese restaurant is usually a fair indication of authenticity and quality. A local guide, *Cheap eats in Sydney*, is published annually and is available from newsagents. In this context 'cheap' means good value for money, not cheap and nasty.

The Chinatown area (the first stop on the Light Rail from Central), the city centre (Town Hall station) and The Rocks (Circular Quay station) abound in good eating places but some are aimed at tourists and prices are therefore 'upwardly adjusted'.

For excellent Greek cuisine try the ***Hellenic Club*** (☎ 02-9264 5128), 5th Floor, 251 Elizabeth St; interstate and overseas visitors are welcome. However, there are many other ethnic restaurants: pick up a copy of the guide to cheap eats mentioned above or simply stroll down the streets and make your own selection.

LONGER DAY TRIPS FROM SYDNEY

To the South Coast (C 9014)

Consider a trip down the coast line to Bomaderry (Nowra) and back. Not much of Australia's coast is visible from its railways, but the Illawarra line is an exception, taking the passenger right to the water's edge or along the cliff tops. North of Wollongong a small section of the coastal scenery is marred by coal mining, but the natural features still predominate.

Trains leave Sydney for Bomaderry (Nowra) at intervals varying between one and two hours (less frequently in the mornings and at weekends), from 04.51 on weekdays, 05.44 at weekends, and arrive at Kiama in about 2 hours 15 minutes and Bomaderry (Nowra) in about 2 hours 45 minutes. Return services depart from Bomaderry (Nowra) just as frequently but at more erratic intervals.

All trains involve a change between local electric and diesel Endeavour units, usually at Dapto or Kiama. Last return times from Bomaderry (Nowra) if you intend catching the Melbourne XPT from Sydney are 17.26 on Saturdays, Sundays and public holidays, or 16.50 on weekdays (the next train at 17.22 misses the Melbourne XPT by two minutes!). Departures from Kiama are 36 minutes later in each case. There are much later trains to Sydney itself.

Between **Oatley** and **Como**, look out for the attractive waterside area of George's River to the east. The Sydney suburbs virtually disappear or become lost in the bush not long after **Sutherland** (25km), where the scenic branch to Cronulla starts. **Waterfall** marks the northern edge of the scenic winding route through bushland which continues through **Helensburgh**, **Otford** and **Stanwell Park**. The route then swings along the coast, winding among forested cliffs and tunnels and bays on the edge of the Pacific north and south of **Coal Cliff**, the only ugly spot, but fortunately very briefly glimpsed. There is a great view over to Port Kembla after Coal Cliff tunnel and another view of the coast, close to, at Scarborough.

Wollongong, featured in the Australian TV *Aunty Jack* series, gave rise to a 'What's wrong with Wollongong' quip. You'll find out, but be prepared for a surprise. Like all hard-earning industrial towns, Wollongong has a warmth about it that many other places lack. You will feel this even more if you go down the branch to Port Kembla (see p129) where the steelworks are.

After Wollongong the line climbs higher and generally a little further from the sea, but descends again right to the beach at Bombo. There are several tempting places to break the journey on this part of the line: at **Bombo** the beach is just over the track from the station platform; **Kiama** is worth a visit to see the nearby blowhole and Cathedral Rocks; **Berry**, the last stop

(Opposite) Top: Bondi Beach, Sydney, a 20-minute walk from Bondi Junction station. **Bottom**: Brisbane CBD Riverside area (see p144) seen from Kangaroo Point across the water.

MADE SUPER
CALL 13 22 95
National
Financial Management
STOP
110
PREPARE TO STOP.
TAXI 1856

before Bomaderry (Nowra), is another little place with its centre of activity near the station – visit the antique shop and enjoy good food at the local pub, ***Berry Hotel*** (☎ 02-4464 1011), Queen St.

At **Bomaderry (Nowra)**, there is time for lunch, a walk round town, and then a choice of trains for your return.

A branch line from **Unanderra** goes to **Moss Vale** on the main line south to Melbourne. Until recently a privately-operated train made this a worthwhile detour. A delightful round trip from Sydney was down the coast past Wollongong, up through the rainforest to Moss Vale and back into Sydney via Campbelltown but the only regular service, operated by 3801 Ltd (☎ 1300 65 3801), now normally involves returning via the coast from **Robertson**, 22.5 km short of Moss Vale. However, continuation to Moss Vale is possible. See p255 for further details.

A side trip from Wollongong or Coniston to **Port Kembla** is also worth considering though is not everyone's cup of tea. You can have a quick beer and say hello to the friendly locals: the pub (***Steelworks Hotel***, ☎ 02-4274 1049) is a short walk from the station and there is usually a good 30 minutes or so before the local train returns to Wollongong.

To the Southern Highlands

Frequent suburban electric trains serve Campbelltown, gateway and changing point (for most trains) to the Southern Highlands, while diesel Endeavour sets of CityRail, plus Xplorer or XPT trains offer a somewhat erratic but roughly hourly service to and from Moss Vale, with some continuing on to Goulburn and intermediate stations, and two to Canberra.

Day trips can be made to all destinations daily except Canberra (see below) from the early morning. The last train for a same-day return from Goulburn is at 19.44 on weekdays (20.41 from Moss Vale), reaching Sydney at 23.09. There is an even later train at weekends (Friday to Sunday) arriving Sydney after midnight.

Attractive places to visit are Picton (for the Thirlmere Museum, see p259), Bowral, Moss Vale, and Bundanoon (see p217).

A day return trip to Canberra is practicable only on Tuesdays, Thursdays and Saturdays: dep Sydney 07.05, Canberra arr 11.23, returning by the 17.07 to Sydney. On other days there is barely half an hour before the train returns.

To the Blue Mountains

Possibly the most scenic part of the continent, at least of readily accessible places, the Blue Mountains west of Sydney feature towering escarpments, waterfalls, deep bush and scenic lookouts, and can be visited on a coach tour from the principal centre, **Katoomba**, or by bush-walking tracks, a steam railway, cable car and the world's steepest funicular railway (see p258). Katoomba is reached by fast and fairly frequent trains from Sydney (C 9014). **Springwood**, with its Norman Lindsay gallery and museum, **Wentworth Falls**, **Leura**, **Blackheath**, and **Mount Victoria** are other convenient stations for access to this National Park.

Just short of the interurban terminus at Lithgow is a tiny platform called **ZigZag**, a request stop and station for the ZigZag Railway (see p260), which operates at weekends. Here you can take a steam train up a private line on the old switchback route which crossed the mountains before they built the present line which pierced the ranges with its ten tunnels.

The line climbs from Bottom Points, adjoining the ZigZag platform, to Top Points, then goes on past Mt Sinai through a tunnel to Clarence.

From Clarence, you return to the bottom and hail the train for the return to Sydney. From Katoomba and Leura there

(Opposite) Top: The tram – an integral part of the Melbourne (see p131) scene.
Bottom: A western grey kangaroo resting on Anglesea golf course near Geelong, Victoria.

are other tours such as the Freedom of the Blue Mountains Explorer bus.

To the central coast and Newcastle (C 9014 and local)

There are frequent trains to **Mount Ku-ring-gai** (for Ku-ring-gai Chase National Park) and the scenic **Hawkesbury River** (55 mins), **Gosford** (75 to 82 mins) and **Wyong** (91 to 102 mins); also to **Newcastle**, normally 122 minutes, at hourly intervals with additional and some faster trains at peak periods; see also p218. You don't have to go back to Sydney if you are going north overnight because the Brisbane XPT calls at Hornsby at 16.56, Gosford at 17.41 and Broadmeadow at 18.45.

There are later trains to the central coast and Newcastle if you intend a longer break of journey by staying overnight. After 21.00 trains stop at more stations and take longer, the last being at 03.00 on week nights and 01.47 at weekends, taking almost three hours to Newcastle, ten minutes less to Broadmeadow.

If travelling south from Sydney that day you will have less time to spare: deadline times to return for the Southern Cross Melbourne XPT on weekdays are 18.02 from Newcastle, 18.11 from Broadmeadow, 19.01 from Wyong, 19.17 from Gosford and 19.41 from Hawkesbury River. Weekend and holiday times are approximately 40 minutes earlier. These connections all involve changing at Strathfield to the Melbourne train. If you have left your luggage at Sydney and not booked it on the XPT you will have to leave earlier, as you must at weekends when connecting trains are earlier.

Day trips further north, to **Dungog** or **Gloucester**, can be made using the XPT to **Maitland** (see p219 or local trains changing at Hamilton, but the area north of Maitland and the Hunter Valley is better covered by a two-day trip or a break of journey northbound or by making excursions from a base in or near Newcastle; some ideas are offered on pp218-20.

The XPT timetable for this area is summarized in Table 8 below.

LONGER TRIPS FROM SYDNEY

A two-day trip from Sydney can take you into the **Northern Tablelands** of New South Wales or to **Moree** (see p222). Daylight travel is by Xplorer air-conditioned diesel train with buffet and all trains require reservations; for times see C 9018 (Table 13, p257).

The limitations on other possibilities for rail travel in New South Wales depend only on how long you have before going on interstate (or home) from Sydney. It is a good idea to make a provincial town your base for part of the time.

Places such as Maitland, Orange, or Goulburn, all rail junctions, will shorten many of your 'away day' trips. If you have to get back to Sydney for an interstate journey, remember the deadlines (see the box opposite).

❑ Table 8: Sydney–Dungog–Gloucester (C 9016, 9017 & local)

Sydney	Dep	07.15	11.35	16.24	Gloucester	Dep	02.33a	12.24	17.40
Maitland	Dep	09.58	14.18	19.09	Dungog	Dep	03.24	13.18	18.34
Dungog	Arr	10.42	15.03	19.55	Maitland	Arr	04.05	14.01	19.17
Gloucester	Arr	11.35	15.58	–	Sydney	Arr	07.13	16.34	21.51

Notes:
Daily XPT trains with buffet.
A more frequent service to and from Dungog only by local CityRail, changing at Hamilton from or to Sydney, is available: see local Newcastle and Hunter regional timetables.
a Stops only as required by prior booking.

On Mondays only an interesting return trip is possible by taking the Broken Hill Xplorer outward from Sydney at 06.20, arriving at the 'Barrier City' (Broken Hill, see p175) at 19.10 for an overnight stop and a good look around town next day before returning at 18.30 on the Indian Pacific, reaching Sydney at 10.15 on Wednesday. This could be covered by an Austrail Flexipass or using ordinary fares.

❏ Deadline departures from Sydney
14.55 The Indian Pacific to Adelaide and Perth (Wednesday and Saturday)
16.24 The Brisbane XPT (daily)
20.43 The Southern Cross XPT to Melbourne (daily)

Melbourne

ORIENTATION

Melbourne has long been Sydney's arch rival and was Australia's administrative capital before the creation of Canberra. The 64 regular street blocks of its central business district are ringed by the railway, serving the main stations of Spencer St (interstate), Flinders St (for all local lines), Parliament, Central (formerly Museum) and Flagstaff. No part of the city centre is more than ten minutes' walk from one of these stations.

An intricate network of tram routes also links the stations with city centre streets and with most of the inner suburbs. Suburban and outer urban rail routes penetrate to the outer suburbs and rural hinterland and go around Port Phillip Bay to Geelong in the west and Frankston and Stony Point in the east.

Spencer St, which was undergoing substantial redevelopment at the time of writing, is reportedly Australia's busiest railway station and is also the terminal for V/Line coach services operating from Melbourne, but Flinders St is in the very heart of the city, adjoining Princes Bridge which crosses the Yarra, linking the southern end of Swanston St with St Kilda Rd.

Batman Avenue runs along the side of the Yarra south of the Flinders St railway yards. On the west of Flinders St to the south of the Yarra is Melbourne's casino, officially the Crown Entertainment Complex, reached on foot or by tram down Market St. The City Circle free tram links Flinders St, Spencer St, Flagstaff, Melbourne Central and Parliament stations.

Information about Melbourne can be obtained from the information booths in Bourke St Mall, City Square and in Rialto observation deck. To book tours and accommodation it is best to go to **Victoria/ Melbourne Visitor Information Centre** (☎ 13 28 42, 03-9658 9658, 💻 www.visitmelbourne.com), Federation Square, on the corner of Flinders St and St Kilda Rd. A useful booklet *The Official Visitor Guide* is available free of charge.

WHAT TO SEE AND DO

Around Spencer St station

Bourke St pedestrian bridge leads over the redeveloped station to the Telstra Dome, Melbourne's newest sport and entertainment centre, and to the adjoining Docklands.

A block east of Spencer St station you can enjoy a panoramic view of Melbourne and Port Phillip Bay from the observation deck on the 55th floor of **Rialto Towers**, claimed to be the tallest building in

Australia (but see Sydney p126). This traditional Sydney/Melbourne rivalry was challenged in the 1970s when there were moves in Brisbane to promote the world's tallest building, not just Australia's. *Up where we belong* was the theme tune, but like the Tower of Babel it never really got off the ground and led to a lot of squabbling.

South of the river from Spencer St (tram No 96, 109 or 112, or a 10-minute walk) on Clarendon St is the **Melbourne Exhibition Building**, an exhibition and conference centre popular with tourists and residents alike, and locally known as 'Jeff's shed'. If you want to know why, ask a Melbournite. Adjoining this is the **Maritime Museum**, where the barque *Polly Woodside*, featured on some Australian stamps, is said to serve 'as a dignified concierge for the whole precinct'.

From the Exhibition Building a walk along the riverside towards Flinders St passes the **Crown Entertainment Complex**, with shopping and dining venues, bars and a variety of gaming and entertainment facilities.

Around Flinders St and Jolimont stations

Just opposite **Flinders St** station is **Young and Jackson's** Prince's Bridge Hotel, where Lefebvre's famous *Chloe* painting, which caused much controversy when first acquired in 1883, is displayed in an upstairs bar.

For nature in a different form, Melbourne's **Royal Botanic Gardens**, open daily until sunset, boast the largest plant collection in the Southern hemisphere; any tram down St Kilda Rd from Flinders St will take you there.

Sidney Meyer Music Bowl is here, too, where Australia's much-loved group, The Seekers, gave their triumphant homecoming free performance to a record crowd of 220,000 on returning from their world tour in 1967.

Also in St Kilda Rd is Australia's largest art collection at the **National Gallery**, open daily, and the **Victorian Arts Centre**, Melbourne's answer to the Sydney Opera House. Day tours or performances must be booked well in advance and are not cheap. From the Arts Centre go along the banks of the Yarra, walk or hire a cycle, or take a ferry boat from Princes Walk (adjoining Batman Avenue) on the northern bank. Alternatively walk or take a tram to the eastern end of Flinders St for a look at **Treasury Gardens**.

Jolimont station, a little further on, is handy for **Melbourne Cricket Ground** and nearby **Fitzroy Gardens**, where Captain Cook's cottage, imported from Yorkshire, honours the discoverer of eastern Australia.

Around Central station

A block to the north-east of Central station, in Russell St, is the **Old Melbourne Gaol and Penal Museum** (open daily) where Ned Kelly (see p209) among 135 others was hanged.

Nearer the station in the block between Latrobe and Little Lonsdale St west of Swanston St is the Melbourne Central shopping complex (being redeveloped at the time of writing), which encloses the old **Shot Tower**, where lead shot was made by pouring molten lead into water from a height.

A little further afield in Carlton, see the exhibit of Australian ceramics, weaving and hand-made jewellery in the **Galaxy of Handicrafts**, 99 Cardigan St. A tram up Swanston St will take you there or it is a short walk from Central station. Nearby **Lygon St** is known for its ethnic restaurants, coffee bars and boutiques.

Around Parliament station

See the **Museum of Chinese Australian History** at 22 Cohen Place, in the heart of Chinatown (between Lonsdale St and Little Bourke St which are close to Parliament station), open daily except Tuesdays.

East of the station is **Parliament House** and beyond it, on Albert St, **St Patrick's Cathedral**, one of the grandest Gothic revival churches in Australia.

Around Flagstaff and Royal Park stations

The heritage-listed **Old Royal Mint Building**, dating from 1872, is now home to the ***Mint Bar & Bistro*** (280 William St, on the corner with Latrobe St) opposite Flagstaff Station. **Flagstaff Gardens** is a pleasant historical site (the site of Melbourne's first cemetery) on the highest piece of land in Melbourne City, and **Queen Victoria Market**, a working market selling a wide variety of foods, though more general products on Sundays, is definitely worth a visit.

For bargain craft wares, try the **Meat Market Craft Centre**, 42 Courtney St, North Melbourne (by tram along Flemington Rd). Just north again is Royal Park and the **Zoological Gardens**, traversed by tram route, or by train to **Royal Park** station (13 mins, C 9023) on the Upfield line.

WHERE TO STAY

Budget/mid-range

Dorms and rooms are available at ***Flinders Station Hotel & Backpackers*** (☎ 03-9620 5100, 🖳 www.flindersbackpackers.com.au), 35 Elizabeth St (between Flinders St and Flinders Lane). At the corner of Spencer St and Flinders St is the ***All Nations City Backpacker Hotel*** (☎ 03-9620 1022, freecall ☎ 1800 222 238, 🖳 www.allnations.com.au), which guarantees the cheapest rates and offers free beer on arrival.

A short walk from Central Station, ***Hotel Y*** (☎ 03-9329 5188, 🖳 hotely@ymca.net), 489 Elizabeth St, is run by the YWCA but is not institutional. It has a variety of accommodation to suit most budgets and is reliably reported to have friendly staff and good food in the attached restaurant.

Toad Hall (☎ 03-9600 9010, 🖳 www.toadhall-hotel.com.au), 441 Elizabeth St, has dorms from $20, singles $50 and doubles $60 (en suite $75).

A three-star hotel two blocks from Spencer St station is ***Hotel Enterprize*** (freecall ☎ 1800 033 451, ☎ 03-9629 6991, 🖳 www.hotelenterprize.com.au), 44 Spencer St, where you should expect to pay $95 for an en suite room.

Spanning the mid- to up-market range is ***Victoria Hotel*** (☎ 03-9653 0441, 🖳 www.victoriahotel.com.au), 215 Little Collins St, where single rooms are $68 with shared facilities and $92 en suite, often cheaper off-season.

Up-market

Almost opposite Spencer St station is ***Batman's Hill Hotel*** (☎ 03-9614 6344, 🖳 www.batmanshill.com), 66-70 Spencer St; prices on application.

Out of town

With anything more than a couple of days in the Melbourne area it is worth thinking of staying a fair way out of town as accommodation is often cheaper. Lilydale, Geelong, Seymour, Kyneton, Ballan and Ballarat are worth considering as they have reasonably frequent trains to the city. There are evening trains to all the places described in Day and longer trips from Melbourne (see pp138-9), so that stopovers of two or more nights can be made.

WHERE TO EAT

Eating places are almost too numerous to mention, with almost every type of cuisine to choose from. In the central city area, north of Flinders St station, Little Bourke St and St Kilda (the last named readily accessible by tram), there are restaurants, snack bars, brasseries, pubs with counter lunch, coffee houses and milk bars. There is no need to go more than a couple of blocks from any of the inner city stations (Flinders, Spencer or a station on the loop) to find something to match your taste and pocket. The **Southgate Arts and Leisure Centre**, reached by footbridge from Flinders St, has restaurants as well as entertainment and a Sunday market.

For a unique culinary and travel experience, try the ***Colonial Tramcar Restaurant***; for lunch or dinner reservations (☎ 03-9596 4000, 🖳 reservations@tramrestaurant.com.au) or call at their office, 566 City Rd, South Melbourne. The

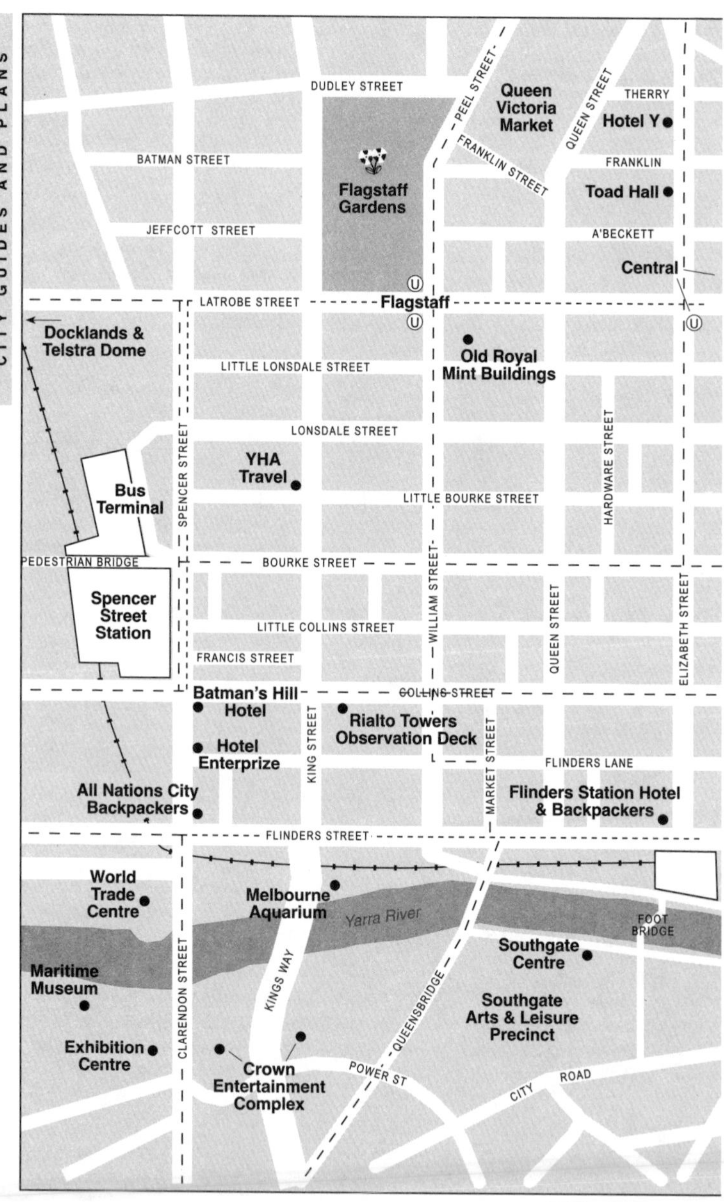
DUDLEY STREET
PEEL STREET
Queen Victoria Market
QUEEN STREET
THERRY
Hotel Y
BATMAN STREET
Flagstaff Gardens
FRANKLIN STREET
FRANKLIN
Toad Hall
JEFFCOTT STREET
A'BECKETT
Central
LATROBE STREET
Flagstaff
Docklands & Telstra Dome
Old Royal Mint Buildings
LITTLE LONSDALE STREET
LONSDALE STREET
HARDWARE STREET
YHA Travel
Bus Terminal
SPENCER STREET
LITTLE BOURKE STREET
PEDESTRIAN BRIDGE
BOURKE STREET
Spencer Street Station
WILLIAM STREET
QUEEN STREET
ELIZABETH STREET
LITTLE COLLINS STREET
FRANCIS STREET
Batman's Hill Hotel
COLLINS STREET
Rialto Towers Observation Deck
Hotel Enterprize
KING STREET
MARKET STREET
FLINDERS LANE
All Nations City Backpackers
Flinders Station Hotel & Backpackers
FLINDERS STREET
World Trade Centre
Melbourne Aquarium
Yarra River
FOOT BRIDGE
Southgate Centre
Maritime Museum
CLARENDON STREET
KINGS WAY
QUEENSBRIDGE
Southgate Arts & Leisure Precinct
Exhibition Centre
Crown Entertainment Complex
POWER ST
CITY ROAD

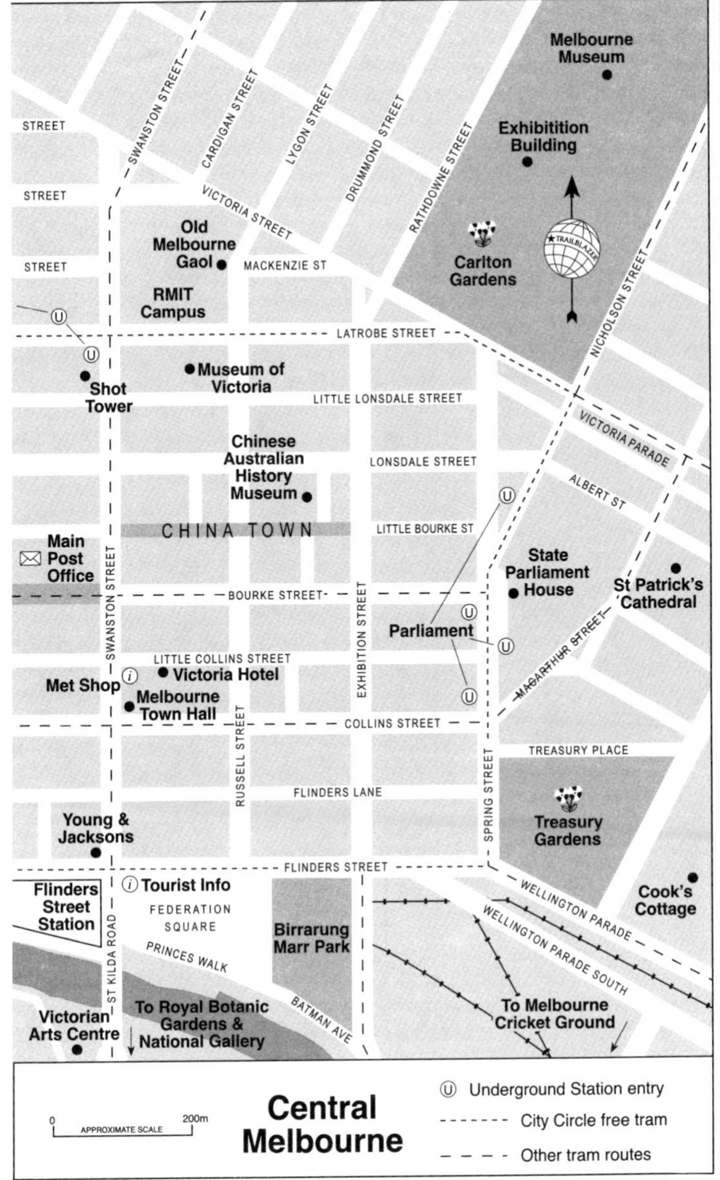

Melbourne Museum
Exhibitition Building
Carlton Gardens
SWANSTON STREET
CARDIGAN STREET
LYGON STREET
DRUMMOND STREET
RATHDOWNE STREET
NICHOLSON STREET
STREET
STREET
STREET
VICTORIA STREET
Old Melbourne Gaol
MACKENZIE ST
RMIT Campus
LATROBE STREET
Shot Tower
Museum of Victoria
LITTLE LONSDALE STREET
VICTORIA PARADE
Chinese Australian History Museum
LONSDALE STREET
ALBERT ST
CHINA TOWN
LITTLE BOURKE ST
Main Post Office
State Parliament House
St Patrick's Cathedral
BOURKE STREET
EXHIBITION STREET
Parliament
MACARTHUR STREET
LITTLE COLLINS STREET
Met Shop
Victoria Hotel
Melbourne Town Hall
COLLINS STREET
RUSSELL STREET
TREASURY PLACE
FLINDERS LANE
SPRING STREET
Treasury Gardens
Young & Jacksons
FLINDERS STREET
Flinders Street Station
Tourist Info
FEDERATION SQUARE
Birrarung Marr Park
WELLINGTON PARADE
WELLINGTON PARADE SOUTH
Cook's Cottage
ST KILDA ROAD
PRINCES WALK
BATMAN AVE
Victorian Arts Centre
To Royal Botanic Gardens & National Gallery
To Melbourne Cricket Ground
TRAILBLAZER
0
APPROXIMATE SCALE
200m
Central Melbourne
Underground Station entry
City Circle free tram
Other tram routes

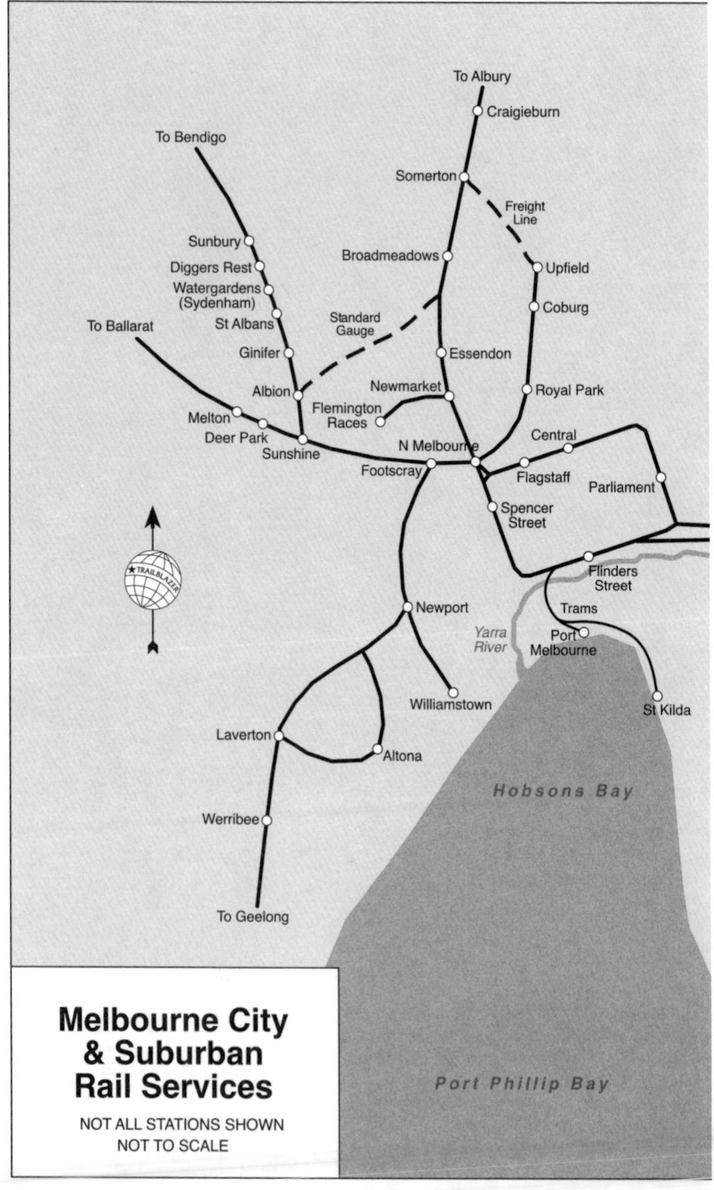

To Albury
Craigieburn
To Bendigo
Somerton
Freight Line
Sunbury
Broadmeadows
Upfield
Diggers Rest
Watergardens (Sydenham)
Coburg
St Albans
Standard Gauge
To Ballarat
Ginifer
Essendon
Newmarket
Royal Park
Albion
Flemington Races
Melton
Central
Deer Park
N Melbourne
Sunshine
Footscray
Flagstaff
Parliament
Spencer Street
TRAILBLAZER
Flinders Street
Newport
Trams
Yarra River
Port Melbourne
Williamstown
St Kilda
Laverton
Altona
Hobsons Bay
Werribee
To Geelong
Port Phillip Bay
Melbourne City & Suburban Rail Services
NOT ALL STATIONS SHOWN
NOT TO SCALE

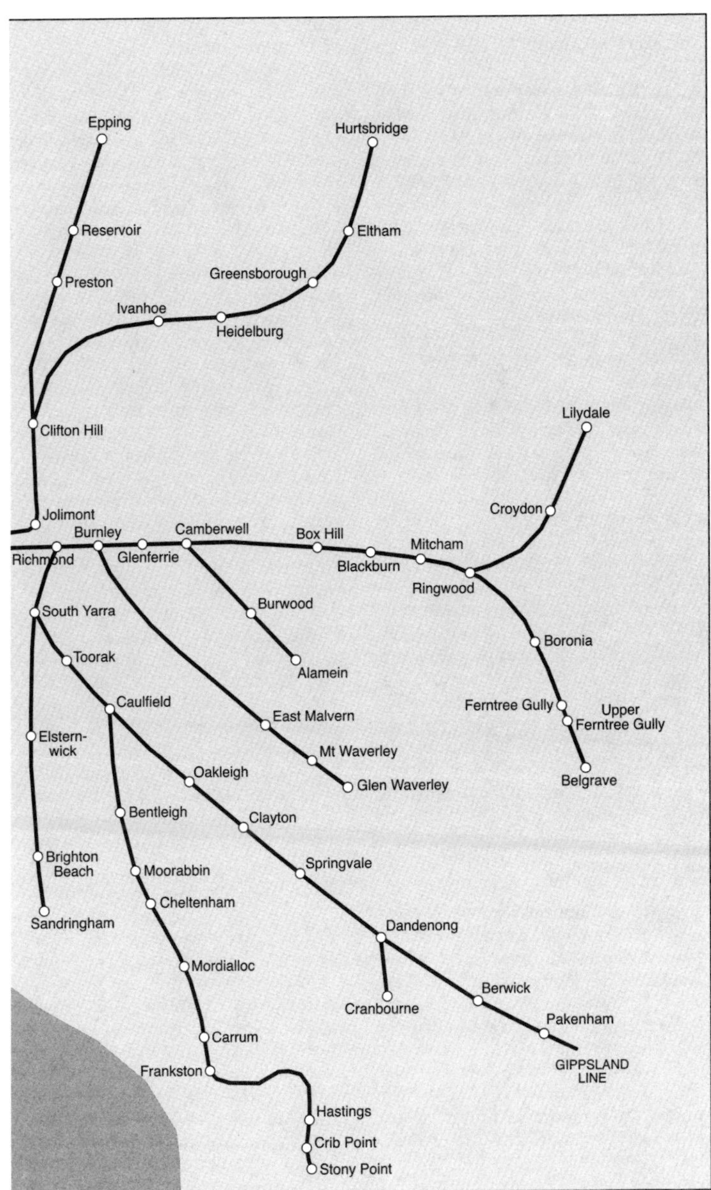
Epping
Hurtsbridge
Reservoir
Eltham
Preston
Greensborough
Ivanhoe
Heidelburg
Clifton Hill
Lilydale
Croydon
Jolimont
Burnley
Camberwell
Box Hill
Mitcham
Richmond
Glenferrie
Blackburn
Ringwood
Burwood
South Yarra
Boronia
Toorak
Alamein
Caulfield
Ferntree Gully
Upper Ferntree Gully
East Malvern
Elstern-wick
Mt Waverley
Oakleigh
Glen Waverley
Belgrave
Bentleigh
Clayton
Brighton Beach
Moorabbin
Springvale
Cheltenham
Sandringham
Dandenong
Mordialloc
Berwick
Cranbourne
Pakenham
Carrum
Frankston
GIPPSLAND LINE
Hastings
Crib Point
Stony Point

gastronomic journey starts at the National Art Gallery just south of Flinders St railway station.

A train out to Eltham will let you enjoy the fare at award-winning chef ***Stephen Mercer's Restaurant*** (☎ 03-9431 1015), 732 Main Rd, a modest walk or short bus ride south from the station (route Nos 152, 281 or 582, covered by Metcard). Specialities are many: the mouth-watering menu is complemented by an extensive wine list. Although not cheap, a culinary experience here will not be forgotten. Booking is essential.

DAY TRIPS IN THE SUBURBAN AREA

Even if you are visiting Melbourne for only one day you have time between the arrival of some overnight trains from interstate and departures the same evening to travel all over the suburban area.

• Go around the bay to **Frankston**, gateway to the Mornington Peninsula with its many attractions, in the south-east (65 mins from Spencer St).

From Frankston there is a local line to **Stony Point** for the ferry to Phillip Island (summer only) with its penguins. The ferry is only a few minutes' trip.

• Take in Flinders St and the underground loop (for city centre sights and shops) and **historic Port Melbourne**, or **St Kilda** (for the beach).

• Go to **Williamstown** at the mouth of the Yarra; Williamstown has both Historic and Maritime museums, not to mention a Railway Museum 500m from North Williamstown station.

• If **races or shows** are on, you can go by train to Newmarket, the showgrounds or Flemington racecourse. The Royal Melbourne Show is held in September and the Melbourne Cup in November, but there are race meetings all year at Flemington.

• The picturesque **Dandenong Ranges**, an hour from Melbourne by electric train to Upper Ferntree Gully or Belgrave (C 9024), are Melbourne's doorstep national park. Here you can see lyrebirds displaying their plumage, or visit the 40-hectare rhododendron garden at nearby Olinda.

For a longer trip, the **Puffing Billy** steam train (see p140 and p261) skirts the south of the Dandenongs from Belgrave to Gembrook.

• North of the Dandenongs is **Lilydale** (a good suburban base 50 to 65 minutes from the city by frequent suburban train), from where a connecting bus serves Healesville with its **sanctuary**: here you can watch kangaroos, koalas, emus, wombats and platypuses in a natural setting.

• The historic town of **Ballarat**, home of the Ballarat Vintage Tramway (see p261), is an easy day-return trip by local V/Line train. The journey takes 1½ hours each way and trains are roughly every 90 minutes from 08.05 to 20.55, slightly less frequently at weekends. Return trains run up to 19.20 except on Saturdays, but if travelling the same day to Sydney the last connections leave Ballarat at 16.25 Monday to Friday, 16.55 on Saturday and 17.15 on Sundays.

Local transport services

Rail/bus/tram passes on the Met system can be obtained for parts or the whole of the Melbourne area by the hour or day at very reasonable rates; $12.30 covers a full day throughout all the zones.

For local train services, fares and timetables visit the Met Shop at Melbourne Town Hall, on the corner of Swanston and Little Collins streets, or call the Met Information Centre (☎ 131 638) between 06.00 and 22.00 any day, or look at the website: www.metlinkmelbourne.com.au.

Trains operate every 10 to 40 minutes depending on the route and time of day or week and trams every 3 to 30 minutes.

• There is a frequent V/Line passenger service, approximately every hour from 05.45 to 23.35 on weekdays but less frequent and extensive at weekends, between Melbourne and **Geelong**, Victoria's second city, with a wool museum, art gallery and some historic buildings. Geelong is an hour's journey on average (C 9024) but is not covered by Metcard tickets. Geelong is also the main centre for touring the Bellarine Peninsula and parts of the south-west coast as well as being a good 'out of town' base for Melbourne sightseeing.

The last return train from Geelong is at 21.15 on weekdays, 20.25 Saturday and Sunday, reaching Spencer St at 22.20 and 21.28 respectively, in all cases too late to catch the night train to Sydney. Table 9 (below) shows all viable connections between Geelong and interstate services.

DAY AND LONGER TRIPS FROM MELBOURNE

To the east

All the stations in Gippsland, east of the Melbourne metropolitan area, are within day-return reach of Melbourne but to see the sights of the region two or three days are needed.

The rail system east of Melbourne serves the Latrobe Valley industrial towns of Moe, Morwell and Traralgon, then goes on through **Rosedale** (see p208) to **Sale** and Bairnsdale (C 9030; see p208), where the Gippsland Wetlands will be of interest to birdwatchers.

(At the time of writing there were plans to restore another branch which used to serve South Gippsland but the date had not been announced; see p262 for details of the private service over part of this route).

❑ Table 9: Connections between Geelong and Interstate services Melbourne–Adelaide and Sydney

Interstate trains must be booked in advance. The Austrail Flexipass is not valid Geelong–N Shore –Melbourne

	Sat	M-F	Sun	M-F	Sat	Fri	Sa,Su	Sat	Thu
Geelong d	06.30	06.58	17.30	18.26	18.32	20.10	20.25	20.25	21.15
N Shore a	—	—	—	—	—	—	—	—	21.21
N Shore d	—	—	—	—	—	—	—	—	22.30
Melbourne a	07.33	08.03	18.33	19.33	19.32	21.10	21.28	21.28	—
Melbourne d	08.30	08.30	19.55	19.55	19.55	22.10	22.10	08.30a	—
Adelaide a	—	—	—	—	—	08.00a	08.00a	—	07.10a
Sydney a	19.53	19.53	06.53a	06.53a	06.53a	—	—	19.53	—

	M-F	Sat	Sun	Thu	Fri	Sat	Sun	Su-Th	Fri	Sat
Sydney d	07.43	07.43	07.43	—	—	—	—	20.43	20.43	20.43
Adelaide d	—	—	—	08.30	10.10	10.10	10.10	—	—	—
Melbourne a	18.55	18.55	18.55	—	—	—	—	07.35a	07.35a	07.35a
Melbourne d	19.20	19.00e	19.00f	—	—	—	—	07.47	08.00	09.40
N Shore a	—	—	—	17.44	19.19	19.31	19.44	—	—	—
N Shore d	—	—	—	18.12b	19.24c	19.52d	20.57	—	—	—
Geelong a	20.23	19.33	19.53	18.20	19.31	20.02	21.07	08.52	08.59	10.42

Notes

a Next day

If connection missed:
b dep 18.44 arr Geelong 18.52 or call a taxi
c dep 20.15 arr Geelong 20.23 or call a taxi
d dep 21.27 arr Geelong 21.37 or call a taxi
e dep 20.35, arr Geelong 21.37
f dep 20.05, arr Geelong 21.07

For catching the overnight service to Sydney or Adelaide at Melbourne, deadline departures on weekdays are 16.45 from Sale (bus connection from Bairnsdale at 15.30), 17.20 from Traralgon, and later from Moe and Warragul. On Saturdays and Sundays times vary so check local timetables carefully beforehand.

The Dandenong ranges (see p138 and map 30, p207) are accessible from Melbourne by frequent Connex trains of the Met system as far as Lilydale, Ferntree Gully and the scenic Ringwood to Belgrave line (C 9024).

Belgrave is the western terminus of the narrow-gauge railway, popularly known as the Puffing Billy Railway (see p261), to Menzies Creek, Lakeside, **Emerald**, Cockatoo and **Gembrook**. Operated by Emerald Tourist Railway Board, the Puffing Billy Railway runs daily except Christmas Day, but on days of total fire ban will be diesel hauled and operate at a reduced service.

The timetable and a detailed route map are available to passengers on this 25km scenic route; the information given is not repeated here. The line penetrates deep into the Dandenongs with many twists and turns, much of it in forest country. The large lake seen to the south between Menzies Creek and Emerald is Cardinia Creek Reservoir of the Melbourne and Metropolitan Board of Works.

There is a refreshment room and toilets at Belgrave Puffing Billy station, refreshment trolleys at Menzies Creek and other stops on the line.

Opposite Gembrook station is ***Ranges Hotel*** (☎ 03-5968 1220); Gembrook also has tea rooms, craft shops, a motor museum and a working pottery. Rambles through the forest and organized tours are available and there is a souvenir kiosk with refreshments on the station.

To the north

The main line from Melbourne to Sydney is also served by V-Line intercity trains as far as the border at Albury-Wodonga.

All Melbourne–Albury local trains stop at **Seymour** (70 mins from Melbourne), **Benalla** (another hour), **Wangaratta** (about 2 hours 40 mins from Melbourne) and **Wodonga**, Albury's Victorian twin city. Albury is reached in a further hour from Wangaratta. For schedules of V/Line intercity as well as Countrylink services see C 9029.

A day trip into the Goulburn Valley is another option. Trains go only as far as **Shepparton** (see p207), from where coaches connect to **Cobram** (see p207) on the NSW border (C 9026). Return times if travelling interstate to Adelaide are 16.10 from Albury, 17.25 from Benalla, and 15.10 from Shepparton, in each case rather later on Saturdays and Sundays; see map 29, p205.

To the west

Warrnambool (see p202) and places in between there and Geelong such as **Winchelsea**, **Colac**, **Camperdown** and **Terang**, are within day-return distance of Melbourne but if visiting this area a two-day trip, perhaps based on Geelong (see p139), gives more opportunities.

If visiting Geelong or the Victorian south-west coast, the last departures to connect with the Southern Cross to Sydney are at 18.26 from Geelong (Monday to Friday), 18.32 (Saturday) or 17.30 (Sunday); see Table 9, p139.

From beyond Geelong (Colac, Camperdown and Warrnambool) there is no convenient connection to the Sydney train but connections to The Overland for Adelaide are reasonably convenient except on Thursday, when The Overland leaves Melbourne at the exact minute the Warrnambool train arrives. It is therefore necessary on Thursday to change to a local at Geelong for North Shore, there to connect with The Overland. The times are as follows: on Thursday, dep Warrnambool 17.45, Colac 1902, Winchelsea 19.29, arr Geelong 20.07, dep Geelong 21.15, arr North Shore 21.21, dep 22.20, arr Adelaide 07.10 Friday.

Since there are over two hours between arrival in Geelong and the departure from North Shore (where there is little other than a platform and telephone box), it is probably worthwhile taking a taxi from Geelong to North Shore nearer the departure time.

On Fridays, Saturdays and Sundays, the train from Warrnambool reaches Melbourne in good time for The Overland departure at 22.10. Depart Warrnambool 17.45 Friday, arr Melbourne 21.10; on Saturday and Sunday, dep Warrnambool 17.05, arr Melbourne 20.18.

To the north-west

Castlemaine (see p203) and **Bendigo** (see p204), on the north-western line, are within day-return distance with trains roughly every 90 minutes but can be made part of a longer trip including Swan Hill and Kerang. The first train leaves at 08.40 from Spencer St, 55 minutes later on Sundays. The last return times from Bendigo are 18.15 on weekdays, 18.50 at weekends, but to catch the XPT for Sydney you need to take the daily 16.25 service; times from Castlemaine are 23 minutes later.

Swan Hill (see p204) and **Kerang** (see p204) are within striking distance and so is **Echuca** (see p206) the last named only on either a day return on Sunday afternoon or a Friday night to Sunday trip. Swan Hill has a daily service but one that was designed for Swan Hill rather than Melbourne residents.

A summary timetable is given in Table 10 (below) and features of these destinations and other excursions are described on pp78-80 and p204-6.

❑ Table 10: Melbourne–Bendigo–Kerang–Swan Hill

		Friday	Sunday	Mon-Thur	Saturday
Melbourne	dep	16.32	17.33	17.33	17.57
Bendigo	dep	18.42	19.30	19.33	19.48
Kerang	arr	20.08	20.56	21.00	21.14
Swan Hill	arr	20.50	21.38	21.42	21.56

		Mon-Sat	Sunday
Swan Hill	dep	07.30	16.40
Kerang	dep	08.09	17.19
Bendigo	arr	09.35	18.47
Melbourne	arr	11.25	20.47

Notes

Intercity trains with buffet. 1st class and economy seating.

The Sunday afternoon train from Swan Hill is too late to catch the overnight XPT to Sydney but is in time for the night train to Adelaide.

❑ Deadline departures from Melbourne

19.55 The Southern Cross XPT to Sydney (daily)
21.10 The Overland to Adelaide (Thursday)
22.10 The Overland to Adelaide (Friday, Saturday and Sunday)

Brisbane

ORIENTATION

Subtropical Brisbane's warmth will greet you as you alight at this northern capital. Founded in the 1830s and now established as Australia's third city,

Brisbane has seen rapid urban growth in the last three decades and its straggling suburbs cover an area equal to Greater London. Unlike Sydney and Melbourne, the city is under one administration: its budget is equal to that of the state of Tasmania.

Brisbane's suburban trains are all modern, smooth, well-furnished electric units. The two main stations, Roma St and Central, are in the city centre and within 15 minutes' walk of each other.

A free inner-city bus route takes the strain out of walking between city centre features (the main strain being having to wait to cross roads at traffic lights) but it takes just about the same time whether you walk or wait for the bus.

The city circle bus follows different clockwise and anti-clockwise routes and gives access to most of the area shown on the map north of the river. The Brisbane City Council (BCC) bus station, off Queen St Mall (Myer Centre) is the main terminus for local buses, but many stop instead at City bus stops in Ann, Adelaide and other central city streets.

Another good way to get around is the CityCat ferry service; take a CityCat to South Bank Parklands and Brisbane Convention Centre (these occupy part of the site of the former World Expo 1988); on foot from Roma St these can be reached in five minutes across Victoria Bridge.

The Information Desk at Brisbane Transit Centre (☎ 07-3236 2020), Roma St, has a Visitors Accommodation Service and can make tour bookings.

WHAT TO SEE AND DO

Around Roma St and Central stations

Climb up to the Old Windmill observatory, built in 1828-9 as a windmill but subsequently used as an observatory amongst other things. It's on Wickham Terrace, north-east of **Roma St** station, which itself is part of Roma St Transit Centre, the terminal for long-distance coaches. Alternatively go down through King George Square and Albert St to Queen St Mall. From the northern end of the Mall take the walkway along the side of Anzac Square or through the square and past the Shrine of Remembrance (Cenotaph) to the old Central station facade, now the entrance to the Sheraton Hotel (as well as to the station itself).

In the area around **Central** station it is possible to see giant old fig trees, particularly at the bottom end of Creek St and at some other road junctions in the inner suburbs.

Walk along Creek St to Eagle St Pier where an outstanding craft market is held every Sunday. About 300m south of Eagle St Pier is Brisbane Botanic Gardens (open daily); the 20-hectare site offers a profusion of sub-tropical flowers and shrubs.

Around South Brisbane and South Bank stations

South Brisbane station, the first stop from Roma St over the Merivale A-frame bridge, adjoins the Parklands where there is an artificial swimming pool, Pauls Breaka Beach, and Stanley St Plaza with shops and cafés and other venues. Right opposite the station is the Cultural Centre with its Performing Arts complex, restaurants and bars. Across the road (by covered walkway) is also Queensland Art Gallery (open daily) with its fine collection of paintings, sculptures, photographs and prints, and Queensland

Museum (open daily) where the exhibits include dinosaurs and the only surviving World War 1 German tank.

On Sidon St at the southern end of the Parklands, near **South Bank** station (the next station after South Brisbane on the Robina and Cleveland lines), you can see many fine ship models and an old frigate at Queensland Maritime Museum, open daily except Christmas Day and Good Friday from 09.30 to 16.30. From here it is a short walk across the Goodwill pedestrian bridge to the Botanic Gardens (see opposite).

Around Brunswick St and Bowen Hills stations

Less than a kilometre north of Central is **Brunswick St**, the station for colourful Fortitude Valley with its many ethnic restaurants and Brisbane's Chinatown. At the eastern end of Brunswick St is New Farm Park, with up to 12,000 rose trees in bloom between September and November (as well as avenues of jacaranda and poinciana trees) beside Brisbane River. Visit St John's Cathedral, open daily, where brass-rubbing workshops are held (check times locally). At nearby Spring Hill are many of Brisbane's dozens of art and craft galleries. Near here, too, is the Brisbane Exhibition site – they call it the Ekka. If an exhibition is on, there will be frequent special trains from all city stations.

Within walking distance of **Bowen Hills** station (the next to the north after Brunswick St) in Jordan Tee is Miegunyah, built in 1884 and now a Folk Museum, open Wednesdays 10.30 to 15.00, Saturdays and Sundays from 10.30 to 16.00. Less than a kilometre away is Brisbane's oldest surviving dwelling, Newstead House (☎ 07-3216 1846, 🖳 www.newsteadhouse.com.au), at the bend of the river in Newstead Park. Look along the river to the wharves in both directions and across to Bulimba Point. Downstream the Gateway Bridge dominates the skyline beyond Hamilton Reach, while the jets loom large overhead on their approach to Brisbane Airport.

Just behind the Breakfast Creek Hotel in Higgs St is a rare Chinese joss-house (☎ 07-3262 5588), built in 1884 and open daily to visitors. It is a one kilometre walk north-east from Bowen Hills station; alternatively you can walk back along the riverside from Bretts Wharf, reached by Citycat, or take a City Council bus.

Around Dakabin station

For exotic animals, birds and plants visit **Alma Park Zoo** and the 13-hectare **Tropical Palm Gardens**, open daily, just over a kilometre from Dakabin station, 50 minutes from the City on the Caboolture line. Some trains have special bus connections to Alma Park – ask for leaflets at Central or Roma St.

For the rail enthusiast

There is a railway shop at the eastern end of the station building at South Brisbane, whilst at **Ipswich** (55 mins by Citytrain) the Workshops Rail Museum (see p264) are open to visitors. The Australian Railway Historical Society (see p254) operates several steam trains in this area.

En route to Ipswich you can hardly fail to note the historic Castlemaine Brewery, home of XXXX beer (tours are held regularly but they need to be booked in advance) on the right at **Milton** station, the first after leaving Roma St.

WHERE TO STAY

Budget/mid-range

The facilities at ***Brisbane Backpackers Resort*** (☎ 07-3844 9956 or freecall ☎ 1800 626 452, 🖳 www.brisbanebackpackers.com.au), 110 Vulture St, West End (west of South Bank station), include a licensed bar, pool, sauna and spa – a five-star backpacker hotel! An en suite single costs $58; dorms are also available.

Palace Backpackers (☎ 07-3211 2433 or 1800 676 340, 🖳 www.palacebackpackers.com.au), right opposite Central station, is a former Salvation Army citadel, now with a licensed bar and grill. Dorm beds cost from $20, single rooms with communal facilities from $36. ***Brisbane City YHA*** (☎ 07-3236 1004, 🖳 brisbanecity@yhaqld.org.au), 392 Upper Roma St, has double /twin rooms from $24 per person, en suite for $35.

Although it is just over 1km from Brunswick St station, the friendly ***Globe Trekkers Hostel*** (☎ 07-3358 1251, 🖳 www.globetrekkers.net), 35 Balfour St, New Farm (in 'The Valley' off Brunswick St) is worth considering because it offers a pickup service from city railway stations (at reasonable hours). Dorm beds cost $19, a twin or double room $44, en suite $50. ***Indooroopilly Hotel*** (☎ 07-3378 1533), 3 Station Rd, opposite Indooroopilly station, has en suite rooms with TV at a moderate price.

A short walk from Roma St station is ***Explorers' Inn*** (freecall ☎ 1800 623 288, ☎ 07-3211 3488, 🖳 stay@explorers.com.au), 63 Turbot St, a small but recommended three-star hotel, where an en suite costs $75 single, $79 twin, while just round the corner in George St is ***Hotel George Williams*** (☎ 07-3308 0700, 🖳 hgw@ymca.org.au), offering friendly three-star service and free use of a gymnasium, with air-conditioned single rooms from $85.

Goodearth Hotel, formerly the Gazebo (tollfree ☎ 1800 777 789, ☎ 07-3831 6177, 🖳 stay@goodearth.com.au), 345 Wickham Terrace, can be reached by bus or by walking up through the Parklands from Roma St station. It is a three-star Flag Hotel with private balconies overlooking the city skyline and Mt Coot-tha ranges: rooms cost from $82.

Up-market

Holiday Inn (☎ 07-3328 2222, 🖳 www.brisbane.holiday-inn.com), at Roma St Transit Centre, was formerly a Travelodge; rooms cost $145. ***The Sheraton*** (☎ 07-3835 3535, 🖳 www.sheraton.com/brisbane), above Brisbane Central Station, is a five-star hotel with single rooms from $169, twin $195.

WHERE TO EAT

Eagle St wharf area (three blocks down Creek St from Central), **Fortitude Valley** (Chinatown) adjacent to Brunswick St Station, **South Bank Parklands** (South Brisbane or South Bank stations), the **City Mall** and areas between there and Central Station; also **Park Rd Milton** (adjacent to the station) and the Toowong station area offer a wide variety of eating places.

Brisbane city centre is also well supplied with restaurants. Take the escalator down from Central station and you are in a food hall. Between there and Queen St Mall, and within and around the Mall, are numerous eating places. Try ***O'Malley's Irish Pub*** for good tucker as well as the real stuff on draught. Then in the middle of the Mall itself ***Jimmy's on the Mall***, and ***The Pig 'n Whistle*** are hard to miss. If time is short and a snack is all you need, the ***Whistle Stop*** bar on Central Station serves tasty meat pies and 'happy hour' drinks at lunch time. There are plenty of eating places at Roma St station also, and over the road right opposite the main entrance is the ***Transcontinental Hotel*** which offers good food and has a well-stocked bar.

You will find other restaurants, rather more up-market, at the **Riverside Centre** on the edge of the CBD (Central Business District). Walk there or take the free city circle bus to Eagle St Wharf, three blocks down Creek St from Central.

In the Newstead area, visit the famous ***Breakfast Creek (Brekky Creek) Hotel***, 2 Kingsford Smith Drive, north of the river, for a beer or big succulent steaks, or try the seafood at the Breakfast Creek Wharf.

On the river side of the railway at Milton (turn left out of the subway from the station), Park Rd is Brisbane's latest hang-out for the 'cafe latte' set, but has something for everyone. Handy places for lunch or dinner include ***Arrivederci Pizza al Metro*** (☎ 07-3369-8500) which means just what the name implies and, almost oppo-

(Opposite) The train on the Kuranda Scenic Railway (see pp250-1) crossing Stoney Creek Bridge, north Queensland. **(Following pages) Top, middle left** and **right**: Uluru (Ayers Rock). **Bottom left**: Tour buses line up for another spectacular sunset at Uluru. **Bottom right**: Kata Tjuta (The Olgas).

1758
1758
1758D

V.I.P
EVIP056

Fish terminology

A word of warning: in Australia 'lobster' always means crayfish, 'trout' may mean Coral trout, a choice white-fleshed reef fish but nothing at all like brown or rainbow trout or sea trout, and 'salmon', unless specified as red, can mean a very unexciting greyish fish called Australian salmon and bearing no relationship to the kind known in North America and Europe.

site, ***La Dolce Vita Ristorante*** offering a great variety of Italian-style dishes.

Slightly further afield at Gailey Five Way Shopping Centre, Taringa (Bus No 411 from Toowong station area) there is a ***Mongolian BBQ House*** where the food you pick is seen cooking in a unique way and, on Oxley Rd a block east of **Corinda Station** (20 mins by Citytrain every quarter-hour), is ***O'Toole's***, a pub-restaurant offering good lunch dishes at table for less than $5.

DAY TRIPS FROM BRISBANE

To the coast

Frequent local trains serve the Moreton Bay coast, **Sandgate** and **Shorncliffe** north of the river mouth (for Moora Park beach and pier), while further north from Caboolture, 60 minutes by City train, buses connect to **Bribie Island** (40 minutes).

South of the river and the industrial area of Fisherman Islands is Manly with its boat harbour, Lota, close to Fig Tree Point on a coastal reserve, and **Ormiston** and **Cleveland** on Raby Bay. Journey times vary from 30 to 50 minutes (C 9013 & local). These bayside suburbs are all on part of the greater Moreton Bay and some are more like commuter suburbs than coastal resorts, but there are good beaches and the usual attractions of sand, surf and sunshine. From Cleveland, Stradbroke Ferries operates a water taxi service to **Stradbroke Island**, with a courtesy bus from the railway station to the ferry terminal. Stradbroke has Point Lookout, Blue Lake National Park, a fish habitat reserve, a conservation park and great beaches.

Day trips (or longer) by catamaran to Moreton Island for the Wild Dolphin Resort at Tangalooma can be made from Brisbane's Pinkenba jetty (courtesy buses from Roma St Transit Centre). Whale-watching cruises are also offered during the migratory season, usually August to October. Whale-watching tours also operate from Redcliffe, 30 minutes from Brisbane by Hornibrook Bus Lines. Details of all such tours and many others can be obtained at the Transit Centre, Roma St station.

The Citytrain network extends south to the **Gold Coast**. Half-hourly express trains serve Coomera, Helensvale, Nerang and Robina. Local timetables give details and reduced fares are available at the weekend.

The Gold Coast, of which Surfers Paradise is the heart, is noted for its surf beaches, its mountainous hinterland, sailing on the Broadwater, the many islands, the famous 'meter maids' in the main shopping area, its casino, and its excellent restaurants – Queensland seafoods are a speciality; try Queensland mud crab or Moreton Bay bugs.

The current terminus of the QR Gold Coast Railway at Robina near Mudgeeraba in the Gold Coast hinterland is 7km west of Mermaid Beach. There were proposals for an extension further south to Coolangatta, perhaps connecting with the NSW system, but these seem to have been abandoned.

The Interurban Multiple-Unit trains of the Gold Coast line are capable of 140km/h though start-to-stop speeds are substantially lower. At intermediate stations on the line between Helensvale and Beenleigh

(Opposite) Top: Views of rainforest and the Pacific Ocean from the Skyrail (see p86). **Bottom left:** Robbs Monument marks the approach to Barron Falls near Kuranda. **Bottom right:** The track for The Gulflander on the Normanton–Croydon railway (see p87).

there are connecting buses to local attractions such as Dreamworld (see p266) at Coomera, a major entertainment park, whilst at Nerang there are connecting buses to and from Surfers Paradise and Broadbeach.

Gold Coast attractions include Seaworld at Main Beach, Warner Bros Movie World at Oxenford, Jupiter's Casino at Broadbeach and Currumbin Wildlife Sanctuary; all are accessible by local Surfside buses.

To the west

Helidon is worth a visit for its mineral springs but apart from The Westlander on two evenings a week, it is now accessible only by railbus from Rosewood. If you don't like natural mineral water there is a pub just opposite the station and a coffee shop a hundred metres down a street of colourful jacaranda trees.

Otherwise **Rosewood** is as far west as you can go in a day by rail at the present time. For further information on Rosewood, including the preserved branch railway, see Part 5 (p268).

To the north

Beerwah is the station for Australia Zoo, awarded Australia's Best Major Tourist Attraction for 2003/4 and famed internationally for TV's Crocodile Hunter series featuring Steve and Terri Irwin (☎ 07-5436 2000 or 🖳 info@australiazoo.com.au for bookings or go to 🖳 www.crocodilehunter.com for further information). Featuring a 5000-seat 'crocoseum' as well as giant pythons, Bengal Tigers and other creatures including the Giant Galapagos Turtle, the world's oldest living resident, the zoo is open daily except Christmas Day from 09.00 to 16.30. Admission is $27 for adults (cheaper for pensioners and children) and there is a café and shopping facilities.

Citytrain Sunshine Coast services from Roma St to Beerwah run on average every 80 minutes from 05.42 on weekdays, though there are barely half as many services at weekends. Journey time ranges from 78 minutes (for a through train) to over 100 minutes when a change is needed at Caboolture. There are additional services with coach connection from Caboolture. Free courtesy coaches meet most morning trains or you can call the zoo from Beerwah station.

The trains leaving at a minute or two past the hour between 07.00 and 15.00 on weekdays have connections to the Zoo itself, and the last daily return connection is at 15.12, half an hour earlier on Sundays.

Travel in the suburban area

The Brisbane **suburban rail network** extends to Rosewood on the south-west, Gympie on the north, Shorncliffe, Cleveland and Robina on the east and includes the branches to Ferny Grove (west) and Doomben.

The **Translink** network can also take you to the coast at Redcliffe, Noosa, Maroochydore, Bribie Island, Broadbeach or Surfers Paradise or, nearer at hand, to interesting inland destinations like Ipswich (see p264), Rosewood, Grandchester, Esk, and south to Beenleigh (for the rum distillery and nearby Lion Park) on the Robina Line.

For exploring the Brisbane area by rail the various tickets offered by Translink (see p31) are the best option, since they cover useful bus and ferry connections as well as trains: the Translink network includes QR Railbus, Trainlink buses, BCC buses, and various private buses which extend the area further (see map pp148-9). The Citycat services on Brisbane River are also covered by Translink – a great way to travel. The airport line is not included, and Translink tickets do not cover QR Traveltrain services, although some local journeys can be made by them (for a separate fare), eg to Nambour, Cooroy, Laidley or Helidon.

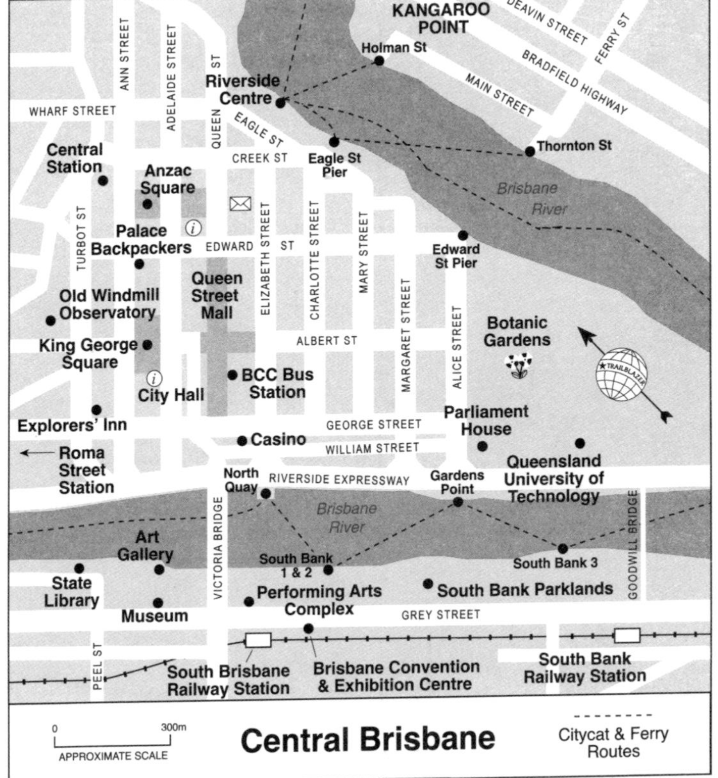

Beerwah Hotel (☎ 07-5494 0555), over the road from the station, is a friendly place to stay or enjoy a meal at its Beerwah Country Bistro.

Landsborough is served by Citytrain Interurban and the Bundaberg and Rockhampton Tilt trains. The ***Landsborough Hotel***, formerly called Mellum Club Hotel, just opposite the station, welcomes you with *'There are no strangers here; only friends you haven't met'* and Trainlink buses (not covered by rail passes) connect with Mooloolaba, Alexandra Headland, and Maroochydore on the Sunshine Coast.

Palmwoods, a little further up the line, has excellent and attractively-priced meals (and accommodation) within sight of the station. The train service is the same as for Beerwah (see opposite), taking about half an hour longer.

Nambour, approximately two hours by QR interurban electric trains (C 9011 & local), is another good place for a break of journey or a day trip, being the gateway to the Sunshine and Sun Coast resorts. A short bus ride from Nambour will bring you to the **Big Pineapple complex** where you can buy local products and ride a cane train (see p264) through the pineapple plantation.

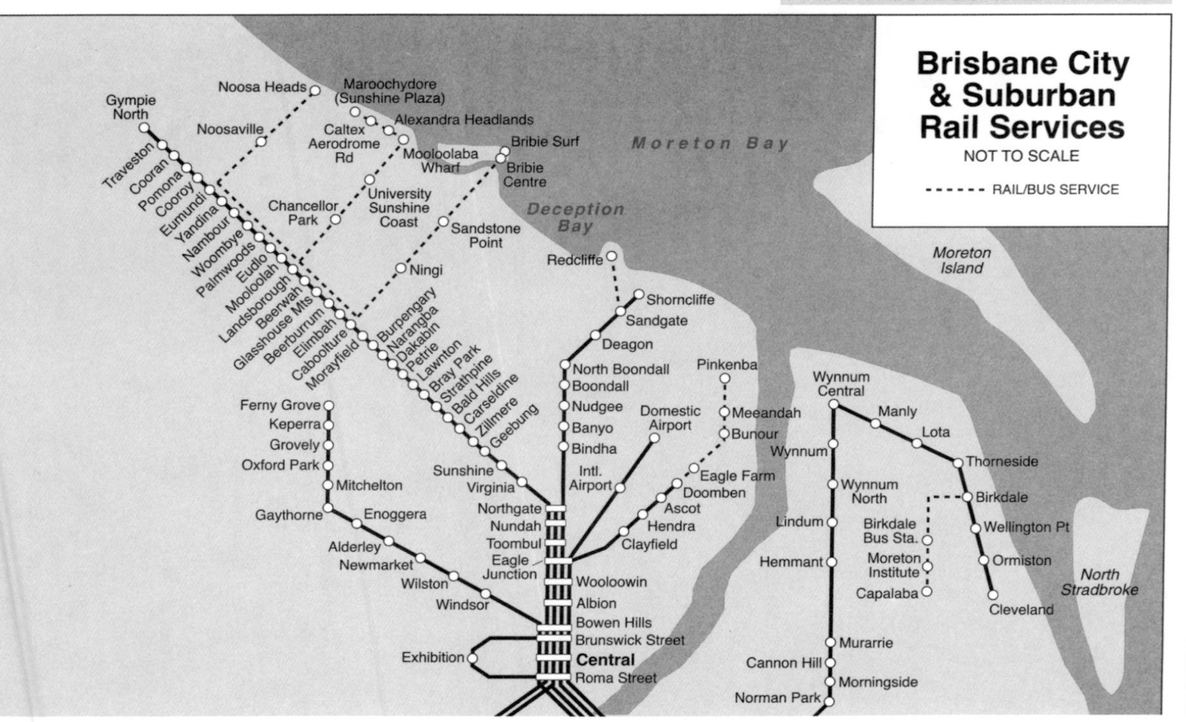

Brisbane City & Suburban Rail Services
NOT TO SCALE
RAIL/BUS SERVICE
Moreton Bay
Deception Bay
Moreton Island
North Stradbroke
Gympie North
Traveston
Cooran
Pomona
Cooroy
Eumundi
Yandina
Nambour
Woombye
Palmwoods
Eudlo
Mooloolah
Landsborough
Beerwah
Glasshouse Mts
Beerburrum
Elimbah
Caboolture
Morayfield
Burpengary
Narangba
Dakabin
Petrie
Lawnton
Bray Park
Strathpine
Bald Hills
Carseldine
Zillmere
Geebung
Sunshine
Virginia
Northgate
Nundah
Toombul
Eagle Junction
Wooloowin
Albion
Bowen Hills
Brunswick Street
Central
Roma Street
Exhibition
Noosa Heads
Noosaville
Maroochydore (Sunshine Plaza)
Alexandra Headlands
Caltex
Aerodrome Rd
Mooloolaba Wharf
Bribie Surf
Bribie Centre
Chancellor Park
University Sunshine Coast
Sandstone Point
Ningi
Redcliffe
Shorncliffe
Sandgate
Deagon
North Boondall
Boondall
Nudgee
Banyo
Bindha
Intl. Airport
Domestic Airport
Pinkenba
Meeandah
Bunour
Eagle Farm
Doomben
Ascot
Hendra
Clayfield
Ferny Grove
Keperra
Grovely
Oxford Park
Mitchelton
Gaythorne
Enoggera
Alderley
Newmarket
Wilston
Windsor
Wynnum Central
Manly
Lota
Thorneside
Birkdale
Wellington Pt
Ormiston
Cleveland
Birkdale Bus Sta.
Moreton Institute
Capalaba
Wynnum
Wynnum North
Lindum
Hemmant
Murarrie
Cannon Hill
Morningside
Norman Park

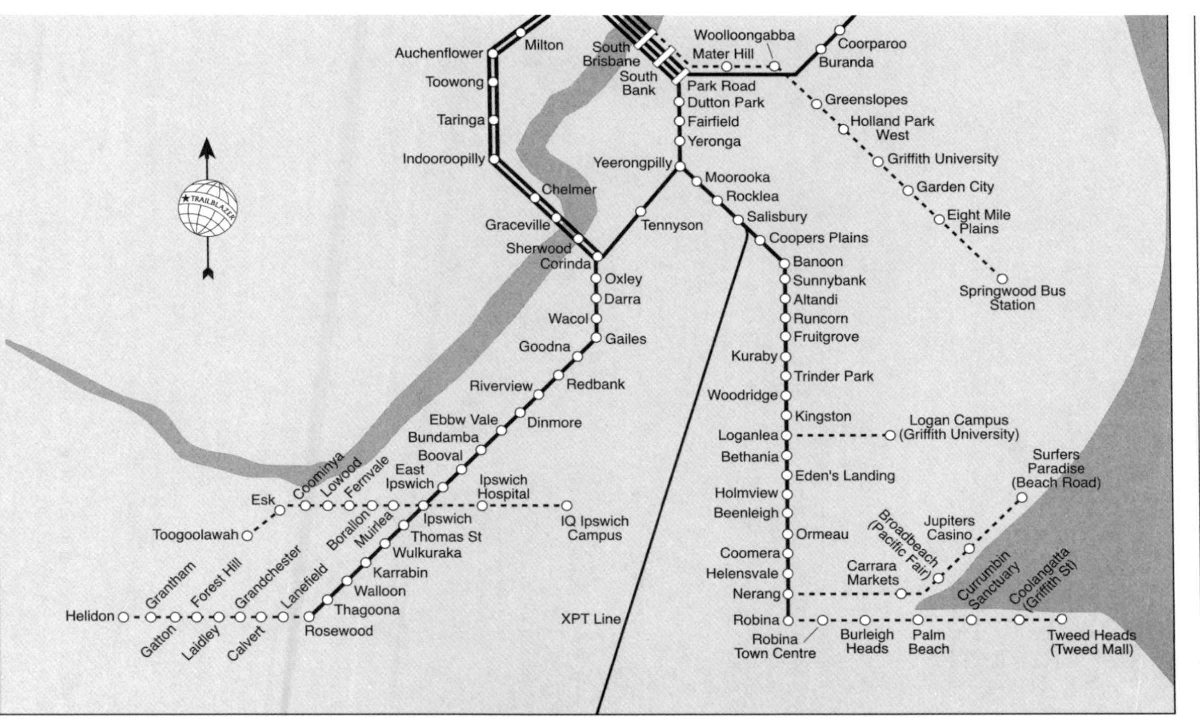

CITY GUIDES AND PLANS

A change from rail travel?

Near the airport you can see the **Southern Cross**, the aircraft in which the first solo flight to Australia was made from England in 1928.

River cruises as well as **ferries** will give you unrivalled views of the City and its bridges, particularly at night. For meals with a difference, try the *Kookaburra River Queens* floating restaurants departing from Eagle St Pier. Lunch or dinner cruises of 2½ to 4 hours are offered daily, with a choice of three-course buffet, seafood platter or Devonshire tea. For sailing times and prices phone ☎ 07-3221 1300 or email 💻 bookings@kookaburrariverqueens.com. A launch trip to Tangalooma on Moreton Island, or a day cruise to Stradbroke are other options if you have a day or more to spare.

Within day-trip reach by coach is the rainforest of **Lamington National Park**, an unforgettable experience of mountains and gorges, breathtaking vistas, cool dense forests, waterfalls, colourful parrots and bowerbirds and little pademelons (these are marsupials the size of rabbits which hop around unconcerned while you feed the rosellas). Visitors can obtain lunch at ***O'Reilly's GuestHouse***, high in the park.

The best panorama of Brisbane is from the viewpoint on **Mount Coot-tha**, a short drive from the city but unfortunately not connected by public transport. You can make a day of it there, exploring the rainforest, then call for afternoon tea or dinner in the restaurant. If you are unable to reach the real thing, there is a simulated rainforest in Mount Coot-tha Botanic Gardens, open daily from 08.00 and served by City Council buses (No 471 from Adelaide St, opposite King George Square). Australia's largest planetarium is also located there: viewing times should be checked locally. There are more lookout points in **Brisbane Forest Park**, further into the ranges.

Equally accessible is Brisbane's most popular tourist spot for overseas visitors, the world famous **Lone Pine Sanctuary** at Fig Tree Pocket. Open daily 08.30 to 17:00, it can be reached by City bus 445 (except Sundays) or 430 from the City or from Indooroopilly Interchange (near the station) or by taking a launch from North Quay (Mirimar Cruises, ☎ 07-3221 0300). Entry is $16 for an adult and there are a variety of concessionary tickets. You can hold a koala, be photographed wearing a snake, feed the kangaroos, wallabies and emus, and see wombats, dingos, sugar gliders and the elusive and unbelievable platypus.

A QR Trainlink bus connects with most trains at Nambour for Noosa on the Sunshine Coast. If your itinerary includes time for a day or more in this area, you do not need to hire a car or take a cab as services operate roughly hourly between Nambour and Maroochydore and the Sunshine Coast at Noosa. Worth visiting if you have your own vehicle are the coloured sands of **Cooloola National Park** but there are many excellent beaches within easier striking distance.

There are also connections to the Sunshine Coast from **Eumundi** (known for its markets on Wednesday and Saturday, selling local and alternative goods) and **Cooroy**. Sunshine Coast Sunbus services (☎ 131 230) meet most train arrivals and departures at Landsborough for Caloundra and Maroochydore, at Nambour for Buderim, Coolum Beach, Alexandra Headland, Perigian and just about the whole of the Sunshine Coast and at Cooroy for Tewantin and Noosa Heads.

The world's largest **ginger factory** (☎ 07-5446 7100 or 💻 buderimg@buderimginger.com) is on Pioneer Rd, **Yandina,** 8km north of Nambour. It is open daily 09.00 to 17.00 except Christmas Day. There are ginger and macadamia nut products for sale, a restaurant and gardens plus an internal narrow-gauge cane railway (see p269) and 'ginger tours' at additional cost. Interurban trains of QR serve Yandina, but not frequently (see Table 15, p269).

Cooroy and Gympie (C 9010, 9011) are within day-return distance of Brisbane but not conveniently by Citytrain. The former is a small friendly town, its centre adjoining the station, where two pubs and the local RSL club combine to tempt visitors to enjoy a lunch break; for comments on Gympie see p227 and p266.

Train services on this part of the North Coast line have been altered several times since the late 1990s and up-to-date details should be checked locally before travel. Table 11 (below) is a summary of day-return possibilities as last advertised. All services except the return journeys at weekends require prior booking, usually only a day or two in advance. This summary gives the longest (or only) possible time available at the places named on the days indicated, by **day return** travel. Otherwise an overnight stop is required. Except on Sunday there are early morning return trains from both Cooroy and Gympie North, the service being better suited to daily commuting to Brisbane than day trips away.

❑ Table 11: Cooroy and Gympie trains

Tuesday	Brisbane dep 08.55	arr Cooroy 11.28 dep 13.27, return arr 15.55
Wednesday	Brisbane dep 11.00	arr Cooroy 12.54 dep 13.27, return arr 15.55
Thursday	Brisbane dep 08.55	arr Cooroy 11.28 dep 12.39, return arr 14.40
Friday	Brisbane dep 11.00	arr Cooroy 12.54 dep 13.27, return arr 15.55
Saturday	Brisbane dep 08.55	arr Cooroy 11.28 dep 21.45, return arr 23.59
	arr Gympie N 12.57 dep 21.06, return arr 23.59	
Sunday	Brisbane dep 08.55	arr Cooroy 11.28 dep 16.39, return arr 19.02
	arr Gympie N 12.37 dep 16.00, return arr 19.02	

Note: All times for Brisbane refer to Roma St station.

❑ Deadline departures from Brisbane

There are no interstate evening departures from Roma St, but the coach connection to Casino for the overnight XPT to Sydney leaves at 15.10 daily from the coach departure level at Roma St Transit Centre. Evening deadline departures are:

17.00 Tilt Train to Bundaberg (except Saturday) and Rockhampton (Fri & Sun)
18.25 Tilt Train to Cairns (Monday, Wednesday and Friday)
18.25 Spirit of the Outback to Longreach (Tuesday and Saturday)
19.20 Westlander to Charleville (Tuesday and Thursday)

The Westlander may be joined (with prior booking) at Corinda (19.34), Ipswich (20.03), or Rosewood (20.19), and the North Coast trains may all be joined at Caboolture, Nambour, Cooroy or Gympie North.

Most long-distance trains from Brisbane leave in the morning, including the interstate XPT to Sydney, which leaves from platform 1. All other long-distance trains leave from platform 10, except the Westlander, which leaves from platform 2. You should allow a good ten minutes to cross to platform 10 with your luggage from the suburban platforms or from or to the coach station.

Adelaide

ORIENTATION

Adelaide is the City of Light, its site being chosen and original plan drawn by surveyor Colonel William Light in 1836. For a panoramic view of Adelaide go to Light's Vision on Montefiore Hill, just three kilometres north of the central station (Adelaide Station).

There is a fairly comprehensive network of suburban services, including buses and a tram in the Adelaide area but from long-distance trains you have first to get to a local station. Adelaide station, on North Terrace, is 3km from the interstate terminal at Keswick; therefore you must first go (a 10-minute walk) to the suburban platform at Keswick. The railway planners have rather overlooked the passengers' need for a direct link between platforms and many of the local trains do not stop at Keswick. Check the times first and consider the expensive option of taking a taxi, or the airport bus (see p97).

Having reached the suburban platform expect to wait up to an hour for a local train: the service is roughly every 30 minutes between 06.20 and 18.50 on weekdays and hourly between 08.00 and 23.00 on Saturdays, Sundays and holidays. You have to walk just as far if you want to catch a city bus. Leave your heavy luggage in a locker at the Great Southern terminal if you are in Adelaide only for the day.

The South Australian Tourist Commission Travel Centre (☎ 08-8303 2200 or ☎ 1300 655 276, 📠 08-8303 2249, 💻 www.southaustralia.com; open daily), diagonally opposite the city station at 18 King William St, has maps and information and provides a booking service. It also has details and prices for state-run tours (see below) to sights such as Cleland Conservation Park (where you can hold koalas and feed kangaroos) and the wineries of the Barossa Valley and the Southern Vales. At Barossa Junction, old railway carriages make an unusual hotel and restaurant complex. For details of the Barossa Wine Train see p57.

Numerous half-day, day or longer tours are available by coach from central Adelaide: Adelaide Sightseeing Travel Centre (☎ 08-8231 4144, www.adelaidesightseeing.com.au) is at 101 Franklin St (the Greyhound terminal).

A free booklet *Adelaide and attractions* is published regularly by Countrywide Tourist Promotions P/L (☎ 08-8232 5433) and is available in tourist offices and hotels and at tourist sights.

WHAT TO SEE AND DO

Once at Adelaide Station you are in the heart of the town. Immediately adjoining is the new **Festival Centre** (☎ 08-8216 8600 or within Australia ☎ 131 246) in King William Rd with its concert halls and theatre, restaurants and plaza. There are hourly guided tours on Mondays to Saturdays from 10am.

Take a **cruise** from here on the nearby River Torrens to the **zoo** (☎ 08-8267 3255, Frome Rd), noted for its birds, or try a ride on the **O-Bahn guided busway**, Australia's first, which runs through some of the parklands of Adelaide's 'green belt'. It passes close to the station, as does a local city centre bus. The O-Bahn, opened in 1986, extends for 12km to Tea Tree Plaza at Modbury and is the longest and fastest guided busway in the world. Service frequency varies from every 15 minutes on Sundays and holidays to one to three minutes at weekday peak; the journey takes 20 minutes.

Near the station see the collection of prints, drawings, sculpture, graphic arts, coins and paintings at the **Art Gallery of South Australia** (☎ 08-8207 7000; open daily 10am-5pm), and the Australian birds and animals in the **South Australian Museum** (☎ 08-8207 7500; open daily 10am-5pm), which also holds the largest collection of Aboriginal artefacts in the world. At the eastern end of North Terrace the **Botanic Gardens** (open daily) feature spectacular water lilies.

Rundle Mall in the centre of the city (one block south from North Terrace) has many attractive restaurants as well as shops. At 5 Rundle Mall is a shop with an underground opal mine: there is another opal shop at 33 King William St.

Suburban trains serve **Port Adelaide** (Historic Port Adelaide is worth a visit for its shops, Sunday market, boat cruises and museums), **Largs** (for Largs Bay historic village) and **Outer Harbour** for the overseas passenger terminal.

WHERE TO STAY

Budget/mid-range

There are several hotels within a short walk of the suburban railway station on North Terrace. Among the cheapest is ***Austral Hotel*** (☎ 08-8223 4660; 🖳 www.theaustral.com/), 205 Rundle St, where rooms cost $35 single, $55 double. Both ***Ambassadors Hotel*** (☎ 08-8231 4331; 🖳 www.sahotels.com.au/ambassadors), 107 King William St, and ***Princes Arcade Motel*** (☎ 08-8231 9524), 262 Hindley St, are two-star places which have rooms from around $60. Further along King William St, at No 401, adjacent to the South Terrace tram stop, is Moore's ***Brecknock Hotel*** (☎ 08-8231 5467, 🖳 brecknock@visp.com.au), with comfortable pub-style accommodation and quality food at modest prices.

At 23 Hindley St, ***City Central Motel*** (☎ 08-8231 4049) is a 2½-star budget hotel where a single room with en suite, TV, and tea- and coffee-making facilities costs $59.

In Glenelg, a tram ride from the city centre, at ***Jetty Hotel*** (☎ 08-8294 4377), 28 Jetty Rd, single rooms cost $55 en suite or $40 with shared facilities, while ***Glenelg Beach Hostel*** (☎ 08-8376 0007, 🖳 www.glenelgbeachhostel.com.au) round the corner in Moseley St has dorm beds at $25 and single rooms at $50, with continental breakfast included.

Up-market

Festival City Hotel Motel (previously Festival Lodge, ☎ 08-8212 7877) at 140 North Terrace, has single en suite rooms

---

Travel in the suburban area

Much of the Adelaide area, including the beach suburbs of Brighton, Seacliffe, Marino, Largs and Outer Harbour, is served by both bus and train. TransAdelaide operates the suburban bus, rail and tram services and Metro tickets are available in several varieties (zonal, multi-trip, day-trip, etc) covering all modes.

A local Day Pass costing a few dollars covers all TransAdelaide suburban buses and trains as well as tram and O-Bahn (see opposite) routes, but not the various privately-run buses which also operate in the metropolitan area.

For all public transport enquiries phone ☎ 08-8210 1000 (07.00-20.00), call at the TransAdelaide Timetable Information Office on the concourse at Adelaide City station, or visit the Adelaide Metro Information Centre (🖳 www.adelaidemetro.com) on the corner of King William and Currie Sts and obtain a copy of *The Metroguide* which gives the whole picture. Alternatively visit TransAdelaide's website: 🖳 www.transadelaide.com.au.

TransAdelaide timetables contain full maps of the areas served by the rail routes and are more informative than those of any other Australian city.

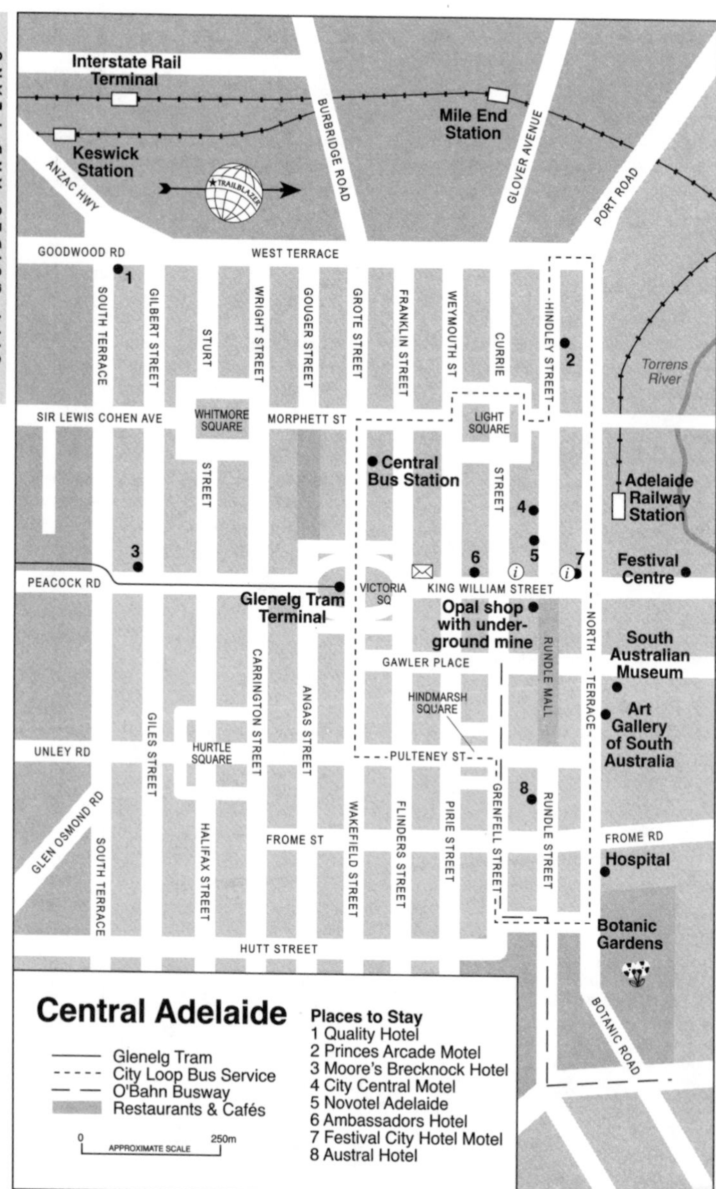

Interstate Rail Terminal
Keswick Station
Mile End Station
ANZAC HWY
BURBRIDGE ROAD
GLOVER AVENUE
PORT ROAD
GOODWOOD RD
WEST TERRACE
SOUTH TERRACE
GILBERT STREET
STURT STREET
WRIGHT STREET
GOUGER STREET
GROTE STREET
FRANKLIN STREET
WEYMOUTH ST
CURRIE STREET
HINDLEY STREET
Torrens River
SIR LEWIS COHEN AVE
WHITMORE SQUARE
MORPHETT ST
LIGHT SQUARE
Central Bus Station
Adelaide Railway Station
Festival Centre
PEACOCK RD
Glenelg Tram Terminal
VICTORIA SQ
KING WILLIAM STREET
Opal shop with under-ground mine
RUNDLE MALL
NORTH TERRACE
South Australian Museum
Art Gallery of South Australia
GAWLER PLACE
HINDMARSH SQUARE
CARRINGTON STREET
ANGAS STREET
GILES STREET
UNLEY RD
HURTLE SQUARE
PULTENEY ST
GRENFELL STREET
RUNDLE STREET
GLEN OSMOND RD
HALIFAX STREET
FROME ST
WAKEFIELD STREET
FLINDERS STREET
PIRIE STREET
FROME RD
Hospital
Botanic Gardens
HUTT STREET
BOTANIC ROAD
Central Adelaide
Glenelg Tram
City Loop Bus Service
O'Bahn Busway
Restaurants & Cafés
0 APPROXIMATE SCALE 250m
Places to Stay
1 Quality Hotel
2 Princes Arcade Motel
3 Moore's Brecknock Hotel
4 City Central Motel
5 Novotel Adelaide
6 Ambassadors Hotel
7 Festival City Hotel Motel
8 Austral Hotel

Gawler Oval
Central Gawler
Gawler
Evanston
Tambelin
To Port Pirie & Broken Hill
Kudla
Munno Para
(Virginia)
Smithfield
Broadmeadows
Womma
Elizabeth
Elizabeth South
Nurlutta
St Kilda
Salisbury
Chidda
Outer Harbour
Parafield Gardens
Parafield
North Haven
Osborne
Midlunga
Taperoo
Green Fields
Draper
Largs North
Largs
Port Adelaide
Peterhead
Dry Creek
Glanville
Alberton
Ethelton
Cheltenham
Kilburn
Cheltenham Race Course
Woodville
Islington
W'ville Pk
Albert Park
Kilkenny
Dudley Park
Seaton Park
West Croydon
Ovingham
Grange
Croydon
North Adelaide
E Grange
Bowden
Adelaide
Mile End
Tram route
Keswick
Glenelg
Goodwood
Clarence Park
Emerson
Unley Park
Mitcham
Edwards-town
Woodlands Pk
Torrens
Tonsley Jcn
Belair
Lynton
(Mt Lofty)
(Bridgewater)
Ascot Park
Oaklands
Mitchell Pk
Pinera
(Route to Melbourne)
Warradale
Marion
Clovelly Pk
Glenalta
Hove
Blackwood
(Aldgate)
Brighton
Tonsley
Eden Hills
Coromandel
Seacliff
Marino
Marino Rocks
Hallett Cove
Hallett Cove Beach
Lonsdale
Christie Downs
Noarlunga Centre
Adelaide City & Suburban Rail Services
NOT TO SCALE

with light breakfast from $90. ***Quality Hotel*** (☎ 08-8212 1277), South Park, on the corner of South and West Terrace and about 15 minutes' walk from the interstate platforms at Keswick, is a four-star Flag-choice hotel with views over parkland; rooms start from $116.

Novotel Adelaide (☎ 08-8231 5552, formerly Hindley Parkroyal Hotel), 65 Hindley Street, has rooms from $185.

WHERE TO EAT

There are numerous eating places of varied ethnic styles (including Australian) in Rundle St, Rundle Mall and Hindley St, all within easy walking distance of the city railway station on North Terrace.

DAY TRIPS FROM ADELAIDE

Among the many interesting day or half-day tours from Adelaide is the tram ride to **Glenelg,** about 20-minutes from Victoria Square in the city or from Goodwood, the next station south of Keswick (C 9031). Trams run about every 15 minutes on average. The fare is not covered by the Austrail Flexipass but will not break you, even if you have neglected to obtain a day Pass (box p153).

The Glenelg tram (see p271) is the only interurban tram-ride left in Australia, and Glenelg, at the seaside on Spencer Gulf, is well worth a visit. At Glenelg North you can watch the sea life at Marineland, then stroll along the beach or take a bus to the pier at Grange. Try the nearby ***Grange Hotel*** (☎ 08-8356 8111), 489 Esplanade, for lunch or an evening meal at their 'Restaurant on the beach' – only 22 minutes from the city by train.

Adelaide is not well situated for day trips much beyond the suburban area, but you can go up into the Mt Lofty ranges, known locally as the Adelaide Hills, by local train as far as **Belair**, 36 minutes, where there is a national park (☎ 08-8278 5477) the entrance immediately adjoins the station.

The view of Adelaide's lights from this railway is particularly good and may be enjoyed by travellers on local services. Although the railway continues much further into the ranges, only buses now serve places east of Belair such as Aldgate, Bridgewater and Mount Barker (but see p271).

❑ Deadline departures from Adelaide

17.15 The Ghan to Darwin on Sunday, also Alice Springs on Friday
18.40 The Indian Pacific to Perth (Wednesday and Sunday)
The Overland, and the eastbound Indian Pacific leave Adelaide in the morning

Perth

ORIENTATION

Perth is Australia's most isolated state capital, with at least 3000km of ocean to the west and about the same amount of desert to the east. Australians refer to residents of Western Australia as 'sandgropers'.

As Saltzman's classic *Eurail Guide* pointed out in briefly commenting on railways worldwide, Perth is known for its 'wide sandy beaches on the Indian Ocean, with good surfing', an apt description. Take the suburban train from Perth City (or East Perth) to Cottesloe or North Fremantle (C 9037), the latter close to Leighton beach, formerly reached by a footbridge over the incongruous and now abandoned railway yards. Choicer beaches are found north and south, reached by Transperth buses.

East Perth Terminal is not in the town centre, but adjoins the suburban station of East Perth from where local trains will take you to Perth city station (four minutes), right in the heart of the city and adjoining the bus terminal. A free city circle bus runs from here, but many of the sights and places you will want to visit are within easy walking distance.

Western Australia Tourist Centre (freecall ☎ 1300 361351, 💻 www.westernaustralia.net; open Monday to Saturday) has an office on the corner of Forrest Place and Wellington St, just opposite the railway station. Also worth looking out for is the free publication *What's on in Perth and Fremantle* or visiting the website: 💻 www.perthtouristcentre.com.au.

For timetables, maps etc for all public transport in the Perth metropolitan area visit the Transperth website: 💻 www.transperth.wa.gov.au.

WHAT TO SEE AND DO IN CENTRAL PERTH

Visit **Hay St Mall**, with London Court, a shopping area recreated as a 16th-century English street; the red London double-decker bus parked in the street is your signpost. Round the corner (to the west) in St George's Terrace see the **historic cloisters and archway**. Walk over Barracks Archway (the bridge over the freeway) and up to the 400-hectare **Kings Park** for the marvellous display of wild flowers and the view over Perth Water. Look for the old **windmill** at the end of Narrows Bridge, then stroll back past **Parliament House**, on Harvest Terrace, to the **markets** in West Perth, where the train will take you back to the city.

North of City station in Beaufort St see the exhibit of large Blue Whale skeletons, meteorites, Aboriginal culture and paintings in the **Art Gallery of Western Australia** (free, open daily), and the old **Gaol and Barracks Museum** in the Western Australian Museum (open daily).

On the other side of the railway, Barrack St leads down to Perth Water and the ferry terminal. Look out for the **Town Hall,** built in part by convicts, **St George's Cathedral**, built in the 1880s, **The Deanery**, a survivor from colonial days, and the lovely Georgian-style Old **Court House** in nearby Stirling Gardens.

WHERE TO STAY

A convenient hostel for City station is ***Britannia YHA*** (☎ 08-9427 5155, 💻 britannia@yhawa.com.au), 253 William St; a dorm bed costs $19-22 and a single room is $35 ($3.50 surcharge to non-members). One block west of City station ***Royal Hotel***

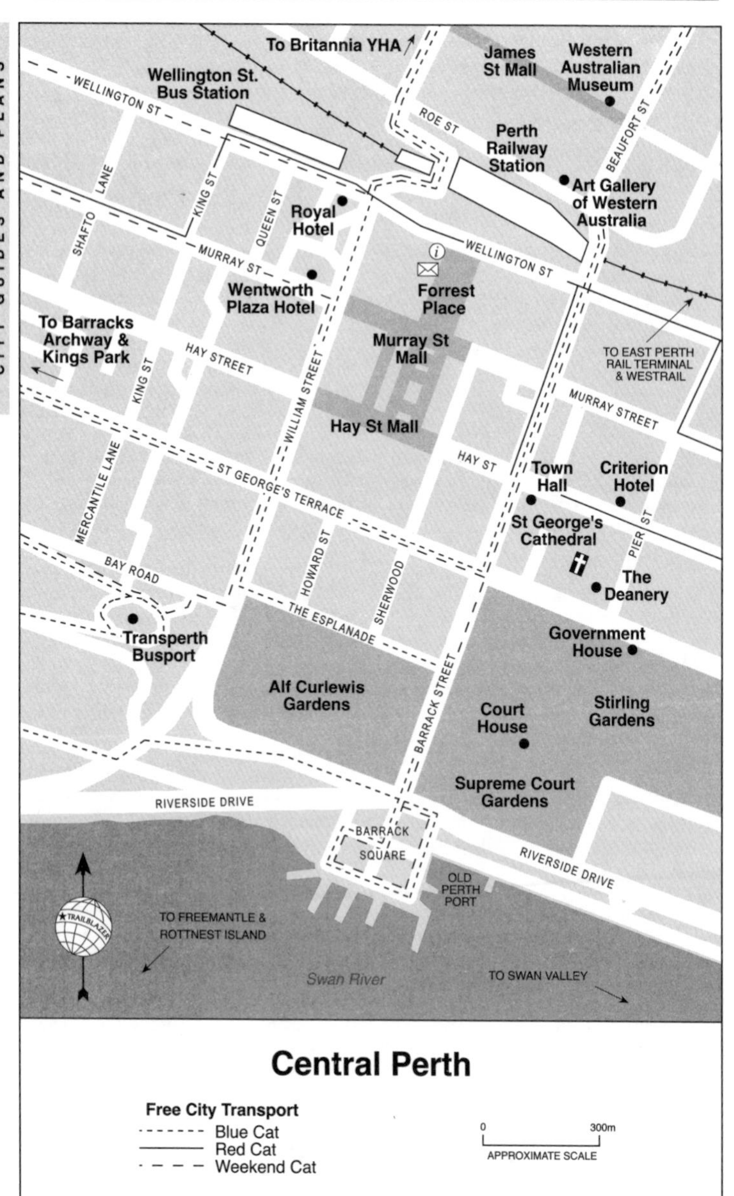

Central Perth

Free City Transport

- - - - - - Blue Cat
———— Red Cat
- — — — Weekend Cat

0 300m
APPROXIMATE SCALE

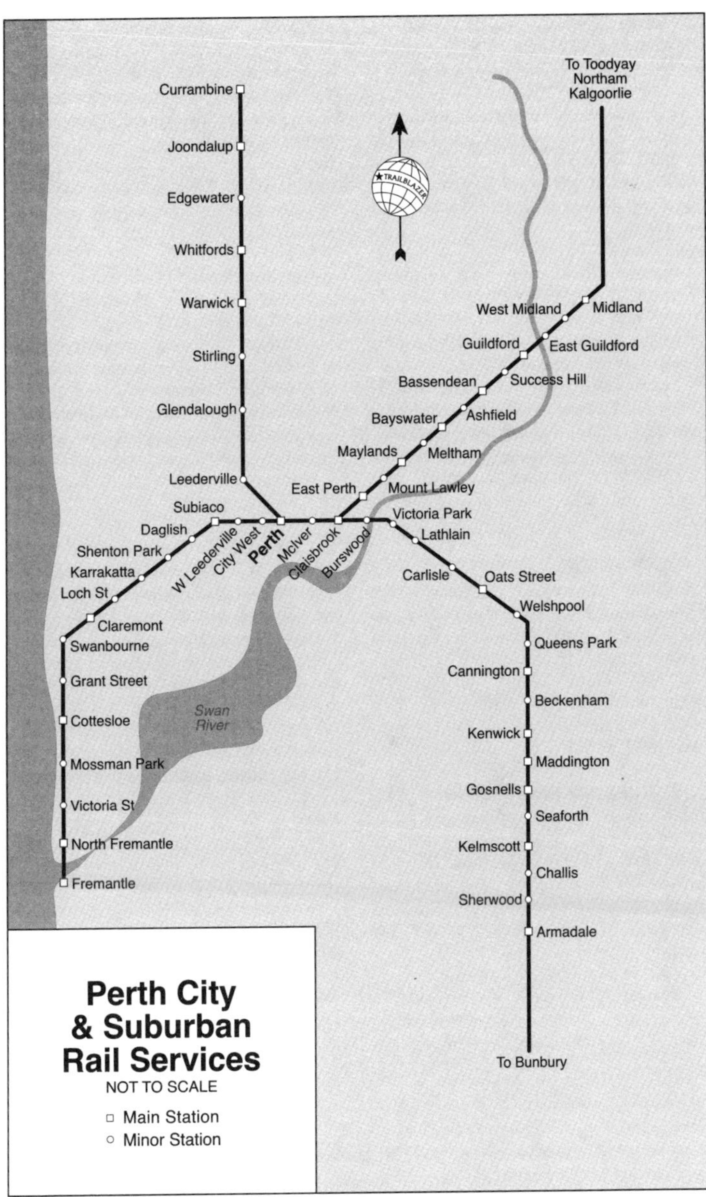
To Toodyay
Northam
Kalgoorlie
Currambine
Joondalup
Edgewater
Whitfords
Warwick
Stirling
Glendalough
Leederville
West Midland
Midland
Guildford
East Guildford
Bassendean
Success Hill
Bayswater
Ashfield
Maylands
Meltham
East Perth
Mount Lawley
Subiaco
Victoria Park
Daglish
Lathlain
Shenton Park
W Leederville
City West
Perth
McIver
Claisbrook
Burswood
Karrakatta
Carlisle
Oats Street
Loch St
Welshpool
Claremont
Swanbourne
Queens Park
Grant Street
Cannington
Beckenham
Cottesloe
Swan River
Kenwick
Mossman Park
Maddington
Gosnells
Victoria St
Seaforth
North Fremantle
Kelmscott
Challis
Fremantle
Sherwood
Armadale
To Bunbury
Perth City & Suburban Rail Services
NOT TO SCALE
Main Station
Minor Station

(☎ 08-9324 1510), on the corner of Wellington and William Sts, charges $45 for a single room with shared facilities, $59 en suite.

A three-star hotel worth considering is ***Comfort Inn Wentworth Plaza Hotel*** (☎ 08-9481 1000), 300 Murray St. It is a short walk from City station; daily rates for single rooms are from $57 (shared bath) to $79 (en suite).

The free bus service within the city area makes it relatively easy to get to ***Criterion Hotel*** (☎ 08-9325 5155, 💻 www.criterionhotel-perth.com.au), 560 Hay St, a three-star hotel which charges from $86 for a room including breakfast.

Bayswater Hotel Motel (☎ 08-9271 7111), 78 Railway Parade, Bayswater (11 minutes on the Midland line) has newly renovated rooms with en suite facilities for $77, whilst at **Fremantle** (see below) there are pub-style hotels reasonably close to the station.

WHERE TO EAT

Numerous eating places are found at the **Down Under Food Hall**, Hay St Mall and the slightly more up-market **Carillon Arcade Food Hall**.

The ***Moon and Sixpence***, in Wentworth Plaza Hotel at 300 Murray St, is a popular place for a good English pub-style meal.

DAY TRIPS AROUND PERTH

From City station the suburban system can take you north to **Stirling** (9 minutes), **Whitfords** (17 minutes), **Joondalup** (23 minutes) or **Currambine** (27 minutes) on Perth's railway where much of the route is in the centre strip of a freeway (C 9037 and local).

Alternatively you can go east to **Bayswater** (11 minutes), **Bassendean** (16 minutes, see p272 for details of Bassendean Rail Transport Museum) or **Midland** (25 minutes), where you are near the Swan valley and you can take river cruises or visit the vineyards near Middle Swan.

Suburban trains also go south to **Kelmscott** (31 minutes) and **Armadale** (39 minutes) on the south-west line to **Bunbury** (see p195); the visitor centre there is in the old 1904 railway station and they can give you details about birdwatching and dolphin spotting in the area. Transperth buses serve most districts and supplement the rail system; within Western Australia phone ☎ 136 213 for local transport information.

Perhaps the most interesting local excursion is to go down the coast to the port of **Fremantle** (28 minutes) where the station itself, built in 1906, is a designated historic building. There are frequent suburban trains between 05.20 and midnight Monday to Saturday, or from 06.58 on Sunday (C 9037 and local). This is an easy half-day trip with plenty to see.

Here you can wander down to the harbour and on to the yacht club, home of the boat which took away the Americas Cup for the first time in 135 years (New Zealand has taken it since then). Visit the Maritime Museum (open daily and has a submarine), and Arts Centre and History Museum (admission free, open daily) and see the great views of the city and harbour from the Round House (the oldest public building in Western Australia and originally a prison; open daily). Have some fish and chips at ***Cicerello's*** (☎ 08-9335 1911), at Fisherman's Wharf on the waterside, before you return to the station for the trip back to Perth.

Another possibility is to take the ferry from Barrack Square jetty to the popular **Rottnest Island resort**, 18km offshore; ferries operate five days a week, daily in summer. See p273 for details of the Oliver Hill Railway on the island.

(Opposite) Top: Transwa's Prospector (see p57) which entered service in 2004. **Bottom left**: The interior of the Prospector. **Bottom right**: Fremantle (see above), historic gateway port to Western Australia.

Transwa
1897
FREMANTLE

IF YOURE
CROOK
COME TO
COOK

❑ Table12: Perth–Toodyay-Northam (C 9033 and local)

Perth–Midland–Toodyay–Northam

	ExSun	MoWeFr	Sun	Mo,Fr	Mon-Fri
East Perth dep	07.20	09.00	14.55	15.15	17.17b
Midland dep	07.40	09.20	15.15	15.35	17.50
Toodyay arr	08.30a	10.10	16.05	–	18.43
Northam arr	08.45	10.25	16.20	16.40	19.10

Northam–Toodyay–Midland–Perth

	Mon-Fri	Sun	Mon	Fri	MoWeFr	TuThSa	MoWeFr
Northam dep	06.30	07.05	07.40	08.05	11.50	11.50	14.45
Toodyay dep	06.50	07.20	–	–	12.10	12.15	15.05
Midland arr	07.50	08.10	08.50	09.10	12.55	13.05	15.55
East Perth arr	08.18b	08.30	09.10	09.30	13.15	13.25	16.10

Notes: Refreshments are available on most trains. Passengers are recommended to be ready to board 15 minutes before departure times.
a Calls Tuesday, Thursday and Saturday only b Change at Midland

Rail excursions beyond the suburban system can be taken either on the south-west line to Bunbury or the main transcontinental route to Kalgoorlie.

Toodyay, 93km from Perth Terminal, in the attractive Avon Valley would be a pleasant stopping place for a night with accommodation close to the station, though a day return to the city can be achieved through Transwa's Avon Link. **Northam** (see p194) is another possible night-stop, though rather far out at 120km. If visiting Perth on the Great Southern there is ample time for a half-day or overnight excursion to Toodyay or Northam while the Indian Pacific is stabled in Perth. The Indian, by arrangement only, can pick up eastbound or set down westbound at Northam.

Table 12 above summarizes the train services on this line.

❑ Deadline departures from Perth

11.55 The Indian Pacific on Sunday and Wednesday from the East Perth Terminal. Allow a good hour to return from Fremantle.
14.40 The Prospector for Kalgoorlie on Sunday (15.30 on Monday, 15.40 on Friday)

(Opposite) Top: On the world's longest straight, the Nullarbor Plain (see p189).
Bottom: The Indian Pacific stops at Cook (see p190) where, according to the message at the station, the 'crook' are welcome. With the hospital having closed this is probably no longer the case.

Canberra

ORIENTATION

If your itinerary includes Canberra, or you have time for a two-day trip from Sydney, there are plenty of interesting features to see.

Australia's Federal capital is famed for its layout and civic buildings, pedestrian ways and new towns which distinguish it from the unplanned city growth elsewhere.

Canberra railway station is on Wentworth Avenue, Kingston, about 6km from the city centre, so taking a taxi or local bus is recommended.

Canberra Visitors Centre (☎ 02-6205 0044, local phone ☎ 1300 554 114 or for hotel bookings freecall ☎ 1800 100 660, 💻 www.canberratourism.com.au) at 330 Northbourne Avenue, Dickson, can provide hotel information and details of local tours, but there is an information centre closer to the city at Jolimont coach terminal.

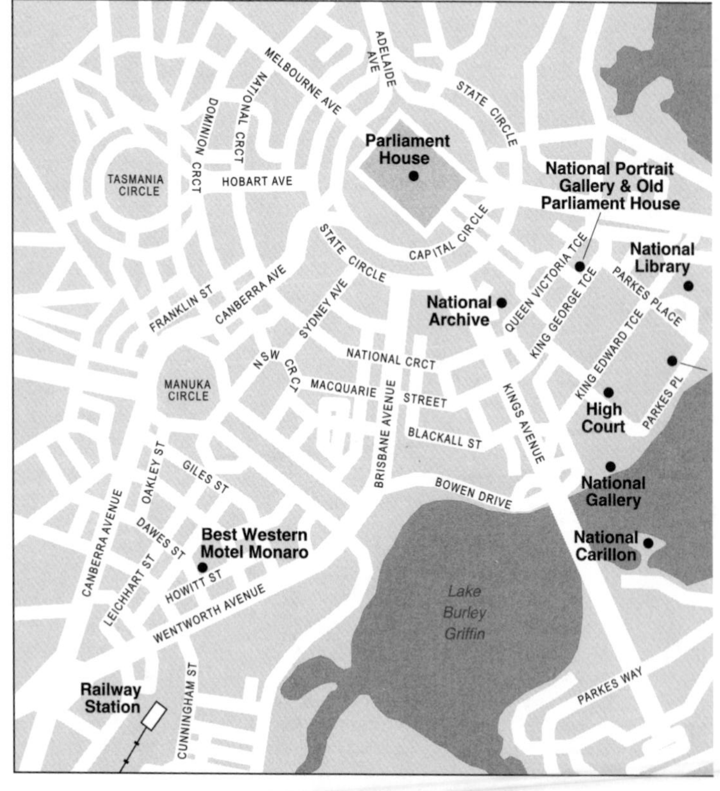

WHAT TO SEE AND DO

In this national capital city you can see **Parliament House**, both the new (free, open daily) and the old ($2 but free guided tour, open daily, and incorporating the **National Portrait Gallery**), the various **foreign embassies** (located around Parliament House and some of which are open to the public), the **National Library** (☎ 02-6262 1111; 1703 Parkes Place, free, open daily) with its modern art display, and the **National Science and Technology Centre** (Questacon, ☎ 02-6270 2800, open daily, $11, family ticket $32).

The **National Archive** (☎ 02-6212 3600, free, open daily) is home to the Commonwealth Government records.

Sittings at the **High Court** (☎ 02-6270 6811; Monday to Friday but not public holidays) are free and open to the public; phone in advance for details. The **National Gallery of Australia** is open daily and the permanent collection can be seen for free.

In September and October a landscape display, **Floriade**, is held in Commonwealth Park, just off Parkes Way. The theme varies, admission is free and it is open daily from 8 or 9am. For information check the festival website (💻 www.floriade australia.com).

Lake Burley Griffin (named after the American architect who won the original competition to design this national capital) and the **Captain Cook Memorial (Water)**

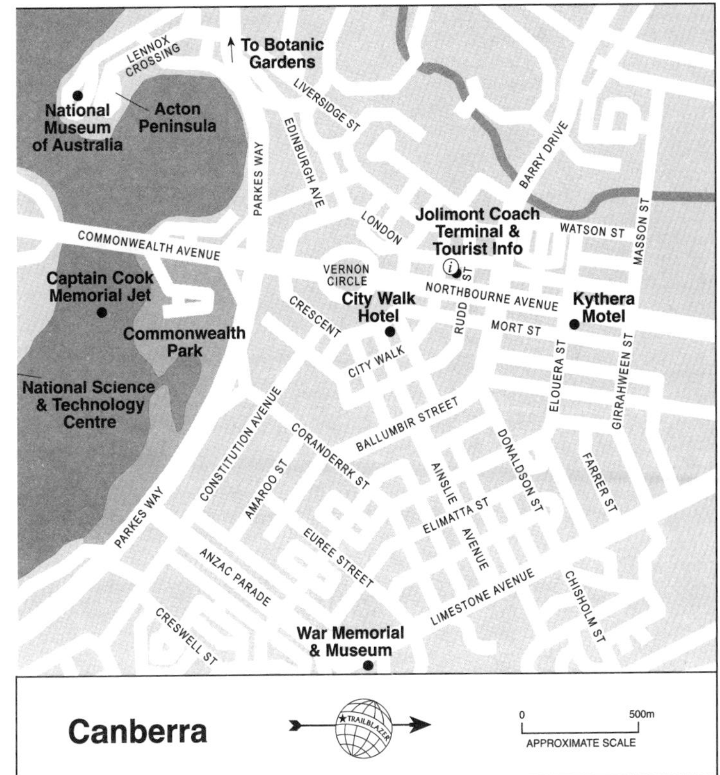

Jet (147-metre high; operates 10.00 to 12.00 and 14.00 to 16.00) are worth a visit. Concerts of the 53-bell **National Carillon** on Aspen Island are held on Tuesdays, Thursdays and weekends.

The **National Museum of Australia** (🖳 www.nma.gov.au; open daily 9am-5pm, free), Lawson Crescent, Acton Peninsula, tells the history of Australia's land, nation and people and is well worth a visit, as are the **War Memorial and museum** (free, open daily), Anzac Parade, Campbell.

If you have time there are marvellous views from Mt Ainslie above the War Museum, and at Telstra Tower on Black Mountain. See the 6000 native Australian plants in the **Botanic Gardens**, or the rather delightful model English village at **Cockington Green** (🖳 www.cockington green.com.au, open daily) in Gold Creek Village, accessible by Canberra–Yass bus from Jolimont Coach Terminal.

Cooma is a gateway to Mt Kosciusko, the highest peak in Australia, where the Perisher SkiTube (see p260) takes tourists by funicular railway to the ski slopes of the Snowy Mountains National Park. The former Canberra Monaro Express continued south from Canberra past Tuggeranong New Town to Cooma, where buses (State Rail operated) connect south to Bombola. Buses have also replaced the train to Cooma.

See p256 for details of Canberra Railway Museum.

WHERE TO STAY AND EAT

Canberra is not well supplied with convenient hotels, being planned as a government city.

Canberra YHA (☎ 02-6248 9155, 🖳 canberra@yhansw.org.au), 191 Dryandra St, O'Connor, has dorm beds ($19) and double/twin rooms; facilities include self-contained kitchens, a common area and a games area and a pick-up service is provided on request.

If you prefer to be located more centrally, ***Canberra City Backpackers*** at 7 Akuna St (☎ 02-6257 3999, 🖳 www.can berrabackpackers.net.au) has dorm beds from $26 and single rooms from $55.

City Walk Hotel (☎ 02-6257 0124), 2 Mort St, has basic rooms for $45 to $70; facilities include a kitchen for self-catering and an Irish-style pub, ***King O'Malley's***, serving Guinness. ***Kythera Motel*** (☎ 02-6248 7611, 🖳 res@kythera.com.au), at 98/100 Northbourne Avenue, Braddon, has en suite rooms and both Italian and Chinese restaurants as well as a swimming pool.

Two places nearer the railway station, which is in Kingston south-east of the city centre, are ***Victor Lodge*** (☎ 02-6295 7777), 29 Dawes St, a B&B Guest House, which offers dormitory accommodation at $25 and single or double rooms with shared facilities starting from $55, and ***Motel Monaro*** (☎ 02-6295 2111), 27 Dawes St, part of the Best Western chain, where rooms start from $99 including light breakfast.

Nearby **Queanbeyan**, 10 minutes away in NSW with twice-daily trains and one return bus trip offers viable alternatives. ***Hotel Queanbeyan*** (☎ 02-6297 3299), 59 Crawford St, within a stone's throw of the railway station, has rooms at $35. ***Sunrise Motel*** (☎ 02-6297 2822, 9 Vriarra Rd) and ***Wallaby*** (☎ 02-6297 1533, 88 Crawford St) motels are all close by.

For further details contact Queanbeyan Visitor Information Centre at 1 Farrer Place (☎ 02-6298 0241 or ☎ 1800 026192, 🖳 www.visitqueanbeyan.com).

❑ Deadline departures from Canberra

12.05 Monday, Wednesday and Friday for Sydney with Brisbane connection at Strathfield

17.07 Tuesday, Thursday, Saturday and Sunday to Goulburn (for Melbourne XPT) and Sydney.

Darwin

ORIENTATION

Darwin only became accessible by rail from the rest of mainland Australia in February 2004 and the new station is in a recently-developing port area over 15 kilometres from the city centre. There are no convenient facilities for accommodation, food or other amenities nearby, and with only one train per week, stopping for a single night is hardly an option. You would have time to do no more than get into town (by courtesy bus or taxi), find a place to stay, then go back out the next morning. To enjoy even a few of the area's many attractions justifies a longer stay.

If Darwin is your port of entry to or exit from Australia, then 'no worries, mate, she'll be right!' You'll have time to do what you like. Otherwise, the options are to stay a week for the next train, fly out, or take a coach: going by coach to the Alice takes over 20 hours (C 9428), to Mount Isa 23 hours (C 9428, 9075), or to Perth over 58 hours (C 9431) – none of them an attractive proposition.

The **Visitor Information Centre** (☎ 08-8936 2499, 💻 www.tourismtopend.com.au; open daily) is at the corner of Knuckey and Mitchell streets in the city centre, a block from Smith Street Mall.

Local buses operate from the bus station round the corner from the south end of the Mall, where there is also an information kiosk. Buses serve most of the attractions in and around Darwin; see map p168 for the main regular Darwinbus routes. Darwin buses offer a **Darwinbus Tourcard** at $5 a day and $25 for seven days, with half price for children and pensioners. This covers most of the city and suburbs including Casuarina beach and shopping centre, Nightcliff, Fannie Bay, Berrimah (but not the railway station), Palmerston, and the Holmes Jungle and Crocodylus Nature Parks. Services between the main interchanges of Darwin, Casuarina and Palmerston are frequent, mostly half-hourly or better, not all by the same route. The direct Darwin–Casuarina service takes 25 to 30 minutes.

WHAT TO SEE AND DO

There are no day trips by rail; the only line being back south through Alice Springs to Adelaide, but there are local buses, as well as tour coaches to the surrounding areas. Various taxis and car-hire facilities are also available.

Visitors to Darwin should not forget the distance involved in Australian travel, if the time taken to get there has not already made an impression. It is no good thinking that you can cover key attractions in a few hours. **Litchfield National Park**, for example, famous for its magnetic termite mounds, streams, waterfalls and rainforest, is over 100km by road; **Kakadu** over twice that. Greyhound has a Kakadu bus service in summer, a four-hour trip via Jabiru to Cooinda for Yellow Water and Jim Jim Falls, the heart of Kakadu. But there are nearer attractions. No visitor to Darwin should miss the fish-feeding frenzy ($7/adult, $4/child) in **Doctor's Gully** on the edge of the Central Business District (CBD) at high tide every day. For further details and feeding times (important to check because the fish can only be fed at high tide) contact Aquascene (☎ 08-8981 7837, 💻 www.aquascene.com.au). If visiting in August, you should be able to witness Darwin's famous '**Beer can Regatta**' (races for boats made from beer cans) and, talking of beer, the '**Darwin Stubby**' (a two-litre bottle of beer) is a real mouthful.

Other attractions within the city area are: the **Australian Aviation Heritage Centre** (☎ 08-8947 2145, 557 Stuart Highway, Winnellie, open daily, $11/$6), which has a collection of aircraft, the highlight being an American B52 bomber; **East Point Reserve and Military Museum** (☎

08-8981 9702, 💻 www.epmm.com.au, open daily 09.30-17.00, $10/$5) focuses on Darwin's wartime history; historic **Fannie Bay Gaol** (☎ 08-8999 8201, open daily 10.00-17.00, free), formerly Darwin's main jail; **Crocodylus Park** (☎ 08-8922 4500, McMillans Rd, Berrimah, open daily, $22/$11) which has a large variety of reptiles as well as other animals. There are also a number of other parks, gardens (including the botanical Gardens, Gardens Rd, free) and coastal reserves.

Markets are a special Darwin attraction; a 'veritable melting pot of South-East Asian and European cultures' as described in the Official Visitors Guide. Both the Nightcliff Market (held every Sunday morning and a good place to have breakfast while browsing) and the Mindil Beach Sunset Market (stalls serving all kinds of food and drink, as well as art and craft stalls; open on Thursday and Sunday evenings in the dry season) are worth a visit.

Even within walking distance of the bus station there are places of interest: less than half a kilometre away is **Darwin Harbour**, a popular diving spot due to the number of wrecks from WWII, and a good place to eat and drink thanks to the many cafés and restaurants lining the wharves; the **Oil Storage tunnels** (☎ 08-8985 6333, open daily May to October, Tue to Sun Nov to Apr) from WWII; the **old Town Hall** (or what was left of it after Cyclone Tracy); **Hotel Victoria** (which survived both Tracy and the earlier Japanese bombing). **Parliament House** (☎ 08-8946 1525) is open daily 09.00-18.00 (free) but tours operate on Saturday only and booking is essential. The **Overland Telegraph Memorial**, on The Esplanade, and the **Chinese Temple**, on Woods St, open daily 08.00-16.00 and still used, are also worth a visit.

From the bottom of Smith St, The Esplanade curves round to the west past the **Anzac Memorial** and extends for a further kilometre towards Doctor's Gully alongside **Bicentennial Park** and **Lameroo Beach** past **Lyons Cottage**, formerly British Australian Telegraph House and now open (daily, free) as a museum with exhibits showing aspects of the early history of Darwin.

WHERE TO STAY

Like all capital cities, Darwin has a range of accommodation for visitors. These range from camping sites and backpacker hostels to 5-star luxury resorts. The Darwin region is referred to as the 'Top End' and most hotels are at the top end of the market. Darwin can be expensive, but even within the heart of the city there are bargains to be found.

Budget/mid-range

Backpacker hostels abound and most have similar facilities including air-conditioning, and offer airport or bus pick-up. Those within or close to the central area, many of which are in Mitchell St and broadly in the $20 to $55 range (dorm bed to single/double room) are the following: ***Chilli's Backpackers*** (☎ 08-8980 5800, ☎ 1800 351 313, 💻 www.chillis.com.au), in the Transit Centre, 69a Mitchell St; ***Darwin City YHA*** (☎ 08-8981 3995, 💻 darwinyha@yhant.org.au), 69 Mitchell St, which has a swimming pool; ***Globetrotters Lodge*** (☎ 08-8981 5385, 💻 www.globetrotters.com.au), 97 Mitchell St, and ***Wilderness Lodge*** (formerly called Fawlty Towers, ☎ 08-8981 8363), 88 Mitchell St, and ***Frogshollow Backpackers*** (☎ 08-8941 2600, ☎ 1800-068686, 💻 www.frogs-hollow.com.au), 27 Lindsay St. Possibly the best value in this range is ***Air Raid City Lodge*** (☎ 08-8981 9214, 💻 pauldich@hotmail.com), 35 Cavenagh St, which offers single en suite rooms with air conditioning, fridge and colour TV for $55 in the low season.

Moving up a bit in cost are ***Don Hotel*** (☎ 08-8981 5311), 12 Cavenagh St, which charges $70 including breakfast, and ***Cherry Blossom Motel*** (☎ 08-8981 6734, 2.5 star, $83), 108 The Esplanade, ***Value Inn Motel*** (☎ 08-8981 4733, 💻 www.valueinn.com.au, around $80), 50 Mitchell St. The ***Best Western Top End*** (☎ 08-898 16511, ☎ 1800-626151, 💻 http://topend.bestwestern.com.au) on the corner of Daly St and Mitchell St, near Doctor's Gully, is a 3-star hotel with rooms from $85.

Up-market

All within the central area and with single rooms at more than $150 are: ***Crowne***

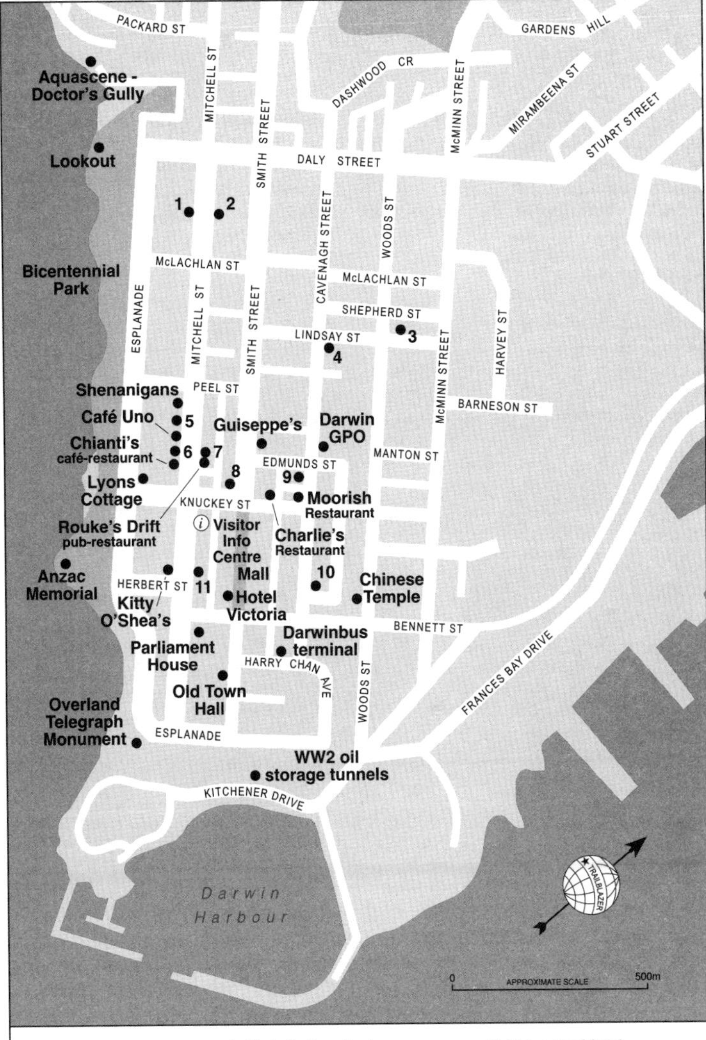

Central Darwin

1 Globetrotters Lodge
2 Wilderness Lodge
3 Frogshollow Backpackers
4 Mirrambeena Resort
5 Darwin City YHA
6 Chilli's Backpacker Hostel & Transit Centre
7 Value Inn Motel
8 Darwin Central Hotel
9 Air Raid City Lodge
10 Don Hotel
11 Crowne Plaza Hotel

Plaza Hotel (formerly Rydges Plaza Hotel, ☎ 08-8982 0000, 🖳 www.ichotelsgroup.com), 32 Mitchell St; ***Mirambeena Resort*** (☎ 08-8946 0111, 🖳 www.mirambeena.com.au), 64 Cavenagh St; ***Darwin Central Hotel*** (previously All Seasons, ☎ 08-8944 9000, 🖳 www.darwincentral.com.au), 21 Knuckey St (on the corner with Smith St), and ***Novotel Atrium*** (☎ 08-8941 0755, 🖳 www.novoteldarwin.com.au), 100 The Esplanade.

WHERE TO EAT

Leaflets from tourist agencies such as *Dining out in Darwin* and *Where to go, What to do* tend to cover the more expensive eating places that pay to advertise. There are, of course, the usual internationally-known restaurants, but Darwin offers food from many cultures as well as good Aussie pub tucker. Some of the following are perhaps less widely advertised but popular with the locals, attractive and reasonably priced – taste and see!

Hotel Victoria, 27 Smith St, at the southern end of Smith Mall is known for its attractively-priced food and (live) entertainment. ***Charlie's Restaurant*** (☎ 08-8981 3298), 29 Knuckey St, just to the right of the top end of the Mall offers good Italian fare. At 37 Knuckey St the ***Moorish Restaurant*** serves Spanish and North African food. In the block between Knuckey and Peel streets on Mitchell St are ***Rourke's Drift pub-restaurant*** (No 46), ***Chianti's café-restaurant*** (No 36-7), and at No 69 (in the Transit Centre) both ***Café Uno*** (Italian food), and ***Shenanigans*** (☎ 08-8981 2100), an Irish-style pub offering attractive counter meals; Shenanigans is right at the corner of Peel St. Another in the same style is ***Kitty O'Shea's*** at the corner of Mitchell and Herbert Streets near The Esplanade.

In Smith St (No 64) just north of Edmunds St is ***Giuseppes,*** quietly offering quality food at reasonable prices.

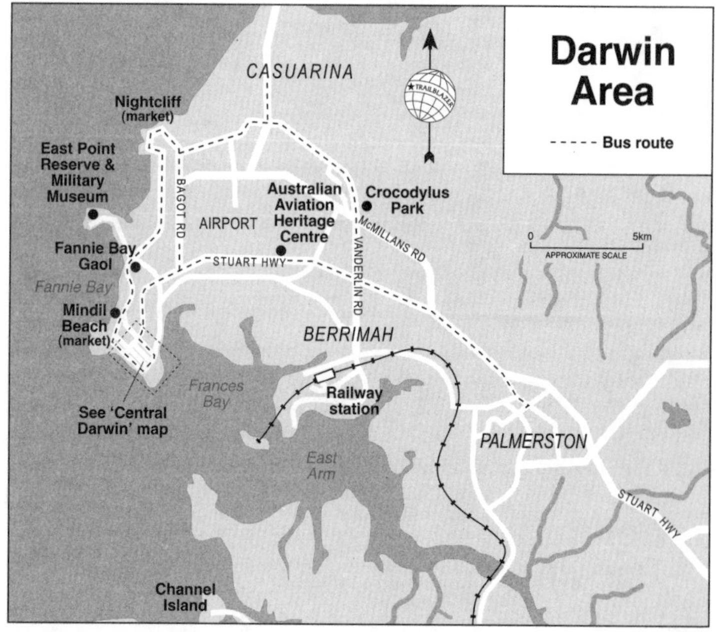

PART 5: ROUTE GUIDES

Using the route guides

The following route guides take the traveller along the routes in one direction following basically the order of itinerary 3 (p68) for a 15-day Flexipass spread over a month, ie, from Sydney up to Alice Springs and Darwin, across to Perth then back through SW Victoria, then up north, but also including all the main regional and branch lines. Major diversions from a predetermined itinerary are suggested where they might be made.

Unless and until some form of automatic global positioning is introduced on trains a rail passenger is unable simply to press a button for a pointer on a screen map to indicate 'you are here'. How then do you find out? There are four ways:

- Check the time and compare it with the timetable (if you have one). On some long-distance services a timetable sheet may be provided on the train.
- Obvious, this one: look out of the window for the names of stations, signal boxes or other railway buildings, place names on hotels, garages or other buildings or road signs. The maps which accompany these notes show places where the trains do not stop but which are included to aid location.
- Look out for line-side distance markers (kilometre posts). These will be little white boards low down close to the track on either side. You need to watch out for them. There should be one every kilometre but there is a problem in that the base point, 0km, may not be the place you started from. Usually but not always it will be a main station and you will not know where it is. Also, as they are intended as identification points for railway operation they may or may not represent the true distance from anywhere because such things as alterations to train workings or yard location and track realignments can change distances.
- Ask the passenger attendant if there is one (and there is nearly always some railway person on board).

Distances where given in the following route guides are from the starting point of the route described except where stated otherwise. They may simply indicate the length of named sections of the route being described. These are not 'sections' in the railway operation sense. The distances given, though correct as far as known, may not correspond to distances shown on kilometre-marker posts.

Places mentioned in the route descriptions that are in the suburban areas of the capital cities are shown on the relevant 'city and suburban rail services' map in Part 4.

Trans-Australia routes

SYDNEY TO DARWIN (VIA BROKEN HILL AND ADELAIDE)

Sydney to Lithgow [See map pp126-7 and Map 1]

(Distances given are from Sydney)

After Strathfield, the busy junction in Sydney's western suburbs, the train passes through Lidcombe, junction for the Olympic Park Sprint shuttle train, Granville, main junction for the south, then the outer suburban and historic town of Parramatta; this is commuter territory. Frequent electric multiple-unit trains (EMUs) serve these and many other intermediate stations but long-distance trains omit most if not all.

Penrith marks the end of the low-lying urban areas, being less than 30m above sea level. The frequent service to town and ***Red Cow Hotel*** (☎ 02-4721 5666), over the road from the station, make Penrith a good base for the Sydney area. Leaving Penrith the line crosses the Nepean River, tributary to the Hawkesbury. The next station, Emu Plains, marks the 1 in 60 start of an 82km climb to the line summit at 1092m in the Blue Mountains.

The short Glenbrook tunnel leads to Lapstone, the first of many popular outer suburban commuter settlements in the mountains. Rugged gorge scenery is visible on the left. The next station, **Glenbrook**, is in the bush but houses can still be seen. Around Blaxland your ears may pop as you reach the 330m (1000ft) contour. A vast expanse of bush is seen on the right and the highway on the left has now crossed to the right. After Warrimoo and Valley Heights the gradient steepens to 1 in 33 and the curves become tighter and more frequent. Speeds here, even for express commuter EMUs, fall to an average of less than 60km/h.

After Faulconbridge is a vast panorama of tree-covered plateau and wooded ravines on both sides of the line. It is best to be in the lounge or dining car on the Indian Pacific for this part of the trip so that you can see out both sides at once. Look out of the window in the direction where the sun is behind you if it is morning or evening time.

Lawson appears as a little village, with a pub (Blue Mountains Hotel) opposite the station. Approaching Bullaburra the panorama widens out to the north-west but for the most dramatic views keep looking out on the south side.

After Wentworth Falls and Leura comes **Katoomba**, 1000m above sea level, near the top of the range on the edge of the Megalong Valley. This is an ideal place to stay for a night or more. It is a stopping place for the XPT but not the long-distance interstate services.

Gearins Hotel (☎ 02-4782 4395, 💻 gearinhotel@bigpond.com, 233 Gt Western Highway), Katoomba's oldest hotel, is just behind the station on the north side and offers good clean accommodation at very reasonable rates (backpackers $20, single with shared facilities $30, en suites $90).

There are many attractions in Katoomba – the Sceniscender cable car, the world's steepest incline railway (see p258), and a new scenic skyway being developed, but even if you stop for only an hour or two (say between the XPT and an interurban train) you can visit Kingsford Smith Park just across the road past ***Metropole Guest House*** (☎ 02-4782 5544, all en suite B&B single $75, for two $130), which is almost opposite the station entrance. In this lovely quiet wooded area a walk of even 50m in either direction will take you into a different world; with the call of the birds and the scent of the trees you really know you are in the mountains.

Around and beyond Katoomba are great views over the gorges. **Mount Victoria**, terminus and depot for many of the commuter services, is the base town for visits to the famous Jenolan Caves. Between here and the little station of Bell is the line's summit, after which the descent begins on the very edge of a ravine, with ten tunnels in quick succession. Between tunnels 4 and 5 you have a brief glimpse of daylight as the train crosses a short bridge over a deep gorge between high walls of bare rock.

Descending towards Lithgow look out, above you to the left, for the viaducts of the ZigZag railway, the original route by which the trains crossed the range. Coming from the east you will see them first on the left, then right, because of the curvature of the route. Now a tourist line, with steam, the ZigZag railway can be reached by road or by local train from Lithgow or Sydney. **ZigZag** is a request stop on the CityRail Blue Mountain service during the hours when the ZigZag railway (see p260) is operating.

Lithgow, 156km from Sydney, marks the end of the CityRail electric service and is an important railway motive-power depot.

Lithgow to Orange [Map 1]

Wallerawang (171km), the junction for the **Mudgee** line (no longer passenger though there

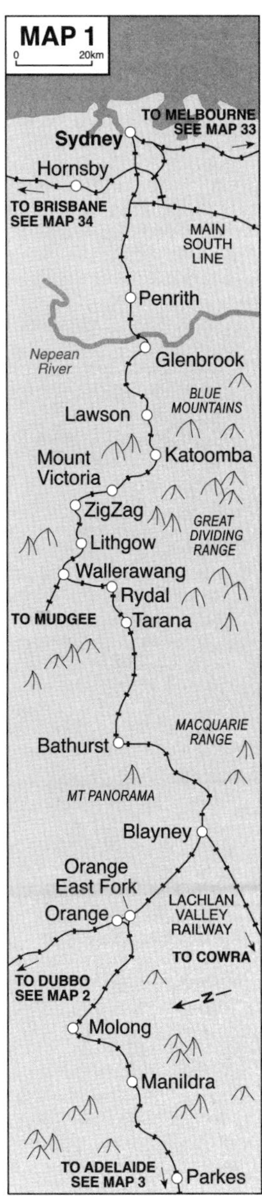

Orange to Dubbo (140km) [Map 2]

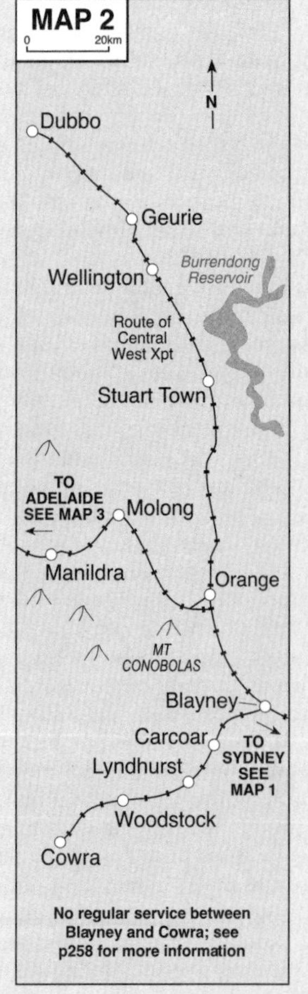

The branch to the north is part of a line which formerly penetrated far into the outback of New South Wales and was the route of a train called the Far West Express. Its route included what must have been another of the longest straight rail lines in the world, 186km without a curve, half as long again as the longest in, for example, the USA.

At one time it was proposed that this route be extended across the border to link with Queensland outback lines and thence on to the Northern Territory. 'Back of Bourke' is an Australian euphemism for the real outback, but now only buses contracted to Countrylink go beyond Dubbo, either north to Bourke, Brewarrina and Lightning Ridge or west as an alternative service to Broken Hill.

The station at **Stuart Town** is the first call for the XPT after Orange. Scene of a former gold rush and immortalized by Banjo Patterson's poem *The man from Ironbark* (its former name) this is a place where the casual prospector can still readily find a little 'colour' in a pan.

Next stop, **Wellington**, has Mount Arthur nearby, and the Wellington caves are within 9km of the town. See the historical museum and the Phonograph Parlour and try the 'Bite-Te-Eat BYO' for fast foods with a difference.

Geurie, 23km north of Wellington and the last stop before Dubbo, is a small town with some interesting antique and craft shops.

In **Dubbo** the well-preserved old Gaol is in Macquarie St in the town centre, a few blocks' walk from the station and round the corner from the police station – so watch your step! Open daily from 09.00 to 16.30 ($5 admission) the Gaol features a self-guided tour and also has a souvenir shop. Almost opposite is the ***Amaroo Hotel*** (☎ 02-6882 3533), one of NSW's 'Pubstay' hotels, with good clean accommodation and an absolutely first-class bistro with a good wine list. Try the Scotch fillet if you like a large, tender steak. Rooms from $50 en suite including breakfast. Other pubs, motels and hostels abound, ranging from the ***Backpackers*** (☎ 02-6882 0922), at 87 Brisbane St, at under $20, to ***Zoofari Lodge*** (☎ 02-6881 1488, 💻 bookings@zoofarilodge.com.au) where the tariff includes entry to the zoo and all meals. Western Plains Zoo is at Victoria Park, 5km south-west of town.

can be some special excursions), is conspicuous for its large power station seen north of the track. Further west, **Rydal** and **Tarana** are request stops for the XPT; the latter is a passing place with a loop line. In this area, particularly on the curves east of Tarana, you may notice double tracking but one line of this section is disused, abandoned and rusting; 12-chain curves abound and you will feel them.

On the downhill run into **Bathurst** (240km) you should see, ahead beyond the town to the south-west, Mt Panorama, scene of the Bathurst 1000 Motor Race held annually in October. Bathurst, the first inland city to be developed by Europeans, is proud of its old buildings, most of which can be seen on a walking tour. See the humble cottage where former prime minister Ben Chifley lived and the steam engine he drove as a railway employee.

To stay in Bathurst, ***Knickerbocker Hotel*** (☎ 02-6332 4500) in the town centre offers motel-style rooms at $60 including cooked breakfast. Closer to the station, ***Shanahan's Family Hotel*** (☎ 02-63331 1353) is an option with single rooms for $30.

Leaving Bathurst the train begins to climb again. After passing through George's Plains the gradient steepens to 1 in 40 and there are more 12-chain curves which keep the speed well down. Just west of the disused but repainted station of Newbridge comes an unscheduled halt (as far as the passenger is aware). At the lineside is a board saying 'replace electric train staff', marking the entry into a double track section. This lasts as far as **Blayney**, junction for the currently unused passenger link through **Cowra** and Young to the main south line (but see p258 for details about Lachlan Valley Railway).

Orange (322km), birthplace of poet AB 'Banjo' Patterson, who wrote the words of Australia's unofficial anthem *Waltzing Matilda*, is the next stop; from here the Dubbo XPT turns north for Wellington and Dubbo while the Broken Hill Xplorer reverses to take the main line west. These trains use Orange main station but the Indian Pacific, if stopping at Orange, calls only at Orange East Fork (see p119).

Orange, named after the Prince of Orange, is an excellent centre for exploring the Canobolas country (not a Greek name as it may sound but formed from two Aboriginal words – Coona and booloo meaning two peaks). The mountain of that name, some 14km south-west of the city, is an extinct volcano and is the highest point between the Blue Mountains and the Indian Ocean.

Hotel Canobolas (☎ 02-6362 2444, 📠 6362 9361), in Summer St, has rooms from $30 and is round the corner from the station, as are the restful civic park, the post office, and the new library and regional gallery. Call at the Visitors Centre (☎ 02-6393 8226 or ☎ 1800 069466), on Byng St, for information on a walking tour of the historic buildings. Coach tours of the surrounding area coordinate with the arrival and departure of the XPT train.

Orange to Broken Hill (802km) [Maps 2, 3, 4 and 5]

After a scenic journey through **Molong** and **Manildra**, the first stop west of Orange is **Parkes**, formerly named Bushman's but renamed Parkes in 1873

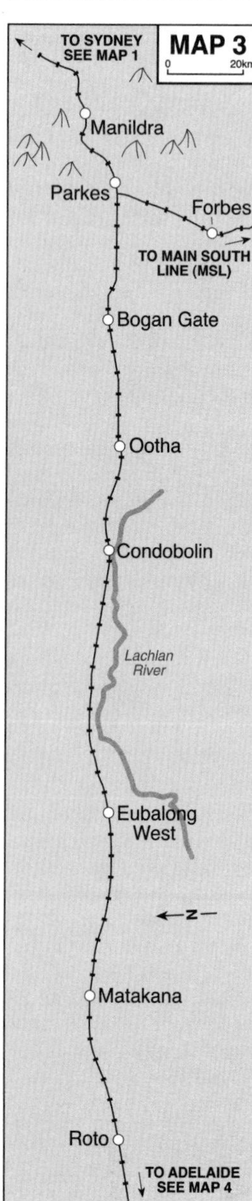

after Sir Henry Parkes, five times premier of New South Wales and popularly regarded as the 'father' of Federation. Parkes was and still is an important railway junction.

For many years the changing station for passengers to or from Broken Hill on the famous Silver City Comet, Parkes is now served once weekly by the Broken Hill Xplorer. The Indian Pacific passes through in the hours of darkness and will take up or set down if required.

The town centre is just over half a kilometre from the station. About as far again to the north-east is Memorial Hill lookout, while 21km north of town is the famous Commonwealth Scientific and Industrial Research Organisation (CSIRO) radio telescope, open daily to visitors.

Condobolin, 547km from Sydney on the banks of the Lachlan River, is another place visited by the Indian Pacific only in the wee small hours but the Xplorer calls in early afternoon on Mondays going west and Tuesdays returning. Countrylink coaches connect to Cootamundra (over four hours) daily from here (C 9111).

If planning to take a break, ***Railway Hotel*** (☎ 02-6895 2650) conveniently and logically adjoins the station, as in many Australian country towns. Between 1898 and 1927 Condobolin was the western terminus of the NSW Western Main railway line.

Grain silos, along with great mounds of grain covered with tarpaulins and possibly a few sandhills, are among the features in a fairly flat landscape you may see by moonlight if awake on this part of the journey.

By day in the distance you may see what appear to be sheets of water – such mirages are common in this part of the country due to the heat and flatness.

During the night the interstate trains pass through **Eubalong West**, **Matakana**, **Roto** (once a junction for a line connecting via Griffith to Melbourne), **Trida**, **Conoble**, **Ivanhoe** and **Darnick**, usually without stopping except perhaps at Ivanhoe, but these are regular stops for the daytime Broken Hill train.

Travelling west on the Indian Pacific you may see kangaroos and emus in the early dawn, or from the Xplorer in the evening as you approach **Menindee** across the Darling River. The Menindee lakes, close by on the south side past the station, contain more water than Sydney Harbour.

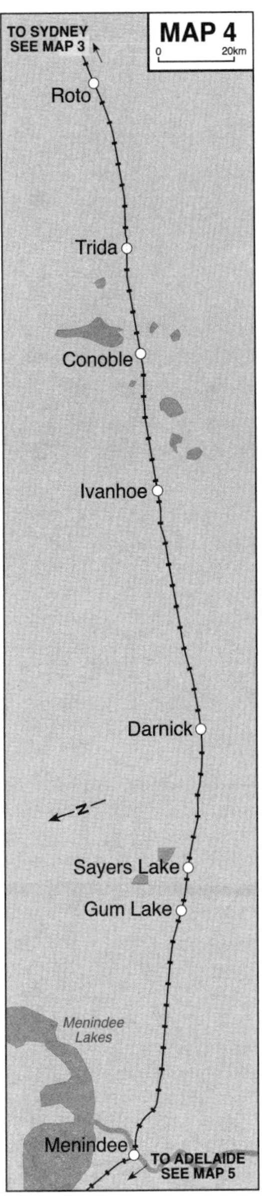

Broken Hill (The Barrier City)

You reach Broken Hill around breakfast time on the Indian but in the evening on The Broken Hill Xplorer (afternoon on the Indian returning east).

The schedules of the Indian Pacific allow an hour or more before the train continues and a coach tour of the city is available. If exploring on your own, note the 30-minute time zone adjustment here, so beware. Check the departure time with the station master or train manager. Broken Hill follows Central Australian Time, half an hour earlier than the Eastern time of the rest of New South Wales.

But Broken Hill deserves more than a one-hour visit: it is worth breaking your journey to stay the night. Unfortunately this may involve up to a three-day break between trains. The range of options is summarized in Table 3, p77.

Being built over rich deposits of silver, lead and zinc, Broken Hill is rich in mining (and railway) history and boasts some of the finest vernacular architecture of the period. Do not fail to look at the magnificent old ***Mario's Palace Hotel*** (☎ 08-8088 1699, single $32, double en suite $67), at 277 Argent St, with its iron verandah, and ask proprietor Marat about the painting on the ceiling.

You can also visit without charge the wonderful Musicians' Club, opposite the railway station at 276 Crystal St; the saxophone chandelier in the entrance lobby is unique. See the many art galleries scattered throughout the city and Silverton.

The restored Afghan Mosque, once used by the camel drivers imported to carry supplies

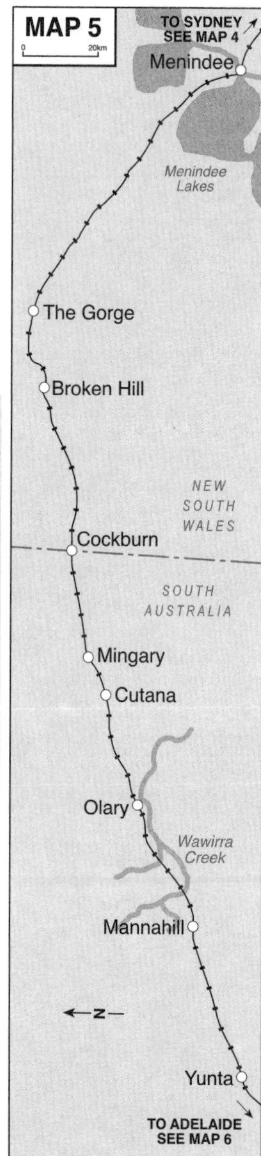

through the region, is open for inspection on Sunday afternoons.

If you would like an underground tour you can visit the original Broken Hill Proprietary (BHP) mine; don a helmet with miner's lamp and descend in the original cage to the levels where first were worked what are among the richest ore deposits of silver, lead and zinc in the world. Delprat's Underground Tours (☎ 08-8088 1604) operate weekdays at 10.30 and on Saturdays at 14.00.

Old timers will tell you that workers in the mines have an easy time of it nowadays. If they do, it is due in large measure to their predecessors who fought hard for the gains now enjoyed. Broken Hill workers were among the pioneers of collective bargaining and other social and industrial issues.

The Broken Hill Company itself, now known as the Big Australian, no longer owns the mines but the Barrier Industrial Council, a grouping of trade unions which once more or less ran the town, is still around. Trades Hall in Blende St is worth a visit to learn something of the Hill's industrial history. The main road from NSW Western Plains to Adelaide running through Broken Hill is called the Barrier Highway, but within the city this and most other roads are named after minerals.

Broken Hill Railway Museum (see p256) has a fine mineral collection as well as local history and railway items. For details of other things to see, tours, free local maps and locally-made souvenirs etc contact Broken Hill Visitor Information Centre (☎ 08-8087 6077 or ☎ 1800 630 008, 💻 tourist@pcpro.net.au) at the corner of Bromide and Blende Sts.

There is a local Citybus service within the town and air-conditioned coach tours are available to various national parks from Broken Hill: Sturt, Mutawintji, Kinchega, Mungo and Paroo Darling. Towns such as Tibooburra, White Cliffs and Menindee add to the mystique of the whole outback experience. Hence the expression: 'Broken Hill the Accessible Outback'. Scenic air tours also operate to places of interest such as the diggings of the world's only source of black opals at White Cliffs.

Twenty-three kilometres north-west of Broken Hill lies the restored ghost town of Silverton and further afield at Mutawintji, 132km to the north-east, are Aboriginal rock carvings.

You will learn perhaps just as much, but not see it all, by simply spending some time in the bar of one of this industrial town's many old hotels and talking to its warm and friendly people. The oldest of these hotels, licensed since 1886, is ***West Darling Motor Hotel*** (☎ 08-8087 2691), at the corner of Argent and Oxide streets. It offers a variety of accommodation, attractive prices and good tucker; a useful adjunct for travellers is a fully-equipped laundromat. A convenient and good eating place near the station is ***Silver City Chinese Restaurant***, 1 Oxide St, open daily for lunch and dinner.

Broken Hill to Gladstone [Maps 5 and 6]

Not long after leaving Broken Hill the train crosses into South Australia at **Cockburn**, 48km from Broken Hill.

For the next 147km from here to Crystal Brook there are traces of the old Silverton Tramway alongside the track. Before 1969 this narrow-gauge line was the only link between

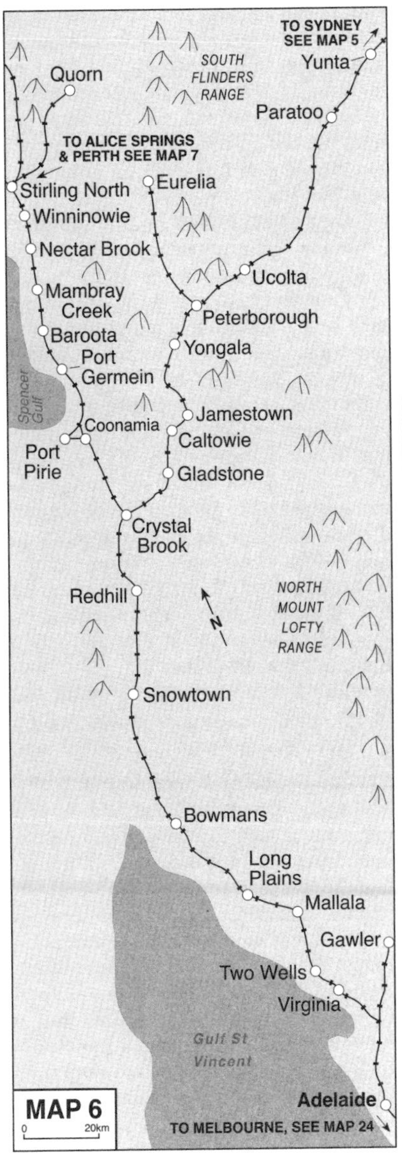

ROUTE GUIDES AND MAPS

Broken Hill and Port Pirie on the South Australian network. On this 'tramway' eight-coupled steam locomotives capable of hauling a thousand tonnes ran up a 1 in 100 gradient, a real railway by any standard! As the late C Hamilton Ellis observed, 'A tramway is simply a form of railway and the term is ambiguous ... freely used to describe lines laid along streets, lines laid over the countryside, lines worked by horses, steam or electricity.' Conversely, the world's largest electric trams in fact operated on a railway named as such: the Swansea and Mumbles Railway in Wales.

Olary, 118km and about 75 minutes after Broken Hill, started life in the 1880s to service the road and railway but little is left other than the pub and general store. The train does not stop.

Peterborough, like its English counterpart, is important in railway history, because it is where three rail gauges met and passengers from Broken Hill formerly joined the train to Adelaide. Unlike Peterborough on Britain's East Coast Main Line, South Australia's Peterborough is now barely a whistle stop, but for enthusiasts there is an operating steam railway and museum (see p272).

Jamestown, a former junction with the South Australian broad-gauge system, is now acknowledged only by a slowing down as the train glides through the old station, now a National Trust museum. The surrounding country is noted for the Euro – not the currency of Europe, but the name of a thick-haired hill-dwelling cousin of the kangaroo, also known as the wallaroo.

At **Gladstone**, until a few years ago, rail buffs had a rare treat: in the yards on the right were triple-gauge tracks of four parallel rails and a complicated system of points and crossings. Three gauges, standard, Irish (1600mm) and narrow (1067mm) met here; all were operational until well into the 1970s and remained until the 1990s.

Gladstone is a centre for the wheat trade in this area but only a request stop on the Indian Pacific. Look out on the left after Gladstone for the remnants of the former narrow-gauge railway between there and Port Pirie.

Crystal Brook to Adelaide (195km) [Map 6]

At **Crystal Brook** the trains now leave the Sydney–Perth direct route for a diversion to Adelaide, which replaced Port Pirie as the turning point after the link to Adelaide was standardized. En route to Adelaide's outer northern suburbs the line passes through rich South Australian farming country with Gulf St Vincent to the right and the Mt Lofty ranges to the left.

After Adelaide, the Indian Pacific from Sydney now retraces 195km of its route; this happens in both directions. Refreshed by the break in South Australia's capital city, you may now have time to notice things you may have missed on the inward journey. The Ghan, starting in Adelaide, also follows this route. After leaving Adelaide's Keswick terminal note on the right the lines to the original station, now the suburban terminal. See the way the edge of the city stands out behind a 'green wedge' on the right as you continue north to the planned suburb of Salisbury and past a Royal Australian Air Force base. You may see some camels in enclosed paddocks, a reminder of earlier transport on the north–south route. A few are still around but many escaped into the wild and roam the Central Australian desert. Packs of wild camels are seen nowhere else in the world, but some are now collected and farmed; eye fillet of camel is worth tasting.

Adelaide to Port Augusta

[Maps 6 and 7]

After leaving the Adelaide environs the train passes through **Bowmans**, at the head of Gulf St Vincent, **Snowtown**, a major junction in narrow-gauge days and a former stop, and Crystal Brook, where the line rejoins the Broken Hill–Port Pirie route.

Coonamia is now the station for **Port Pirie** (about 3km). The town itself is worth visiting to see the former station's long platform and, down the main street, the original station preserved as a museum. Port Pirie boasts the largest lead-smelting plant in the world; you can see its tall chimney to the left after leaving Coonamia. Little tubes of smelter slag containing traces of lead, silver, zinc and gold can be purchased in town. Port Pirie was formerly a compulsory stop on the Trans-Australian route where three rail gauges met.

Between Port Pirie and Port Augusta, Spencer Gulf is close on the left and the attractive Flinders Ranges are on the right. At **Port Germein** you may see on the left the 4km-long timber jetty, relic of the days when the tall ships crowded this former busy port.

Four kilometres before Port Augusta is **Stirling North**, junction for the old route to Alice Springs via Quorn and Marree. The part between Stirling North and Woolshed Flat, a little west of Quorn has been re-opened by the Pichi Richi tourist railway (see p271). Stirling North is also the junction for the later standard-gauge route to Marree, followed by The Ghan until 1980 with a change to narrow gauge for the last 870km to Alice Springs. That line now ends at Leigh Creek coal mine, 245km from Stirling North.

Port Augusta at the head of Spencer Gulf holds an important place in Australia's railway history, being a major operating and workshop centre of the former Commonwealth Railways. It is still an important railway centre and worth a visit even though trains now call only in the early hours or late at night and sometimes only if passengers are booked.

Port Augusta to Alice Springs (1243km) [Maps 7, 8, 9, 10 and 11]

At Spencer Junction, a major goods yard 3km beyond Port Augusta, is a 73km branch to **Whyalla**. This branch line was approved for construction by the former Commonwealth Railways before 1970 and opened with great pomp and

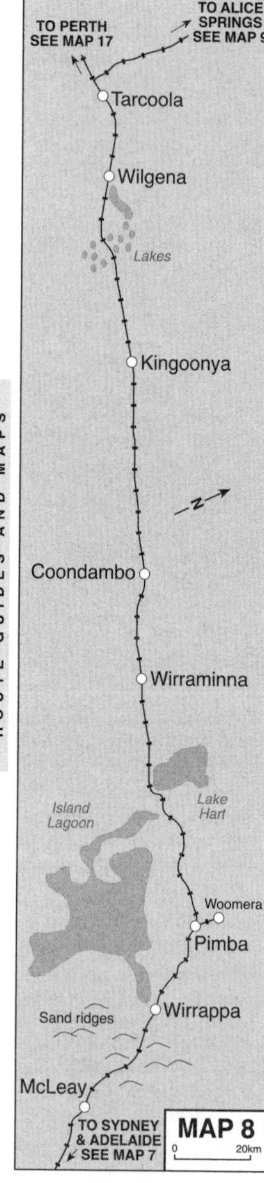

circumstance. By 1973 a daily passenger service from Port Augusta was in operation, using railcars and with a self-serve buffet, but it was withdrawn, then re-opened, then withdrawn again. Since 1979 only goods trains have remained.

West of Port Augusta the train winds its way at night through numerous sand hills and past salt pans and scrub forests, an eerie scene by moonlight if you happen to be awake. A brief stop may be made at **Pimba** but this is best looked for on an eastbound journey on the Indian Pacific when in late evening off to the left you may catch a glimpse of the disused rail branch to **Woomera**. Lying 6km to the north, this was the site of a Defence Department rocket-testing range and more lately it has been notorious as a detention centre for 'illegal' refugees. The name is an Aboriginal word for a throwing stick.

The Ghan but not the Indian Pacific calls at **Tarcoola** (412km from Port Augusta) in the early morning hours but in late evening on the way back east. Until a few years ago Tarcoola had the only hotel, the Wilgena, between Port Augusta and Kalgoorlie, 1277km further west. Now there is none. The town is named after a horse that won the Melbourne Cup in 1893 and at one time there was an annual horse race here on which there were reputedly no bets and no-one knew which horse won. To get the real feel of being in the middle of nowhere, if your conductor will allow it, step down from the train and breathe the pure air of the outback. The sky will be brilliant with stars. Before sunset you may already have seen the stars shining against the brilliant red sky. Dawn will be similar, golden red above the brown earth all around.

Tarcoola is where The Ghan diverts from the Trans-Australian route to reach Alice Springs, replacing the original route from Port Augusta at Stirling North through Quorn and Marree. **Manguri**, most likely noticed in the late evening on the return journey, is the stop for nearby Coober Pedy, famous for opals, where the daytime temperatures are so high that many inhabitants live underground.

Highlights of the line between Tarcoola and Alice Springs include the crossing of the Northern Territory border just south of **Kulgera**. You may see the signboard first thing in the morning or in the evening on the return journey. Then around 40km north of Kulgera look out on the right for the **Iron Man**, a monument to the railway workers who built the new line and where the Alice used to stop for photographs. This impressionistic sculpture of twisted steel rails and concrete created by the builders of the line marks the site of the millionth sleeper to be laid on this track, built in 1980 to replace the old flood-prone line.

Further on you are unlikely to miss the 15-span bridge over the **Finke River**; this follows a course millions of years old and although usually fairly dry, it can become a raging torrent after heavy winter rain. Finke river crossing is about the nearest place on the railway to Ayers Rock; it's only about 90km to the bus stop at Erldunda Resort and then less than a three-hour ride! The sheer size of Australia is brought home on a journey like this.

Approaching Alice Springs the train passes through the **Heavitree Gap** in the MacDonnell Ranges, outcrops of special interest to geologists. **Todd River** is also close by east of the track, and the Old Ghan Rail Museum is visible on your right as the train approaches the Gap.

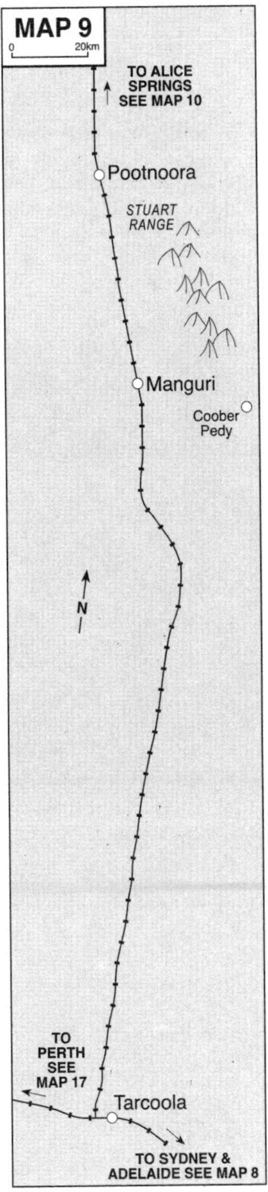

Alice Springs

Alice Springs, capital of the Red Centre, was for many years the railhead and gateway to the Northern Territory. Although there was a North Australia Railway, reaching 502km from Darwin south to Birdum, it was never extended further south. It fell into disuse and was closed in 1976, finally to be replaced by the new standard-gauge line north from Alice Springs, opened in 2004.

By any standards Alice Springs, or simply The Alice as Australians say, must be regarded

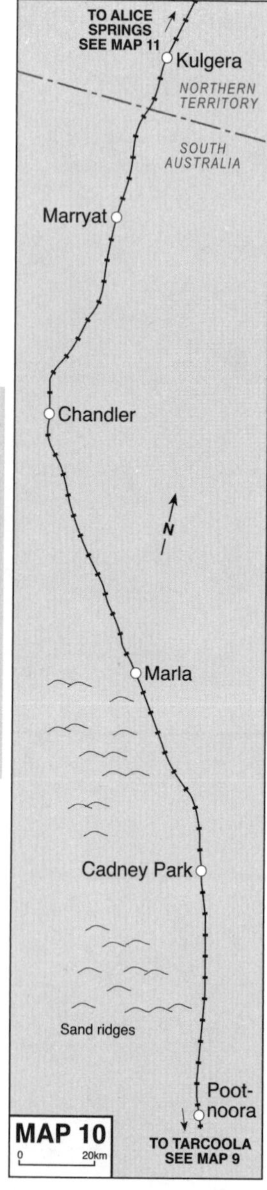

as part of the Australian Outback. It certainly looked like it in the film *A Town like Alice* although the scenes were mostly shot in Broken Hill and Silverton in western New South Wales. The Alice is over 650km as the crow flies from any town with a population of more than 20,000 (and even that is Mount Isa in far western Queensland). It is located in the very centre of the continent, nearly a thousand kilometres from the nearest reach of the sea. The Darwin Ghan allows travellers three to four hours here and those in Gold Kangaroo class have an outback tour thrown in. Perhaps better still is a two-night break at The Alice by changing from the Alice Ghan to the Darwin Ghan northbound, or vice versa southbound.

Even if you are on an out-and-back trip on the Alice Ghan with only two hours to spend here, there is still time to mooch around town. You can do a walking tour of the town centre in an hour or so; see the Aviation museum, the School of the Air, the Panorama 'Guth' and the Old Gaol, or walk up to Anzac Hill Lookout to view the surroundings. The Panorama 'Guth' is unique, an art gallery featuring a 360-degree painting-cum-bas-relief of the country around Alice Springs, the desert floor, the flora and fauna, the distant mountains. Admission is only $5.50, representing time and money well spent. You should still have time for a couple of beers or lunch in one of the pubs or restaurants, where you may sample some of the more unusual meats found in the Northern Territory, like camel, buffalo, crocodile, emu and kangaroo. Eye fillet of camel is superb, whilst roo steaks are fat free, as tasty as venison, and low in cholesterol. The ***Overlanders Steakhouse*** (☎ 08-8952 2159), 72 Hartley St, offers such exotic dishes as buffalo steak with witchetty grub dressing or, if you really want to indulge, their speciality 'Drover's Blowout' has the lot! Among other attractive watering holes offering good tucker at lunch or dinner are the ***Firkin and Hound English Tavern*** (☎ 08-8953 3033) on Hartley St, also ***Bojangles*** (☎ 08-8952 2873;

with music and live broadcasts in the evening), the ***Red Ochre Grill***, ***Al Fresco*** and ***Todd Tavern*** (see below), all in Todd St.

For something completely different, you can indulge in an afternoon camel safari followed by a barbecue, or you can go out on a bush-tucker excursion to watch boomerang throwing, Aboriginal dancing, and eat witchetty grubs live.

An unusual bus service, the Alice Wanderer, offers 70-minute 'Hop on Hop off' tours of major attractions around the city, with commentary, including the Old Telegraph Station (site of the original Alice Springs), the old Ghan train (p274), Anzac Hill and many others. The fare is $35 and it starts from Todd Mall in the city centre every 70 minutes from 09.00 to 16.00 with connecting services to The Ghan on Mondays and Thursdays. The journey may be broken at any stop so the tour can be made to last a whole day and it includes an extra day free. For further details phone ☎ 08-8952 2111, freecall ☎ 1800 722 111, or look at their website 💻 www.alicewanderer.com.au.

For a stopover there are many places to choose from, ranging from budget and backpacker style to expensive luxury hotels. The Central Australian Tourist Industry Association (☎ 08-8952 5800) offers helpful information and advice and can make bookings. A little noisy at times but worth trying is the ***Todd Tavern*** (☎ 08-8952 1255, 💻 www.toddtavern.com.au), at 1 Todd St Mall, where a room costs $48 to $60. Somewhat nearer to the station is the ***Desert Rose Inn*** (☎ 08-8952 1411, 💻 www.desertroseinn.com.au), 15 Railway Terrace, where single rooms with air-conditioning, shower and TV cost $56 and backpacker rooms with shared kitchen facilities are only $40.

The Alice Wanderer (see above) also offers longer tours covering places like Simpsons Gap, the Desert Park, the West MacDonnell Ranges and Glen Helen. Prices range from $65, subject to change without notice and to minimum numbers.

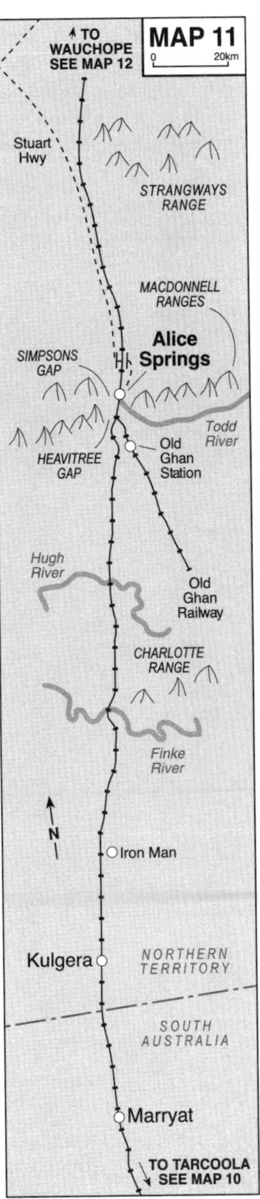

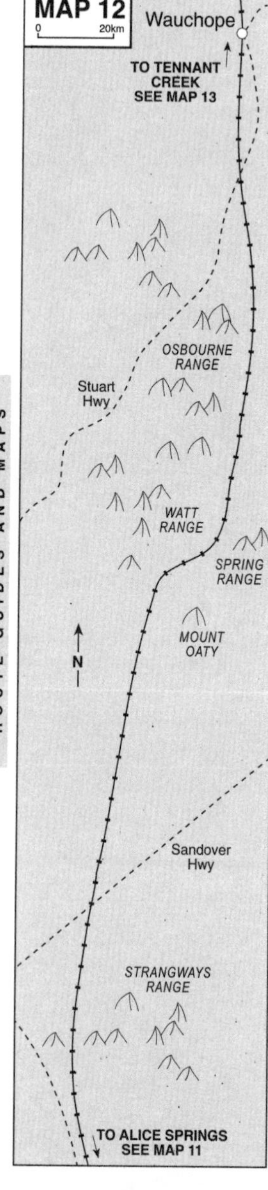

Other coach tours and regular flights from Alice Springs serve all the surrounding natural attractions including Uluru (formerly Ayers Rock) and Kata Tjuta (formerly the Olgas), the MacDonnell Ranges and Kings Canyon; Uluru is six hours by coach.

If time permits, stay at Yulara, its modern township; there is everything from a Sheraton hotel to camping sites; you can listen to an Aboriginal folk group and learn how not to play a didgeridoo, or you can take a three-day bus pass from Ayers Rock Touring Company for conducted tours of the Rock and the Olgas. The Red Centre is not quite the traditional outback, but it is not to be missed.

If you are fortunate enough to be in Alice Springs at the right time of year, around the first Saturday in October, you may have an opportunity to witness its unique boat race, the Henley-on-Todd Regatta. Held in the dry bed of the Todd River, with contestants carrying their boats, this had to be cancelled in 1994. The reason it could not be run? The river was full of water!

Alice Springs to Darwin (1420km) (C 9034) (Maps 11-16)

(Distances from Alice Springs)

The train moves slowly out of Alice Springs and runs close to the highway for the first sixteen kilometres.

The track then swings east, affording views of the **Strangways Range**, and then crosses some minor highways and property access roads. From 79km north of Alice Springs the line is dead straight for 115 kilometres, but there are few really noticeable curves anywhere on the route.

About three hours after leaving The Alice, a stop may be made at Illoquara to allow a southbound train to cross. Illoquara is 225km from Alice but is not marked on any map so far discovered.

Night will have fallen by the time the train passes **Wauchope**, after again crossing to the west of the highway. Just north of Wauchope, if the moon is bright, it might be possible to catch a glimpse of the **Devil's Marbles**, despite the broken and hilly terrain. The scenic reserve is about nine kilometres east of the track, adjoining the Stuart Highway.

Tennant Creek (475km) is a regular stop, reached just after ten at night northbound and in the middle of the night southbound. Although the station adjoins the Stuart Highway, it is over six kilometres from the town centre.

Tennant Creek has long been connected by McCafferty's coach services (C9075, 9428) to Alice Springs, Darwin and also Mount Isa, the last-named of course being on the Queensland Rail system. It is therefore possible to connect twice weekly between the Darwin and Mount Isa lines via Tennant Creek, but the times are far from attractive. The current timetables would allow one possible connection, leaving Mount Isa at 19.45, arriving at Tennant Creek at 03.00 next day. Change there to the Alice Springs bus at 03.35, which should reach the station in good time for the southbound Ghan at 04.27. Unfortunately, at the time of writing, the coaches did not stop at the station, but this could change: check with McCafferty's on ☎ 07-4690 9888. Connections in the other direction or to or from Darwin are simply not viable without a hotel booking, wake-up call and taxi ride at night.

Another stop may be made near **Newcastle Waters**, although the point on the railway is 30km or more west of the little town shown on the map. Here there is a further crossing loop. If you wake up around three in the morning to find the train has stopped, that is why. In the morning the scenery is different.

The rather barren wastes of the Red Centre give way to the more lush scenery of the tropics. People notice the 'anthills' (properly 'termite mounds') which have grown in size, and the greater abundance of trees.

At **Katherine** (1108km), 'where the outback meets the tropics', the station is 6km from town, but GSR operates a shuttle bus *Raillink* to the Springvale Homestead via the town centre (BP Roadhouse) approximately half-hourly

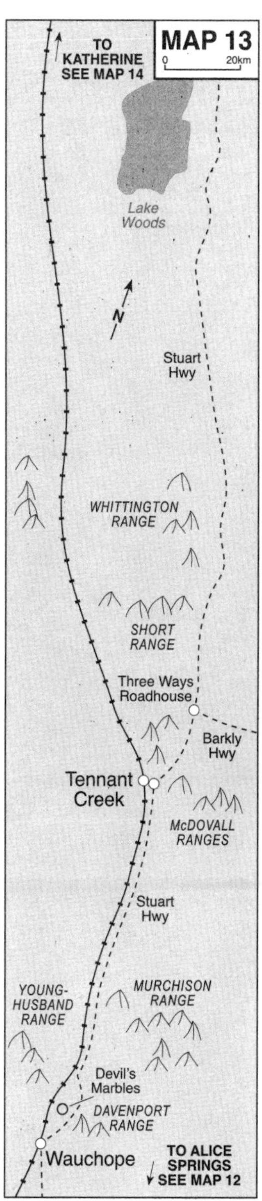

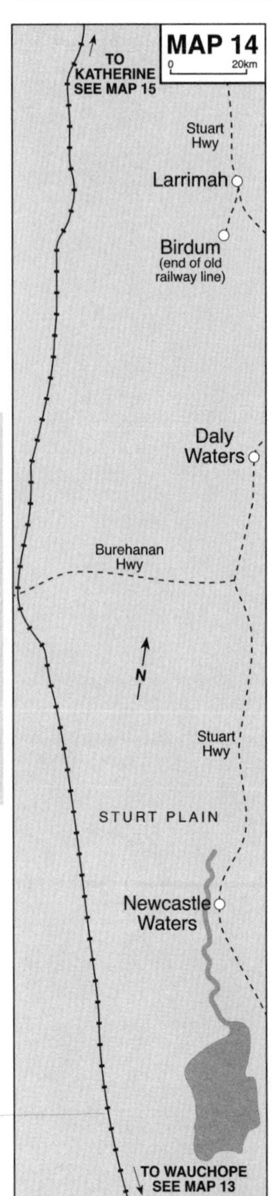
MAP 14
0
20km
TO KATHERINE SEE MAP 15
Stuart Hwy
Larrimah
Birdum
(end of old railway line)
Daly Waters
Burehanan Hwy
N
Stuart Hwy
STURT PLAIN
Newcastle Waters
TO WAUCHOPE SEE MAP 13

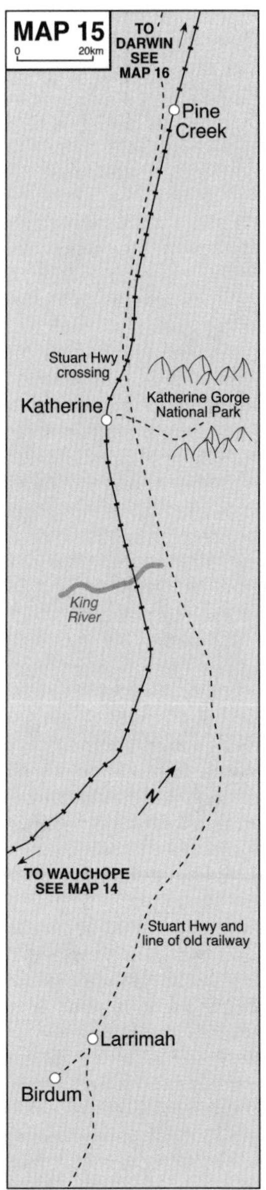
MAP 15
0
20km
TO DARWIN SEE MAP 16
Pine Creek
Stuart Hwy crossing
Katherine
Katherine Gorge National Park
King River
N
TO WAUCHOPE SEE MAP 14
Stuart Hwy and line of old railway
Larrimah
Birdum

from 20 minutes after the train's arrival, the last return bus being 40 minutes (55 minutes from the Roadhouse) before The Ghan's departure. The return fare is $8.

More exciting (and expensive) options range from coach tours to helicopter flights over Nitmiluk (**Katherine Gorge National Park**). This can also be explored at ground level on the water. Take suitable footwear and a hat. Springvale Homestead (☎ 08-8972 1355) is a historic house, reputedly the Territory's oldest cattle station, featuring among its attractions groups of monster Indian Raintrees *(Samanea Saman)*, whose massive trunks support huge branches spreading as much as 10 metres outwards. Canoeing is available here, but swimming togs are advisable if going on the water, and there are holiday cabins and a café.

Other accommodation is in the town centre on Katherine Terrace at ***Crossways Hotel*** (☎ 08-8972 1022) and ***Katherine Hotel Motel*** (☎ 08-89721622, 💻 www.katherinehotel.com).

Pine Creek (approx 1200km) is not a stop for The Ghan but may be seen about an hour and a half after leaving Katherine heading north towards Adelaide River, since the new line closely follows the original route on this sector. Pine Creek owes its existence to a 19th-century gold rush. Mining continues today.

About an hour and 20 minutes before reaching Darwin The Ghan crosses the Stuart Highway again 19km south of **Adelaide River** (1312km). The old station and yard, preserved by the National Trust, may be seen on the left of the train at the township, which is named after the river itself and was a major stop on the old railway.

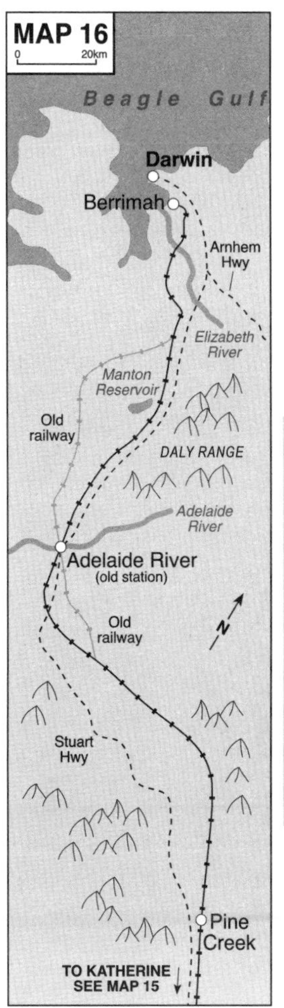

The suburbs of Palmerston on the right signify the final approach to **Darwin**, Australia's most modern capital city, having been largely rebuilt after the devastation caused by Cyclone Tracy in 1974. Darwin, 1420km from Alice Springs and 2979km from Adelaide, is a genuinely multicultural community with a current population of around 87,000 but its railway station appears to stand isolated and remote on a bleak peninsula – yet to witness the surge of industrial activity which, following the already evident boost to tourism, the railway must surely bring.

Notes on Darwin appear on pp165-8.

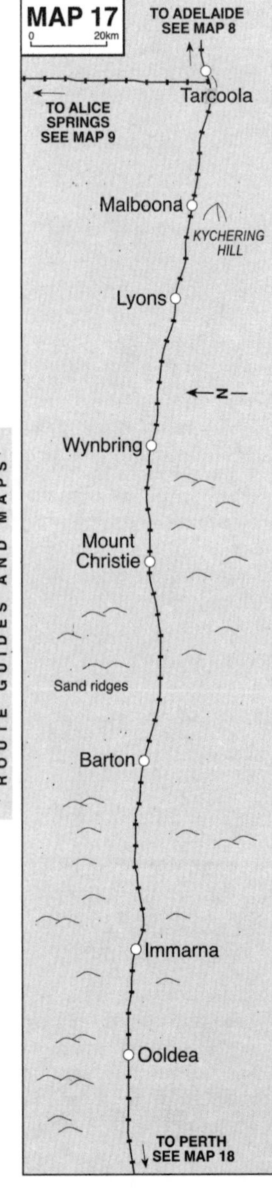

TARCOOLA TO PERTH (ACROSS THE NULLARBOR)

Tarcoola to Cook (410km)

[Maps 17 and 18]

West from Tarcoola the landscape begins to change. Around **Wynbring** the track enters an area characterized by long sand ridges, which are the principal landscape feature for the next hour or so. This is the edge of the Great Victoria Desert which stretches 1000km to the north-west.

Barton, which the eastbound train passes around breakfast time, is one of a number of railway settlements along the route named after former prime ministers of which Barton was the first; he was sworn in on 1 January 1901, the day of Federation. Barton is also close to an important Aboriginal ceremonial area.

Near **Ooldea** (pronounced Oolday) is the only natural source of water on the Nullarbor, believed to come from an underground river over 400km away to the north. Ooldea is where the construction teams building the line met in 1917.

To the north, not long after Ooldea, you may see a vehicle coming towards the track in a cloud of dust; the vehicle will cross the track at the next siding, **Watson**. This could be from Maralinga, 40km away on the low ridge to the north, the long-guarded site of a once-thriving

❑ **The way to the west – watch your time!**

There are time changes between South and Western Australia. The train timetable follows the correct time, whether Central (CST) as in Adelaide or Western (WST) which, subject to the one-hour adjustment when summer time applies in South Australia, is normally 1½ hours different; the train time may not be the same.

To even out the change and avoid things like having two meals only a couple of hours apart, the train operates in its own internal time zone and the conductor will tell you what time it is. Any clocks on the train will usually be wrong, as will your watch!

township of scientists and service personnel. Maralinga (meaning 'thunder') is a place of shame. In 1956/7 a series of atomic bomb tests was carried out by Britain. Australian, Canadian and British soldiers were used as guinea pigs, entering the area just after a blast.

Although the site was finally cleared of radiation hazard and rehabilitated on 1 March 2000 some personnel are still awaiting compensation, as are survivors from the unknown number of Aborigines then living in the locality. These literally did not count as far as officialdom was concerned (see p95).

You will notice that vegetation has now virtually completely disappeared. So have curves; if you were allowed to look out of the door of the train you would see that the line is straight as far as the eye can see. The Indian Pacific has now entered the longest straight line of railway in the whole world and there will be no more curves for at least the next six hours.

The long straight starts 705.6km from Port Augusta and 293km from Tarcoola and it extends for the next 477.6km, ending just before **Nurina**. Most of this whole day on the train will be spent riding smoothly across the Nullarbor Plain, past little sidings or passing loops named after Australian prime ministers such as O'Malley and Fisher.

This would be a good time to get your 'train legs' if you started the journey in Perth, but if you came from the east you would be well adjusted by now. The only walking you need to do is backwards and forwards along the corridor to and from the toilet, lounge or dining car. You can stretch your legs a bit further at the next stop, Cook.

Cook

Around mid-morning westbound or mid-day eastbound the train will stop at Cook, where you put your watch back again (or forward if returning east).

Cook (Queen City of the Nullarbor) is known among other things for its jail cells.

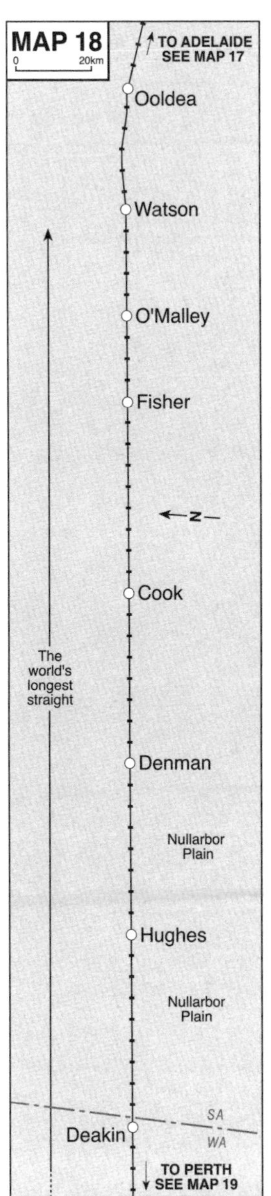

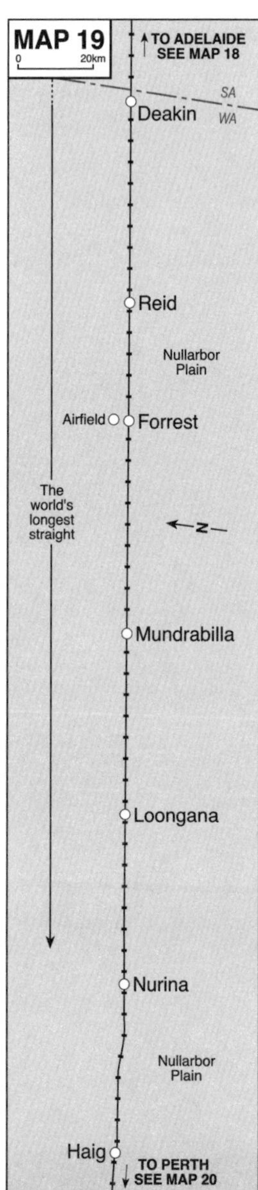

These now adjoin the station; one for males and one for females, and they look very much like the little tin sheds people used to have at the bottom of the garden before the advent of piped sewage disposal.

Cook until recently also had a hospital, but with such a small population (a few dozen at most) it was hard to keep enough patients (let alone doctors and nurses, one would imagine). Travellers were therefore invited to 'go crook at Cook' – the Australian colloquial for getting sick.

The resident population is now only three but they will still ply you with souvenirs when the train stops there for half an hour or more, as it always does. Like souvenirs everywhere, not all will have been made in Cook. The Cook interlude is a good time to get out and stretch your legs, but don't forget to look along the track. You won't see a longer stretch of straight line anywhere.

If you are able to look along the straight at night towards the headlights of an oncoming train, it is an unbelievably long time before it reaches you. This would be possible only if your train is running extremely late, or you are travelling in the truck drivers' carriage of a freight train.

Cook to Kalgoorlie (867km) [Maps 18, 19, 20 and 21]

Around mid-morning on Mondays the Saturday train from Sydney, if on time, may stop 87km beyond Cook at a passing loop called **Hughes** to allow another Indian Pacific going in the opposite direction to pass by; this will probably be announced.

Approaching the small siding of **Deakin**, about 139km from Cook, the train crosses the South Australia/Western Australia border. This, like other lineside features, is likely to be announced, but look out for the welcoming hoarding at the lineside. Perched on top you may see a wedge-tailed eagle, the Indian Pacific's logo. To watch these mighty birds swoop down on seemingly invisible prey is an experience long remembered.

About an hour after passing Deakin the train reaches **Forrest**. Named after a former Australian Prime Minister, Forrest is nothing to do with trees, being in the middle of the Nullarbor – Null Arbor, the plain with no trees (Latin, not Aboriginal, as is sometimes thought). Forrest is noted for its international-standard airfield, used during World War II and occasionally more recently as an emergency alternative to Perth.

Loongana is the last station (or rather, passing loop – trains rarely stop) before the end of the long straight. This was a watering stop in steam train days. The locality is noted for its stalactite caves which hold some of the earliest evidence of human settlement in Australia.

Rawlinna, the next place of interest going west, was noted for its social club, which boasted the largest car park in the world – space for a million cars at least: north, east and west from the club the empty car park reached to the horizon and beyond – the Nullarbor plain. Apart from the station, the club and the railway rest house (if still there), there is not a tree or building in sight.

Zanthus, 169km further on, was once a major stop for trains like the Tea and Sugar supply train (see p38), which in the 1980s waited there for over three hours while the residents would do their weekly shopping, but the next scheduled stop for the Indian Pacific is not until Kalgoorlie.

Kalgoorlie (The Golden City)

Kalgoorlie, rich in history and present-day interest, is the evening stop of the Indian Pacific. The current schedules allow plenty of time to look around and there is much to see. A coach tour is an optional extra for passengers but many find it interesting enough to walk around on their own.

Kalgoorlie should be a prime choice for a stopover of even two or three days to appreciate

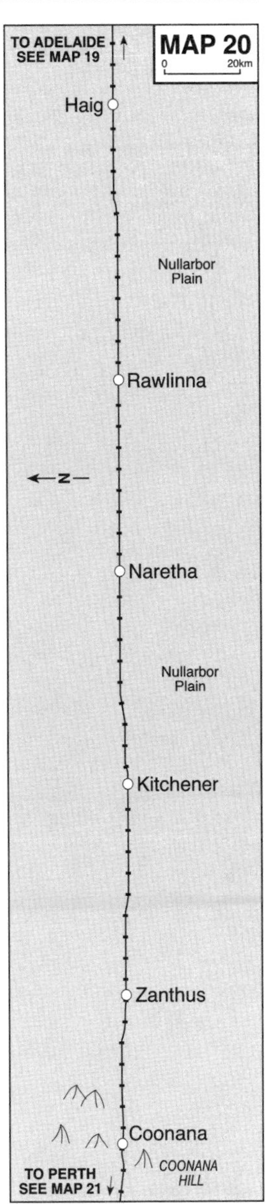

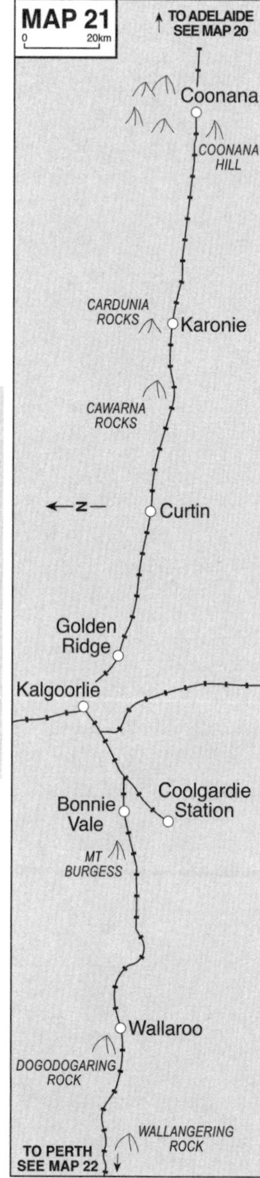

its real atmosphere. There are comfortable historic hotels where you can stay the night, such as ***The Palace*** (☎ 08-9021 2788, 🖳 ddrummond@palacehotel.com.au), the ***Exchange*** (☎ 08-9021 2833, 🖹 9021 7459) or the old ***Australia*** (☎ 08-9021 1320, 🖳 oah@iinet.net.au), some just opposite the station.

There's another kind of accommodation in Hay St, to your right from the station; not very prepossessing externally, but it is said to include the very best in personal comfort. Coach tour guides will be sure to point it out but be warned – a night there will not appeal to all and it is very expensive.

More gold has been won in Kalgoorlie than anywhere else on earth and if in Kalgoorlie for even just as long as the train waits, follow Paddy Hannan's golden footsteps to his monument; he was the bloke who discovered gold in this area.

You can also see the old brewery bearing his name, a historic building but, alas, no longer producing the pale amber fluid.

If staying a day or more, visit the Museum of the Goldfields (open 10.30-12.30, 14.30-16.30), Boulder and the 'Rattler' train on the Golden Mile (see p273), Hainault gold mine and the lookout.

The **tourist bureau** (☎ 08-9021 1966), in Hannan St, four blocks from the station, is open daily though at varying times.

While waiting for your train to depart you may see a freight train thundering by on an outside track. These mostly ignore Kalgoorlie, having their own stations at Parkeston 5km to the east and at West Kalgoorlie on the other side.

Kalgoorlie station has other features of interest. Notice the standpipes for watering the passenger trains; there are enough for a train of around 20 coaches.

Some of the longest passenger trains ever put together ran on this route (that is before the advent of the Darwin Ghan), when floods caused delays which resulted in the running of combined Indian Pacific/Trans-Australian sets.

There are historical notes about the railways of this area in the booking hall and you might be interested to learn that Kalgoorlie boasts the longest railway platform (526.5m) in Australia still in use, which you will know about if you try walking its length with your heavy luggage! Actually, the *Guinness Book of Rail Facts and Feats* states that Perth Terminal main platform is 762m. Someone has it wrong!

Around Kalgoorlie Some 40km from Kalgoorlie and 14km south of **Bonnie Vale** railway station is historic **Coolgardie**, well worth a visit if you are staying in the Goldfields region for a day or two.

Kalgoorlie to Perth (655km) [Maps 21, 22 and 23]

Most of the line between Kalgoorlie and Perth can be viewed in daylight on the return journey, or from the Transwa Prospector train in either direction. The views are similar on both sides of the train, but with slightly more of interest on the north.

Vast lakes and salt pans around **Koolyanobbing** are visible on the north side, as well as great mounds of salt at the lineside. Look out also for the vermin-proof fence, an historic and famous feature of Australian outback regions which like so many other attempts to curb nature, was not a howling success.

Southern Cross is a busy town where in the southern springtime the surrounding area is ablaze with wild flowers. Named after the constellation featured on the Australian flag (see box p46) and vividly displayed in the night sky of the outback.

Merredin is an important junction on the West Australian narrow-gauge rail system and, like Southern Cross, an optional stop for the Indian Pacific.

If travelling west on the Indian Pacific, you will probably be asleep most of this part of the journey, and therefore not notice **Cunderdin**, Meckering, or **Grass Valley**, optional stops only for the Prospector.

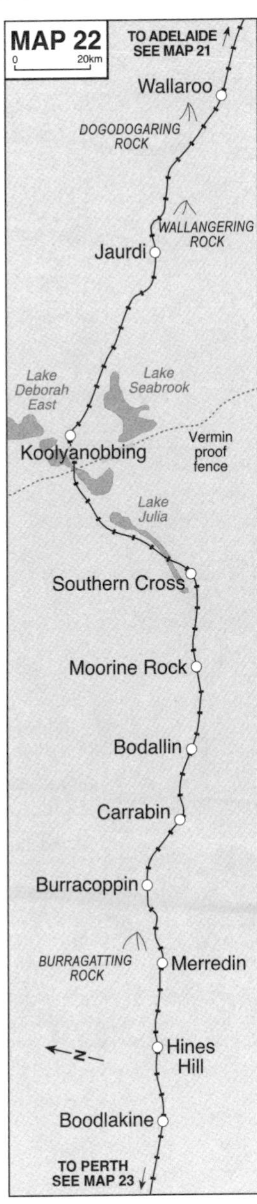

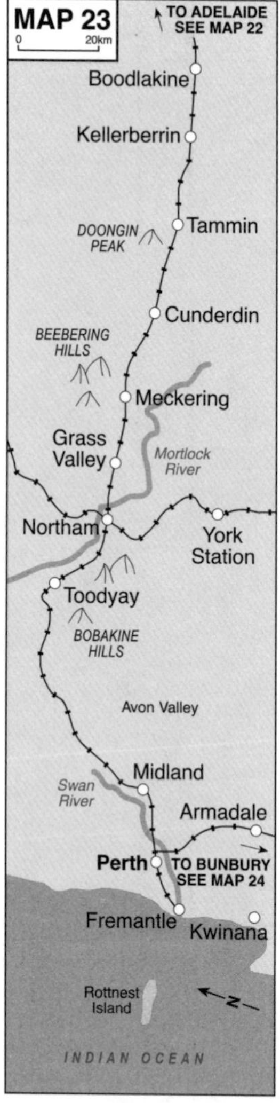

Meckering was the scene of one of Australia's worst earthquakes, which devastated the town in 1968. A low escarpment which it created is visible in the area.

You should notice **Northam** if you're awake a few hours before the final approach to Western Australia's capital city. On the banks of the Avon River, Northam is noted for its white swans – these may be familiar to visitors from northern Europe but are rare in Western Australia, home of the famous Black Swan.

If breaking the journey here, there are hotels near the station. For a breakfast snack, try the refreshment room at the station.

Look out after Northam for the picturesque and pleasantly-winding Avon valley with its brightly-coloured parrots and flocks of black cockatoos.

Rail buffs will be interested in the combined-gauge track between Perth and Northam; standard and 1067mm (3ft 6in) gauge together.

Toodyay, a regular stop for the Prospector and the express commuter service, the Avon Link, would be another good place for a night stopover.

Notes on Perth appear on pp157-61.

PERTH TO BUNBURY [Map 24]

Instead of staying in or around Perth, a pleasant day trip by rail takes you 181km south down to Bunbury.

Commercial development, however, seems to be the main feature in the first 15km or so of the line south from Perth City station; the line is shared by Transperth electric trains as far as **Armadale**, 30km, where transfer can be made to the Australind service.

Mundijong, junction for a disused branch to **Jarrahdale**, is the nearest station to Jarrahdale National Park. Jarrah is one of the tallest of the Eucalypts, producing hard durable timber, logged extensively in this area.

At **Pinjarra**, 87km, the Hotham Valley Tourist Railway (see p273) runs to **Dwellingup** in the Darling Range east of the coastal plain.

Harvey is the centre of a fruit-growing and popular bushwalking area, close to Yalgorup National Park.

Around this area and generally north of Bunbury the country is full of wild flowers. You can hardly miss them even without taking one of the special wildflower bus tours put on by Transwa.

Brunswick Junction was the connecting station for a vast network of rail routes in the south of Western Australia, including Collie, Narrogin and Albany, connecting north to the main eastern line at Northam and Merredin; those that remain are now only freight lines.

Bunbury is now the most southerly terminus of the passenger rail system in Western Australia, although the line through Donnybrook to Bridgetown, some 102km further south, was briefly re-opened in 1995 for an experimental weekend extension to the Australind service.

Bunbury is on the Indian Ocean. Worth seeing are the basalt rock formations on the beach, the many historic buildings like ***Rose Hotel*** (☎ 08-9721 4533, 🖷 9721 8285) near the old station (try a counter meal there). Commercial redevelopment unfortunately displaced Bunbury station to Wollaston, about 2km away, but a free bus service connects with the trains.

See p273 for details of Boyanup Transport Museum.

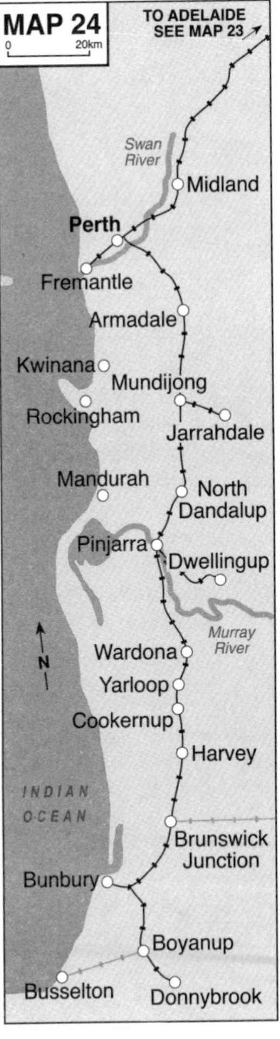

South-eastern Australia

ADELAIDE TO MELBOURNE

Adelaide to Murray Bridge [See Map p155 and Map 25]

(Note: distances given are from Keswick but may not correspond to present kilometre posts at the lineside owing to route realignment.)

The Adelaide–Melbourne line has never been noted for speed; the first 50km out of Adelaide reveal why. Minutes after leaving Keswick terminal the track swings east away from the coastal suburban lines to climb into the Mt Lofty ranges, known in this area as Adelaide Hills. At **Torrens Park** (9km) the line swings south-west bringing the coastline of Gulf St Vincent into view ahead. It then curves through 180°, climbing all the way up to **Belair**, 18km, which marks the present-day end of the TransAdelaide system. Suburban trains formerly continued a further 12km through the ranges past **Mount Lofty** and **Aldgate** to **Bridgewater**. This was a conditional stop for The Overland as well as for the then existing Mount Gambier Bluebird trains.

After Bridgewater the next places of interest are **Mount Barker Junction** (the northern end of the privately-run SteamRanger branch to Victor Harbor, see p71) and Nairne (52km), one of South Australia's oldest settlements.

Before the introduction late in 1998 of the short-lived Melbourne extension of The Ghan, and a year later the rescheduling of the eastbound Overland, leaving Adelaide mid-morning, most of the then 774km journey between Adelaide and Melbourne was by night. Passengers could look back on the lights of the city (Adelaide or Melbourne depending on the direction) as the trip commenced and then wake to greet the dawn among the hills around Ballan in Victoria eastbound, or the Adelaide Hills of the Mt Lofty ranges westbound. But the rescheduling made it possible to see the whole Adelaide–Melbourne route by train in daylight for the first time in more than 20 years.

Still today, westbound on The Overland, passengers wake to an early morning crossing of the Murray. After climbing again up to Mount Barker Junction, the rail route winds down through the national park area of the Mt Lofty ranges between Bridgewater and Adelaide, giving views on the final approach to Adelaide over Gulf St Vincent.

Murray Bridge to Bordertown [Map 25]

Just beyond Murray Bridge station (93km) the eastbound train crosses the 576m-long Murray Bridge, over the Murray. This crossing is 40km from the entry of Australia's greatest river system into Lake Alexandrina from which it flows into the Southern Ocean.

East of the Murray lies **Tailem Bend** (117km), junction for some of South Australia's remaining broad-gauge lines. From here branches ran north to the

Riverland irrigation districts around Berri and Renmark, major wine- and fruit-producing areas. The present railhead is at Loxton, 159km from Tailem Bend, but passenger trains have not used this line since the early 1970s. Another branch still runs through to join the Victorian system at Pinnaroo but passenger trains had been replaced by buses even before 1970.

Tintinara (208km) and **Keith** (245km) are former stops on The Overland and were also served by the Mount Gambier Bluebird railcar until the latter's controversial withdrawal in the spate of rail closures in the 1970s. Now served only by V/Line's Speedlink bus between Adelaide and Melbourne, these little towns are full of history.

Bordertown (290km) was never in fact on the South Australia/Victoria border which is 19km further east. Although originating in the 1850s as a gold-mining camp, Bordertown's main claim to fame is probably as the birthplace of RJ Hawke, former trade union leader and one of Australia's best-known prime ministers (from 1983 to 1991).

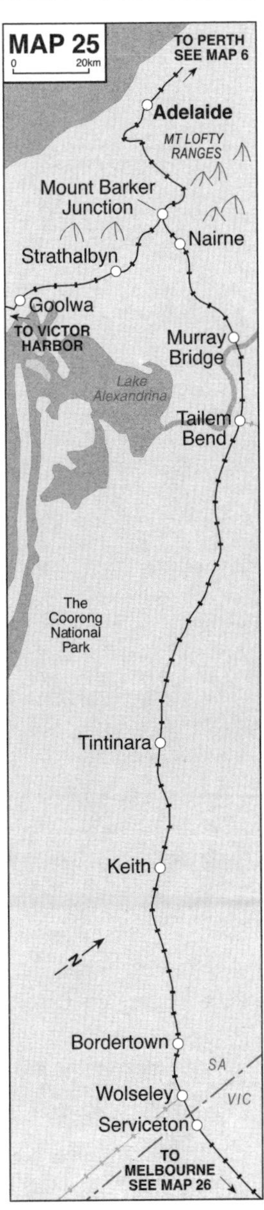

Bordertown to Nhill [Map 26]

Wolseley (304km), originally named Tatiara, which was the Aboriginal name for the district meaning 'good country', is the junction for the currently disused Mount Gambier line.

Serviceton (312km from Keswick, 462km from Melbourne by the original route through Bacchus Marsh and Ballarat) was the scene of arguments between smugglers and customs in the days before the border had been accurately surveyed. The 1889 station building, classified (listed) by the National Trust, is built over former dungeons and doubles as Serviceton Hotel. Kaniva (335km) was in the same disputed territory in the 1880s. It is also gateway to the area known as The Little Desert.

Nhill, 374km from Keswick and 400km from Melbourne on the old route, has three distinctions; it is exactly halfway between Melbourne and Adelaide on the Western

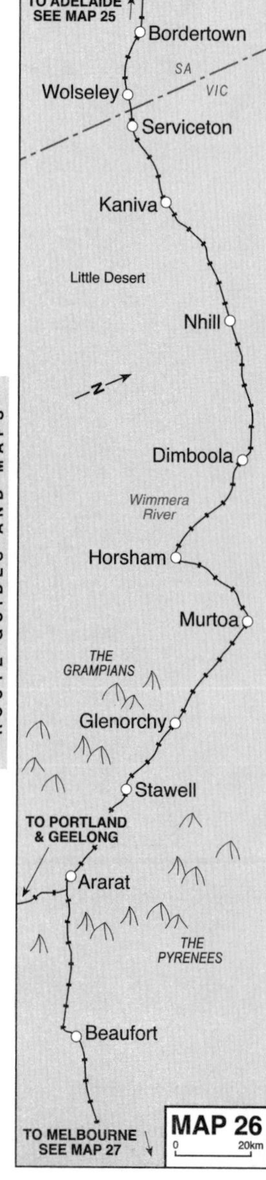

Highway, it claims to have the largest single-bin grain silo in the Southern hemisphere and it was the first Victorian country town to have electric street lighting.

Nhill to Geelong **[Maps 26 and 27]**

(Note: From here on, kilometre distances are to Melbourne via Cressy, the new route taken by The Overland.)

Dimboola, 423km from Melbourne via Cressy and 412km from Keswick, is one of the few remaining stops on this route. It was reached by the railway in 1882 and was the terminus of the former V/Line passenger train, the Wimmera Limited. Wimmera is the name of the surrounding district, noted for waterfowl. Dimboola dates from the 1840s and acquired a certain fame from a satirical play of that name first staged in Melbourne in 1969.

Horsham, 388km, regional capital of the Wimmera and on the banks of the Wimmera River, hosts conventions and sporting meetings. It is the birthplace of Kevin Magee, famed in the motorcycle-racing world. Wimmera wool factory is open from 10.00 to 16.00 almost every day of the year. **Murtoa**, 359km, considered the centre of Victoria's wheat district is a small town, with a population of about 1000, on the edge of Lake Marma.

Stawell, 302km from Melbourne, is accessible now only by V/Line coach from Horsham or Ararat (C 9093). Attractions include a unique chiming clock on the town-hall tower, a 'world in miniature' and the winding Gold Reef Mall. This has been a good centre from which to explore Grampians National Park since the former railway to Fyans Creek, the heart of this scenic area, was abandoned. The Grampians are clearly visible here to the south from the eastbound train.

Ararat, 265km by marker post but in fact closer to 272km, is the junction of the standard and broad gauge and may regain some of its former rail importance following the return of V/Line trains in July 2004. It is 563km from

Keswick and 211km from Melbourne on the old route. Ararat station adjoins the town centre. From here until 1981, Australia's then fastest train served Hamilton, the wool capital of the world and a good centre for a Western Victoria stay. Hamilton is now served by bus from Ballarat (2¼ hours, C 9408).

Maroona, 250km, is the junction where the line to Melbourne via Geelong swings east from the Hamilton and Portland branch which is now used only by goods trains.

You can watch out for **Nerrin Nerrin** (211km), **Pura Pura** (202km) and **Vite Vite** (192km) but these former stations will be hard to find. A passing loop should enable the vigilant to locate Vite Vite around six in the evening on the Friday, Saturday or Sunday Overland from Adelaide.

After the Berrybank loop (156km) the train runs downhill for about 5km to the crossing of the Hamilton Highway. About 8km south of the line from here as the train approaches **Cressy** (150km) is one of Victoria's largest salt lakes, Lake Corangamite. Cressy was once an important rail junction, the east–west line being crossed by a north–south link between Ballarat and Colac on the West Coast line. That route was abandoned in November 1953 and passenger trains have not served Cressy on the Geelong–Ararat route for longer still, the last train being a car goods train in January 1952.

The standard-gauge line from Adelaide to Melbourne joins the Victorian broad-gauge route from Victoria's west coast at **Geelong North Shore** (72km) where a new platform was constructed in 1999. The various authorities argued for four years over who should pay for this since the interstate line was standardized. Although Geelong is Victoria's second city there is nothing much at North Shore; if leaving the train there it might be wise to have a taxi waiting; not all local trains stop at North Shore and there could be as much as two hours wait for a connection. For North Shore connections see Table 9 (p139).

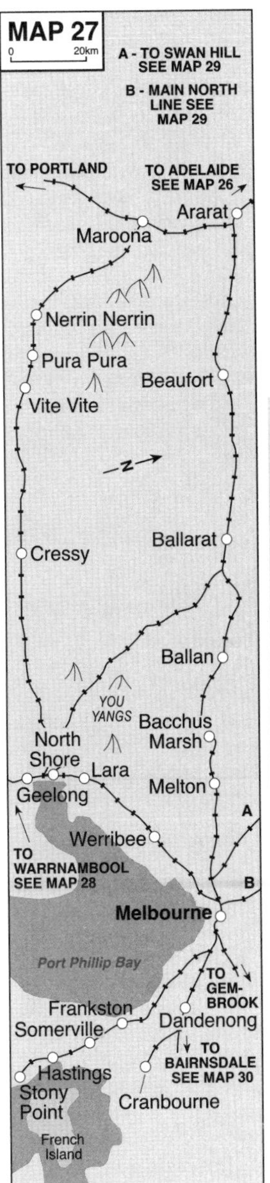

Geelong to Melbourne [Map 27 and map pp136-7]

North of Geelong is a major industrial area. Geelong itself is a pleasant and busy city with a throbbing nightlife. At **Corio** (64km), the station after Geelong North Shore, Australia's own whisky was produced for a while. Very popular (it was cheaper than imported Scotch) in the 1960s it is rarely heard of today.

The hills to the left seen north of **Lara** (58km) are the You Yangs, of volcanic origin and a designated national park, rich in wildlife, particularly birds, koalas and kangaroos.

Werribee (32km) marks the start of Melbourne's suburban system. Connex trains operate the Met services from here right round the bay to Frankston. The route between here and Melbourne is marked by the wharves and industry which are mostly on this side of Port Phillip Bay. At Newport (11km), a junction of suburban passenger and goods lines, you are barely 20 minutes from Spencer St, so be ready to leave the train. On the Bay side of the train are Newport Railway Workshops (see p263) and ahead to the right you should see Melbourne's Westgate Bridge which carries a freeway over the Yarra.

For information on Melbourne see pp131-41.

Coastal and inland routes in Victoria

MELBOURNE TO ARARAT [See map pp136-7 and Map 27]

Sunshine (13km), in the inner western suburbs, was for many years the transfer station for passengers from Adelaide joining the daylight train to Sydney, the western line to Ballarat being the original interstate route.

Deer Park, Rockbank and **Melton** are in commuter territory though not served by The Met system as such. V/Line passenger trains offer a service that is just enough to make work or shopping trips to Melbourne attractive. **Bacchus Marsh** (51km) on the Werribee River is the terminus for most commuter services on this line. The marsh itself was drained long ago and now produces vegetables.

The route west to Ballarat features a steep climb towards **Ballan** half an hour to an hour after leaving Melbourne Spencer St station, with views back over the lights of the city, specially impressive at night-time.

Ballarat (119km), one of Victoria's major regional cities, reeks with history. South-east of the town is the site of the Eureka Stockade of 1854 where Peter Lawler, later a member of parliament, led the miners in a revolt against government licensing policies. Sovereign Hill (☎ 03-5337 1100, 💻 www.sovereignhill.com.au; a recreated mining settlement where you can pan for gold) commemorates this event. The Ballarat 'Eureka Pass' ($35.50 adult, with various concessions) gives two days access to Sovereign Hill, the Eureka Centre, and Ballarat Fine Art Gallery. The white on blue Eureka flag still symbolizes this successful insurrection which led to the institution of the 'Miners' Right', an official licence to dig for gold.

Other attractions in Ballarat include the vintage tramway and museum (see p261), many historic buildings, and the railway station; the station is a particularly fine building with arched roof, old-fashioned level-crossing gates, signal cabin and gantry, classics of industrial archaeology. There's also an excellent licensed refreshment room.

The station itself is conveniently located in the heart of the city. Basic pub accommodation ($40 single) is opposite at ***Irwin's Hotel*** (☎ 03-5332 1845) on Lydiard St. Further down Lydiard St is the ***George Hotel*** (☎ 03-5333 4866) with single rooms at $50, en suite $60. Light breakfast is included but it can be noisy at weekends. A little further, at the corner of Lydiard and and Mair Sts is ***Sebastians***, a popular coffee bar, fully licensed and open daily except Mondays for lunch and dinner. The Begonia Festival is held in early March, and there is also the Yellowglen Winery, specializing in *méthode Champenoise* sparkling dry wine of fine quality.

At Ballarat North Junction (120km) the line to St Arnaud and Mildura leaves the main western line. A little further on, Linton Junction marks a former branch to Linton and Skipton. After passing the long abandoned stations of Wendouree and Windermere, Lake Burrumbeet may be seen near the track on the left.

Beaufort (165km) is the only re-opened station between Ballarat and Ararat; the former intermediate stations of Trawalla (157km) and Buangor (188km) being now only bus stops. The ***Beaufort Railway Hotel*** and two others are close to the station at Beaufort.

Between Beaufort and Ararat are several sharp gradients at 1 in 50 as the track crosses the foothills of Victoria's Pyrenee range; note also the wind farms in this area. **Ararat** is 211km from Melbourne by this route, formerly traversed by The Overland and Victoria's Wimmera Limited, and once again facing a future as an important rail junction.

GEELONG TO WARRNAMBOOL [Map 28]

(Distances quoted are from Melbourne Spencer St except where stated.)

Geelong (73km) is the starting point for Victoria's west coast line (C 9028). South Geelong is a commuter station serving the suburbs less than 2km away. Inter-City trains do not stop here.

Winchelsea (114km) on the Barwon River has an unenviable claim to a place in history; rabbits were first imported into Australia here. To the south are the Otway Ranges. Fifteen kilometres beyond Winchelsea the railway swings across the adjoining highway to the small township of Birregurra (134km) at which only some trains stop. A 90° curve brings the line back to cross the highway again at Warncoort (the station is long gone).

The next station is **Colac** (153km) on the lake of that name; Lake Colac is the largest freshwater lake in Victoria. Colac Botanic Gardens are on the foreshore and the lake is a popular swimming and boating area. The town centre is close to the station on the north.

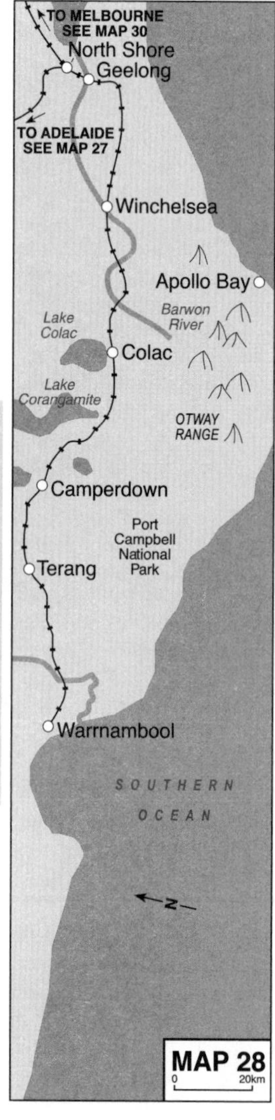

The rich agricultural country around here is part of a vast basalt plain. Crater lakes abound. Pirron Yallock (168km) is at the southern tip of Lake Corangamite, the largest in Victoria and three times as salty as sea water. The station here no longer exists.

Camperdown (198km) is surrounded by crater lakes. The main street has a shaded avenue of English elms and is dominated by an imposing clock tower. Dry stone walls bounding paddocks around Camperdown are reminiscent of north England. They were in fact built by Scottish and Irish immigrants and dug well into the ground to stop the spread of the rabbit pest. Vain hope!

Terang (221km) is a rich dairying centre; Glenormiston Agricultural College is open to visitors.

Warrnambool (267km) marks the end of the passenger line operated by V/Line. It features safe, wide, surf beaches and a lookout from which, during winter (June to October), the rare southern right whales can be seen coming in to calve in the sheltered waters. Southern Right Charters (💻 www.southernrightcharters.com.au) have boat and coach tours covering Logan's Beach where whales are most likely to be seen close by in season.

Flagstaff Hill Maritime Museum, seen on the right as the train approaches the station, recreates the days of sail. The nearby historic fishing village of Port Fairy (29km) is reached by V/Line coach.

The tourist information centre (☎ 03-5564 7837) next to Flagstaff Hill in Merri St has information on other tours, mostly of one day but also overnight at weekends. These cover, among other attractions, the Twelve Apostles and 'London Bridge' on the Great Ocean Road, and a visit to Logans Beach where whales are most likely to be seen close by in season.

MELBOURNE TO SWAN HILL AND ECHUCA (C 9032)
[See map pp136-7 and Map 29]

Watergardens (25km) is the station for Sydenham and the northern terminus of the Met trains, although there is some inter-availability of ticketing in that Metcards can be used on V/Line trains to Sunbury, as well as Melton on the west and Craigieburn on the north. ***St Albans Hotel*** (☎ 03-9366 2066) adjoining the station is a good spot to break a journey for a counter lunch. The line from here to Bendigo was built between 1858 and 1862 and was one of the most expensive country railways built in Australia, being double track with easy curves and gradients (none steeper than 1 in 50), stone bridges and station buildings, a line of the highest engineering standard almost worthy of an engineer such as Isambard Kingdom Brunel of Britain's Great Western fame.

Watergardens and **Diggers Rest** (33km) are the nearest stations to Organ Pipes National Park, which contains a wall of basalt columns somewhat reminiscent of the Giants' Causeway in Antrim, Northern Ireland.

Sunbury (38km), reputedly the place where test cricket's ashes were created, marks the start of the climb up over the Dividing Range with a 1 in 50 gradient for the first 2km after the little platform at Rupertswood (39.5km). This is possibly the only remaining stop on an Australian main line exclusively for school students, serving the Salesian Catholic College there. Look out for the superb old stone buildings of Rupertswood situated in park-like grounds on the right, 1.5km north of Sunbury. The foundations were laid in 1874 and Rupertswood is on the Victorian Heritage Register.

Climbing steadily through Clarkefield (50km), Riddell's Creek (57km), Gisborne (64km) and **Macedon** (70km) the line reaches the summit at 580m above sea level just before **Woodend** (78km), from where connecting coaches run to Trentham, Daylesford and Ballarat. **Mt Macedon**, a 1013m-high extinct volcano and a forest park, is clearly seen about 10km off to the right, whilst about 7km north-east of Woodend station is Hanging Rock, scene of the ill-fated picnic. It is said to be worth the climb for the view alone.

Malmsbury (102km) is heralded by a magnificent bluestone viaduct by which the railway crosses the Coliban River.

A steep descent leads into **Castlemaine** (125km), a place that is full of railway and other history, and is now the last station before Bendigo. In the railway yard left of the track is a historic preserved signal box and behind that an old pub, ***Railway Hotel*** (☎ 03-5472 1250) – unfortunately its opening hours are limited but other pubs are in the main street close by. It is the junction for the old railway to Maldon (see p262), opened in 1884, closed in 1976 but since restored by a preservation society formed that same year. In contrast to the several 'recreated' historic townships, Maldon is a living example of a small mining town of the 19th century, where an enlightened local council maintains strict control of all new building. Castlemaine rock (a peppermint sweet, not a geological feature) is still manufactured here. It gave its red and yellow colours to the cans of a now well-known beer of the same name, Castlemaine XXXX, first produced here at Fitzgerald's Brewery, but now at Milton Brewery in Queensland. A recent colour change proposed for these cans by a management out of touch with history and tradition has been widely criticized in Queensland.

The former stations of Kangaroo Flat and Golden Square herald the approach to **Bendigo** (162km). Scene of a gold rush in 1851, this city has a wealth of Australian history, perhaps typified by its magnificently opulent Shamrock Hotel. The original Chinese joss house is worth a visit. Take a ride on the tram (see p262), visit the pottery and climb to the top of the Central Deborah Gold Mine. Large mullock heaps are a reminder of the 1852 gold rush, which was the start of Eaglehawk (170km), the next station north on the line to Swan Hill. Now a suburb of Bendigo, it is the junction of freight lines to Robinvale and Sea Lake on which the last passenger trains ran in the late 1970s, but Eaglehawk has one train a day.

Pyramid (249km), is the station for Pyramid Hill, a pyramid-shaped hill of white granite. Stud farms and merino sheep are the mainstay of the area. ***Victoria Hotel*** (☎ 03-5455 7391) adjoins the station.

Kerang (289km) on the Loddon River borders an area of wetlands where protected migratory ibis and other birds come to breed. Sir John Gorton, Australian Prime Minister 1968-71, was a former Shire councillor here.

Lake Charm (307km), **Mystic Park** (317km) and **Lake Boga** (330km) are no longer passenger stops but the lakes and features of this area are clearly visible from passing trains. Caravans fringe the water line and the lakes are popular holiday and recreational areas for swimming, boating and fishing, and on Lake Boga, water skiing, wind surfing and the like. During World War II Lake Boga was an RAAF flying-boat base. A restored Catalina commemorates those days.

Swan Hill (345km), population around 9000, is a major market centre for this part of the Murray River irrigation area. Its attractions include the recreated Pioneer Settlement on Horseshoe Bend which features the largest paddle steamer to operate on the Murray. River cruises at Swan Hill operate daily between 10.30 and 14.30. There are numerous restaurants, a military museum, and historic homesteads. ***Oasis Hotel*** (☎ 03-5032 2877 or Freecall ☎ 1800 658 380), 287 Campbell St, opposite the station, has motel rooms from $56. The former, popular Swan Hotel with its Irish Bar has been converted into a supermarket. Such is progress!

Bendigo to Echuca [Map 29]

Leaving the Swan Hill line at North Bendigo Junction, the rail route to Echuca is almost straight and not far from level. It descends very gradually from over 200m to less than 100m in 86km, a mean gradient of about 1 in 1000. Despite such easy conditions, the average speed is markedly lower than the preceding run to Bendigo, possibly because the track saw no passenger trains for nearly 20 years from 1978.

Elmore (207km from Melbourne) and **Rochester** (223km) are the only intermediate stops before Echuca. At both places the town centre, pubs, banks and shops are opposite the railway station.

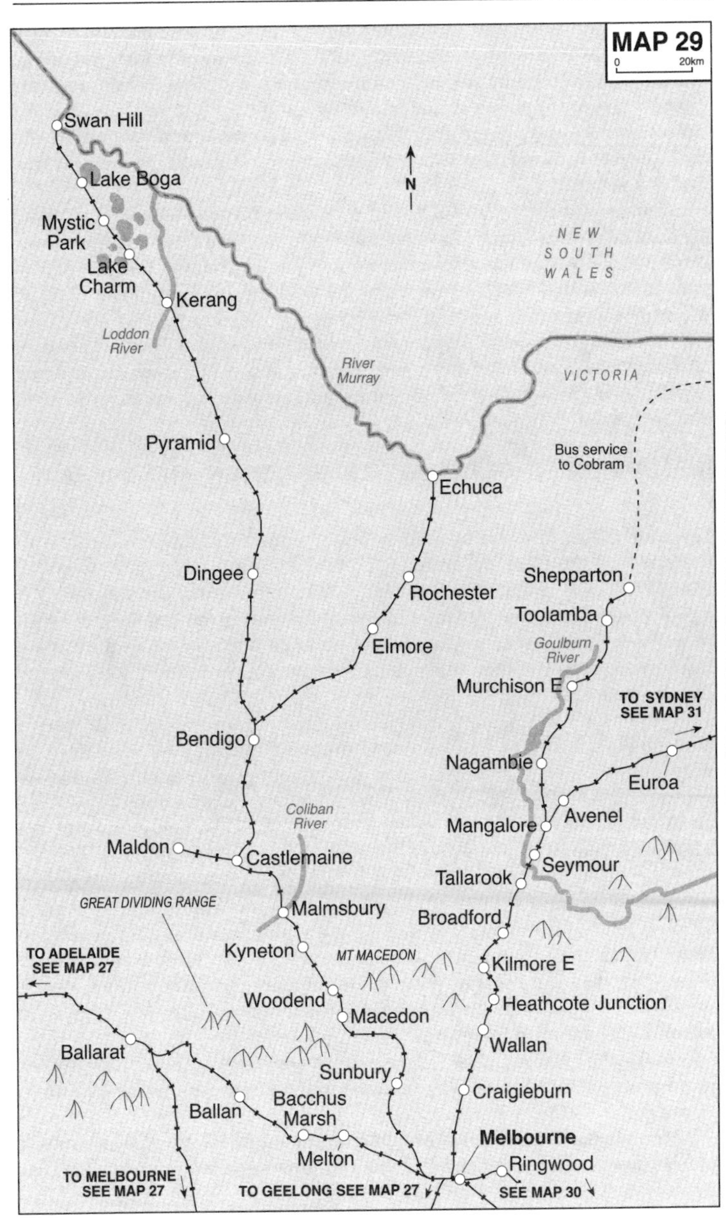
MAP 29
0
20km
N
Swan Hill
Lake Boga
Mystic Park
Lake Charm
Kerang
Loddon River
River Murray
NEW SOUTH WALES
VICTORIA
Pyramid
Echuca
Bus service to Cobram
Dingee
Rochester
Shepparton
Toolamba
Elmore
Goulburn River
Murchison E
TO SYDNEY SEE MAP 31
Bendigo
Nagambie
Euroa
Coliban River
Avenel
Mangalore
Maldon
Castlemaine
Seymour
Tallarook
GREAT DIVIDING RANGE
Malmsbury
Broadford
Kyneton
MT MACEDON
Kilmore E
TO ADELAIDE SEE MAP 27
Woodend
Heathcote Junction
Macedon
Wallan
Ballarat
Sunbury
Craigieburn
Ballan
Bacchus Marsh
Melbourne
Melton
Ringwood
TO MELBOURNE SEE MAP 27
TO GEELONG SEE MAP 27
SEE MAP 30

Echuca (233km) was the location for the TV series *All the Rivers Run*. Established as a working steam port in 1865, Echuca was the first port on the Murray to be reached by rail and is full of history. Numerous hotels, souvenir shops, wine-tasting places etc are in and around the historic port area. See the old wharves of massive red gum logs, the historic buildings, and the art and craft shop. You could also take a river cruise on a paddle steamer or visit Tisdall's winery.

Pastoral Hotel (☎ 03-5482 1812), with motel accommodation, is opposite the railway station, which is a short walk from the town centre and port area, passing the visitor information centre on the way. The railway formerly shared right of way with the road across the bridge to Moama and Deniliquin in NSW, where passenger trains used to go.

Since the reintroduction of passenger trains, Echuca has had services only on Friday and Sunday but this could improve. Meanwhile there are bus connections to Echuca from Bendigo and from Murchison East on the rail line to Shepparton.

(MELBOURNE TO) SEYMOUR TO SHEPPARTON (AND COBRAM) [Map 29]

Seymour (99km from Melbourne on the Victorian broad-gauge route through Essendon) is the effective junction for the Goulburn Valley line (C 9026), though the actual rail junction is at **Mangalore**, 10km further north. Seymour is a good place for a break of journey, the station adjoining the middle of the main street, with shops, pubs, accommodation etc right opposite. Cross the railway line by the subway at the south end of the platform so that you don't get run over by the train!

Nagambie (126km) adjoins the lake of that name, one of five in this part of the Goulburn Valley, rich in fauna and flora and catering to a wide range of water activities. Among the attractions of this area are several wineries, including some of Australia's best known. The railway station is on the edge of town, about 700m from the Central Business District (CBD) which is itself on the edge of the lake.

Murchison, on the Goulburn river, was established in 1840 and is the oldest town in the region. In 1969 an unusual meteorite with a cell-like organic structure crashed in fragments around the town. Murchison has another claim to fame, boasting the largest plane tree in the world. The River Bank Gardens, Strawberry Farm, Longleat Winery and ***Gallery Tea Rooms*** are among Murchison's other attractions for the visitor. The station (147km) is at **Murchison East**, 2km from town.

Toolamba (166km) is no longer a passenger station but was formerly the junction for the Murchison–Echuca line on which passenger services were withdrawn in the 1980s.

Mooroopna, 26km north of Murchison East, might be regarded as a suburb of Shepparton. This is the heart of the fruit-growing area. The Ardmona cannery, a name well known in Australia for tinned fruit, adjoins the railway station just south of the town centre.

Shepparton (182km) is home of the Shepparton Preserving Company (SPC) and famed for its SPC tinned fruit. This is also a vegetable growing area and the major city of the Goulburn Valley. The Visitors Centre (☎ 03-5831 4400 or 1800 808 839, 🖹 5822 2311) is at Victoria Park Lake, Wyndham St.

Cobram is about an hour's ride by coach from Shepparton and, if on a day trip from Melbourne, an interesting alternative to spending several hours in Shepparton. The coach passes Numurkah and Strathmerton en route. At Cobram, ***Cobram Hotel***, on the corner of Main St and Station St, opposite the station, offers a good Chinese counter lunch and the chance of friendly conversation with the locals, many of them ex-railway workers.

MELBOURNE TO SALE AND BAIRNSDALE (GIPPSLAND LINE)

[See map p137 and Map 30]

The first stop from Melbourne's Spencer St on the Gippsland line (C 9030) is **Flinders St** (1.2km), for long the main hub of the suburban rail network. Gippsland trains call here to pick up only, as they do also at **Caulfield** (12km) and **Dandenong** (31km); the latter is an industrial suburb bearing little relationship to the Dandenong Ranges, 18km to the north.

Pakenham (58km) is the terminus of the suburban system. Among interesting places between here and the next major station, Warragul, are Nar-Nar-Goon (66km), believed to be an Aboriginal word for the koala, Garfield (75km), named not after the cartoon cat but an American president who was murdered, and **Bunyip** (79km), on the river of that name. Bunyip is the name of a legendary water-dwelling, man-eating monster believed to have inhabited the area. After Bunyip comes Longwarry (83km), then **Drouin** (92km), a

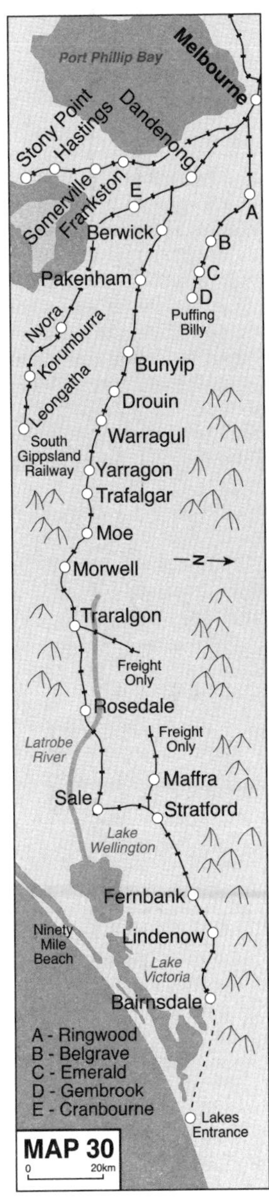

major centre for locally-produced gourmet foods and site of one of the largest milk-processing plants in Australia.

Between Longwarry and Warragul gradients of up to 1 in 50 flank the summit of this otherwise fairly level route. Recognizable by the way the 'down' and 'up' lines diverge just after Drouin station, the 'down' track reaches 19m higher than the 'up', at 167m above sea level.

Warragul (100km) is a major station, once the junction for a branch up into the hills of the Dividing Range. For decades after the branch line closed in 1958 a board on the station announced 'Change here for the Noojee line'.

The major towns in the Latrobe Valley in Gippsland are Moe, Morwell, and Traralgon. **Moe** (130km) is the main residential centre for the brown coal-mining area, where the site of a former town, Yallourn, was 'resumed' for coal mining. Moe is also the junction for the former narrow-gauge Moe–Walhalla branch, part of which has been restored (see p263). ***Moe Hotel*** adjoins the station.

Morwell (144km), a centre for the dairying industry, is best known for its open-cut mine, formerly producing around 15 million tonnes of coal annually, and the group of power stations including the largest in Victoria. Morwell power station was also a briquette factory; coal briquettes were one of the principal traffics on the railway for many years, but coal is no longer the economic base of the area and the factory branch is closed, the power stations moving to alternative fuel sources.

Traralgon (158km) is an industrial town but with a pleasant and quiet main street near the railway station. It is the junction for the freight-only line through Maffra to Bairnsdale in East Gippsland.

Rosedale (180km) on the Latrobe River is a quiet, pleasant town; it is the gateway to Holey Plains State Park and the last station before the former dead-end terminus, now replaced by a new station at Sale (207km). **Sale** is the administrative centre for Bass Strait oil, which is treated and stabilized at nearby Longford. It is also a gateway to the Gippsland Lakes and Victoria's Ninety Mile Beach stretching from Seaspray to beyond Lakes Entrance.

At Sale the line turns north to Stratford, then east again.

Stratford (222km) is where the direct line from Traralgon is joined by the route via Sale just short of Stratford station. After leaving Stratford the route now starts to climb and after briefly descending to cross Sandy and Paisley Creeks, climbs again to **Fernbank** (246km) before descending through **Lindenow** and **Hillside** to Bairnsdale (274km). The undulations are barely noticeable as the line is mostly straight. You may spot some wildlife as the route crosses the Macleod Morass Game Reserve.

Bairnsdale is a pleasant town, close to Lake Victoria and only 34km by road from Lakes Entrance. V/Line coaches connect to Lakes Entrance and to Orbost further east. Try the ***Grand Terminus Hote***l (☎ 03-5152 4040) near the station if staying in Bairnsdale.

Melbourne to Sydney and branches

MELBOURNE TO BENALLA [See map p136 and Maps 29 and 31]

The broad-gauge and standard-gauge lines follow different routes for the first half-hour of the journey north from Melbourne. The shortest route is the broad-gauge line through Essendon (10km) used by V/Line and Met services. The standard-gauge line, after swinging over the Essendon route on a flyover in the first two kilometres, runs west to Sunshine where a platform allowed connection with The Overland from Adelaide in its broad-gauge days.

Just beyond Sunshine at Albion (14km) the new route swings east to cross the Essendon route by another flyover south of Broadmeadows (17km via Essendon, 28km via Sunshine). In Assisted Passage days migrants arriving at Port Melbourne were first taken to an army camp at Broadmeadows via a short spur line just north of the station. Tullamarine Airport is close by to the west. North from Broadmeadows the two lines run more or less parallel but with fewer platforms serving the newer standard-gauge line.

Suburban (Met) services terminate at Broadmeadows. V/Line outer urban trains run as far as Seymour (99km via Essendon) serving up to eight further stations as the line climbs through the tail end of the Great Dividing Range. The summit of 349m is reached 5km after **Wallan** (47km) at **Heathcote Junction**; the 60km branch to Heathcote itself closed in 1968.

Further on as the line descends towards the Goulburn Valley is **Tallarook** where a former branch led east beside the Goulburn River into the hills around Lake Eildon, serving the townships of Yea, Alexandra and Mansfield. The first named of these was the site of the long-running Australian TV series *Bellbird* which occasionally featured a railcar at Yea station (renamed Bellbird for the occasion).

Comments on Seymour have already been made (see p206); it is a stopping place for all the broad-gauge trains. There is a platform for the standard gauge but this is used only in an emergency.

The next stop for some V/Line trains is **Avenel** (116km), named after a village in Gloucestershire, England, and the town where bushranger Edward (Ned) Kelly went to school.

All V/Line trains then call at **Euroa** (151km), a small town in a pastoral area around Seven Creeks, famed as the place where the Kelly gang successfully raided a bank in 1878.

Most V/Line trains stop at **Violet Town**, 169km, which is more a village than a town with a population of only 590. In season, fresh blueberries are plentiful here.

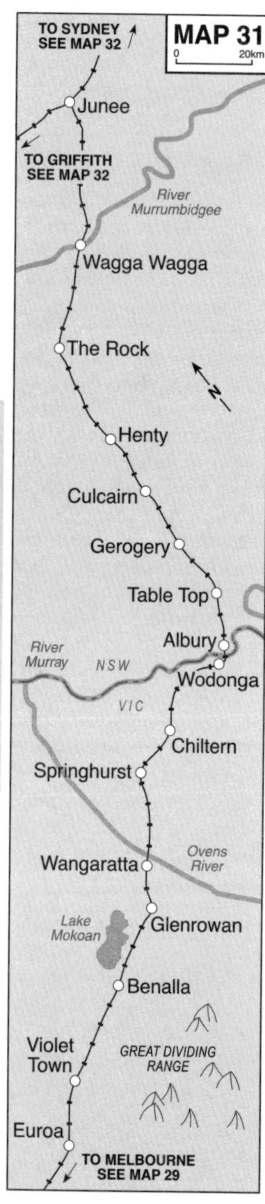

Seymour, Benalla and Wangaratta are gateways to the Goulburn Valley on the west and the mountains (the Victorian Alps) on the east. The valley can be reached by train from Seymour (p206) or bus from Benalla but the Alps only by bus or hired transport.

Benalla (195km) is a major stop, being formerly a junction for a connecting line through Yarrawonga on the River Murray to Oaklands in NSW. The standard-gauge line has a short platform down in a cutting just east of the station forecourt – not easy to find if you do not know where it is and the quiet XPT may not even be heard approaching until it arrives. So if breaking a journey here, be in good time for the connection.

The town centre of Benalla, with a bakery, eating places, banks, a well-stocked second-hand bookshop, and Benalla Gardens Park adjoining Lake Benalla on Broken River, is about 500 metres east of the station. Opposite the station is ***Victoria Hotel*** (☎ 03-5762 2045 or 5762 1233) and 100m or so down the road to the right is ***North-Eastern Hotel*** (☎ 03-5762 3252), with excellent food and motel-style accommodation at very modest rates.

BENALLA TO ALBURY/WODONGA [Map 31]

Most of the way from Benalla to the state border the railway appears to be double track, but in fact it consists of two single parallel lines, broad gauge on the left, standard on the right; it is flanked by the Hume Highway. Lake Mokoan is the large watery swamp on the west just north of Benalla.

Between Benalla and Wangaratta it has been known for the train to be held up by a character with an upturned bucket covering his head and armed with pistols; this might have been for real long ago but any such events in recent years have only been re-enactments – for example at **Glenrowan**, famous in Australian history as the haunt of bushranger Ned Kelly; trains no longer stop nor are passengers robbed at gunpoint. To visit Glenrowan two connecting bus services operate to and from Wangaratta on Wednesdays only. A V/Line Melbourne to Albury bus also calls there at 17.10 on Fridays (local timetable).

Wangaratta, on the Ovens River, has a standard-gauge platform somewhat hidden like that at Benalla, and the town is similarly slightly distanced from the railway. Also like Benalla it has a ***North-Eastern Hotel*** (☎ 03-5721 3741) near the station. The town's economy is dominated by textiles, two woollen mills being the main source of employment. The branch railway to Myrtleford and Bright up in the Victorian Alps no longer exists but V/Line coaches connect with trains daily and a 1½ to 2½-hour trip can have the visitor within striking distance of Mt Buffalo or Mt Bogong in the heart of the Great Dividing Range.

Chiltern, 31km beyond Wangaratta, is a quiet remnant of a once-thriving gold-rush town.

The 'Twin Town' of Albury/Wodonga is the largest urban centre on Australia's mightiest river, the Murray, and was nominated a planned growth centre in the 1970s. Here the Victorian railway meets up with the NSW system. In years past passengers had to change trains, usually in the early hours of the morning. All trains on the standard gauge now run right through, but you can break the journey at Albury by taking a V/Line intercity service for the Melbourne–Albury section and the NSW XPT between Albury and Sydney. But note – Austrail Flexipasses are not valid on V/Line. If you also have a V/Line Victoria pass you are covered. **Wodonga** has its own railway station; 3km further on the line crosses the river and border for the last kilometre into Albury on the NSW side.

Albury is 307km from Melbourne by V/Line, 318km on standard gauge via Sunshine and 646km from Sydney, although the latter depends not only on which route is followed through Sydney's suburbs but on whether the 'up' or 'down' line is followed. The former, from Albury to Sydney, is 3km shorter than the down line. This shows how kilometre posts on the lineside can be rather misleading.

Albury is a centre for tours of the historical gold towns, river centres, wineries, and the snowfields of north-eastern Victoria. Attractions include Albury's fine railway station, Hume Weir (for trout fishing), historic Beechworth and Yackandandah, and the many wineries around Rutherglen. There is a free bus tour of Albury/Wodonga and coach tours operate to the surrounding places of interest.

Ettamogah

A magazine, *Australia Post,* featured a cartoon about the goings-on around a ramshackle bush pub called Ettamogah; a real-life replica may be seen at Ettamogah, a former station 9km north of Albury. The name is alleged to be Aboriginal for 'let's have a drink'. Copies of the same crazy building (drinks can be obtained at all) are found in other places in Australia.

ALBURY/WODONGA TO JUNEE [Map 31]

Culcairn enjoys Australia's largest artesian water supply and is also shire capital of what is often called Morgan Country, another example of the grudging respect still held in Australia for bushrangers of the past among whom Mad Dan Morgan was one of the most notorious and brutal. The heritage-classified ***Culcairn Hotel*** (☎ 02-6029 8501) adjoins Culcairn railway station.

At **Henty** note the curiously-named ***Doodle Cooma Arms Hotel*** (☎ 02-6929 3013) adjoining the station; Doodle Cooma was Henty's original name but it was changed to avoid confusion with Cooma in the Snowy Mountains. Henty has a memorial to Sergeant Smythe, a policeman shot and killed by Mad Dog Morgan just west of the town in 1864.

The Rock is a small township named after a 360m-high rocky outcrop which stands above the surrounding plain about one to two kilometres west of the railway approaching the station. Originally called Hanging Rock, its name was changed to avoid confusion (see p203); the rock itself is a nature reserve and a popular recreation area.

Wagga Wagga is part of the Riverina agricultural area and the largest inland city in NSW with a population around 40,000. It boasts Australia's only inland surf lifesaving club beside its beach on the Murrumbidgee River and is also known for Charles Sturt University which has its own winery and a viticulture course in its curriculum. The station is handy for hotels and restaurants, being at the southern end of Bayliss St, the main street. The city's name is usually shortened to Wagga, pronounced Wogga; Wagga means crow in Aboriginal language and there are many crows in the area. Wagga is also a major air force and military base.

Immediately north of Wagga station the railway crosses a series of six viaducts over the river. After passing the now abandoned stations of Bomen and Harefield the line reaches **Junee**, an important junction and railway town past and present.

The town centre with hotels and shops is just outside the station. There is a railway refreshment room with a tourist information centre. The railway roundhouse with 47 repair bays and a large turntable is to the left of the line on the

A record-breaking line

Between Albury and Wagga Wagga are racetrack sections of line where the former Riverina XPT twice broke the Australian train speed record; in 1981 at 183km/h and again on 18 September 1992 when it reached 193km/h, since surpassed by the QR electric tilt train (see p111). For several years from 1985, when the XPT regularly stopped at the intermediate stations of Culcairn, Henty and The Rock, Australia held a place in the *Railway Gazette* World Speed League (p111). The normal running speeds on this part of the route were 110 to 160km/h yet only a few years earlier trains had to slow down to exchange 'tokens' between sections.

These stations are all now mere request stops.

Junee – from the foreword to *Traincatcher*

'Recently I did one of my Sunday morning programs at the town of Junee, in of all places, the railway refreshment rooms. The RRRs are still there, but the local baker now runs the rooms, not to service the trains, but for the people of Junee.

I was reminded of the glory of the age of steam, and the days of rail. Families came to town on Saturday night to watch the trains come and go – The Albury Mail, The Riverina Express and many others. You could stay at the Hotel, upstairs from the refreshment rooms.

Yes, Junee was a Railway Town, and apart from the station it had the 'Roundhouse' where up to 150 men and apprentices – fitters, boiler makers – worked repairing the rolling stock.

While we were there (on the Saturday actually) an XPT whose brakes had jammed was pulled into a siding at Junee. The engine had a 'flat tyre' as it's called, a flat spot caused by the brakes jamming.

In the old days, that is up until 1993 when the 'Roundhouse' closed, that engine could have been repaired right there. Now all repairs, even the most basic like changing a fuse, have to go to Sydney. That XPT was towed at 20km/h to Sydney. And that's progress? No, that's stupidity.'

Ian McNamara of ABC Australia All Over in the foreword of *Traincatcher* by Colin Taylor. IPL Books, Sydney and Wellington, 1996.

'... the refreshment room at Junee ... Macca talked about that, and I have a little bit of empathy for that because my Dad was the stationmaster at Junee for many years in the days, the great old days of the railways when the refreshment rooms were open and you charged in off the train and spilt your coffee on the platform, trying to catch the train. It was blowing the whistle, with guys like Trevor Campbell up front driving – or his Dad, driving the train, and all those great days of yesteryear.'

Vince O'Rourke, Chief Executive of QR at the launch of *Traincatcher*, 16 April 1996 at Roma St Station, Brisbane

approach from the south. Although the roundhouse was closed in 1993 it has been partly re-opened for use by the private rail company Austrac and it remains a monument of industrial archaeology. It is also open daily (10.00-16.00, $6, $4 for concessions) except Monday and Friday as a museum. For further details phone ☎ 02-6924 2909 or visit their website 💻 www.rhta-junee.org.au/. ***The Locomotive Hotel*** (☎ 02-6924 1327) is, naturally, opposite the station.

Much of Junee's glory lies in the past, thanks to misguided economic rationalism but it is still important as a regional office for Freightcorp, as a train control centre and a crew changeover station. For many years it was one of the only stops (unadvertised because it was used for essential railway purposes only) on the supposedly non-stop Melbourne–Sydney Southern Aurora express. It is the junction where the once-weekly Griffith Xplorer turns to enter the branch line formerly served by 10 weekly trains including the Riverina Express.

JUNEE TO GRIFFITH [Map 32]

Branching from Junee, the train to Griffith first stops at **Coolamon** (37km from Junee), a delightful small town in turkey-breeding country. A general air of prosperity seems matched by the appearance of the freshly-painted station facing the main street, with its waiting room reopened in 1996 when the trains returned.

Not all the former stations have enjoyed the new lease of life experienced by Coolamon. Thirty-nine kilometres beyond Coolamon lies **Grong Grong**, yet another of those double-barrelled place names of Aboriginal origin.

Grong Grong is best known to motorists as the place where the adjoining Newell Highway from the Victorian border to Queensland makes a sharp 90° turn to the north.

Narrandera is one of the oldest settlements in the Riverina. First developed in the 1850s, it grew in importance 30 years later as the railways arrived, first from Melbourne, then from Sydney, adding to its strategic position as a river port.

More recent products of the area are goat mohair and ostriches (for meat, skin and feathers). Narrandera boasts a Royal Doulton fountain, of which there are only two worldwide.

Yanco is no longer a passenger station but remains a junction for the truncated Hay branch of the railway. **Leeton** is the administrative centre of the surrounding Murrumbidgee irrigation districts. Fruit and wine growing are important here; it is the home of the Letona tinned-fruit cannery and Quelch citrus-juice factory. Sheep's milk is another speciality.

Griffith, the largest centre in NSW west of Wagga, is regarded as the centre of Australia's wine and food country, the Riverina. Originally the home of the Wiradjuri tribe, it soon became the domain of squatters following in the wake of explorers Oxley and Sturt. Irrigation from the Murrumbidgee River since 1913 stimulated its growth and the original town plan was the work of American architect Walter Burley Griffin, well known as the designer of Canberra but perhaps less so as architect for a large number of incinerators in various parts of the country.

Italian migrants and their descendants give the area its justifiable reputation for good food and wine. There are plenty of wineries to visit and restaurants to enjoy the region's produce. The area produces 15% of Australia's wine and 90% of its rice as well as 70% of NSW's wine and citrus fruit.

Pioneer Park open-air museum is just over 1km north of the railway station; the station is right in the town centre one street north of the main street, Banna Avenue. The museum, which adjoins Rotary Lookout above the town, commemorates the life and times of early pioneers and is one among many attractions for the visitor. Accommodation ranges from luxury motel units to shearer's quarters at Pioneer Park. The information centre (☎ 02-6962 4145) is just 200m from the station.

JUNEE TO GOULBURN

[Maps 32 and 33]

Between Junee and Cootamundra watch out for the **Bethungra loop**, where the northbound line describes a complete circle to overcome the gradient while the line south follows a more direct route.

Cootamundra is the junction for a cross-country route to Parkes on the main west line from Sydney, sometimes used by interstate trains when engineering work or other factors affect the usual route. It is also a junction for other branches on which the passenger trains have been replaced by buses, such as Gundagai (famous for its dog on the tucker box and the song 'The Road to Gundagai') and Wyalong. It was Cootamundra's position as a main junction that turned it from a small village to an important town in the late 1800s. It is now a main rail/bus interchange. It even has a refreshment room and shop in the station where leaflets, maps and information on places of interest can be obtained, mostly free of charge.

Countrylink buses connect south to Tumut and Tumberumba (via Gundagai), east to Canberra and north to Cowra, Bathurst, Orange, Griffith and Condobolin. Hotels and other town centre features are within 200m of the station.

The ***Glebe Hotel*** (☎ 02-6942 1446), five minutes' walk straight out from the station, has rooms from $25 including continental breakfast. For a good pub lunch try the ***Railway Tavern***, a couple of blocks left on leaving the station.

A graceful wattle tree takes its name from Cootamundra, while a restored nursing home, now a museum, at 89 Adams St, commemorates the birth here of Australia's cricketing great, Sir Donald Bradman, in 1908. The Cootamundra Heritage Centre (☎ 02-6942 2456) is at the former Railway Barracks in Hovell St.

After Cootamundra, the Melbourne–Sydney mainline passes **Harden**, from where State Rail bus services replaced trains in 1983 on the former branch through the fruit country of Young and Cowra to the western mainline at

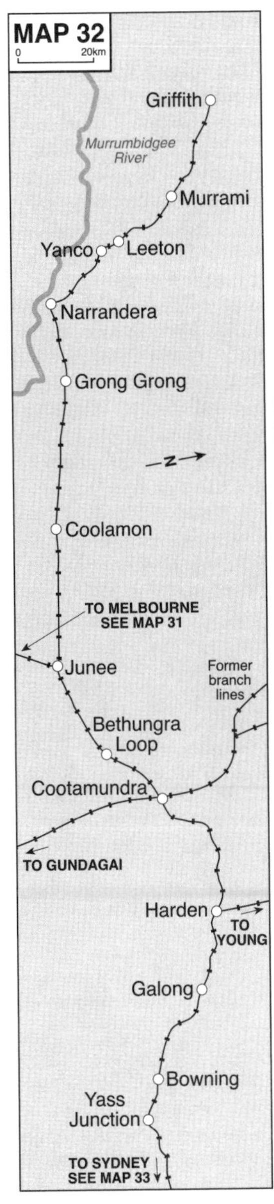

Blayney. For reasons known only to anonymous bureaucrats the connection has since been moved back to Cootamundra, making the bus journey longer. The town of Harden is seemingly inexplicably also known as Murrumburrah, but the Readers Digest *Illustrated Guide to Australian Places* gives a fascinating account of how it happened, largely to do with the coming of the railway in 1877.

Until late 2004, **Yass Junction** offered an alternative link to Canberra, for rail passengers from Victoria or the Riverina, by changing to a connecting Countrylink coach instead of continuing to the rail junction at Goulburn. Yass Town is a little over 3km away, the branch railway long disused. Although there are private buses between Yass and Canberra, Countrylink coaches no longer call at Yass station and passengers are expected to change at Cootamundra. The coaches do, however, stop at Harden in Albury Street which is only a couple of blocks from Harden station, but passengers contemplating this saving of bus travel should check carefully first.

Gunning, more a farming village than a town, is a request stop for the daylight Melbourne XPT. After leaving Gunning the track climbs steadily up through curves of down to 280m radius (14 chain) towards the former station of **Cullerin**, the highest point on the line at 256m, before descending more gradually through Breadalbane (also now closed) to the junction for Canberra.

Goulburn itself is a major regional centre with a visitor centre (☎ 02-4823 4492) and plenty of places to eat or stay within walking distance of the station; try ***Astor Hotel*** (☎ 02-4821 1155), on Clinton St, a block from the station, with single rooms at $55. If staying in Goulburn, the historic Waterworks Museum

Goulburn to Canberra [Map 33]

At Goulburn (or more accurately at Joppa Junction 6km earlier coming from the south) the line for Canberra and the Southern Highlands branches from the main south line. Goulburn is an important railway centre and terminus for CityRail's interurban Endeavour services from Sydney. It is also served by Countrylink Xplorer trains to Canberra. Goulburn began life as a garrison town for guarding convicts: it has since become an important farming and pastoral centre. Its several claims to fame include being the last town in the British Empire to become a city through Royal Letters Patent and having the only pre-Federation brewery still operating.

Features of the Canberra route include **Lake Bathurst**, on the east near the first stop, **Tarago**, the much larger but frequently dried up **Lake George** on the west approaching **Bungendore** and the scenic Molonglo Gorge, on the right after Bungendore. The former Canberra–Monaro Express divided at **Queanbeyan**, the main part continuing south to Cooma on the edge of the Snowy Mountains.

Cooma and places further south are now served by Countrylink coaches from Canberra station. Queanbeyan town centre, unlike that of Canberra, is close to the station, making it a handy base for exploration of the region including the Federal Capital itself. Queanbeyan is in NSW; so is Canberra geographically but not politically, being in a separate enclave known as the ACT (Australian Capital Territory). See p164 for places to stay in Queanbeyan, and p259 for details of Michelago Tourist Railway.

Canberra, the end of the line, is Australia's national capital, although Sydney is the largest urban area and Melbourne was the original capital in 1901 at federation. Notes on what to see and do in Canberra are in Part 4, pp163-4.

(☎ 02-4823 4462, 🖳 museums@goulburn.nsw.gov.au) with its steam beam engine is worth a visit – it is usually open at the weekend.

GOULBURN TO SYDNEY [Map 33 and map pp126-7]

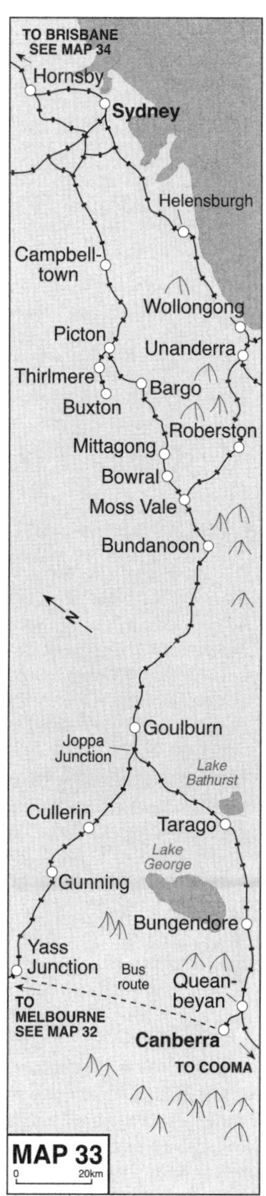

Goulburn Gaol is conspicuous on the left as you leave the city for Sydney. After Goulburn the main line descends from the Southern Highlands through Bundanoon, Moss Vale and Bowral, pleasant little destinations for a day trip from Sydney or a break of journey. The XPT stops only at Moss Vale but the Canberra and Griffith Xplorer trains stop conditionally at the others. At **Bundanoon**, ***Bundanoon Hotel*** (☎ 02-4883 6005) has a well-deserved reputation, reasonably-priced accommodation, first-class meals and well-stocked bars. In the Morton National Park nearby is a feature locally called The Grand Canyon, where lookout points give views over the deep gorges and sandstone outcrops.

Bus connections from here provide a link to the Illawarra district at Wollongong (see p128).

Moss Vale, junction for the scenic line through the mountains down to Wollongong, now traversed only by special tours of 3801 Limited (see p255), is still connected by Countrylink buses to the coast. It is the main regional centre and the station is conveniently located just off the main street. ***Moss Vale Hotel*** (☎ 02-4868 1007), opposite, has accommodation.

Bowral, another busy little centre is next, with shops, café, and ***Grand Hotel*** (☎ 02-4861 4833) just up the road from the station. Five kilometres further on at **Mittagong**, look out on the left of the track for the original line of the Great Southern Railway of 1867 which descends from the highlands more directly than the present mainline built in 1919. The former line proved too steep for most trains (1 in 30 as against 1 in 75 maximum for the new line). NSW Rail Transport Museum at Thirlmere (see p259) operates trains on part of this old route from the southern end at **Picton**. A loop bus service links Bowral and Mittagong with Thirlmere and Picton.

Campbelltown, a modern planned new town, marks the beginning of the greater Sydney area and from here on in (or rather from Macarthur, a more recent purely suburban station 2km south), the line is shared by electric multiple-unit trains of various shapes but all double deck.

Trains into Sydney from Campbelltown can and do follow different routes, The newest and shortest is via East Hills, used by Cityrail trains from Goulburn. Other routes are via Sefton Park Junction, the most usual in recent years for Countrylink services, or via Granville, the longest. By either of the older routes, a stop may be made at Strathfield, making connections with trains to or from the north and west possible.

Notes on 'the big smoke' (an affectionate if rather derogatory name for Sydney) appear on pp120-31.

Sydney to northern NSW and Brisbane

SYDNEY TO NEWCASTLE/MAITLAND [see map pp126-7 and Map 34]

(Distances given are from Sydney via Strathfield)
Climbing north out of Strathfield in Sydney's western suburbs and once clear of the northern suburbs beyond **Hornsby** (30 minutes after leaving Sydney), the trains follow the edge of Ku-ring-gai Chase National Park (on the right) through Berowra and **Cowan**, then descend steeply through the Boronia tunnels until the waters of the Hawkesbury River come into view (on the left and right as you cross the bridge). Delightful forest and lake scenery of Brisbane Water National Park flank the line (mostly on the right) from **Hawkesbury River** (57km) to **Gosford** (81km), a useful turning point for a day trip. Just north of the bridge over the Hawkesbury the line curves along the west shore of Mullet Creek. For many years the old lady who lived in a small cottage between the railway and the water waved to the passing train. The Woy Woy tunnel which follows, 13km south of Gosford, will be of interest to rail fans. Look out for the oyster beds in the waters of this area (and try some in a local restaurant when you return to Sydney!). Oysters are a favourite seafood and are plentiful on Australia's eastern seaboard.

Some surprisingly fast running will be experienced on the far from straight track north from Gosford through **Wyong** and **Morisset**.

Broadmeadow (two hours from Sydney) is the junction for Newcastle, a coal port and the birthplace of Australia's railways (see p103). This is the gateway to Hunter Valley, one of Australia's premier wine regions west of Maitland. Perhaps incongruously, coal is also a feature of Hunter Valley, particularly around Newcastle and Maitland, and heavy coal trains can be observed on the freight lines parallelling the route between Broadmeadow and Maitland.

Here also is one of the straightest and fastest parts of the main North Coast line, on which the XPT will quickly achieve and maintain its permitted maximum of 160km/h; at one time the train conductor would proudly announce 'The train is now travelling at 100 miles an hour'. Slow to fully adapt to metric measurement, everyone on board understood but the news appeared to frighten some older passengers and the practice ceased.

Newcastle, terminus of the electric interurban services from Sydney, is a coal town, but has maritime, local history and shell museums as well as an art gallery.

Nearby **Hamilton**, first stop on the spur line to Newcastle and where you change trains for the locals to Maitland, is an attractive place for a break of journey, being regarded as Newcastle's 'Sunset Strip' or 'Bondi', a major night activity spot offering an impressive selection of good, mostly ethnic, restaurants as well as cheap hotel accommodation all within a stone's throw of the railway station. A 'Pubstay' hotel in the main street is ***Northern Star Hotel*** (☎ 02-4961 1087).

Maitland, 31km west of Newcastle and 193km from Sydney, is a historic town with a thriving city centre just north of the station. Visit the Grossman House Historical Museum, just past the pubs north of the station forecourt.

There are several Pubstay hotels on High St, a kilometre's walk north from the station. Contact the Information Centre (☎ 02-4933 26611) on the corner of New England Highway and High St for information about the city and its heritage. ***Grand Junction Hotel*** (☎ 02-4933 5242) is right opposite the station and offers comfortable accommodation with shared facilities at rock-bottom prices.

From Maitland you might then afford to take a taxi to the Pokolbin wine district, 31km away. Alternatively, there is a bus service to Kurri and Cessnock (see p220).

North Coast and Tableland trains go direct to Maitland from Sydney and the Brisbane XPT

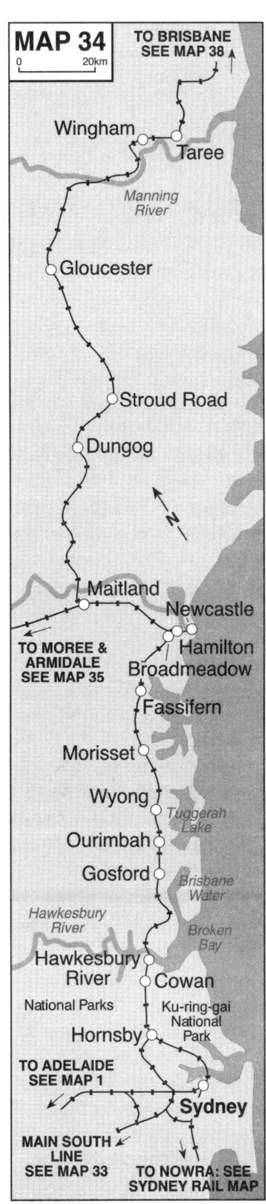

leaves there at 19.09 so make sure you book a taxi for the journey back to Maitland Station from Pokolbin if you are continuing north.

The Hunter Valley wine-growing area is also served by the stations at Branxton, Singleton and Muswellbrook, reached by CityRail local services on the Hunter Valley route or by Countrylink Tableland Xplorers, branching from the North Coast line just beyond Maitland.

MAITLAND TO WERRIS CREEK (218km) [Map 35]

Branxton, just east of Singleton, is the nearest station for the Pokolbin vineyard district but the local train service is vestigial and there are no reasonable connections with buses. Cessnock is the major centre but passenger trains ceased running there over 20 years ago. However, there are regular buses to Kurri and Cessnock from Maitland station by Rover Motors (☎ 02-4990 1699) which make even a day-return trip possible.

Most big names in Australian wine are in this area, between Rothbury and Bellbird, 10 to 16km south of the railway. Most wineries are open every day of the week. There are holiday cabins, a wine village and motel-type units where, if in a hired car, you can stay the night to sober up before going back to the train. Whether visiting the Hunter vineyards by taxi, hired car or public transport, an overnight stop is recommended since rail and bus schedules are not conducive to a quick visit. See p258 for details of Hunter Valley Railway Museum.

Singleton, where the railway crosses the Hunter River, has a long history being one of the oldest towns in the state and with a varied economic base: vegetable and fruit growing, viticulture, timber milling, an army base and tourism all contributing. The railway station itself is one of particular interest while the giant Liddell power station with its 132m-high cooling towers and 10km-long conveyor belt is a reminder that Singleton is the state's main producer of opencast coal.

Muswellbrook is 96km beyond Maitland. The town centre is just north of Muswellbrook station on the New England Highway. This is a good centre for visiting the wineries of the Upper Hunter Valley, of which the nearest, Queldinburg, open daily, is less than 2km away, and there are pubs with accommodation immediately opposite the station. Muswellbrook has a colourful display of jacarandas in bloom in the last two months of the year. It is the junction for a freight and mineral line inland to Gulgong.

A further 26km brings the train to **Scone**, a town associated with horses and noted for breeding because of the many studs in the area. There is a Thoroughbred Carnival in May, a Polo Carnival in July and a Bushmans Carnival in November. The early European settlers were Scots, hence the name from the original crowning place of Scottish kings. Scone is the current limit of the Hunter Valley local Endeavour diesel train services.

Some 17km north of Scone, on the right you should see **Mt Wingen**, the burning mountain, in which a coal seam well below the surface has been burning for thousands of years. Wingen station no longer exists but here the uphill gradient steepens as the line climbs through Murulla towards **Murrurundi**, which lies in a narrow valley in the Liverpool Range. Like many places inland from Australia's east coast Murrurundi's growth was spurred on in the 19th century when for a time it was the railhead. Bushranger Ben Hall spent his childhood here.

A further steepening of the gradient with many twists and turns brings the line to the summit of this section at **Ardglen**, 632m above sea level, just after the short Ardglen tunnel through the Liverpool Range.

Willow Tree is the next station after a downhill run of 12km and then comes **Quirindi**: the origin of the name and its original spelling are matters of debate. Like Muswellbrook, Quirindi has hotels and pubs opposite the station and a wealth of jacaranda trees.

Werris Creek is a railway junction where the Tableland Xplorer divides, the front half going north-west to Moree and the rear north to Armidale. Another branch, freight and grain only, goes 190km west to Merrygoen. The station is heritage listed, and on the remnant of a loop line south-west of the station may be seen what appears to be a locomotive graveyard.

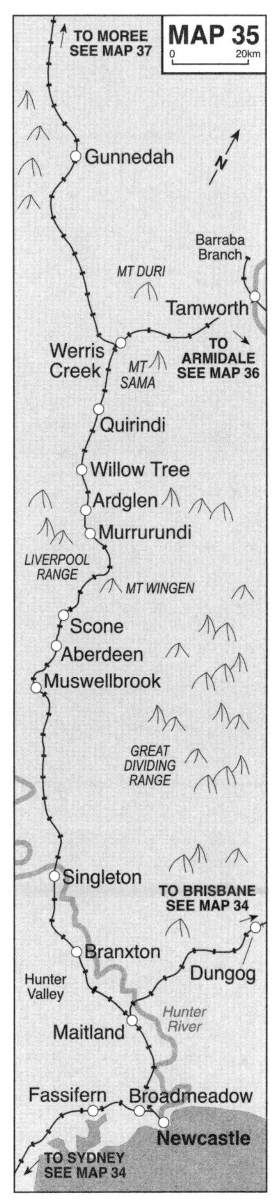

WERRIS CREEK TO ARMIDALE

[Maps 35 and 36]

Tamworth, 455km from Sydney, is famous for its country music festival held over 11 days in January. Historic buildings, galleries, friendly family pubs and surrounding bush walks are other features. ***Tamworth Hotel*** (☎ 02-6766 2923) is opposite the station, or call the Information Centre (☎ 02-6755 4300).

After the small station of **Kootingal** the track goes along the west side of the attractive valley of the Cockburn River, climbing steeply after about 13km through successive curves to cross the Moonbi Range near **Walcha Road**. This is the station without a town; there is nowhere to go without transport. The town is

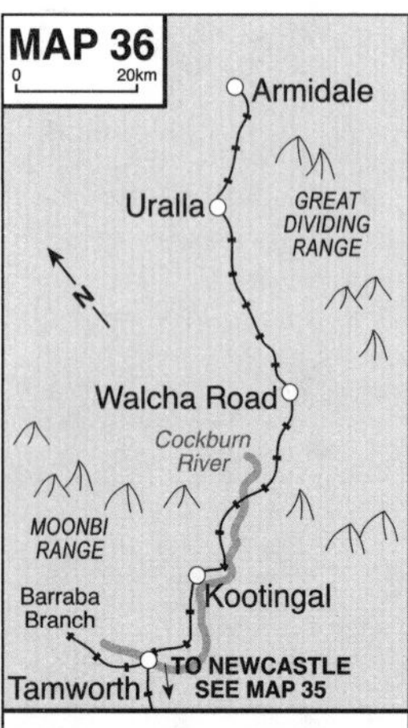

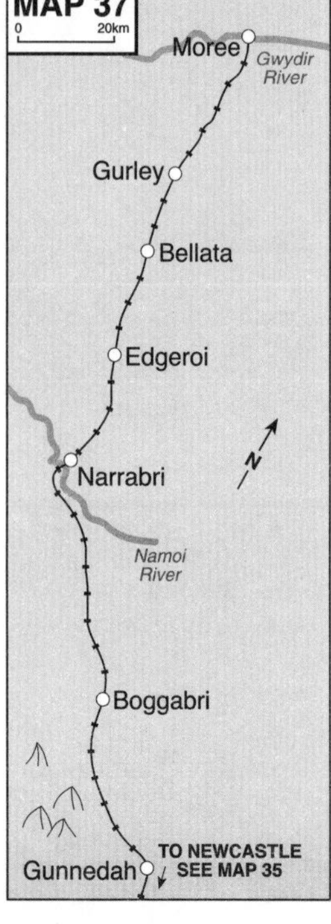

20km to the east on the other side of the Great Dividing Range. However, Walcha Taxis have a service which meets the train. The 1106m line summit is 15km beyond Walcha Road where the line crosses to the eastern side of the range. Pleasant rolling country heralds the approach to Armidale from the south.

Uralla, the last intermediate stop was the final resting place of the bushranger, Thunderbolt.

Armidale holds a people's market in the mall on the last Sunday of each month. Worth visiting too is the Folk Museum on Faulkner St. Follow Barney St east from the station to reach the town centre but it is a long way: to reach most of the hotels in Armidale it is worth taking a taxi. ***Wicklow Hotel*** (☎ 02-6772 2421, close to Beardy St Mall in the town centre) has comfortable rooms at budget price, making the taxi ride affordable. Armidale Visitors' Centre (☎ 1800-627736) is nearby at 82 Marsh St.

On returning south by train, be in the buffet car early for breakfast, particularly if you want a bacon sandwich because they are very popular.

WERRIS CREEK TO MOREE [Maps 35 and 37]

Gunnedah, **Boggabri**, **Narrabri** and Bellata are the main stations on this route. These, and others (ie Edgeroi and Gurley) no longer open, are marked by grain silos: wheat is a major crop and Gunnedah is one of the largest centres in Australia for wheat and stock sales.

From here the line follows the Namoi River, with the Nandewar Range away to the east after Boggabri. Narrabri is the junction for the line to Walgett, mainly used by wheat trains.

At **Moree** on the Gwydir River there are hotels close to the station: ***Moree Hotel*** and the ***Royal Hotel Motel*** are both Pubstay (💻 www.pubstay.org.au) hotels. Take your swimming togs (cozzie, bathers): no visitor to Moree should miss an early morning bathe in the spa pool just a block or two away from the station.

Why the railway?

Prior to Federation there was no greater achievement for the local member for a bush electorate than to get a railway line – or two or three – cutting across his constituency. And they tried and vied with all their might.

It's not hard to see why railways were so popular. The same year as the decision to extend the line to Werris Creek was made, the Hon Thomas Dangar, on his way to Sydney to that very session of parliament, had to cross the Breeza Plains by coach.

It was a foul autumn night, raining fiercely, and the road was an interminable bog. The horses knocked up time and time again. As they floundered across the plain, the wind strengthened to gale force and eventually the horses lost their footing, breaking the pole and releasing the team from the coach.

Armed with lamps and tomahawks, Mr Dangar and the driver searched for a sapling to repair the broken pole, while the other passengers searched in the dark for the horses.

Cold, wet, mud splattered, bedraggled and far too late to catch the train, the travellers arrived at the railhead – then at Willow Tree.

Such a journey was not uncommon and the mania for the railway had its roots in people's experience of the alternatives.

Rail was not just quicker, it was far quicker. It was not just cheaper but immensely cheaper. Not just safer and more comfortable but unbelievably so.

And rail was the great technological wonder of the age. It was fashionable to be fascinated by railways.

From *Werris Creek railway station Conservation Management plan* by J Carr and J Perry, published in *This Month in New England Country* in December 1999 and reproduced here by kind permission of This Month Publications Pty Ltd.

Moree water comes from underground, the Great Artesian Basin. The song *We are Australian* featured by The Seekers refers to 'the black soil of the plain': Moree is in the middle of it, one of the most fertile areas in the country. Cotton has in recent years overtaken wheat and wool as the major product of the region.

THE NORTH COAST ROUTE (MAITLAND TO BRISBANE)

Maitland to Casino [Maps 34, 38 and 39]

(Distances given are from Sydney)

After **Maitland**, 193km, a good place to break the journey for a night-stop, the North Coast line swings away from the valley and curves northwards among bush-covered hills past **Dungog** (245km) and **Stroud Rd** (267km) to **Gloucester** (309km) from whence it follows the attractive river valley through **Wingham** (367km) to Taree.

Taree (379km), on the Manning River, is the connecting point for a Countrylink bus service on an alternative route from Newcastle via the coast and Great Lakes district. It is a convenient place for a break of journey (see Itineraries 1, 2 and 4, pp65-71). A Pubstay hotel ***Exchange Hotel*** (☎ 02-6552 1160), 154 Victoria St, is a 10-minute walk from the station; single rooms cost

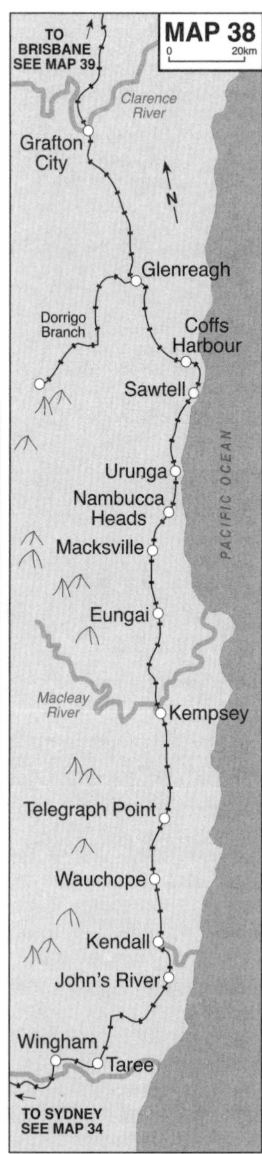

under $30. There are other hotels in the same locality. An old signal gantry in the station forecourt will interest enthusiasts.

On the right of the track, if travelling in daytime, you should catch glimpses of the coastal lakes north of the abandoned station of **Johns River** just before the next stop at **Kendall** (433km).

Wauchope (455km), pronounced War-hope (one would hope not!) is an old timber town. You may see traces of an old timber rail siding a kilometre before the station. Though the town itself is small, Wauchope station serves the coastal resort of Port Macquarie, 20km away by road.

Kempsey, a large town on the Macleay River, was the terminus of the Mid-North Coast XPT, forerunner of the Brisbane XPT. Like Taree, Kempsey serves the surrounding farming area. It has a special claim to fame as the original home of Australia's distinctive Akubra hat.

Most of the scenery on this part of the line is pleasant and varied, with numerous creeks, plantations and small settlements. North of **Macksville** (552km) there are glimpses of the Pacific Ocean between **Nambucca Heads** (565km), **Urunga** (581km; the best area) and **Sawtell** (601km), and it would be well worth breaking a journey at one of these intermediate stations.

Coffs Harbour (608km), self-named capital of 'the Banana Republic' (due to the many plantations in the locality), is noted for the beauty of its coastal scenery, its rich hinterland and magnificent beaches.

North of Coffs (Australians typically shorten names) the track climbs at a steady 1 in 80 through numerous curves and a series of short tunnels to a minor summit (just over 100 metres) at Landrigan's loop.

Rail buffs should watch a few kilometres further on for the historic Dorrigo branch (see p256) to the left at **Glenreagh** (652km), on the left about 35 minutes north of Coffs Harbour.

Grafton City (696km), terminus of the Grafton XPT and built on both sides of the Clarence River, is noted for its colourful jacaranda trees, smothering the roads and footpaths in season with their beautiful blue-purple blossoms. The Grafton Jacaranda Celebration takes place around October/November.

Casino (805km) is where the line into Queensland breaks from the NSW North Coast route which here veers right to the coast.

Casino to Byron Bay Before the 1980s, passengers for the coast had to change trains. Later, a motorail service, the Gold Coast Motorail Express, ran direct from Sydney. This became the route of the Murwillumbah XPT, without car-carrying facilities, but even this popular service was withdrawn in mid-2004 despite the vehement opposition of the local people, and the line closed indefinitely.

A scenic route, serving important centres of the NSW Northern Rivers district such as Lismore and the coastal resort of Byron Bay, the branch to Murwillumbah may yet reopen, as politicians bow to the will of the people, as so often happens.

Although at the time of writing there are not even any excursion trains using the line (the popular Ritz Rail Tourist Train of Northern Rivers Railroad introduced in 1999 being an early casualty), it is worth recording some features of the route in case it reopens.

The first station is **Lismore** (836km), the main dairying centre of NSW, while 30km north is the small town of Nimbin, which acquired widespread fame in 1974. It has since become a haven for alternative lifestyles, on which its residents, now second generation, have capitalized to make it quite a tourist centre.

Byron Bay is the furthest point east on Australian railways and is a popular surfing resort. In fact nearby Cape Byron is the furthest point east on the mainland of Australia.

A break of journey here is worthwhile even if it has to be by Countrylink coach. Even with

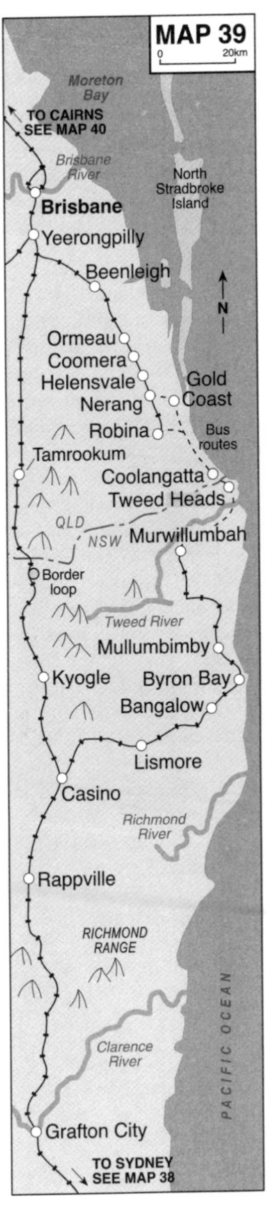

ROUTE GUIDES AND MAPS

only a few hours or a brief nightstop in Byron Bay you would have time to walk to the beach (where you will see the surfies with their multi-coloured boards, sun-bleached hair and bronzed skin) and back, have a good meal, or enjoy the nightlife with the locals at the swinging bar lounge of the ***Railway Friendly Bar*** (☎ 02-6685 7662); this occupies most of the former station refreshment and waiting rooms. Also worth seeing is the extinct volcano, Mt Warning, which stands out on the west above the farmlands of the Tweed River valley.

For details of coach services linking the Northern Rivers, coastal resorts and Queensland's Gold Coast see p81. Notes on the Gold Coast appear on p145.

Casino to Brisbane [Map 39 and map p149]

Between **Kyogle** (834km) and **Tamrookum** (909km) the railway passes through the magnificent border ranges, timber and mist covered with small waterfalls, bridges and rivers. If travelling from NSW to Brisbane, look out in the early morning, or later if travelling south, for the Border loop. This is of interest because of its spiral tunnels by which the differences in altitude crossing the NSW/Queensland border ranges are overcome.

Throughout the whole border-range crossing of 23km the train negotiates a series of 241m (12 chain) reverse curves on a constant 1 in 66 compensated gradient and traverses five tunnels. The first, spiral No 1, is 38km north of Kyogle, then comes spiral No 2 and the summit within the next 3km.

The former **Border Loop** station is at the 271m summit, immediately followed by the border tunnel and two more tunnels a few kilometres north. Set in wild country, the border loop area is only accessible, apart from the railway, by an unsealed gravel road. Before the advent of the XPT it was best viewed in the morning mists from the northbound Brisbane Limited but is now best seen from the southbound XPT about an hour out from Brisbane.

Rail enthusiasts may note the dual- and combined-gauge track on the right between Rocklea and the city (after the branch from the Gold Coast joins the interstate line. At **Yeerongpilly**, 8km from Roma St, local Gold Coast trains are likely to swing over onto combined-gauge track west of the suburban lines.

Approaching Brisbane you will see the city centre on the right as you pass through South Brisbane station to cross the Merivale Bridge. In the foreground just before South Brisbane are the South Bank Parklands, developed on the site of the 1988 World Expo while on the other side of the track is Brisbane Convention Centre.

The Sunshine Route: Brisbane to Cairns

BRISBANE TO BUNDABERG [Map 40]

Going north from Brisbane the first stop is **Caboolture** which marks the end of the Citytrain intensive suburban network, though outer urban services continue further north. North of Caboolture look out for the **Glasshouse Mountains**, curious volcanic peaks so named by Captain James Cook on 17 May 1770. They are to the left ahead about 21km after leaving Caboolture following a section where very fast running is noticeable after leaving the comparative congestion of suburbia. There are pineapple farms in the foreground. You may also notice **Beerwah** shortly after, on the right, home of the famous Australia Zoo (see p146).

Inter-urban trains and the Rockhampton Tilt Train stop at **Landsborough** (82km from Brisbane), from where Trainlink buses (not covered by rail passes) serve the Sunshine Coast up to Maroochydore. **Nambour** (104km) is the main transfer station for Trainlink buses to the coast further north at Noosa Heads. (These services are covered by Translink tickets).

After **Yandina** (112km; see p269), a local stop just north of Nambour, there is a long slow climb up the Eumundi Ranges, past **Cooroy** and Pomona to the old gold-mining town of Gympie. In **Pomona** note the old cinema in the town street on the right, whilst on the west of the track appears the distinctive shape of Mt Tiboorbargan, popular with hill climbers. The walking track to the top is clearly visible from the train.

The main station at Gympie is now **Gympie North**, 173km from Brisbane and some 3km from town, which replaced the original station when this part of the North Coast line was electrified and realigned in 1989. A bus link (covered by your ticket) connects with all trains and serves the old station at the north end of the town centre. From here the **Mary Valley Heritage Railway** (see p266) operates to **Imbil**.

Although Gympie itself is by-passed by the realigned North Coast line glimpses of the town may be seen on the left before Gympie North. **Gympie** is a friendly town, full of historic relics. They hold an annual show in late May and a Gold Rush week in mid-October. Local fruits, orange and pineapple, are plentiful and cheap. Gympie is worth a day trip from Brisbane or a break of journey en route to north Queensland. However, the train service is limited and better suited to an overnight stay in Gympie (see timetable p151). The ***Railway Hotel*** (☎ 07-5482 7677) adjoins the old station, with bedrooms at $20 a night. North of Gympie the train passes, but no longer stops at, Theebine Junction for the line to Kingaroy.

The next stop is **Maryborough West**, 262km, the station for Fraser Island. QR operates the Trainlink bus service to Maryborough and Hervey Bay, includ-

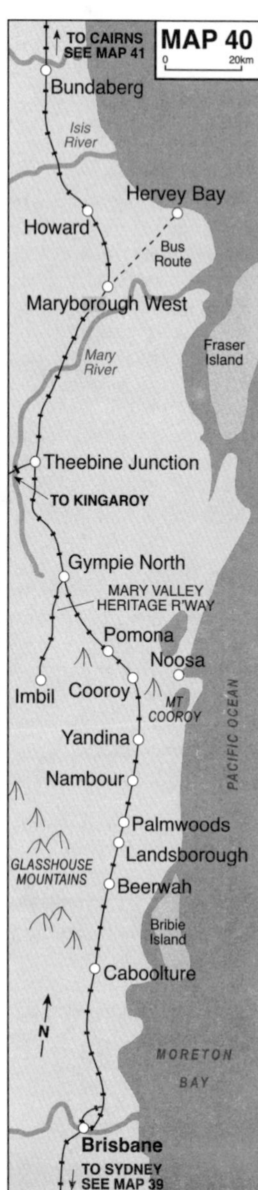

ing Urangan with its long pier to which the railway used to extend. Buses connect with the Sunlander and the Rockhampton Tilt Train. Maryborough, established in 1843, is one of Queensland's oldest cities with many historic buildings, traditional Queensland homes and pub-style hotels.

Hervey Bay, one of the world's best places to view migrating humpback whales between August and October, is 40-45 minutes by connecting bus from Maryborough West station and is the ferry embarkation point for the nearby World Heritage site Fraser Island, the world's largest sand island covering 16,300 square kilometres.

After Maryborough there follows some fast running, with possibly a conditional stop at **Howard**, a pleasant little town with historic buildings and a friendly little ***Grand Hotel*** (☎ 07-4129 4906) in the main street a few hundred metres from the station. Single rooms cost $30 a night and they serve a good lunch in the dining room.

Bundaberg, a major stop and main terminus of the evening Tilt Train from Brisbane is in the heart of the sugar country and home of Queensland's famous rum. Tours at the distillery are held hourly between 10.00 and 14.00; for further details contact the Visitor Centre (☎ 07-4131 2999, 💻 www.bundaberg.com.au). If you want to see how they make the rum, and to taste it, you should stay the night, since the days on which a break of several hours can be taken during daytime are limited. A six-hour break northbound from 15.25 to 21.25 is possible on a Sunday while a longer break, leaving Bundaberg for the north around midnight is possible on Tuesday, Friday and Saturday. Southbound no break longer than just over an hour is possible without staying overnight or leaving after midnight.

There are numerous motels within a couple of hundred metres of the station. ***Chalet Motor Inn*** (☎ 07-4152 9922) offers quiet comfort and convenience for less than $70. Next door is Best

Western's ***Bundaberg Motor Inn*** (☎ 02-4152 5011 or ☎ 1800 814 930) with rooms from $76, and nearby the ***Rendez-vous*** licensed restaurant forms part of the ***Sugar Country Motor Inn and Convention Centre*** (☎ 07-4153 1166); turn left at the level crossing along Bourbong St for these and several others. Alternatively, right opposite the station is the ***Federal Hotel*** (☎ 07-4151 6010), which has only backpacker accommodation but its ***Squatters Bar & Bistro*** offers great meals and snacks at attractive prices (from chicken burger at $3 to 'reef and beef' for $18. Being popular with railway workers is usually a good sign. Adjoining it, ***Matilda Motel*** (☎ 07-4151 4717) offers excellent moderately-priced single and twin units. Two blocks further down Bourbong St to the right, ***Grand Central Bar & Grill*** (☎ 07-4151 2441) has good pub tucker but with only backpacker accommodation.

Bundaberg is also famous for whale watching. Tour packages are available covering arrival and departure transfers, two- or three-nights' accommodation, breakfasts and lunch and cruises to Platypus Bay off Fraser Island and Lady Musgrave Island in the coral reefs of the Capricorn group. For the prices of these and other attractions, the tourist information centre (freecall ☎ 1800 060 499) near the station on Bourbong St is your best source.

BUNDABERG TO ROCKHAMPTON [Map 41]

On leaving Bundaberg the train swings over the wide Burnett river, from which, looking back to the east you should see the whale mural covering the flank of a large building in the town centre. At North Bundaberg the railway runs for a short distance along the street. The next stop, except for the Cairns Tilt Train, is **Miriam Vale**, a beef cattle and tobacco-producing area.

Gladstone, reached on most northbound services in the evening, bustles with railway activity. It is a colourful town, with its juxtaposition of massive industrial development and a

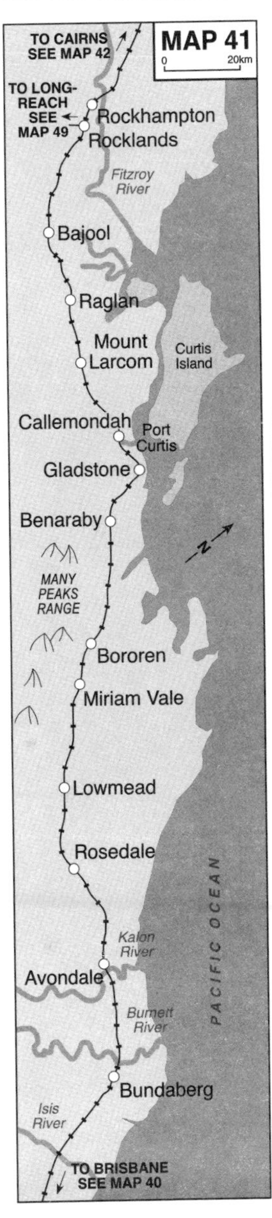

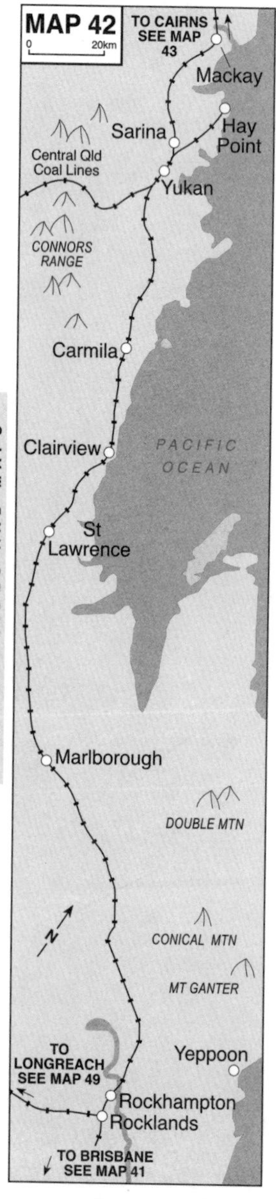

small boat harbour in a beautiful natural setting of tree-clothed hills. Break your journey at Gladstone and take a cab up to the vantage point on Round Hill. The coal terminals, as modern as any in the world, and the railway marshalling yards set in undulating bushland at **Callemondah Yard** (see p265) just north of the river present a most unusual picture.

Further north there may be a stop at **Mount Larcom**, centre of a dairy-cattle-producing area, which is a pleasant place for a stopover, with ***Mount Larcom Hotel*** (☎ 07-4975 1154) just a short walk from the station offering rooms at $35 a night.

Most northbound trains reach **Rockhampton** (see also p268) in the evening. This is the first stop north of the Tropic of Capricorn. If new to Queensland, this is a place to get out of the train and stretch your legs. You will probably feel its warmth even at night. The Sunlander and Spirit of the Outback trains have a 20-minute break here but the station is a 10-minute walk from town so there is not enough time to look around unless changing trains; this is now readily possible since the advent of the Rockhampton Tilt Train, which reaches there at 18.15, with two hours clear before the departure of the northbound Sunlander. The station refreshment room now opens only for an hour or so in the early morning.

The nearest hotels are within a kilometre: go straight out from the station on George St, turn right into Derby St and the ***Commonwealth Hotel*** (☎ 07-4922 1835), a few hundred metres on the right at No 45, has cheap meals and accommodation from $18; booking is essential. A little further on, turn left into Denison St and you will see ***O'Dowd's Irish Pub*** (☎ 07-4927 0344, 💻 www.odowds.com.au) over the road. Motel rooms cost $79, singles with shared facilities about half that, and the restaurant serves top-class meals of abundant proportion.

Great meals and entertainment can be found at ***Great Western Hotel*** (☎ 07-4922 1862, freecall ☎ 1800 006344), just north of the station rail yards where the line curves into Denison St. A bullring is one of the features (a rodeo is held most Fridays), perhaps echoing Rockhampton's reputation as the beef capital of Australia.

On leaving Rockhampton station the line curves west to run along the middle of Denison St, flanked by motor cars and pedestrians, before swinging across the Fitzroy River to continue northwards.

ROCKHAMPTON TO PROSERPINE [Maps 42 and 43]

Unfortunately, the current timetables mean that whatever train you travel on, most of this part of the coast route is traversed only at night.

St Lawrence, 173km north of Rockhampton, is the first stopping place where the station cat is likely to be the only living thing in sight. Nearby **Clairview** is one of only two places on this route where the Pacific Ocean could be visible from the train; the other is north of Townsville at Cardwell, passed in daylight.

Sarina is an important railway junction where the electrified line from the central Queensland coalfields crosses the north coast line to **Hay Point** coal terminal. There is also a large distillery, but only for industrial alcohol. Sarina is not a major passenger stop, and although the scenery is attractive between Sarina and Bloomsbury to beyond Mackay, this part of the line is most often traversed at night. **Mackay**, on the Pioneer River, is a sugar-exporting port with the largest bulk sugar terminal in the world. You may see the burning cane fields light up the sky after harvest, though different harvesting methods have largely transcended this feature and in 1999 it was outlawed for environmental reasons, though it can still be seen. Taxi travel is needed here, as the new station is at Paget, 3km away on the edge of town.

Proserpine is a major tourism centre. It is also only a short bus ride away from Shute

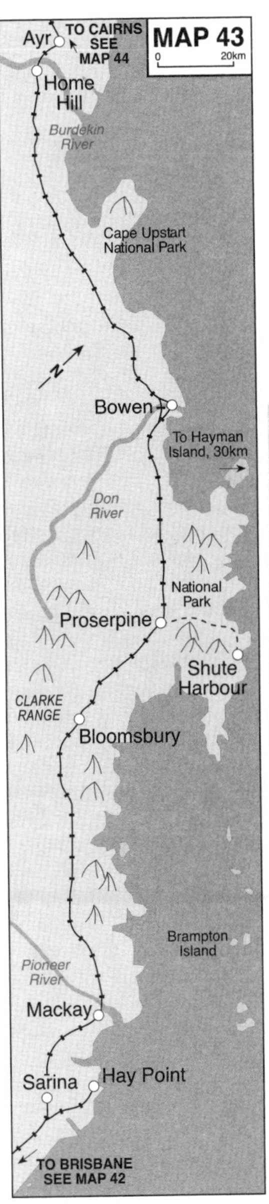

Harbour (see Table 14, p265) in Conway National Park and gateway to the tropical islands of Hayman, Daydream, Hamilton, Lindeman and South Molle in the Whitsundays. A QR Trainlink service meets all the trains, even the northbound Sunlander at 04.00. Sugar is important in this area; there is a close up of the sugar mill and its sidings on the right going north on leaving the station. Mackay and Proserpine are both good places from which to visit parts of the Barrier Reef and the tropical islands.

PROSERPINE TO TOWNSVILLE [Maps 43 and 44]

Bowen, on the Don River and a centre for fruit (it's famous for its mangoes), is 65km north of Proserpine, although the station at New Bowen is some way from town with no obvious sign of transport. From there on you are in sugar-cane country most of the way.

Home Hill is 100km further north and the station adjoins the main street. The ***Crown Hotel*** (☎ 07-4782 1007) is handy for a night's stopover. Between the twin towns of Home Hill and Ayr the train crosses the Burdekin River, the mightiest of the Queensland rivers east of the Great Dividing Range. Rice cultivation is a recent venture in this area.

At **Ayr**, the ***Grand National Hotel*** (☎ 07-4783 1200), right opposite the station, offers budget pub-style accommodation. An unusual pastime is pursued here – table bowls: ask the friendly landlord about it – contests are held locally.

About 20 minutes after leaving Ayr the train crosses the Haughton River, renowned among the angling fraternity for its barramundi, one of the choicest of table fish. On the left you may notice a large building named ***Giru International Hotel*** (☎ 07-4782 9166); if your itinerary allows a break here, you will have a memorable stay in this lovely example of a typical Aussie country pub. The train stops at **Giru** only by prior booking.

Wild birds including the dancing brolga or native companion are a feature of the marshy flats north of Giru approaching **Cromarty**, half an hour or so before the train starts its slow crawl alongside the main road into Townsville. Cromarty is no longer a train stop but you may glimpse among the trees on the left an old house which has an interesting history. The train conductor may know about it – try asking if local history is your interest. At **Stuart**, no longer a stop, the line to Mt Isa branches to the west. The large building group on the left is Stuart Jail.

Townsville is Queensland's fourth largest city. Here you should make time to look around town and get used to the tropical heat, as you can do if changing to or from the Mount Isa train. Flinders Mall, the town's commercial centre, is ten to fifteen minutes' walk from the new station, but there are local buses from a nearby stop on Flinders St. Cross the railway, then the road and the bus stop is on your right: the service runs every half hour on Saturdays, more frequently on weekdays and less on Sundays. ***Midtown Hotel Motel*** (☎ 07-4771 5121), rooms from $49 single, is within about a hundred metres of the station but, if you have time, make your way to the original station, where Ogden St crosses

Flinders St. This is near the central area. There is a small park in front of the old station building, historically the terminus of the former Great Northern Railway and looking very much the part. From the little park you can look up towards Castle Hill, a pink granite peak which towers over the city, while on the right is ***Great Northern Hotel*** (☎ 07-4771 6191) with single rooms at $25, or $45 twin en-suite air-conditioned. You can get good tucker in the pub dining room, while at weekends, when the dining room is closed, ask for John's Beef Stuff, a nourishing stew at less than $3 a bowl. Counter meals at ***Newmarket Hotel*** on the other side of the road are also good, and on Sundays the whole of Flinders Mall is turned into a busy open-air market.

Just to the right from the northern near the end of Flinders Mall you will find Ross River, dotted with a myriad of small boats. The quayside is lined by an excellent restaurant and bar complex; you have ample time to visit ***Tim's Surf 'n' Turf*** open-air restaurant if changing at Townsville for the train to Mount Isa. Steaks of unbelievable size, with accompaniments, cost less than $16 while a dozen oysters cost little over $7: you would pay that for half a dozen in most restaurants. For something more up-market, ***Winstons*** piano-bar and restaurant is almost opposite.

Day cruises operate from Townsville to the outer Barrier Reef but for less expense you can enjoy an hour or two among the marine wonders of the Great Barrier Reef Wonderland near The Strand, or take a ferry from Hayles Wharf on Ross Creek over to nearby Magnetic Island.

TOWNSVILLE TO CAIRNS
[Maps 44 and 45]

Once past Townsville's northern industrial suburbs, the railway crosses under the Greenvale Railway bridge, a mineral line built to a high standard but now abandoned. Rollingstone, where trains no longer stop, has nothing to do

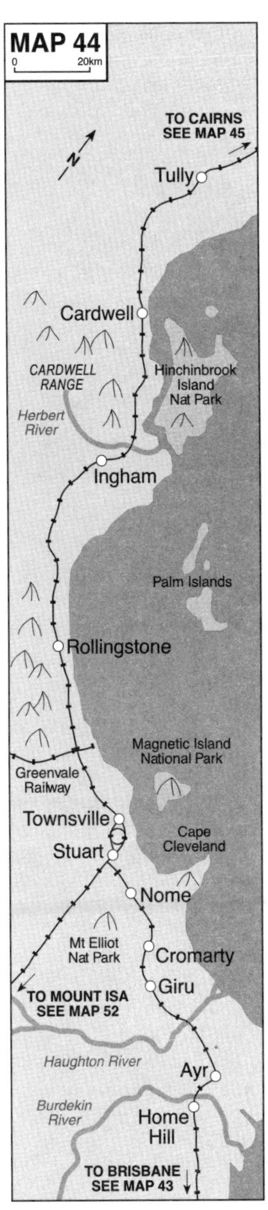

ROUTE GUIDES AND MAPS

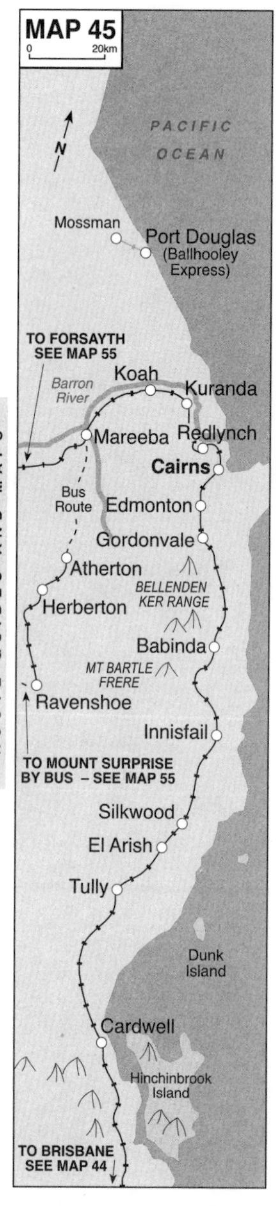

with Mr Jagger and his friends. The next stop, 1½ to 2 hours away, is **Ingham** (see Table 5, p84) on the Herbert River, original home of the 'Pub with No Beer', made famous the world over in Gordon Parsons's ballad. This was a local hotel which American servicemen were reputed to have drunk dry during World War II. There is a rival claim: at Taylors Arm, 26km from Macksville on the NSW North Coast main line, the Cosmopolitan Hotel claims this title but Ingham is right on the railway and an easier place to visit – if you go for pubs with no beer. In general, Australians don't.

In any case, the historic pub is no more. ***Station Hotel*** (☎ 07-4776 2076), just over the road at the southern end of Ingham railway station, is cool and more convenient, serving excellent home-made pies (as well as beer) if you decide to stop there for lunch or stay the night. Here, as at many places on this route, narrow-gauge cane lines cross the roads and the railway, and you may see cane trains even longer than the Sunlander on their way to the mill.

There is a brief glimpse of the coast 53km further north at **Cardwell**. You should also see some of the many islands on parts of this route. Hinchinbrook Island National Park is particularly prominent, appearing as a mountain range on the seaward side of the railway. The scenery is mostly excellent on both sides: the coast is on the right going north, but a recent scar is the controversial development of the Port Hinchinbrook resort near Cardwell which is plainly visible from the train.

Tully, a major sugar centre, has Australia's highest annual rainfall of 4267mm (68 inches). A stop of around 10 minutes is often made here; this is useful for smokers. Tully is a centre for white-water rafting: the people in the station refreshment room can give details. A walk of a few hundred metres past the bus station brings you to the main street where ***Mt Tyson Hotel*** (☎ 07-4068 1088) can supply a cold beer or a bed for the night at $20 or less.

North of Tully the train passes slowly through lush sugar-cane fields amid tree-clothed mountains, and passes the little town of **El Arish**, once a 'pub-visit' stop for the Great South Pacific Express and gateway to Mission Beach and Dunk Island, and **Silkwood**, traditionally where scraps from the Sunlander's dining car were thrown out to 'feed the chooks'.

Innisfail, 253km north of Townsville in sugar-cane country, is set between the ranges and the sea and is noted for its Chinese temple and Pioneers' monument. Nerada tea plantation, several miles inland, was Australia's first venture into this crop; the plantation is now well established and successful. Palmerston National Park is further inland on the road to Millaa Millaa and Ravenshoe on the Atherton Tableland. Accommodation in Innisfail is plentiful and mostly inexpensive but requires a longish walk up the street to the right of where the train crosses the main road.

Mt Bartle Frere, Queensland's highest peak in the Bellenden Ker Range, is between Innisfail and Babinda. **Babinda**, 59km short of Cairns, features a nature reserve, The Boulders, where a small river plunges among rocks, scene of both legend and tragedy some years ago when a foolhardy swimmer ignored the warnings. If visiting, keep to the excellent deep pool where it is safe.

Closer to Cairns, at **Gordonvale** (32 minutes by train), set among canefields and backed by rainforest, with the prominent monolith known as Walsh's Pyramid to the south is the last stop before Cairns. Mulgrave Mill is open for inspection tours even if the Mulgrave Rambler steam train (see p267) is not taking its scenic 15km narrow-gauge rail trip to Orchid Valley.

CAIRNS

Originally known as Trinity Inlet, Cairns is the essence and heart of north Queensland. Warm and extrovert, it is a thriving town with a population of over 60,000, a major centre of game fishing, and gateway to the Barrier Reef and the Atherton Tableland.

A Visitor Information and Booking Centre (☎ 07-4031 4355, 🖳 www.cairnsvisitorcentre.com) is on the Ground Floor at The Pier Complex, Pier Point Rd, or you can phone Tourism Tropical North Queensland (☎ 07-4031 7676). Attractions of Cairns include the harbour with the marlin jetty and sailing club, the surrounding cane fields and exciting hinterland of misty mountains and tropical rain forest.

There are many excellent restaurants and eating places ranging from the really cheap to the very expensive, the latter being particularly noted for seafood. And, of course, the easily accessible islands of the Barrier Reef, including Green Island with its underwater observatory. Cairns has many fine hotels, but within reach by rail or bus are smaller places where accommodation can be cheaper: Redlynch, Kuranda, Edmonton, Gordonvale and Babinda.

For a convenient night-stop try ***Grand Hotel*** (☎ 07-4051 1007) at the corner of Shields and McLeod Sts, close to Cairns Station (a short walk through Cairns Central, a shopping-centre complex). The hotel opened in 1928 just after

Cairns was first connected to Brisbane by rail. Music, singing and dancing, in the now famous ***Crocodile Bar***, are a feature of most nights. The hotel boasts an 11m-carved wooden crocodile as the main bar; this was carved, in the bar, from north Queensland yellow siris timber by a Papua New Guinean master carver, Ekielus Kambae. Rooms are cheap, and a self-serve continental breakfast is included. On the other side of the station, at the corner of Spence and Bunda streets, is ***Cape York Hotel*** (☎ 07-4051 2008) with rooms for around $35 and excellent counter meals.

Other eating places handy for the station are ***John and Di's*** in Sheridan St where a cooked breakfast costs as little as $6, ***Fasta Pasta*** for budget-priced Italian fare on Shields St, and ***Mrs Robbb's Kitchen*** on the station platform itself.

Around Cairns

Despite all the attractions of Cairns itself, it would be almost unforgivable to visit this area and fail to make the rail trip to Kuranda. A round trip from Cairns takes three hours, not counting time spent in Kuranda, but Kuranda is also worth an overnight stop. Depending on which train you join for the return trip, there will be time to visit the markets, the ***'Top Pub'*** for a good lunch (it lacks accommodation but has music while you eat), or the ***'Bottom Pub'*** for a cold beer or a bottle of Kuranda Hotel-Motel claret; don't believe everything it says on the label – it's a fine drop and if it knocks you over, you can stay the night in a comfortable motel room (***Kuranda Hotel-Motel*** ☎ 07-4093 7206) and eat extremely well there. For more on Kuranda see pp250-1.

Cairns is a useful base for other local trips, by train, coach, launch or hired car. A day trip to one of the islands on the Great Barrier Reef is easily undertaken from Cairns if you have a whole day there. Full-day coach tours are available to Atherton Tableland, with its crater lakes, orchid gardens and waterfalls; or to Cape Tribulation and Mossman Gorge.

On the north Queensland coast Ballyhooley Express (see p263) is the name of a train on the Mossman Mill sugar-cane railway at Port Douglas north of Cairns. The Queensland caneline network of so-called tramways extends over 1600km north to south, with over 3000km of track route, much of it interconnected. Its obvious tourist potential is capable of much greater development.

Narrow-gauge railways similar to the cane lines operate at two of Queensland's island resorts, Hayman and Brampton (see p265), to bring visitors from the ferries to the motel.

Referring to sugar-cane lines as tramways and their trains as trams can lead to some curious concepts. In Nambour a sign in the main street warns of 'tram crossing'. A visitor seeking public transport waited ages for a tram until he learned the truth!

Routes in outback Queensland

BRISBANE TO CHARLEVILLE

Brisbane to Toowoomba [See map pp148-9 and map 46]

Distances are from Brisbane Roma St.

At Roma St, The Westlander, alone among QR's Traveltrain fleet, leaves not from the main long-distance platform No 10, but from a platform at the other side of the station, closer to the interstate platform, since the western line exits in the same direction as the line going south. The latter swings away across Brisbane River whilst the western line of four tracks, the main western 'up' and 'down' lines and the adjacent suburban lines, follow the north bank of the river past the Castlemaine XXXX brewery at Milton, through Toowong to cross the river seven or eight minutes after leaving Brisbane at Indooroopilly.

Toowong is the modal interchange for Queensland University; shuttle buses operate from just over the road from the station. Opposite the station is ***Royal Exchange Hotel***, a favourite watering place for students (and staff) after lectures and exams, but without accommodation. At **Indooroopilly** the river is crossed by four bridges side by side; two double-track rail, one for cyclists and pedestrians, and one for road traffic, the latter noted for its entry towers and a road surface which seems to be almost constantly under repair.

The river is seen again on the right approaching **Ipswich**, some 45 minutes after leaving Brisbane, a historic town with convenient places for a lunch or dinner break within sight of the station, and with the unique Workshops Rail

The Westlander – survival of the fittest

The Westlander is possibly the most threatened of all the major inland air-conditioned services of Queensland Rail, but which has survived in spite of the worst efforts of government commissions, economic rationalists, treasury 'razor gangs' and the efforts of rival transport operators.

The Westlander's non-air-conditioned cousin, the Dirranbandi Mail described in earlier editions of this book, was the first victim of the branch line closure mania when it hit Queensland in earnest in the early 1990s. That the Westlander still survives, despite truncation of its route, two relocations of a major station, alterations to the timetable and days of running, withdrawal of booking facilities from country stations and downgrading of on-board catering from a grill-restaurant car to a club-buffet serving mainly pre-packed snack meals, is something of a testimony to the determination of country people to survive and hold fiercely onto their tangible links with the rest of the world, of which the railway is one of the most symbolic and well-loved. By travelling on a train like the Westlander you become part of a clan, identifying yourself with local interests and learning about a way of life that is a far cry from the suburban rat race that is now all too typical of the Australia most people know.

Museum (see p264) a short bus ride away. From here the first railway in Queensland ran to Grandchester, or Bigge's Camp as it was then called, 31km further on and just past the end of the electrified suburban system which extends to Rosewood.

Rosewood, 56km from Brisbane, is also a request stop for joining the Westlander and an excellent place for budget accommodation and hearty pub meals. The ***Rising Sun***, ***Rosewood Hotel***, and the ***Royal George*** are all within an easy walk from the station. Half a kilometre back alongside the railway takes you to Museum Junction, southern terminus of Rosewood Railway (see p268). **Grandchester** itself, with its preserved station, is served now only by Railbus from Rosewood or nearby **Laidley**, just 8km away as the crow flies but over 12km by rail where the line crosses the Little Liverpool Ranges. Here is one of the oldest tunnels and the longest single-bore tunnel on Australian railways. West of Laidley are **Forest Hill** (88km), then **Gatton** (96km) in the heart of the fertile Lockyer Valley, noted for quality fruit and vegetables. Nearby Gatton College is part of Queensland University, served by the QR-contracted railbus. (Rail passes are valid).

Helidon (115km), at the foot of the main (Great Dividing) range, is a pleasant little town famous for its spa waters and a good place to break the journey. Try the ***Criterion Hotel*** (☎ 07-4697 6213) opposite the station. The train now climbs the ranges towards Toowoomba, a long, winding deviation while the highway climbs much more steeply on a shorter but less scenic route. There are good views to the south and east. The best side for viewing is the left going west; however, on the westbound journey it will be dark and you will probably be concentrating on having a snack or drink in the club car. You can see this part of the ranges by day from the eastbound Westlander.

Spring Bluff, a picturesque little station right in the middle of the ranges, is always winning the competition for the best-kept station and is worthy of a look on the return trip when its profusion of flower beds is evident on both sides of the track. In late September during Toowoomba's Festival there are usually

Warwick

Warwick, once gateway to the south by rail on the former 'main line' is 94km south of Toowoomba on a scenic route and can be reached only on a special excursion or McCafferty's bus. It is the outlet for the fruit-growing area of Queensland's 'Granite Belt' centred on **Stanthorpe**. For many years the Sydney Express followed the NSW Tableland route as far north as Wallangarra. Here the station still stands, the former junction of the Queensland and New South Wales systems, 103km south of Warwick and five hours away in the old days. The orchards, wineries and scenic lookouts in these granite ranges are worth visiting.

Inglewood, which the Dirranbandi passenger train used to reach in the early hours, was the junction for Queensland's own Texas, a small border town once served by regular freight trains but an early victim of the closures of the last two decades.

Dirranbandi was the end of the south-western line, served now only by the occasional freight train. There are not even any substitute buses offered west of Warwick in place of the former mail train.

special 'Carnival of Flowers' excursions to Spring Bluff from Toowoomba; phone Toowoomba Station (☎ 07-4631 3380 or 4631 3381) for details.

Toowoomba (161km), Queensland's third largest city and the garden city of the Darling Downs, sits atop the Dividing Range escarpment. It is well worth a break of journey. Not only has it excellent restaurants and a pleasant climate, it is a colourful town proud of its trees and flowers. On the edge of the escarpment is a great view out across the ranges towards Brisbane.

The station refreshment room is a relic of the gracious living of the past. You will still get silver service, a tablecloth, and a very substantial meal for a ridiculously reasonable price, but unfortunately in the most recent change to the Westlander's itinerary, the Toowoomba stop is either early morning or late at night and the refreshment room traditional lunch is at midday. So spend a night or two!

Norval Hotel (☎ 07-4639 2954) and ***Irish Club Hotel*** (☎ 07-4638 9770) are close to the station and have budget accommodation. Rather further away but worth taking a taxi there, is ***Weiss's Restaurant***, famous for its unlimited buffet specializing in prawns and oysters.

Toowoomba to Charleville [Maps 46, 47 and 48]

There are many places of great interest, historically and otherwise at **Oakey**, **Jondaryan**, **Dalby**, **Chinchilla** and **Miles**, all on the rail line through the fertile Darling Downs west of Toowoomba – but all unfortunately served by train in either direction only in the middle of the night, with Jondaryan no longer even a stopping place.

McCafferty's coaches (C9073 and local) greatly increase the accessibility of these places. Jondaryan Woolshed is a must if stopping in this area because you can see shearing and other aspects of rural life.

This route is also noteworthy for the intriguing names of small siding stops, some of which

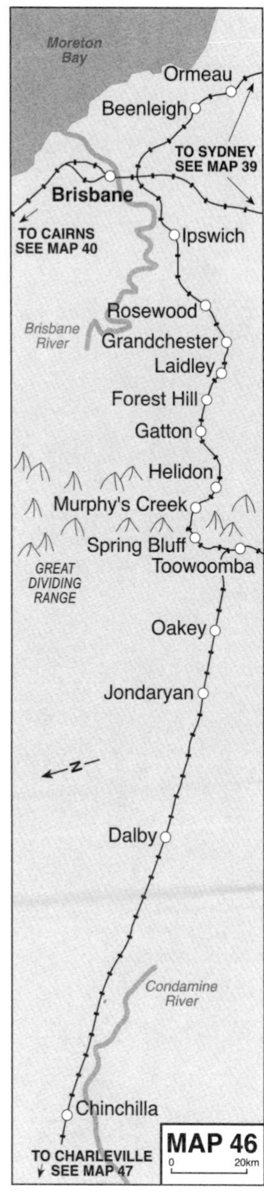

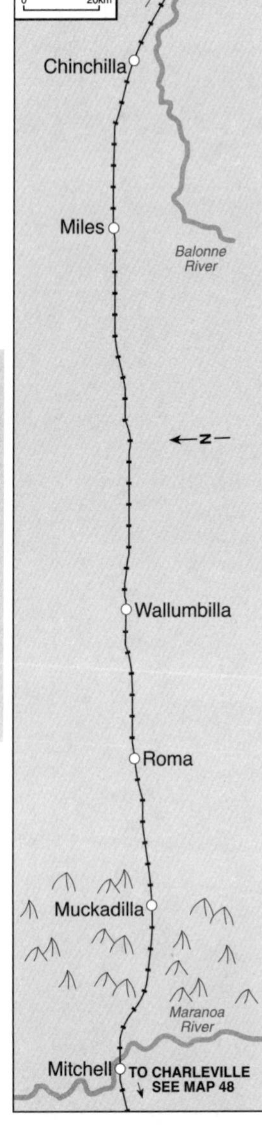

have almost a poetic quality; **Muckadilla**, **Womalilla**, **Amboola**, **Mungallala**, **Dulbydilla**, **Angellala**, **Sommariva** and **Arabella**; most if not all are of Aboriginal origin.

En route to the current terminus of the Westlander at Charleville, is a stop in the early dawn (or late evening on the return) at **Roma** (512km), a flourishing grazing town, centre for gemstones and home of Bassetts winery, long known for its rich Sauternes-style white wines.

Further on are Mitchell and Morven, both worth a visit and linked by bus as well as rail services (C 9009, 9073).

Mitchell (598km), on the banks of the Maranoa River, was named after Sir Thomas Mitchell, explorer and surveyor-general of NSW. The late Frank Forde, who enjoyed the quaint distinction of being Australia's shortest-serving prime minister (one week only), was born here. Well-loved by all who knew him, Forde was deputy prime minister for many years and represented Australia at the inaugural meeting of the United Nations. The tourist information centre (☎ 07-4623 1133, 🖷 07-4623 1145) is in Kenniff Courthouse.

Morven, two hours and 90km further on, has a small open-air historical museum. ***Morven Hotel-Motel*** is just along the road from the station.

Charleville

Heart of Queensland's mulga (small acacia) country and the second-largest outback town in the state, 777km from Brisbane by rail, Charleville is where the train now turns around but formerly divided in two, one part going further west to **Quilpie**. Passengers on the Quilpie portion of the train, for many years consisting of a single coach and known locally and affectionately as the 'Flying Flea', faced five hours rolling uncertainly along the slender track which itself almost disappears – they call it 'two wires in the grass'.

In the main street of Quilpie a road sign tells you how far it is to places further west. If you can face the long bus ride go to the end of the line in Quilpie station yard and look out west. This is the nearest you can get on Australia's rail system, over 500km (albeit by bus) to Birdsville, that remotest of all outback settlements on the edge of the Simpson Desert, famous for its annual races and the four-wheel drive Birdsville Track down to South Australia.

If you intend to stay the night out west, be sure to pack some mosquito repellent; you'll need it. Duchess (see p249), a stop on the Mt Isa line, is almost as close – and still served by train, and Yaraka, on a freight branch from Jericho in Central Queensland, is a little nearer but has no passenger rail or coach access.

The other branch from Charleville leads to **Cunnamulla** which, like Quilpie, is served by connecting buses on charter to Queensland Rail and covered by the Austrail and QR rail passes.

There is time for a quick out and back trip with about half an hour in either place while the train turns around and is cleaned and watered in Charleville, but you can spend a little longer and get a good taste of life out west by stopping off instead at one of the smaller places en route such as Wyandra, Cooladdi (Aboriginal for 'Black Duck'), or Cheepie ('Whistling Duck').

You will feel the heat if wandering far from the pub or roadhouse in this area in the middle of the day. Don't walk too far, the ground is full of tiny, prickly, grass-like shrubs. Go back and have a drink before the bus returns. That would be difficult in Cheepie, where the only hotel burned down over a decade ago. But **Cooladdi** has the little ***Fox Trap*** roadhouse, almost all that remains of a once-thriving little railway town, where you can get a drink and something to eat, while at **Wyandra**, ***Gladstone Hotel*** has good counter meals and there is plenty of historic interest in its surroundings.

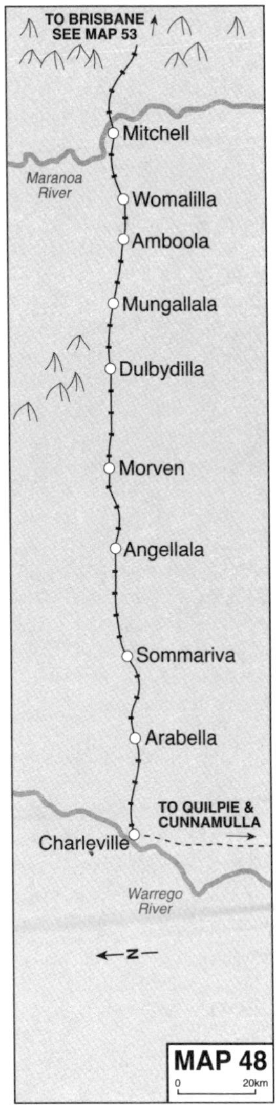

On the other hand, if you wait with the train in Charleville there is much of interest by just taking a walk up the main street, Wills St, across the road from the station.

In ***Hotel Corones*** (☎ 07-4654 1022) on the right you will find souvenirs of the major floods which inundated the town a few years ago but, although you may see thunder clouds piling up in the afternoon sky, drought is more of an experience in this sunburnt outback country than floods. Bradley's Gully, running through the centre of town, is more often dray than full of water. When there has been 'good' rain, the land can be green here: at other times it is burned bronze.

Charleville Information Centre (☎ 07-4654 3057, 🖹 07-4654 3970) is just up the road from the station, and the ***Railway Hotel*** (☎ 07-4654 1091), commonly known as The Rocks, is handy for a drink while waiting for the train. It also offers a good lunch, as do other pubs in Charleville: ***Hotel Charleville*** (☎ 07-4654 1076), at the corner of Wills St and Alfred St, opposite the post office, and ***Cattle Camp Hotel/Motel*** (☎ 07-4654 3473), 149 Alfred St. This is worth visiting even if only for a look at the fascinating and humorous mural behind the bar. At the corner by the post office, turn right along Alfred St to the east, past the ***Ming Court*** Chinese restaurant and the Historic House Museum on the left. It is about half a kilometre to the hotel.

Charleville also has an RSL Memorial club which welcomes visitors. In August, camel races are a feature of the area, but Charleville has year-round attractions; the School of the Air, the Royal Flying Doctor Base and the C.D.E.P Aboriginal art shop among them.

A recent innovation is the Cosmos Centre, off Airport Drive, reached by a ten-minute walk along Mitchell Highway south over the railway. With simulated space displays this is a modern museum well worth visiting. For details phone the Information Centre (see above) or try the website 🖳 www.cosmos.centre.com.au.

The Westlander runs twice weekly: to stay overnight in the far south-west means spending either two or five days between trains, but this would be time well spent and memorable.

ROCKHAMPTON TO WINTON

Rockhampton to Barcaldine [Maps 49, 50 and 51]

Other inland long-distance trips by air-conditioned train are from Rockhampton and from Townsville. The Spirit of the Outback from 'Rocky' actually starts its journey at Brisbane's Roma St, covering the North Coast sector overnight and in the morning turning to make its leisurely way west through the Bowen Basin coalfields to Longreach, 'border to the far outback'.

At Rockhampton the electric locomotive is detached and another engine takes over, attaching to the rear to pull the train back six kilometres to **Rocklands**, junction for the Midland line.

In times of severe flooding affecting Rockhampton and particularly the low-lying parts of the track between there and Rocklands, passenger trains may use the **Gracemere** diversion (as all coal trains do) to by-pass Rocky and detour inland via the central Queensland electrified coal lines. The Spirit of the Outback's next major stop, after negotiating the coastal ranges between **Kabra**, **Westwood**, **Duaringa** and **Dingo**, is **Bluff**, 170km from Rocklands, a major staging post for the coal trains which run almost hourly through this section and where three or more may often be seen together in the four passing 'roads' of the station yard.

Blackwater, a tad further west, is where the mine branches start to peel off the main midland route, south to Laleham and Koorilgah, north to Curragh and at Rangal south again to Boorgoon and Kinrola. Blackwater is a mining town, somewhat famous, or notorious, in Australia's political history. It is where the locals showed a prominent politician, then Federal Treasurer, in no uncertain terms what they thought of his bright idea to tax miners' free housing, a move as unpopular as taking away miners' free coal in Britain or depriving sailors of their rum ration! ***Black Diamond Motel*** (☎ 07-4982 5944) is opposite the station here, with a pub, ***Blackwater Hotel*** (☎ 07-4982 5133) on the next street corner.

Burngrove, 13km beyond Blackwater but not a train stop, is a junction made conspicuous by a major electricity substation for the power to the overhead catenaries. The main coal line swings north here through Bowen Basin. After passing German Creek it joins other coal lines from Blair Athol, Riverside and Goonyella at Copabella, before winding back down the ranges to the loading terminal at **Hay Point**, south of Mackay, crossing the main coast line at **Yukan**.

After the small town of **Comet**, at which the train stops but rarely, the line crosses the Comet River and in a further hour covers the next 41km to **Emerald**, the chief town between Rockhampton and Longreach, noted and named for the gemstones mined in the area. The station is on the south side of the main street and is handy for hotels, shops and other amenities. While the train stops (usually for at least 15

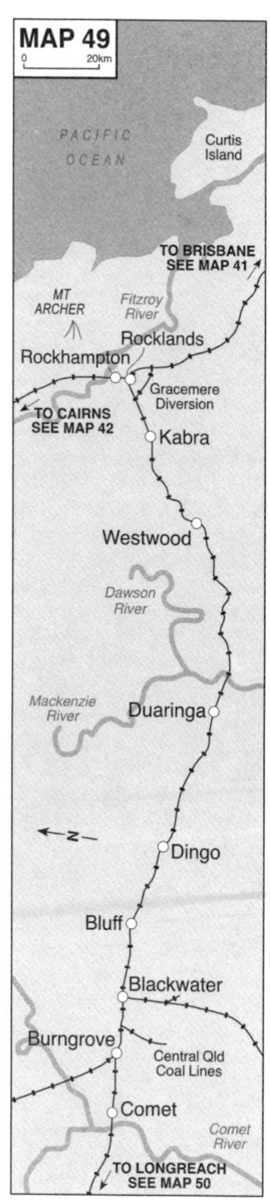

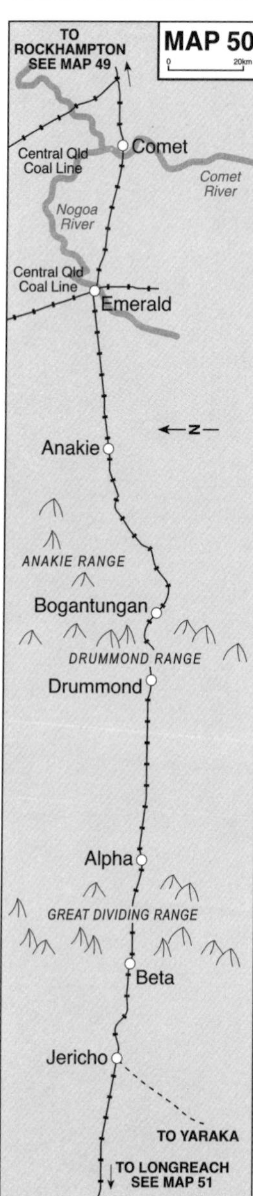

minutes) there is time to nip in to one of the pubs opposite the railway station for a quick glass of beer or to buy a postcard from a local shop. But warn the conductor if leaving the train and intending to reboard; passengers have been known to be left behind and forced to beg a lift from local police to catch up with the train further west.

Anakie, nothing to do with lawlessness, is a place name taken from the Aboriginal for 'twin peaks'. The largest sapphire field in the world is here and it is where, in 1935, the 'Star of Queensland' black star sapphire was discovered; this is now kept at the Smithsonian Institute in Washington. ***Anakie Hotel*** is conveniently near the station.

After possibly a brief stop at **Bogantungan**, which years ago boasted a railway refreshment room, the line, which has for the last 15km been winding its way through the Zamia Range, starts its climb into the Drummond Range. The track here is full of sharp curves which means you can look out of the window from anywhere in the train to see either the locomotive end or the rear or both, curving one way or the other. The curves are as tight as 80m (four chain) radius and the track, which has been climbing steadily for the preceding 26km, steepens to an average 1 in 70 for the 13km up to Hannan's Gap from where it descends at just under 1 in 100 to the tiny station named **Drummond**, The route here is being gradually re-aligned. On the first part of the climb you can see the formation of the original route.

Shortly after Drummond comes **Alpha**, a small settlement but (relative to the scale of things out west) a reasonably important railway centre, where freight trains are marshalled and train staff vans are attached or detached. Both the ***Alpha Hotel*** (☎ 07-4985 1311) and ***Criterion Hotel*** (☎ 07-4985 1215) are opposite the station. The former has air-conditioned units ranging from \$30 to \$70, the latter offers pub rooms at \$20 including a do-it-yourself continental breakfast.

Between Alpha and Jericho the only other station, now merely a passing loop, is **Beta**; presumably they knew no more letters of the Greek alphabet after that. Trains for the remote **Yaraka** branch (see p270) may start or finish at Alpha, unless at Emerald further back, and they enter and leave the branch at **Jericho**, a slightly larger settlement 55km further west.

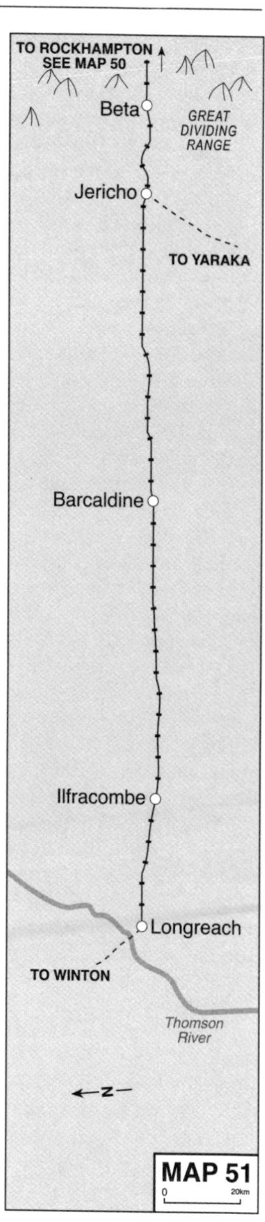

At **Barcaldine**, 'Garden City of the West', see the Tree of Knowledge just outside the railway station in Oak St. The Australian Labor Party was founded here after the Shearers' strike of 1891, of which Barcaldine was the centre. The Australian Workers' Heritage Centre (open daily 09.00 to 17.00), commemorating the role of workers in Australian social and political history, is one block away in Ash St. Barcaldine also has a folk museum and good outback-style hotels where a counter tea and a bed can be obtained at very reasonable cost. In fact, you will not see many outback main streets with so many hotels in view from one spot. From the station entrance you look out and, from left to right over the road, are the ***Union Hotel/Motel***, ***Railway Hotel***, ***Artesian Hotel***, ***Shakespeare Hotel***, ***Commercial Hotel*** and ***Globe Hotel***. There is no shortage of accommodation, prices ranging from as low as $15 a night. Just take your pick!

If staying the night is not on your agenda, there is just time to see and photograph the tree while the train pauses at the station. The tourist information centre (☎ 07-4651 1724, 🖹 07-4651 2243, 💻 tourinfo@tpg.com.au) is on Oak St, about 100 metres from the railway station.

Barcaldine to Longreach and Winton [Map 51]

Between Barcaldine and Longreach you may be offered high tea in the train's dining car (see box p52). At the risk of missing high tea, but with compensations, you may decide to curtail the trip at **Ilfracombe**. Developed from a railway construction camp on part of Wellshot sheep station (the biggest in the region with 400,000 sheep on 6000 square kilometres) the town now has a small open-air museum (Ilfracombe Folk Museum). ***Wellshot Hotel*** (☎ 07-4658 2106) was formerly a 'must' on any tour of outback Queensland, offering cheap unit accommodation and meals; features of the bar would captivate any visitor even if the pub had no beer! Unfortunately, the hotel closed in 2003 and for seven months the town suffered a drought (of beer). Now there is a new owner and it should be reopened before this book is printed: check with the local police station (☎ 07-4658 2176) if you are unable to contact the hotel by phone.

At **Longreach**, visit the Qantas Founders Outback Museum, the Australian Stockman's Hall of Fame and Outback Heritage Centre, open 9am to 5pm every day except Christmas Day. Australia's own airline, Qantas (Queensland and Northern Territory Air Service) was based in Longreach from 1921 to 1930 and the hangar is preserved at the airport precinct.

Excellent meals and cheap accommodation can readily be found in Longreach.The historic ***Commercial Hotel*** (☎ 07-4658 1677, 🖹 07-4658 1798) housed the original Cobb & Co stagecoach booking office. Rebuilt after a disastrous fire, it is just one block away from the station in Eagle St (the station master will point the way) and has motel-style units at under $70 a night, rooms with shared facilities much cheaper. Longreach has several modern motels with all the amenities and even a night club. It is a place in which it is worth staying more than the one night you would have if returning by the train on which you arrive. Immediately opposite the station is ***Longreach Motor Inn*** (☎ 07-4658 2322) where the train crew stay; single rooms are $88. The visitor information centre (☎ 07-4658 3555, 🖹 07-4658 3733, 💻 info@longreach.qld.gov.au), open daily, is opposite the post office in Eagle St.

From Longreach station, Alan and Suzie Smith's Outback Aussie Tours (☎ 1300 787 890) offer excursions to Winton and beyond (including Lark's Quarry – see below). Since the withdrawal of passenger trains between Longreach and Winton, QR has charter buses which connect with the arrival and departure of trains, although allowing less time in Winton than there is in Longreach, unless the return journey is postponed to the next of the twice-weekly services.

Winton, a major sheep and cattle centre, is the birthplace of Qantas (the airline) and the song *Waltzing Matilda*; the latter is based on a story about a swagman who stole a sheep and jumped into the Combo Waterhole, 145km from Winton, to escape the police. Written by 'Banjo' Patterson, a visiting solicitor who was staying at nearby Dagworth cattle station a few years later, in 1895, it was first publicly sung in Winton's North Gregory Hotel (☎ 07-4657 1375 or for reservations freecall ☎ 1800 801 611 or 💻 northgregoryhotel@hotmail.com). Rooms are $33 to $55 including continental breakfast.

An enthralling account of events connected with the origin of this song, Australia's folk 'anthem', is given in the book *Matilda my Darling* by Nigel Krauth in which, incredibly, the publishers were not allowed to include the words known by heart and loved by all Australians, because some American person or body has apparently acquired the copyright.

Visit the Waltzing Matilda Centre (☎ 07-4657 1466, 💻 waltzing.matilda@bigpond.com) in the main street, 10 minutes from the station, for a journey into history. With money and time to spare you could hire a car to visit the dinosaur tracks 111km south of town at Lark's Quarry Environmental Park on the Jundah road. Winton's water supply comes from boreholes over a kilometre deep and has a temperature close to boiling point.

The original rail link to Winton was from Hughenden on the QR Great Northern line, and this was the only way it could be reached by rail since the former Midlander train through Longreach was replaced by The Spirit of the Outback, though even that was not without difficulty (see p84). Reinstatement of a regular passenger train has been urged locally, though without result.

TOWNSVILLE TO MOUNT ISA [Maps 52, 53 and 54]

The Inlander links Townsville and Mount Isa, through Hughenden and such romantic places as Charters Towers, Julia Creek and Cloncurry, not to mention Nonda. One of Queensland's first fully air-conditioned trains, The Inlander first ran in 1953.

Distances are from **Stuart**, the junction south of Townsville. Some of the places marked are now merely passing loops where trains stop only to allow others to pass in the opposite direction.

At **Charters Towers**, population 10,000, you are back in gold-rush history. Legacies of past glories include more National Trust buildings than anywhere else in Queensland. Seen from the top of Towers Hill and worth a visit, 2km from the station, is the Venus Gold Battery, a stamping mill restored by the NT. See also the old German Church in Ann St, or simply visit one of the old pubs of which there were 80 in the town's heyday. Gold was discovered here by accident in 1871. The soldier poet known as Breaker Morant lived here during the subsequent gold rush when the population was 30,000.

For more information contact the Visitor Information Centre (☎ 07-4752 0314, 💻 www

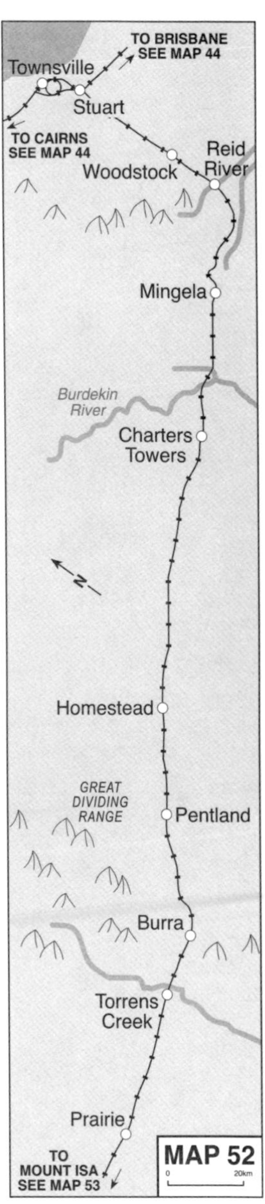

ROUTE GUIDES AND MAPS

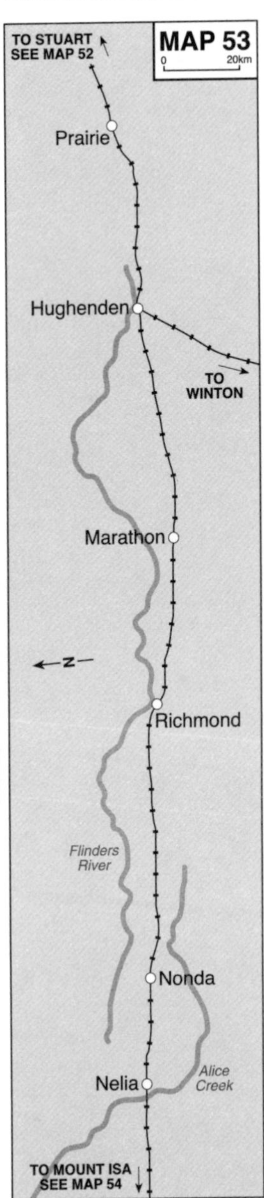

.charterstowers.qld.gov.au, or, if you want to stay the night, ***Enterprise Hotel*** (☎ 07-4787 2404) is just beside the station, with air-conditioned motel-style rooms for $54, or self-contained units (do your own cooking) at $62.

Hughenden is a place you are only likely to visit by rail en route to or from Winton (see p270), unless joining or leaving a train at a rather isolated station in the middle of the night has irresistible appeal. Many freight trains bypass the station, but stop for brake tests and crew changes on sidings on an avoiding loop to the west. Porcupine Gorge National Park is 63km to the north, while at the Dinosaur Display Centre (☎ 07-4741 1021) in Gray St, the exhibits include a life-size replica of Australia's own bird-footed dinosaur Muttaburrasaurus, relics of which were found at Muttaburra between here and Longreach. ***Royal Hotel Motel*** is close to the railway station.

Marathon, which is 48km or about 45 minutes on the train before Richmond, invites the visitor to 'step back 100 million years'. See Australia's best-preserved dinosaur fossil and the 'moon rocks' of limestone displayed at Lions Park. **Richmond** is a small town (population 800) approximately midway between Townsville and Mount Isa by road and on the banks of Queensland's longest river, the Flinders. It is described as the heart of the ancient inland sea, and the Marine Fossil Museum (☎ 07-4741 3429) here has some rare or unique examples found at Marathon.

An hour or more before Julia Creek going west, or 40 minutes or so after midnight going east, the train may stop at **Nonda** (561km). This is a depot for railway freight and mineral train crews which, a few years ago, still boasted a station master and a waiting room with refreshments (a soft drink slot machine). Cartoon postcards, obtainable at the station, cynically advertised it as 'Nonda by the Sea'.

Julia Creek (638km), described as being in the middle of nowhere, is reached either in early morning or late at night on The Inlander. This small outback town features in Scyld Berry's book *Train to Julia Creek*, representing to his mind 'the end of a journey in search of the spirit of Australia'.

Cloncurry, (770km), is known locally simply as 'The Curry'. Australians habitually shorten place name: 'The Creek', 'The Curry', 'The Isa', in this area and, of course, 'The Alice' in 'The Territory'. Cloncurry boasts the remains of the 'Great Australian' copper mine of 1867. See also the Cloister of Plaques in Uhr St, site of the Flying Doctor's first base in 1928. Tourist information is available from the Council Chambers (☎ 07-4742 1251), Scarr St. Cloncurry is the junction for the disused Kajabbi branch and a good place to break the journey if intending to take the bus (if running, see p284) to Normanton and the Gulf Country. Cloncurry also has links with Qantas, Australia's airline which, it is asserted, was 'conceived in Cloncurry, born in Winton and grew up in Longreach'.

The train may stop briefly for operational purposes at **Bungalien** (866km). Three kilometres further on is Flynn, junction for the 66km Phosphate Hill branch on the left, one of the main revenue sources for this line.

Between Cloncurry and Mount Isa the scenery is particularly rugged. You may see wandering camels, one of which was said to be a customer at the pub nearby at Duchess, where a brief stop may be made by The Inlander. **Duchess** (879km) has few inhabitants but is a base for railway workers. The Duchess hotel, adjoining the station, sports the name ***The Thirsty Camel*** (☎ 07-4748 4833) and has basic accommodation, good home-cooked tucker and a friendly welcome.

Mount Isa, the largest city in the world (by area 40,977 sq km or 15,822 square miles), is roughly twice the size of Wales but with only a fraction of the population, about 25,000. This is an industrial complex which looks almost incongruous in the middle of nowhere.

You will be acutely aware of the giant chimneys, but don't miss the Underground Museum

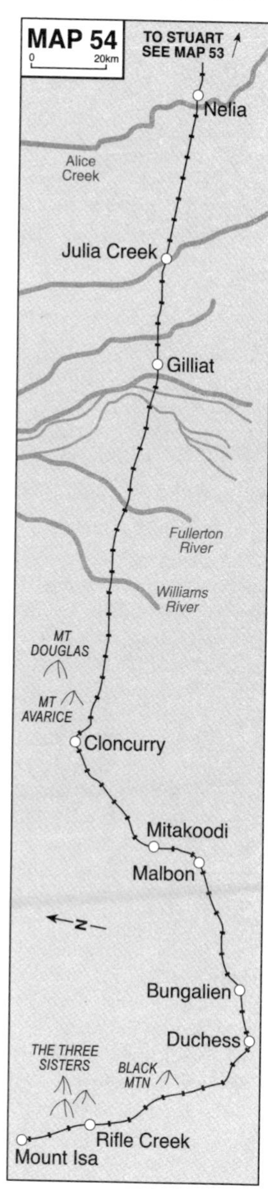

in Shackleton St. A nearby lookout offers a good view of the city and mine.

There are many tours available here if your stay is longer than it takes the train to be turned and refurbished. This includes a full 24 hours if you arrive on the Wednesday train from the east. Tours range from the two-hour Mount Isa Explorer covering the world's largest silver, lead and zinc mine to the three-day/two-night all-inclusive Lawn Hill and Riversleigh Safari, visiting world heritage Riversleigh fossil fields and Lawn Hill National Park. Contact Campbell's Tours & Safaris (☎ 07-4743 2006, 🖹 4743 6903 or, better still, freecall ☎ 1800 242 329) before leaving Townsville on the Mount Isa train.

Mount Isa has several pubs and hotels with accommodation but nothing close to the station. Excellent motel-style accommodation and good food is found at the ***Mt Isa Irish Club*** (☎ 07-4743 5678, 🖹 4743 5665 or 💻 eileenm@matilda.net.au for booking) on Twenty-third Avenue where visitors are welcome. A single room costs as little as $33, whilst two can share a double with three meals for $115.50 a day. A regular taxi service links the club with the town centre and railway station. Details from the club office (☎ 07-4743 2577, 🖹 4743 0310).

KURANDA SCENIC RAILWAY [Map 55]

Only 33km long, the Kuranda railway line (see photo opposite p144) first runs for 12km along the flat coastal strip north of Cairns to **Redlynch**, where the climb up the coastal ranges really begins. Redlynch came to notice during World War II when it was the site of the largest field hospital in the Southern hemisphere. Before the war, some of the cars on this train had sideways seating arranged like a grandstand for better viewing, but facing out from one side of the train only. The cars were converted for ambulance use during the war but the unusual seating was never restored – and no need! There are great views on both sides.

In the next 19km the line rises 318 metres up the side of the Barron River Gorge, first negotiating a horseshoe bend to the right, the Jungara loop, then a series of tight curves and 15 tunnels. The opening up of this rail route into the hinterland in 1891 gave Cairns the edge over its former rivals, Port Douglas and Geraldton (since named Innisfail). First surveyed in 1882, the line took nearly 10 years to construct and enormous difficulties were faced by the workers. A small booklet on the line's history, and including a map, is available to passengers on booking.

Mostly clinging to the edge of a 45-degree slope the line then enters Stoney Creek station, now merely a passing loop but where the train stops to ensure the line ahead is clear. Stoney Creek is crossed by a trestle bridge on another tight bend, almost in the spray of the waterfall. Next, after curving round the bluff past a rock column known as Robbs Monument (see photo opposite p145), the line comes out above the wide amphitheatre above Barron Falls, where the train stops for passengers to look out at the view and take photos. These falls are somewhat disappointing except in heavy rain, because most of the water has been diverted for hydro-electric power.

Kuranda is famous for its railway station, which is like a botanical garden, for the 'Bottom Pub' (***Kuranda Hotel-Motel*** see p236) where you can meet some of the locals, for the craft markets (open on Wednesdays, Thursdays, Fridays and Sundays) a hundred metres or so up the main street past the 'Top Pub', and just beyond, the butterfly sanctuary. Close to the station on the lower side is the river, while on the higher side just past the pub is the Skyrail terminal. There are many attractive bush walks around Kuranda and there are 'stations' on the Skyrail route, with pathways through the rainforest.

KURANDA TO FORSAYTH

Kuranda to Almaden [Map 55]

Unless the train calls at **Koah**, where the line crosses the Clohesy river, Mareeba is the next stop. **Mareeba**, the Aboriginal name for 'meeting of the waters' (the Barron and Granite rivers), is a former stopping place of Cobb's coaches and a centre for timber and tobacco. The sawmill yard to the right of the station is worth a look.

The town centre adjoins the station. ***Highlander Hotel*** (formerly Dunlop's ☎ 07-4092 1032), just over the road, has a reputation for offering the 'best tucker in town'. Mareeba is a useful base for an excursion through tobacco country to Dimbulah or coach trips south into the Atherton Tableland. Mareeba Rodeo is held every July in nearby Kerribee Park. A granite gorge, west of the town, has boulders the size of eight-storey buildings.

The railways west of Mareeba in north Queensland were built by the Chillagoe Railway & Mining Co. The Chillagoe line to the then copper mines was completed in 1901 and the Etheridge Railway to Forsayth goldfields in 1911. The whole lot was taken over by the government of Queensland eight years later when mining declined.

The opening of one of the world's most remarkable natural wonders, the Lava Tubes at Undara (see p252), has helped to bring new life to this almost forgotten remnant of a once-thriving

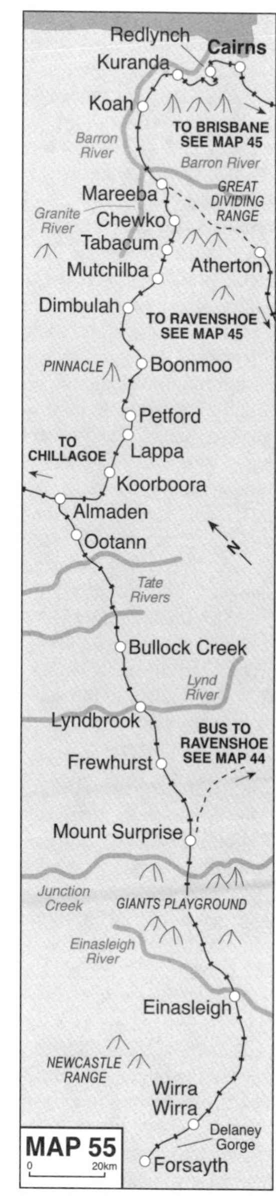

railway system, where in the old days the Cairns Express was the pride of the line and drivers were fined if it ran late.

Chewko, 12km beyond Mareeba, was once the major tobacco-growing area in Australia. The Chewko Range is part of the Great Dividing Range; from here on the creeks flow to the west. Watch out beyond Chewko for Arriga Junction, where a new line serves a sugar mill opened in 1998.

Tabacum, from the Latin *nicotina tabacum*, is appropriately named. **Dimbulah** is the first comparatively major settlement after Mareeba. It was originally the junction for the line to Mount Mulligan, scene of Queensland's worst mine disaster in 1921. It is an important local centre for fruit and vegetable produce. Conveniently ***Junction Hotel*** (☎ 07-4093 5206) is opposite the station. Near **Boonmoo** you will hardly miss Mt Pinnacle on the right ahead. This leads to Cape Horn where, in the gorge on the right, is Australia's shortest telegraph pole. The story has it that you can see the Pacific Ocean, 100km to the east, through a gap in the ranges but you would need to know the exact spot or spend a fair while in the area to prove it. **Petford** boasts a shop and a post office. It is also the site of a former work camp for troubled youths which, during 1999, was a source of controversy in the media, and which has since closed.

At **Lappa**, short for its original name Lappa Lappa, you may note a siding on the left, a remnant of the former branch to Mount Garnet. In the old days this was a railway refreshment stop. The disused pub is still occupied and maintained privately by the owners as a historic feature. If the train stops there, passengers are welcome to enjoy a drink at the bar – but it is strictly BYO.

Almaden or Alma Den, also known as Cow Town (you will soon see why) is the last junction on the line and the current overnight stopping place for the westbound Savannahlander. You can stay at ***Railway Hotel*** (☎ 07-4094 8307), over the road from the station, but many opt for the bus connection to the old mining town of **Chillagoe** (see box opposite), 33km to the north along a very rough unsealed track.

Almaden to Forsayth [Map 55]

After Almaden the route meanders among the hills and creeks, through **Ootann**, **Bullock Creek**, **Lyndbrook** (a former railway staff station in the 'Last Great Train Ride' days), to Fossilbrook Creek where at one time the train would stop to allow passengers to take a dip; the freshwater crocodiles did not seem to mind. After passing **Frewhurst**, the train reaches **Mount Surprise** where there is a welcome half-hour break in which to visit one of the two cafés or the pub for lunch.

In offering meat pies the landlord may ask whether you want cat or kangaroo. Don't be afraid; you will not be poisoned! Roo meat is highly nutritious, tasting a bit like venison and low in cholesterol, but all the pies are said to be normal beef. Mount Surprise is the overnight stop on the return journey when there is the option of transferring to a bus for a visit to the nearby Undara Lava Tubes, an outstanding system of volcanically-formed caves, believed to be around 200,000 years old but only recently rediscovered. The Lava Tubes are visited by full day, half-day or two-hour tours from ***Undara Experience*** (formerly Lava Lodge), where accommodation is available ranging from tents to

Chillagoe

Chillagoe is conspicuous with its old smelter chimney. Until 1999 this was fired once a year by the locals as a memorial to the past. In the town centre there are two hotels to choose from: ***Chillagoe Hotel*** (formerly the Black Cockatoo, ☎ 07-4094 7168) and ***Post Office*** (☎ 07-4094 7119), and there is also ***Eco-Lodge*** (☎ 07-4094 7155), at 37 Queen St, on the northern edge of town; a connecting coach serves them all on request.

There is time here to visit the Royal Arch Cave National Park or one of the other caves close to town, or the Balancing Rock, the old smelters or marble quarries (the quality matches that from Carrara in Italy). The museum is especially worthy of a visit, where among other things you can learn something of Queensland politics of the past.

The re-opening of the 28.5km rail line to Chillagoe may not be out of the question. If you travel on The Savannahlander, write to support it. Politics have a lot to do with railway openings and closures. People power can, in the end, defeat economic rationalist ideology, as the history of this whole route has demonstrated more than once. For updates, try the website 🖳 www.savannahlander.cairnsteam.com.

berths in railway sleeping cars; for further details phone ☎ 07-4097 1411 or freecall ☎ 1800 990 992 for bookings.

At **Junction Creek**, after leaving Mount Surprise, the line cuts through one of the main lava flows. Between Mount Surprise and the next stop, **Einasleigh**, the train wanders through an area known locally as the Giants' Playground. Huge boulders are balanced on the top of rugged crags and you wonder how they got there. Shortly before Einasleigh is the crossing of the Einasleigh River, one of the most photographed and fascinating on the line. The train may stop here for a short while. The line curves and dips down to the bridge and in periods of heavy rain the rails can be under water.

Einasleigh was formerly a copper-mining town and gold was also found in the river. The Kidston Gold Mine, 40km south, is among the top gold-producing mines in Australia. There is a break here in order to visit the pub, the remains of the old town hall (so they tell you) which until blown down in the late '90s in a violent storm was known as Einasleigh's very own 'leaning tower'. Passengers can also visit the adjoining gorge of the Copperfield River; if breaking the journey to stay the night, a dip in its deep pool between the rocks is an exhilarating experience – the fresh-water crocs are said to be harmless unless provoked or disturbed while mating. The train crew will point out various other features and there will be some surprise stops during the final 66km across the Newcastle Range to Forsayth, the end of the line. **Wirra Wirra** is the only intermediate station, where the train hardly ever stops.

On the approach to **Forsayth** the line twists its way along the side of Delaney River Gorge; the shrieking of the wheels on the tight curves announcing its approach to the townsfolk waiting to greet its arrival. ***Goldfields Hotel*** (☎ 07-4062 5374) is across the road from the station at Forsayth. On the same side as the station you will see one of the diesel mechanical locomotives similar to those used to haul the trains until well into the 1980s.

PART 6: FOR THE ENTHUSIAST

For the enthusiast (in particular)

This section is obviously misnamed. Of course **all** railways are of interest to enthusiasts, but some are perhaps of more interest than others. This chapter therefore deals with historic, preserved and unusual railways with which Australia abounds. Many of these not only appeal to enthusiasts but are immensely popular with tourists. Without enthusiasts, however, most of the railways here would not exist. Abandoned by decision-makers mesmerized by so-called micro-economic reform, they are restored by volunteers who recognize and give weight to social need and tourist potential alike.

Restored branch lines help feed passengers to the main routes. Recognizing this, the travel centres and enquiry offices operated by the various rail systems at the main stations provide information on private railways in their area and also on special excursions. These are run quite frequently by the Australian Railway Historical Society (ARHS) and other societies, often on lines normally used only for freight or primary produce such as wheat, wool, pineapples etc.

An excellent and comprehensive guide to private and preserved railways as well as rail museums for the whole of Australia, including many not listed in this guide, is published by the NSW Division of ARHS as *Guide to Australian Heritage Trains and Railway Museums*. The most recent edition should be obtainable from most specialist railway bookshops, eg the Railfan Shop in Flinders Lane, Melbourne, or direct from the publishers, ARHS New South Wales Division (☎/📠 02-9699 4595), 67 Renwick St, Redfern, NSW 2016. However, at the time of writing, the latest edition was the 7th, published in 2000, since when there have been many changes.

Most preserved railways have been threatened in recent years by spiralling insurance costs arising from unreasonable court decisions on outrageous compensation claims from irresponsible people – mostly nothing to do with railways. A notorious example was where a swimmer sued the local council because he hit a sandbank while diving in the surf. Recent world events have also played a part, and some of the railways listed may not be operating by the time you wish to travel. Details of operating times, fares etc, given here, and indeed, even whether the railway still operates, should be checked carefully before planning a journey.

Some earlier editions of *Australia by Rail* offered an outline itinerary for those rail enthusiasts or any other tourists who might wish to experience some of the best of such railways without spending unnecessary time finding out what there is, where it is, when it operates and how to get there. Most enthusiasts prefer to work out their own itinerary, so this guide now gives details, state by state, of some of the major rail museums and historic or unusual railways that are reasonably accessible, especially by public transport. It also names the nearest regular station and, where appropriate, the distance or journey time from there to the item of interest and advice on how to get there.

As with preserved and private railways the world over, some are now unfortunately totally disconnected from the rest of the system and can only be reached by private transport. Particularly saddening in recent times has been the isolation of the former South Australian railways broad-gauge Mount Barker Junction–Victor Harbor branch from the Adelaide suburban network by the conversion to standard gauge of the Adelaide–Melbourne line east of Belair. This prevents the former loco-hauled SteamRanger (see p271) making a full day-return trip from Adelaide up over the Mt Lofty Ranges which, at 264km each way, was the longest tourist rail route in Australia and one of the most scenic.

NEW SOUTH WALES INCLUDING CANBERRA

3801 Limited and the Cockatoo Run [see map pp126-7]

The Cockatoo Run is the name given to regular tours operated in New South Wales' scenic South Coast and Southern Highlands by 3801 Limited, a name derived from Australia's preserved C-38 Class 4-6-2 Pacific steam locomotive, built in 1943.

Locomotive 3801 is as famous in Australia as ex-LNER number 4472 is to British enthusiasts, and is the frontispiece of Leon Oberg's definitive *Locomotives of Australia* (Sydney, 1975, AH & AW Reed Pty Ltd). The locomotive, along with other preserved steam engines, is used on various excursions offered by the company, though not usually on the Cockatoo Run itself. This normally uses a 49-Class diesel loco with traditional 1930s- and 1940s-style carriages, including a buffet car and operates on Sundays and Wednesdays from Sydney at 09.00, taking the Illawarra line past Royal National Park and along the coast to Wollongong, then ascending the forested ranges from Unanderra on an almost steady gradient of 1 in 30 through a succession of ten-chain curves up to Summit Tank, where there is a break to allow passengers to walk to the lookout above Lake Illawarra. The line continues climbing to Robertson, home of the famous pig in the film *Babe*, where passengers have the option of stopping for lunch before returning, or continuing on the more gently-graded line to Moss Vale. This line was formerly worked by NSW railmotors and was a useful link between the Illawarra region and the main south line to Melbourne.

The Cockatoo run calls to take up at Thirroul, Wollongong and Unanderra on the south-coast line. Current fares are $85 return ex-Sydney, $40 from Thirroul, Wollongong or Unanderra, with reductions for persons aged over 60 and children.

Excursions further afield hauled by locomotive 3801, perhaps even double-headed with its sister (non-streamlined) locomotive 3830, operate at weekends, based on Sydney, at fares ranging from around $70 upwards. For tour details and all bookings phone ☎ 1300 65 3801, visit www.3801limited.com.au or email trains@3801limited.com.au.

Broken Hill Railway Museum

Located in the former Sulphide St station of Silverton Tramway, opposite the tourist information centre at the corner of Blende and Bromide streets, this museum is open daily from 10.00 to 15.00 for a nominal charge. The static display includes one of the large 4-8-2 steam locos formerly used on the Silverton Tramway and cars from the old Silver City Comet diesel express.

The museum is an easy walk from Broken Hill station, which is served by the Indian Pacific from Sydney or Adelaide twice weekly and the Broken Hill Xplorer once weekly. On other days the only access to Broken Hill is by coach to and from the XPT at Dubbo (an 8½-hour bus journey connecting with a 6½-hour train journey!) or by Hazelton Air Services. For a summary of rail connections see Table 3 (p77).

Canberra Railway Museum

Run by the ARHS, the museum at Geijera Place, Kingston, near Canberra station is open at weekends and on public holidays. Rail tours are available on selected dates. Phone ☎ 02-6284 2790 or email tours@arhsact.org.au for details.

Cooma–Monaro Railway

Cooma, gateway to the Snowy Mountains region of NSW, lost its regular train service, the Canberra–Monaro Express in 1988, and the Monaro area saw no trains again for the next ten years. In December 1998, the Cooma–Monaro Railway (CMR) was established using CPH Railmotors which formerly served country and outer urban branches of the State railways. The CMR operates over 19km of the line between Cooma and Chakola on the banks of the Numerella River, the return trip taking 90 minutes. Trains are also available for hire for special parties. A unique feature is a trailer car converted into a lounge/diner.

Trains run on Saturdays, Sundays and public holidays. For booking check with the Cooma Visitors Centre on ☎ 1800 636 525 or cmri@snowy.net.au. Cooma is 75 minutes by Countrylink coach from Canberra station.

Dorrigo Railway Museum

This museum (☎ 02-6657 2176, www.dsrm.org.au) claims to have the largest collection of railway vehicles in the Southern hemisphere, including 54 locomotives and over 300 other rolling stock items but at the time of writing was not open to the public.

Glenreagh Mountain Railway **[see Map 38, p224]**

There have been plans for several years to operate steam-hauled tourist trains on the 70km former State Rail branch which linked the main North Coast line at Glenreagh, 43km south of Grafton, with Dorrigo. A start has now been made with restoring parts of the track between Glenreagh West and Ulong, 35km of the 69km steeply-graded and sharply-curved line, first opened in 1924 but closed after flood damage in 1972.

Initially it is planned to operate 'trike' services over stretches of two or three kilometres at each end of the half route. These are fairly level sections compared to the steep climb further west including two tunnels and many 8-chain curves up to Timber Top, which will be something to look forward to when railcars and steam-hauled trains can be introduced.

Glenreagh is no longer a stop for mainline trains nor is there a feeder bus service as originally provided when the XPT first replaced the loco-hauled North Coast trains, but this may change in the near future. The sidings at Glenreagh may be observed, if the trains are on time, on the right side of the southbound Grafton XPT at about 07.15 or the southbound Brisbane XPT around mid-day. Phone ☎ 02-6652 6998 or visit the website 💻 www.gmr.org.au for progress information.

Hunter Valley

Hunter Valley was the scene of some of Australia's earliest railways (horse-drawn tramways carried coal to Newcastle as long ago as 1827) and, like northern England's Tyneside after which so many of its places are named, it is a fascinating area for the industrial archaeologist as well as the rail enthusiast.

Places of particular interest include Newcastle, Maitland, Morpeth, Hexham, East Greta, Rothbury and Kurri Kurri but, with some exceptions, the

❑ Table 13

Sydney–Newcastle–Maitland–Branxton (C 9016, 9018 and local)

		Mon-Fri	Mon-Fri	Mon-Fri	Mon-Fri	Sat, Sun
Sydney	dep	04.56	10.05a	13.17	14.47	15.17
Hamilton	arr	07.39	—	15.55	17.27	17.41
Newcastle	arr	07.46	—	—	17.34	—
Newcastle	dep	08.07	—	—	17.39	—
Hamilton	dep	08.13	—	15.59	17.44	17.50
Maitland	arr	08.50	12.46a	16.28	18.13	18.18
Maitland	dep	08.50	16.28	16.28	18.13	18.18
Branxton	arr	09.10	16.48	16.48	18.33	18.38

Branxton–Maitland–Newcastle–Sydney (C 9016, 9018 and local)

		Mon-Fri	Sat, Sun	Mon-Fri	Mon-Fri	Mon-Fri	Mon-Fri	Sat, Sun
Branxton	dep	07.06	07.47	11.02	11.02	19.42	21.27	21.50
Maitland	arr	07.28	08.08	11.23	11.23	20.03	21.48	22.12
Maitland	dep	07.28	08.08	11.23	14.21a	20.03	21.48	22.12
Hamilton	arr	07.56	08.36	11.51	—	20.23	22.23	22.40
Newcastle	arr	—	—	11.58	—	—	22.30	22.47
Newcastle	dep	—	—	12.37	—	—	—	—
Hamilton	dep	08.03	08.42	12.41	—	20.26	—	—
Sydney	arr	10.21	11.10	15.10	17.00a	23.12	—	—

Notes

Services arriving or departing after midnight are not shown in this table.

a Countrylink service with buffet, runs daily, booking required. Change at Maitland. All other services change at Hamilton or Newcastle where times are shown.

major attractions are not readily accessible by public transport. In April, the annual Steamfest (PO Box 351, Maitland NSW 2320, ☎ 02-4933 2611) is based on Maitland, from where tours by rail and road take in most places of interest.

• **Hunter Valley Railway Museum** The museum (☎ 02-4932 5086, PO Box 37, Branxton NSW 2335) is at the former Rothbury Colliery, North Rothbury, 5km by private line from Branxton which is 10km west of Maitland on the main north line. It has a large collection of NSW passenger carriages, including some complete sets and also houses seven out of the ten Beyer-Peacock 2-8-2 locos formerly used on South Maitland Railway. Inspection by appointment is most welcome.

Frequent electric trains link Sydney with Newcastle and a diesel service links Newcastle with Maitland and the Hunter Valley. Trains serving Branxton are few and far between. Table 13 on p257 summarizes the current timetable.

• **Richmond Vale Railway Museum** This museum, 4km south of Kurri Kurri, operates steam trains on the first three Sundays of each month over 4km of line between Richmond Main and Pelaw Main collieries (a route on which steam-hauled coal trains operated regularly until as late as 1987). For further details write to PO Box 224, Kurri Kurri, NSW 2327 or phone ☎ 02-4937 5344 or 4358 0190. Frequent local buses, operated by Rover coaches (☎ 02-4990 1699) run between Kurri Kurri and Maitland.

Katoomba Scenic Railway (C 9025)

A 1219mm-gauge railway which was built to serve a coal mine, this 0.45km (1/4 mile) incline railway is the steepest in the world with a maximum gradient of 128 per cent (1 in 0.78). A frequent service operates daily between 09.00 and 16.50; $14/$7 adult/child return. The railway is reached by bus from opposite Carrington Hotel outside Katoomba station, or by a 2.5km walk. The top station (where the trip starts) adjoins the Katoomba Skyway terminal, the descent gives magnificent views of Blue Mountain scenery and the bottom station gives access to walking tracks in Jamieson Valley and to the Sceniscender cable car as a return option. For further details visit their website: 🖳 www.scenicworld.com.au.

Katoomba station, 110km west of Sydney, is served by fairly frequent interurban EMUs from Central (C 9014 and local).

Lachlan Valley Railway, Cowra [see Map 1, p171]

The museum and roundhouse is open daily from 09.30 to 17.00. Charters and tours operate from the Railway Depot, Campbell St, to various points along the Harden–Cowra–Blayney line at weekends, usually once or twice monthly; phone ☎ 02-6342 4999 or email 🖳 inquiries@lvr.com.au for further information. Cowra is reached by Countrylink coach connections, 70 minutes from Blayney or 90 minutes from Orange on the western line from Sydney Central, or 100 minutes from Cootamundra on the southern mainline, all at different times on different days of the week. Although Countrylink trains call at Blayney, the 'connecting' buses to or from Cowra miss the western line train by just a few minutes in each direction: one of those seemingly deliberate non-connections some railway systems achieve so effortlessly! But a night-stop in Blayney can avoid an extra 35 minutes of bus travel from Bathurst. If you are happy with extended bus travel, they also connect from Cityrail at Lithgow, a 125-minute bus ride away but extending the range of optional times.

Coaches stop in the middle of town just off Kendal St. ***Lachlan Hotel*** (☎ 02-6342 2355) offers budget accommodation in Cowra just 100 metres up the road from the coach stop.

Metro Monorail, Sydney [see map pp122-3]

The Metro Monorail, of the straddle type, circles the central area of the city and the Darling Harbour complex.

The nearest CityRail station is Town Hall (three minutes from Central), just one block away. A day pass costs $9 and the complete circuit takes approximately 15 minutes, trains running every few minutes. A trip on the Monorail is an excellent way to get a snapshot of Sydney's many attractions.

Michelago Tourist Railway, Queanbeyan

This railway usually operates on Sundays over 48km of the former Queanbeyan–Cooma–Bombala branch of State Rail, a scenic route including a 1 in 40 climb and affording views of Tuggeranong, one of Canberra's satellite 'new towns'. Excursion trains may operate to scenic Molonglo Gorge and various centres in the Southern Highlands. Details and bookings from ARHS Tours (☎ 02-6239 6707 or ☎ 02-6295 7909 or visit 💻 www.arhsact.org.au/mtr.phtml). Queanbeyan station is reached by Countrylink's Xplorer services from Sydney or Canberra.

NSW Rail Transport Museum, Thirlmere [see map p127]

Whatever Dorrigo Museum may have claimed, NSW Rail Transport Museum (☎ 02-9744 9999 or 💻 rtm@accsoft.com.au), is regarded as Australia's largest. The Thirlmere Rail Heritage Centre includes Thirlmere Railway Museum, the Picton to Mittagong Heritage Railway and heritage-listed Thirlmere station (named Redbank for the first year after its opening in 1885).

Heritage tourist trains, steam hauled, operate on the first and third Sunday of each month from March to November. Diesel-hauled trains may operate on other occasions. The normal Sunday timetable is for three return services over 7km of the steeply-graded original south main line between Thirlmere and Picton. It is a steady 1 in 40 for all but the last 2km near the junction with the present main line. On special occasions, trains run beyond Thirlmere to Buxton, a further 6.7km south. The final section of the old main line to Mittagong, which includes a formidable 3km climb to Hill Top at 1 in 30, is no longer open but regular CityRail coaches serve the whole loop between Picton and Mittagong. On market days, the third Sunday of the month between May and October, a steam train is run between Thirlmere and Campbelltown or Sydney, called the 'Thirlmere Flyer'. The centre also operates day and weekend tours on the 'Southern Aurora', which formed the first Sydney–Melbourne through service in 1962. These tours visit various places in New South Wales, including some like Cowra or Mudgee no longer served by regular trains.

The museum is open daily (except Good Friday, Christmas Day, Boxing Day and New Year's Day). Adult admission costs $10, the return train ride is $12, or combined train and museum ticket $20, with reductions for pensioners, students and families. For further details phone ☎ 02-4681 8001, 📠 4681 8410, email 💻 thirlmere@nnswrtm.org, or visit the website 💻 www.nswrtm.org. Picton is reached by CityRail electric trains from Central via East Hills, taking an average of about one hour.

The Heritage Centre also has a branch in the Blue Mountains, the Valley Heights Locomotive Depot Museum, phone ☎ 02-4751 4638 for details.

Perisher Skitube Railway (C 9019)

An 8.6km standard gauge on Voll Rack system, electric, offering a 17- to 30-minute journey mostly every 20 minutes (less frequent out of the ski season) from Thredbo (Bullocks Terminal) to Perisher Valley and Mt Blue Cow, much of the route being in tunnel; for further details phone ☎ 02-6456 2010 or visit 💻 www.perisherblue.com.au/skitube. Reputed to have the widest rail-passenger vehicles in the world, it is also the world's fastest rack railway and Australia's highest railway, reaching 40km/h and an altitude of 1900m.

Bus connections by Greyhound and others from Canberra (Jolimont bus station), take about 3 to 3½ hours (C 9099).

Powerhouse Museum, Sydney

A museum of transport and technology (☎ 02-9217 0111), including rail exhibits, open daily from 10.00 to 17.00. Located in Harris St, Ultimo, and a short distance from the Metro Monorail (Haymarket Station).

Sydney Tramway Museum, Loftus, and Sutherland Tourist Tramway [see map p127]

Open on Wednesdays, Sundays and public holidays, except Christmas Day, the Tramway Museum adjoins Loftus Station, 36 minutes from Sydney Central by frequent electric trains. Vintage trams from not only Australian cities but also as far afield as Nagasaki and Berlin operate on two lines, one alongside the railway back to Sutherland and another on the former 2km Royal National Park branch of State Rail.

Adult all-day tickets cover the museum and unlimited tram rides, with discounts for seniors and school children. For details phone ☎ 02-9542 3646.

ZigZag Railway, Lithgow [see Map 1, p171]

Vintage railmotors and trains hauled by steam locos like ex-QR BB18 class or by DH diesels, operate on 7.5km of the historic Blue Mountains former zigzag route, one of the engineering wonders of the 19th century, now converted to 1067mm gauge.

The service operates throughout the year (except on Christmas Day) from around 09.00 to 18.00. The full return trip from Bottom Points to Clarence takes 1½ to 2 hours and costs $18. ZigZag is a request stop on the regular Sydney–Lithgow interurban services (C 9014 and local). The 11.35 train from Sydney Central is the recommended connection. For further details phone ☎ 02-

6353 1795, 🖷 02-6353 1801 or for recorded information ☎ 02-6351 4826. Check the website 💻 www.zigzagrailway.com.au or 💻 zzroffice@pnc.com.au.

Lithgow is conveniently near ZigZag for a nightstop, with budget hotels like ***Lithgow Hotel*** (☎ 02-6351 3379) a few metres from the station. There is also the 3.5-star ***Zig Zag Motel*** (☎ 02-6352 2477) on Bell's line of road, near the railway.

VICTORIA

Ballarat Vintage Tramway [see Map 27, p199]

Ballarat Vintage Tramway (☎ 03-5334 1580), 1.3km through Botanic Gardens, is part of Ballarat's original tramway system which opened in 1887 and closed in 1971. The tramway is open from around noon on Saturdays, Sundays and holidays and can be reached by bus No 15 from Post Office Corner near the railway station, itself a historic monument. Ballarat is 119km from Melbourne Spencer St and is reached by a fairly frequent V/Line train service taking about 90 minutes (C 9024).

Puffing Billy Railway, Belgrave [see Map 30, p207]

The Puffing Billy Preservation Society (☎ 03-9754 6800, 🖷 03-9754 2513, 💻 info@pbr.org.au, www.puffingbilly.com.au), part of a statutory body known as the Emerald Tourist Railway Board, operates this narrow-gauge (762mm or 2ft 6in) branch of the former Victorian Railways (VR) system.

The pioneer and best known of Australia's preserved railways, it was extended in 1998 deep into the Dandenong Ranges to the original terminus at Gembrook, 24km from Belgrave. Mostly operated by steam, such as a 2-6-2 Prairie Tank, and manned by volunteers, trains run at least twice daily except on Christmas Day. The adult return fare Belgrave–Gembrook (around five hours) is $39.

Shorter trips may be made, eg to Menzies Creek, where the Society has a steam museum, to Emerald or to Lakeside at Emerald Lake Park (around three hours). Luncheon trains operate every day (except Christmas Day), while a night train with licensed dining cars is available on most Friday and Saturday evenings or for special charter.

Access is by frequent suburban train from Flinders St, or stations on the City Loop, Melbourne, to Belgrave, 60 to 70 minutes (C 9024), Information leaflets are available at Spencer St station and Belgrave. ***Ranges Hotel*** (☎ 03-5968 1220), opposite the station in Gembrook, is convenient for an overnight stay or a lunch break.

Bellarine Peninsula Railway, Queenscliffe–Drysdale

The 16km remnant of the former Geelong–Queenscliffe branch is reached by frequent trains from Melbourne to Geelong (60 minutes, C 9024, 9028 and local). The railway operates return services on Sundays and public holidays with additional days during school holiday periods.

For detailed timings, current fares and other details including bus connections from Geelong, phone ☎ 03-5258 2069 or 03-5351 3725.

Bendigo trams

The trams go through the city centre, within walking distance of Bendigo station, passing historic buildings, the old tram depot and Central Deborah gold mine. The service runs from 10.00 daily except Christmas Day; a travelling restaurant tram may operate at weekends. For further details phone ☎ 03-5443 8117. Bendigo is 162km from Melbourne and is served by regular V/Line trains (C 9032).

Victorian Goldfields Railway [see Map 29, p205]

This railway (formerly Castlemaine and Maldon Railway) runs on Sundays, Wednesdays and most holidays, except during total fire bans, on 8km of the former Victorian Railways branch. Maldon station is a National Trust listed building and the town itself is subject to special preservation policies.

For details phone ☎ 03-5475 2966 on operating days, or ☎ 03-5475 1451 at other times, email 💻 cmr@vgr.com.au or visit the website: 💻 www.vgr.com.au. Castlemaine, 16km from Maldon and 125km from Melbourne on the Bendigo line (C 9032), is the nearest station to Maldon; there is a very limited bus service but there are plans to extend the service to link with the main line at Castlemaine.

Central Highlands Tourist Railway (Daylesford Country Spa Railway)

Ex-VR vintage railmotors operate approximately hourly every Sunday except Christmas Day from 10.00 to 14.45 on a partly-restored 1600mm-gauge branch line between Daylesford and Musk or Bullarto.

On Saturday evenings once monthly the Silver Steak champagne train is an added attraction. For further details phone ☎ 03-5348 5475 or 03-5348 1759, or look at the website (💻 www.chtr.org.au). Daylesford railway station in Raglan St is 125km from Melbourne, reached by V/Line train and bus, changing at Woodend (C 9032 and V/Line local timetable), a two-hour journey overall.

There is no bus service on Sunday until the evening, so prospective travellers on this railway must stay overnight on Saturday in Daylesford if relying on public transport.

South Gippsland Railway, Korumburra [see Map 30, p207]

This railway operates diesel railcars from South Australia and railmotors ex-Victorian Railways, as well as loco-hauled heritage carriages, on a 38km section of the twice-closed South Gippsland line between Nyora and Leongatha. Normally operating every Sunday, with extra days in December, January and during school holidays, all trains have refreshments, but no alcohol. Evening trips may include a 'sausage sizzle' and charter trips may be arranged.

Current timetables and fares are obtainable from major V/Line stations in the Gippsland area, such as Traralgon, or by phoning ☎ 03-5658 1111, 🖹 03-5658 1511 or freecall ☎ 1800 630 704. The website is 💻 www.sgr.org.au. Korumburra station, the main base of the railway, is just over an hour's journey by V/Line coach from Dandenong east of Melbourne (C 9024, 9030, 9098), though the service necessitates an overnight stay in South Gippsland.

The Vintage Train

Based at Newport Workshops (not a museum), Melbourne, Steamrail Victoria operates heritage steam-, diesel- and electric-hauled day and overnight train tours throughout Victoria. Steamrail has the largest collection of operational heritage locomotives and rolling stock in Victoria, dating back to the 19th century. For further information phone ☎ 03-9397 1953, or visit 💻 www.steamrail.com.au.

Yarra Valley Tourist Railway

The Society, of volunteers, is currently running Trolley Trains from Healesville through the historic tunnel to Tarrawarra Winery. Other sections of the track are being restored to enable trolleys and, later, steam trains, to run to Yarra Glen and in the longer term, Lilydale, current terminus of the Melbourne Met system; phone ☎ 03-5962 2490, or look at the website 💻 www.yarravalleyrailway.org.au for further details. The railway can be reached by frequent suburban electric trains from Melbourne to Lilydale (a 55-minute journey, C 9024), thence by private bus to Healesville (32 minutes).

Walhalla Goldfields Railway

Once a thriving gold-mining town, Walhalla is 44km north of Moe in Gippsland and two hours' drive east from Melbourne. Even though the railway cannot be reached by public transport mention must be made of the 42km narrow-gauge (762mm) line between Moe and Walhalla through spectacular mountain scenery which was operated by Victorian Railways between 1910 and 1954.

Closed and pulled up in 1956, it has been progressively restored since 1993 by an enthusiast group, the Walhalla Goldfields Railway Inc. At that time, little remained other than derelict bridges but operations commenced with the restoration of Thomson station and yard, and in March 2002 the line was reopened from Thomson to Walhalla, 4km, on which services run mainly at weekends. Adult return fare is $15. For recorded information phone ☎ 03-9513 3969 or check the website 💻 www.comu.net.au\wgr.

QUEENSLAND

Ballyhooley Express, Port Douglas, north Queensland

A commuter service of period carriages hauled by a 12-tonne diesel loco on 3km of the narrow-gauge (610mm) Mossman Central Mill sugar-cane line between Marina Mirage station and St Crispin's in Port Douglas; a 15-minute journey including two intermediate stops with five departures each day; booking is not required.

For further details phone the mill at ☎ 07-4098 1400. Coral Coaches operates a regular bus service between Cairns, Mossman (1 hour 20 minutes) and Port Douglas (1 hour 50 minutes).

Beaudesert Rail

In O'Reilly's Guest House up on the Lamington Plateau on the Queensland /NSW border (see p150) a poem by James McGrath, *The Wild Beaudesert*

Train, recalls one which, from 1885 to 1996, carried passengers, livestock, timber and just about anything else between Brisbane Melbourne St (now South Brisbane) and Beaudesert, gateway to the plateau in the early days.

At the time of writing Beaudesert Rail operated steam-hauled excursions of heritage carriages at weekends on the southern 32km of the line between Logan Village and Beaudesert. Return fares were $20 for adults, with reductions for children and pensioners. However, just before going to print all services were suspended though it seemed probably only temporarily. For an update on the situation phone ☎ 07-5541 0000 or visit the website 💻 www.beaudesertrail.com.au.

Big Pineapple Railway, Nambour

A miniature rail circuit of pineapple plantations, built on the lines of sugar-cane railways. The railway features a steep climb on a reverse curve and is situated 6.4km south of Nambour on the Bruce Highway, 10 minutes by local bus from Nambour railway station.

For a stopover here, try ***Commercial Hotel*** (☎ 07 544 1114, 69 Drayton St) across the main street near the station for motel units at budget price. Nambour is 100 minutes by electric train from Brisbane, with an average of 12 trains a day each way (C 9011 and local).

The Moreton Central Sugar Mill, until its closure in 2003, operated cane trains. The lines can still be seen crossing the main street south of the station.

Brisbane Tramway Museum, Ferny Grove [see map p148]

This is an operating electric tramway and museum (☎ 07-3351 1776), 500m from the railway station on Brisbane suburban electric line and 25 minutes from Central station.

The museum is open on Sundays from 12.30 to 16.00 and admission costs $10 for adults, with concessions for pensioners and children.

The Workshops Rail Museum, Ipswich [see map p149]

Open daily from 09.30 to 17.00 except Christmas and Anzac Day, the Workshops Rail Museum is a unique heritage attraction, combining a rail museum with the only Australian rail workshop from the 1860s still operating. A walking tour of two or more hours offers a fascinating insight into the bygone era of steam and much more.

As well as an extensive collection of heritage items, there are working locomotives, a blacksmiths' shop, an extensive model railway layout, videos, special features for children and interactive computer simulations. It's a working world of steam and sound, advertised as 'BIG-LOUD-FUN', where QR's heritage fleet of steam locomotives undergo restoration. There is a choice of conducted tours or you can wander around at leisure: the admission price varies from $16 for an adult ($9/child) up to $30 for the 'First Class Pass' which includes a barbecue lunch at the heritage-listed Workers' Canteen.

For further details phone ☎ 07-3432 5100 or email 💻 info@theworkshops.qm.qld.gov.au. Trains to Ipswich operate at least half-hourly from Roma St and Westside buses run from opposite Ipswich station on Bell St.

❑ **Table 14: Brisbane/Cairns to Proserpine and Shute Harbour (C 9010)**

Brisbane to Proserpine/Shute Harbour

		Sunlander	Tilt Train	Tilt Train	Sunlander	Sunlander
		Tu,Th,Sa,Su	Mo,We,Fr	We,Fr,Su	Tue,Sat	Mon,Thu
Brisbane (Roma St)	dep	08.55	18.25	–	–	–
Rockhampton	dep	18.15	02.15a	–	–	–
Cairns	dep	–	–	08.15	08.35	–
Townsville	dep	–	–	14.35	15.55	15.55
Proserpine	arr	03.52a	09.06a	18.05	20.05	20.05
		coach	coach	coach	coach	coach
		Mo,We,Fr,Su	Tu,Th,Sa	We,Fr,Su	Tue,Sat	Mon,Thu
Proserpine	dep	04.00	09.15	18.15	20.15	20.15
Shute Harbour	arr	04.45	10.00	19.00	21.00	21.00

Shute Harbour/Proserpine to Brisbane

		Mon,Thu	Wed,Sun	Tu,Th,Sa	We,Fr,Su	Mo,Tu,Th,Sa
Shute Harbour	dep	02.35	02.35	07.40	16.30	18.30
Proserpine	arr	03.10	03.10	08.15	17.15	19.15
		Sunlander	Sunlander	Tilt Train	Tilt Train	Sunlander
Proserpine	dep	03.57	03.57	09.11	18.10	20.10
Townsville	arr	08.20	08.20	12.50	–	–
Cairns	arr	16.00	–	19.20	–	–
Rockhampton	arr	–	–	–	01.25a	04.40a
Brisbane (Roma St)	arr	–	–	–	09.10a	15.55a

Notes: a: next day

- All trains carry refreshments
- Proserpine–Shute Harbour adult fare $8.80 if bought in conjunction with a rail ticket

Brampton Island Railway/Hayman Island Resort

This line runs from the jetty to the resort on Brampton Island, reached by launch from Mackay, but the railway station is somewhat distant from the jetty. There is a similar railway at Hayman Island Resort in the Whitsunday Islands near Proserpine, which is perhaps more accessible, involving a 45-minute Trainlink bus ride from Proserpine station to Shute Harbour, followed by a short sea crossing. Proserpine Mill, close to the station is a major centre for Queensland cane-train activity. For reasonably-priced accommodation in Proserpine, the ***Grand Central Hotel*** (☎ 07-4945 1021), ***Metropole*** (☎ 07-4945 1167) and ***Prince of Wales Hotel*** ☎ 07-4945 1912) are all in Main St. Table 14 (above) shows the connections at Proserpine from Brisbane and Cairns.

Callemondah Yard, Gladstone [see Map 41, p229]

Gladstone is full of railway interest, both in the layout of the tracks through, around and behind the town, in the variety of trains you will encounter, and in the almost constant activity.

At Callemondah Yard, 5km north of Gladstone station, is a vast complex of sidings, where electric and diesel locos are assigned their respective tasks. From Callemondah, the catenaries reach north and west to Emerald and, via the Bowen Basin coalfields, to Hay Point on the coast; also south to Brisbane, while diesel-operated routes strike inland to the mines of the Callide and Dawson valleys.

Gladstone is worth a break of journey for the enthusiast but much may be observed merely passing through. The Sunlander and other long-distance trains pass Gladstone but the best viewing is in daylight on the all-electric Tilt Train (C 9010).

Dreamworld, Coomera [see map p149]

On the Pacific Highway, west of Gold Coast city, the Dreamworld complex includes a 3km railway at 610mm-gauge with ex-Canefield locomotives. Local buses meet QR Citytrain's Gold Coast expresses at Coomera Station. The trains take one hour from Brisbane and run hourly from early morning till nearly midnight (half hourly on Saturdays and Sundays). Dreamworld is open daily except Christmas Day. Admission to the park includes other features and shows.

Durandur Railway and Museum, Woodford

A 610mm-gauge railway which operates on the first and third Sundays of a month on 1.2km of the former Wamuran–Kilcoy branch at Woodford, 24km west of Caboolture. Caboolture is 50 minutes by a half-hourly service from Central station, Brisbane, on the regular Citytrain network, but a taxi or hired car may be needed from there. Phone ☎ 07-3278 9110 or visit 💻 www.angrms.org.au for further information.

Dee River Railway, Mount Morgan

What might have been the slowest passenger train in the world (Thangool–Rockhampton, 178km at an overall mean speed of 11.25km/h) ran on this line in central Queensland until the mid-1980s. Among the few still operational remnants of the former Callide Valley branch of QR from Kabra Junction to Thangool is the ARHS Mount Morgan Railway and Tourist Information Centre, with 3.5km of railway between historic Mount Morgan and Cattle Creek siding. Four bridges and a tunnel, plus Mount Morgan's imposing railway station building, are features of the route. The complex is open daily and trains operate from 10.00 on Saturdays and Sundays, with group specials on request. For more details phone ☎ 07-4938 2312.

Mount Morgan can be reached by Young's bus service from Rockhampton, 38km to the north-east.

The Gulflander, Savannahlander and Kuranda Scenic Railway

These are a 'must' for every rail enthusiast, not to mention the everyday tourist, and are covered on p53, pp86-8, pp250-1 and pp251-3).

Mary Valley Heritage Railway, Gympie [see Map 40, p228]

Steam-hauled trains, the Valley Rattler, run every Sunday and Wednesday, from Gympie's historic old station to Kandanga (29.5km) and Imbil (39.6km) on the former Brooloo line in the Mary Valley. The line descends through Gympie suburbs to Monkland, where the track once joined the QR main north coast line, which it parallels for a short distance. The timetable allows a good lunch break at Imbil, and a local wine and cheese tasting at Dagun on the way back.

The ***Railway Hotel*** (☎ 07-5484 5202) at Imbil is directly opposite the station and offers an extensive menu including a smorgasbord at tempting prices. Accommodation is also available.

The adult return train fare is $29.50. There is the additional option of half-day return trips on Saturdays, morning and afternoon, but only as far as Dagun (20.17km) and Amamoor (23.18km). For further details, phone ☎ 07-5482 2750, email 💻 rattler@mvhr.org.au or visit the website 💻 www.thevalleyrattler.com. Gympie old station, home of the Rattler, contains a historic model railway, 'Elliotville', which is open daily. It is reached by QR courtesy bus connecting with interurban and Traveltrains at Gympie North but timetables favour a Gympie nightstop: the ***Railway Hotel***, with budget accommodation, is opposite the old station and other hotels are in the town centre.

The Mulgrave Rambler, Gordonvale

Often operated only as a charter train or by excursions advertised locally, this cane line was the most accessible of all since the station, which can still be seen, immediately adjoins QR's Gordonvale station, 22km south of Cairns and a regular stop for the Sunlander. Hauled by the Nelson, a restored Fowler 0-4-2 oil-fired steam loco, the train followed a route past canefields, river and rainforest to Orchid Valley where tropical plants, entertainment and refreshments were among the attractions.

The Mill management has abandoned the Rambler activity and sold off the carriages since the previous edition of this book so unless some other body such as Tourism Tropical North Queensland takes an interest this delightful tourist experience will remain history.

RAILCo, Ravenshoe [see Map 45, p234]

The Ravenshoe–Atherton Insteam Locomotion Company Ltd (☎/📠 07-4097 6005 or email 💻 railco@cyberwizards.com.au), to give it its full title, operates a weekend and holiday service between Ravenshoe and Queensland's highest railway station at Tumoulin, 965m above sea level. This is the southern 7km of the former QR Atherton Tablelands branch from Mareeba.

The train departs Ravenshoe station at 13.30, for a 1½-hour trip, adult fare $15, family $30. The company also operates Section Car journeys over the 12km between Herberton station and Carrington Falls. The route includes a 7km climb at 1 in 33 through the ranges. For Section Car bookings phone ☎ 07-4096 2124. Herberton and Ravenshoe were until recently accessible from Cairns or Kuranda by coach, but at the time of writing this service had been withdrawn and private car hire may be the only access to the Atherton tableland. Mareeba remains accessible by the Savannahlander railcar.

Rockhampton

Rockhampton, 630km and seven hours by train from Brisbane, is the northern limit of the QR electrified mainline, and terminus of the daily Intercity Tilt Train service, a place of great interest to rail enthusiasts (C 9010).

Most long-distance trains stop at least 20 minutes in Rockhampton (the Cairns Tilt only 10 minutes), where there can be time to explore the station environs. Just beyond the station, the railway goes along the middle of a public street before swinging north across the river. Near the station is the original roundhouse, built in 1915 with a central turntable serving 52 locomotive bays, and other historic buildings.

If changing trains or staying overnight a visit to the Central District Train Control Centre at Rocky (always learn what the locals call it) is a must, but you would have to ask permission. See Rockhampton's station master and tell him you've heard so much about it you want to tell your people back home. As they say, flattery will get you everywhere.

Other Rockhampton railway attractions include the Archer Park Railway Museum and Rockhampton Steam Tramway.

Rosewood Railway [see map p149]

The Rosewood Railway operated by ARHS has, since the last edition of this Guide, extended its services on the remnant of the former QR Marburg branch by re-opening 2.35km of line from Perry's Nob south to Museum Junction, a new station barely 400m from Rosewood Citytrain station. Formerly, this historic route was accessibly only at Cabanda, reached by car or a 4km walk from Rosewood. A gap of 750 metres between Perry's Nob and Cabanda remains to be restored, which the society hopes to achieve in the medium term if authorities co-operate.

On the last Sunday of each month, ex-QR railcars leave Museum Junction hourly from 09.40 to 14.40 for Perry's Nob, where a free bus takes only a few minutes to Cabanda, where more passengers (who have come by road) join the steam-hauled trains which leave every hour from 10.15 to 15.15. Eleven minutes are allowed for the last twisting 1.6km to Kunkala, a station to be proud of, with more facilities than many a larger station on QR main lines. A souvenir shop, clean toilets, refreshments and picnic tables are among its facilities. The museum, with all these facilities and an outstanding collection of railway vehicles and equipment, is open every Sunday.

The return services (last Sunday of the month only) leave Kunkala hourly from 10.39 to 16.39 and Perry's Nob from 10.10 to 15.10. Advance booking is usually unnecessary. Return fares for either section are $8, or for both $14 with half price for children, and include entry to the museum. Trains may be run at other times, by special request or on special occasions. Contact the ARHS on ☎ 07-3252 1759 or visit the website 💻 www.arhs-qld.org.au.

Rosewood is 18 minutes from Ipswich, 80 minutes from Brisbane, by hourly electric Citytrain (C 9013).

Buderim Ginger Factory, Yandina

[see map p148]

There is a 1km loop railway of 610mm-gauge at this factory, about 200m walk from the station. A day-return trip from Brisbane is only just possible. It allows less than 40 minutes at Yandina on weekdays, over three hours on Sunday, and 2½ hours on a Saturday evening. Otherwise, it is worth staying a night: ***Yandina Hotel*** (☎ 07-5446 7341) provides pub-style accommodation and adjoins the station. If time is limited, Noosa Heads Trainlink bus services (covered by Translink but not by rail passes) connect with at least four additional local train services daily each way at Nambour. Journeys using these connections, some involving rail bus between there and Caboolture, take up to an hour (or more) longer than by direct train.

Table 15 below summarizes the Yandina train services.

Sunshine Express

Sunshine Express is the name of a monthly magazine published by ARHS Queensland Division, and also of frequent rail tours organized by the society, which also runs Winelander tours to Queensland's Granite Belt south of Toowoomba and operates both the 'Iron Road Restaurant' evening steam train tours around Brisbane suburbs and the Rosewood Railway Museum (see opposite).

Tours by steam- or diesel-hauled trains or railcars are run over many lines no longer served by regular passenger trains, eg to places like Wandoan, Kingaroy, Biloela and as far afield as Cunnamulla. These are advertised by leaflets displayed or obtainable at major suburban stations, or by calling ☎ 07-3252 1759 between 10.00 and 15.00 on Tuesdays, Wednesdays or Thursdays. Tours vary in duration from evening or day trips to week-long excursions including overnight stops at motels en route. Prices vary from as little as $20 to over $1000.

❑ **Table 15**

Brisbane–Yandina (local)

		Mon-Fri	Sun	Sat	Mon-Fri	Sun
Brisbane	dep	10.58	11.24	17.25	17.30	17.36
Caboolture	dep	11.49	12.16	18.16	—	18.28
Nambour	dep	12.44	13.24	19.15	19.22	19.27
Yandina	arr	12.55	13.33	19.26	19.31	19.36

Yandina–Brisbane (local)

		Mon-Fri	Sun	Sat	Sat	Mon-Fri
Yandina	dep	13.33	16.53	21.59	06.52	06.53
Nambour	arr	13.41	17.02	22.09	07.01	07.02
Caboolture	arr	14.40	18.14	23.08	07.58	08.01
Brisbane	arr	15.40	19.02	23.59	08.50	08.52

Notes: Brisbane times are at Roma St but all trains call at Central.

Yaraka branch, Hughenden to Winton and Kingaroy branch, QR [see Map 51, p245, and Map 53, p248]

The Yaraka branch is one of only three in Queensland on which, until a few years ago, scheduled goods trains still carried 'passenger accommodation', at least notionally; the others being the Kingaroy branch and the Hughenden–Winton line. The Yaraka branch extends for 271km from Jericho on the midland route from Rockhampton. Just under halfway along from Jericho is Blackall, where shearer Jackie Howe hand-sheared 321 sheep in one day. Also at Blackall is the 'Black Stump' in the grounds of the state school: the only problem being that almost every state in Australia claims its own black stump. But Blackall does have a 225-million-year-old fossil tree stump in Shamrock St.

Hughenden to Winton is 212km, while Kingaroy is 131km from Theebine, itself 34km from Gympie North, the nearest regular passenger station on the North Coast line. Although these branches commence at mainline junctions, connections in the normal sense of the word are usually non-existent; departure and arrival times tending to be at unattractive hours.

Thomas Cook's *Overseas Timetable* listed trains on two of these branches until 2002. The Winton–Hughenden branch was particularly useful as a connecting link between Midland and Northern routes; a grey-painted crew van would be attached to the weekly freight, an almost unique feature which attracted rail enthusiasts world-wide. But not only might the train not run to time (or at all); it might not carry such accommodation. Trains tend to run only according to customer requirements and current QR policy is to restrict passengers to QR employees. You would not want to get off the comfortable *Spirit of the Outback* only to find the weekly Yaraka 'mixed' not running, or that you were not allowed on. Enthusiasts should therefore enquire from the appropriate district headquarters of Queensland Rail or the stationmaster's office at Emerald (☎ 07-4983 8351) before contemplating travel on such lines, and complain about it if refused.

Railways concerned about passenger patronage should realize the importance of enthusiast interest, which has kept many lines going worldwide. Special excursions may be advertised from time to time on such routes (see under 'Sunshine Express' above), but these are expensive, covering accommodation as well as travel.

SOUTH AUSTRALIA

National Railway Museum, Port Dock

The Port Dock Station Railway Museum is 10 minutes' walk (or a short bus ride) from Port Adelaide station. The precinct, designated as the First State Heritage Area, offers a 'walk through history' with the Museum at its centre. It houses an outstanding collection of locomotives and rolling stock. Trains operate around the site, including on sections of the unique triple-gauge track which were a feature of the triple-gauge station yards formerly in use at Peterborough, Gladstone and Port Pirie (see pp178-9).

For further details contact the Manager, Port Dock Station, PO Box 3153, Port Adelaide SA 5015 or phone ☎ 08-8341 1690.

St Kilda Tramway Museum

A museum and 2km operating tram track to the seafront, which is best reached by taxi from Salisbury station on the suburban system (Gawler line, C 9031). The museum is open from 13.00 to 17.00 on Sundays and most public holidays.

Glenelg Tramway **[see map p155]**

A frequent and daily service on the 11km former private railway from central Adelaide (Victoria Square, 600m or Bee-line bus from City station) to the seaside suburb of Glenelg.

To avoid the walk or local bus, take a local TransAdelaide Belair or Noarlunga train from City station or from Keswick suburban station to Goodwood, near to which the tram route intersects the railway route (C 9031).

Pichi Richi Railway, Quorn

Narrow gauge (1067mm), mostly steam, (including a steam motor coach, the Coffee Pot), this was part of the original Great Northern Railway intended to link Port Augusta with Darwin. It was at Quorn that the Great Northern Express to Oodnadatta was first nicknamed the Afghan Express, later shortened to become the legendary Ghan.

Historic trains consisting of former SAR or Commonwealth Railway heritage vehicles, steam or diesel hauled, and vintage railcars run on various sections of the line between Port Augusta and Quorn on various dates between March and November. The *Afghan Express* runs most Saturdays between April and October from Port Augusta. There is also the *Transcontinental*, the *Pichi Richi Explorer*, and a Barwell Bull railcar and trailer which runs between Quorn and Woolshed Flat (16.5km). In December, special dinner trains run from Port Augusta. For other details including fares or bookings write to the Society (Railway station, Railway Terrace, PO Box 111, Quorn, SA 5433), phone (☎ 1800 440 101, or L J (Bill) Hart on ☎ 08-8276 6232) or use the Internet: the Society's website is 💻 www.prr.org.au or email 💻 bookings@prr.org.au.

Quorn is accessible from Port Augusta, a major stop on the route of the Indian Pacific and The Ghan (C 9033/4). Stateliner buses operate three days a week (Sundays, Wednesdays and Fridays, returning Sundays, Thursdays and Fridays, a 40-minute journey, C 9427) but overnight stays in both Port Augusta and Quorn would usually need to be taken into account by those wishing to travel on the railway.

SteamRanger Heritage Railways, Goolwa (C 9022) **[see Map 25, p197]**

The SteamRanger depot which formerly adjoined Dry Creek station on the Adelaide suburban network had to be relocated in 1996 following standardization of the Adelaide–Melbourne line. The new depot is at Mount Barker, 5.2km from Mount Barker Junction.

The SteamRanger Tourist Railway (1600mm), run by ARHS South Australian Division, now operates over 82km of former South Australian

Railway track between Mount Barker Junction, Mount Barker, Goolwa and Victor Harbor. A variety of services are available, almost always on Sundays but also on many other days. The services include: the Highlander from historic Mount Barker station to Strathalbyn and back; the Southern Encounter between Mount Barker and Victor Harbor via Goolwa and Port Elliot; the Cockle Train between Goolwa and Victor Harbor (over a line first opened in 1854); the Winelander from Mount Barker to Gilberts siding where a coach takes passengers on a visit to Currency Creek Estate Winery; and the Junction Jogger, which covers the northern part of the route between Mount Barker and the junction with the main Adelaide–Melbourne line where, unfortunately, trains no longer stop.

Trains are mostly hauled by historic steam locos but diesel may be used, particularly during days of total fire ban, or services may consist of one of Adelaide's historic 'Red Hen' railcars. A buffet car is usually attached to the main services, but alcohol and smoking are not permitted on the trains.

At Goolwa, once an important inland port, a boat trip on the lower reaches of the Murray may be offered and at Victor Harbor there is a horse-drawn tram ride to Granite Island on Encounter Bay.

For details of fares, travel times, etc and bookings phone ☎ 1300 655 991 or, on running days, ☎ 08-8552 2782 or 8555 2691. The steamranger website is 💻 www.steamranger.org.au, email either 💻 info@steamranger.org.au or, for bookings, 💻 bookings@steamranger.org.au. or write to PO Box 960, Mount Barker, SA 5251. The only public transport access to Mount Barker is by TransAdelaide buses from Adelaide via Aldgate, Bridgewater and historic Hahndorf (C 9031). These run several times daily; single fare is $5.

Steamtown, Peterborough [see Map 6, p177]

Excursions were operated over the southern 57km of the Peterborough–Quorn 1067mm railway until insurance companies imposed intolerable and unreasonable burdens on such enterprises. Now all that remains is a museum, open normally on weekdays between 08.30 and 16.30. Guides are available at weekends. For further details phone ☎ 08-8651 3355.

The triple-gauge roundhouse at Peterborough is National Trust classified and a short section of triple-gauge track is still used by the museum. Peterborough is a conditional stop on the Indian Pacific.

WESTERN AUSTRALIA

Bassendean Rail Transport Museum [see map, p159]

Bassendean Rail Transport Museum (☎ 08-9279 7189), 136 Railway Parade, is an ARHS railway museum which is 400m north of Ashfield station, on Perth's suburban system (Midland line, local timetable). It is open on Sundays and public holidays from 13.00 to 17.00.

(Opposite) Top: The Rattler (Mary Valley Heritage Railway, see p266) at Dagun where passengers have time to sample local produce including wine and cheese. **Bottom:** Stoking the boiler on the Rattler.

GYMPIE
45
CLASS
C 17

Bennett Brook Railway [see map, p159]

Bennett Brook Railway (☎ 08-9249 3861) is 8km north of Perth, a 5.7km long 610mm-gauge loop line through bushland, linking items of railway interest in Whiteman Park. It operates all weekends and holidays between 11.00 and 16.00 or 17.00. The **Whiteman Park Tramway Museum**, including a 4km standard-gauge electric tramway operational on Thursdays to Sundays and holidays, is part of the park complex. Access is by taxi from Guildford station on the Transperth suburban system (Midland line C 9037 and local).

Boyanup Transport Museum [see Map 24, p195]

Home of the historic steam locomotive, the *Leschenault Lady* and other relics. Steam and diesel trains operate on the 17km, 1067mm-gauge Boyanup–Capel branch line. Boyanup station is 18km from Bunbury; access is by Transwa coach from Bunbury station or Brunswick Junction, both served by the Australind service from Perth. Boyanup is halfway between Bunbury and Donnybrook on the Western Highway (C 9036); phone ☎ 08-9731 5250 for further information.

Golden Mile Railway, Boulder

A narrow-gauge (1067 mm) loop line, linking Boulder, Golden Gate and Trafalgar. For details phone (mobile phone) ☎ 0407 387 883, or enquire at Kalgoorlie–Boulder Tourist Bureau (☎ 08-9021 1966). Kalgoorlie is on the Sydney–Perth TransAustralian rail route served by both the Indian Pacific and the Prospector from Perth (655km). The Goldenlines bus service operates between Kalgoorlie and Boulder (5km) daily except Sunday.

Hotham Valley Tourist Railway and Etmilyn Forest Railway [see Map 24, p195]

Dwellingup Forest Ranger and Steam Ranger trains operate into the Darling Range on the 24km Pinjarra–Dwellingup line between May and late October. Forest Ranger trains depart Perth City and Pinjarra stations on Sundays and Steam Ranger trains depart Pinjarra at 11.00 on Wednesdays, with connections from Transwa's Australind (C 9036).

Etmilyn Forest Railway operates from Dwellingup on Tuesdays, Wednesdays, Thursdays and weekends including public holidays and daily during school holidays. Restaurant trains are available on Friday and Saturday nights. Hotham Valley Tourist Railway also operates steam and diesel excursions on other routes within Western Australia. For further details and bookings phone ☎ 08-9221 4444, visit the website: 🖳 www.hothamvalleyrailway.com.au, or email 🖳 info@hothamvalleyrailway.com.au.

Oliver Hill Railway, Rottnest Island

A re-built military railway links the Settlement at Kingstown to the Oliver Hill gun batteries. Four trains run daily; the adult fare includes a tour of the gun

(Opposite) Workshops Rail Museum, Ipswich (see p264) **Top:** The Blacksmith Shop. **Bottom:** The Powerhouse, dating from 1904.

emplacements. For more information phone ☎ 08-9372 9752. Rottnest Island is in the Indian Ocean 20km off the coast, accessible by ferry from Perth and Fremantle and by airbus.

NORTHERN TERRITORY

The Old Ghan [see Map 11, p183]

The Ghan Preservation Society formerly operated a service over 26km from MacDonnell Siding, Alice Springs, to Ewaninga Sidings on the original Marree–Alice Springs narrow-gauge line, but, like so many others, insurance costs have led to its demise. There is still a museum at MacDonnell Siding, open 09.00 to 17.00 daily, admission $5.50.

For further details phone the society on ☎ 08-8955 5047, or the Northern Territory Tourist Commission on ☎ 133 068. Alice Wanderer (see p183) bus services from the town centre call at the siding regularly during the day.

Katherine Railway Station Museum

A short walk from the Ghan Raillink BP stop in the town centre is one of the oldest buildings in Katherine, the preserved railway station. Owned by the National Trust, this houses memorabilia from the former North Australia Railway closed in 1976. An old black 2-6-0 locomotive stands on the track outside, which extends south across the preserved railway bridge over the Katherine River, and which originally continued to Birdum, 502km from Darwin. Phone ☎ 08-8981 2848 or 8972 2650 for further details.

Adelaide River Railway Heritage Precinct

The original station at Adelaide River is well preserved and has long been visible from the adjoining highway. Now it is passed closely on the left by the northbound Ghan, which crosses west of the highway earlier, but Adelaide River is unfortunately not a stopping place on the new railway.

TASMANIA

There are no mainline passenger services in Tasmania; so access to any private or preserved railways has to be by other forms of transport. TT Line shipping services cross the Bass Strait from Melbourne to Devonport, and TWT coaches link Devonport with most of the places where preserved railways remain. Full information on those described here and others is found on 💻 www.railtasmania.com/pres/group/php.

The **Tasmanian Transport Museum** at Glenorchy (☎ 03-6272 7721), reached by northern suburbs bus from Hobart is a good starting point, being another source of information on Tasmanian heritage railways generally. Short rides at weekends operate over 0.5km of the former Launceston–Hobart main line. Some 30km north-west of Glenorchy, at New Norfolk, the **Derwent Valley Railway** operates steam excursions to Mt Field National Park or Plenty on alternate Sundays. Details are published in Hobart's paper *The Mercury*, or phone ☎ 03-6261 1946.

The old railway workshops at Launceston are preserved, while near Devonport the Van Dieman Light Railway Society Inc operates the **Don River Railway**, a 4km, 1067mm-gauge branch which was closed in 1963 and restored in 1971. Trains run alongside Don River to Coles Beach, 3.5km west of Devonport. Diesel units are used on weekdays, with steam-hauled vintage trains on Sundays and public holidays. There is also a museum open daily. On selected dates, special trains venture onto the mainline system. For further details contact the Don Museum (☎ 03-6424 6335, ☎ www.donriverrailway.com.au).

Some 22km to the south at Sheffield, the **Redwater Creek Steam & Heritage Society**, formed in 1993, is developing a steam rail and heritage museum, with tourist trains running on 4km of the long-abandoned Roland Branch line to Redwater Creek, to be linked eventually to Railton and via the former TGR main line from there to Devonport. For information on progress contact the society by fax (🖹 03-6491 1613) or email ☎ vivmart@bigpond.com.au.

In Tasmania's rugged south-west, the **West Coast Pioneers Memorial Museum** (☎ 03-6471 6225) in the main street of Zeehan contains relics and memorabilia from the former complex rail and tramway network of the area while at Tullah, near Strahan, the **Wee Georgie Wood Steam Railway** operates on Sundays over 1.6km of a former 610mm gauge tramway (for details phone Strahan Visitor Centre ☎ 03-6471 7622).

Last but far from least, the unique historic and dramatic **West Coast Wilderness Railway** through the rugged gorge of King River between Strahan and Queenstown (C 9517), which was closed in 1963 after 67 years serving the mines of Mount Lyell, has been recently restored and re-opened as a tourist attraction. The 32.8km route extends from the restored original station of Regatta Point beside the old quays of Macquarie Harbour through rainforest along the King River, past the once thriving but now derelict old town of Teepookana, where the original iron bridge has been restored to its former glory. Trains are diesel hauled between Strahan and Dubbil Barril, start of the uphill, 1 in 20 gradient, rack section to the summit station of Rinadeena. Here one can watch trains from a high bridge over the cutting, visit the original mine built by Cornish miners in the 1890s, or relax at the Paddymelon Tearooms. The rack section descends at 1 in 16 to Halls Creek. The line then follows the banks of Queen River to the magnificent Queenstown Central Station, the largest in Tasmania with facilities worthy of a mainline terminal on the mainland. The Abt steam locomotives, which haul the trains over the rack sections and into Queenstown, were imported from Scotland in 1895. They are capable of climbing gradients as steep as 1 in 5.

Fares on the Wilderness railway are not cheap, but modest in proportion to the cost of getting there and well worth it. The Tasman Limited no longer links Hobart and Launceston with Burnie, where the Emu Bay Railway's mixed service formerly ran south to the wilderness region. However, scheduled coach services of Tassielink (☎ 03-6272 7300) connect Queenstown with Hobart, Launceston and the Bass Strait ferry terminal at Devonport (C 9062, 9520). For enquiries and bookings phone Strahan Activity Centre ☎ 03-6471 1700 (Freecall within Australia ☎ 1800 628 288).

Envoi

Perhaps you lose yourself somewhere in the heart of Australia, in the bush, in the vast emptiness of the Nullarbor, the lush greenery of the tropical rainforest, the sun and surf of Australia's miles of golden beaches or the bustling brashness of the major cities. Maybe you are just caught up with the excitement of a party, the 'footy', the fever of the Melbourne Cup when all Australia stands still, or you succumb to the rich variety of food, from witchetty grub soup to mud crab, from king prawns to barbecued Western beef steak, or you are busy 'looking at' (as the wine buffs say) the fine Australian wines – the golden yellow of Coonawarra Chardonnay or the rich ruby purple of the Hunter Valley reds with, what is described as, the flavour of a well-worn saddle (it may not sound very appealing until you taste it). Or you are enchanted by the wildlife, the myriad of brightly-coloured birds, the possums and the wallabies, not to mention the crocodiles and snakes which are best seen from a protected position.

You may even just be taken by the people, the friendliness, mateship and trusting attitude you meet in so many places, especially in small towns and in the bush, or when travelling, or in a pub. Even in major cities a person can buy a drink at the bar and leave the change on the counter while attending to a call of nature or some other matter. That pile of change, reserved for the next drink, will remain untouched. To violate it would provoke outrage. And in a pub, especially in the outback and in provincial towns, you will hear stories in abundance, tall tales and true ones – the latter often the strangest. Too true, mate, don't you worry about that!

You could even be listening to our radio programmes, such as the ABC's 'Australia all Over', on which you will hear similar stories of the outback and ballads of the bush, or tales of trains, old and new.

For whatever reason, or for none you can put a finger on, some places will make you want to linger, will draw you back, and if you go there by rail in the first place you can probably go there again. You can see much of the country and feel its spirit without ever going far from a railway or spending much more time out of a train than it takes to wait for the next one – but remember that this may not be until the following day, or week!

So have a good trip, stay a while, and come again. See ya!

APPENDIX A: FLEXIPASS DEADLINES

This table shows the minimum number of days of **Austrail Flexipass** usage needed to return to your port of departure from places mentioned in this book that can be reached using a Flexipass. The figures given are on the basis that the train journey is the quickest possible, using the most immediate connections between one train and another where a change is required. But, be warned, **do not assume** that this minimum applies to starting your homeward journey at any time on any day of the week, or that the trip will take the same number of **calendar days**.

For example, suppose you are in Canberra and that you are booked to leave Australia from Cairns Airport on a Monday. The table shows three flexidays of rail travel as the minimum required. You might therefore decide to leave Canberra by train on Friday to reach Cairns on Sunday, the day before your departure. Between Canberra and Cairns you need to change trains first at Sydney or Strathfield, then at Brisbane. On a Friday there are two Sydney departures from Canberra, at 06.37 and at 12.05, the latter needing a change at Strathfield. Either will get you to Brisbane by 06.35 the next day, Saturday. But there is no Cairns train from Brisbane on Saturday, so you must wait for the Sunlander the next day. This does not reach Cairns until Monday at 16.00 and you have probably missed your plane home. To be in Cairns before Monday, you would need to leave Canberra no later than by the 06.37 train on Thursday. This would have you in Cairns by 19.20 on Saturday, taking the Friday Tilt Train from Brisbane – still only three flexidays used up but with an extra calendar day in Cairns (and an extra fare to travel business class on the Tilt!). On the other hand, should you think of leaving Canberra on an evening train, which departs at 17.07 on Tuesday, Thursday, Saturday and Sunday, your quickest journey to Cairns would take four flexidays; one to Sydney, another to Brisbane, then two more (25 or 31 hours) from Brisbane to Cairns.

The following table is therefore merely a guide. It is **essential** to check actual times and days in every case, but especially if the expiry date of your pass is close to the calendar end of your stay, because the calendar days needed may exceed the 'flexipass' days in extreme cases by **over a week**.

This may sound incredible but suppose you have been exploring outback Queensland, based on Mount Isa where you arrived on the Sunday train from Townsville. Not wishing to go back on the same train a few hours after arriving, since you want to visit the mine and places of interest in the region, you opt for the Friday Inlander to start your journey back to Darwin, your port of entry to and departure from Australia. The table shows you need a minimum of seven flexidays to get there, so you start off on the Inlander, connecting in Townsville with Saturday's southbound Sunlander to Brisbane, arriving on Sunday; two flexidays' travel spread over three calendar days. You then catch the Monday XPT to Sydney, but the next train west is not until Wednesday, and you reach Adelaide on the Thursday, another two flexidays but four more days real time. The Friday Ghan only goes to Alice Springs, so you have to wait till Sunday for the Darwin Ghan, arriving Tuesday. Two more flexidays, but your total calendar travelling time, from Friday until Tuesday over a week later, amounts to 12 days, to which the three days before you leave Mount Isa have to be added.

NOTE: The minimum flexidays shown in this table refer only to journeys covered by the Austrail Flexipass, and to travel by train except where a quicker connection may be made using Countrylink buses for links such as Brisbane–Casino, Canberra–Cootamundra or Blayney–Cootamundra, or where the starting place is itself only reached using coach services contracted by Countrylink or QR Traveltrain, such as Cowra, Cunnamulla, Byron Bay and Surfers Paradise.

Minimum flexidays travel to port of departure in Australia

From: / To:	Brisbane	Cairns	Darwin	Melbourne	Perth	Sydney
Adelaide	2	3	2	1	2	1
Albury	1	3	4	1	3	1
Alice Springs	3	5	2	2	3	2
Almaden	3	1	8	5	7	4
Alpha	1	2	6	3	5	2
Ararat	2	3	4	1	3	1
Armidale	1	3	5	2	4	1
Ayr	1	1	6	3	5	2
Babinda	1	1	6	3	5	2
Barcaldine	1	2	6	3	5	2
Bathurst	1	3	3	1	3	1
Benalla	2	3	4	1	3	1
Berry	1	3	4	1	4	1
Blackwater	1	2	6	3	5	2
Blayney	1	3	3	1	3	1
Bowral	1	3	4	1	4	1
Brisbane	–	2	5	2	4	1
Broadmeadow	1	2	4	1	4	1
Broken Hill	2	3	3	2	3	1
Bundaberg	1	1	5	2	4	1
Bundanoon	1	3	4	1	4	1
Byron Bay	1	3	5	2	4	1
Cairns	2	–	7	4	6	3
Canberra	1	3	4	1	4	1
Casino	1	2	5	1	4	1
Charleville	1	3	6	3	5	2
Charters Towers	2	3	7	4	6	3
Cloncurry	2	3	7	4	6	3
Coffs Harbour	1	2	5	1	4	1
Condobolin	2	3	3	1	3	1
Cook	3	4	3	2	1	2
Coonamia	3	4	2	1	2	2
Cooroy	1	1	5	2	4	1
Cootamundra	1	3	4	1	3	1
Cowra	2	3	5	1	3	1
Culcairn	1	3	4	1	3	1
Cunnamulla	1	3	6	3	5	2
Darwin	4	6	–	3	4	3
Dubbo	2	3	4	1	3	1
Dungog	1	2	4	1	4	1
Emerald	1	2	6	3	5	2
Forsayth	4	2	9	6	8	5
Geelong N Shore	2	3	4	1	3	1
Geurie	2	3	4	1	3	1
Giru	1	1	6	3	5	2
Gladstone	1	1	5	2	4	1
Gloucester	1	2	5	1	4	1
Gosford	1	2	4	1	3	1
Goulburn	1	3	4	1	4	1

From:	To: Brisbane	Cairns	Darwin	Melbourne	Perth	Sydney
Grafton	1	2	5	1	4	1
Griffith	2	3	4	1	4	1
Gympie North	1	1	5	2	4	1
Hamilton	1	2	4	1	4	1
Henty	1	3	4	1	3	1
Home Hill	1	1	6	3	5	2
Horsham	2	3	4	1	3	1
Hughenden	2	3	7	4	6	3
Ilfracombe	1	2	6	3	5	2
Ingham	1	1	6	3	5	2
Innisfail	1	1	6	3	5	2
Julia Creek	2	3	7	4	6	3
Junee	1	3	4	1	3	1
Kalgoorlie	4	5	4	2	1	3
Katherine	4	6	1	3	4	3
Katoomba	1	3	4	1	3	1
Kuranda	3	1	8	5	7	4
Lismore	1	3	5	2	4	1
Lithgow	1	3	3	1	3	1
Longreach	1	2	6	3	5	2
Mackay	1	1	6	3	5	2
Maitland	1	2	4	1	4	1
Mareeba	3	1	8	5	7	4
Maryborough West	1	1	5	2	4	1
Melbourne	2	3	3	–	3	1
Miriam Vale	1	1	5	2	4	1
Moree	1	3	5	2	4	1
Moss Vale	1	3	4	1	4	1
Mount Isa	2	3	7	4	6	3
Mount Larcom	1	1	5	2	4	1
Mount Surprise	3	1	8	5	7	4
Murray Bridge	2	3	4	1	3	1
Muswellbrook	1	3	4	1	4	1
Nambour	1	1	5	2	4	1
Newcastle	1	2	4	1	4	1
Nowra	1	3	4	1	4	1
Orange	2	3	3	1	3	1
Parkes	2	3	3	1	3	1
Perth	4	5	4	3	–	3
Port Augusta	3	4	2	1	2	2
Port Kembla	1	3	4	1	4	1
Proserpine	1	1	6	3	5	2
Queanbeyan	1	3	4	1	4	1
Quilpie	1	3	6	3	5	2
Richmond	2	3	7	4	6	3
Rockhampton	1	1	5	2	4	1
Singleton	1	3	4	1	4	1
Strathfield	1	2	4	1	3	1
Surfers Paradise	1	3	5	2	4	1
Sydney	1	2	4	1	3	–

From:	To: Brisbane	Cairns	Darwin	Melbourne	Perth	Sydney
Tamworth	1	3	5	2	4	1
Tarcoola	3	4	2	2	2	2
Taree	1	2	5	1	4	1
Townsville	1	1	6	3	5	2
Tully	1	1	6	3	5	2
Wagga Wagga	1	3	4	1	3	1
Wangaratta	2	3	4	1	3	1
Wellington	2	3	4	1	3	1
Werris Creek	1	3	5	2	4	1
Winton	2	2	6	3	5	2
Wollongong	1	3	4	1	3	1

APPENDIX B: BIBLIOGRAPHY

General guidebooks have already been mentioned (see p10). There are more detailed guides for specific areas, eg the Thomas Cook Travellers series: *Sydney and New South Wales*. Lonely Planet has guides covering *New South Wales and Australian Capital Territory*, *Victoria*, *Queensland*, *South Australia*, *Western Australia*, *Northern Territory*, *Outback Australia* and *Tasmania*. Jasons' Accommodation Guides contain useful city maps.

There is also a map folder recently published by Hema Maps entitled *Rail Journeys of Australia* which has every railway shown on a detailed cartographic base at 1 to 5,500,000 scale (1cm represents 55km). It also contains information on heritage railways, railway museums and miniature railways. Other suggestions for further reading are:

GENERAL

Blainey, Geoffrey *The Tyranny of Distance*, Sun Books, Melbourne 1966
Culotta, Nino *They're a Weird Mob*, Ure-Smith, Sydney, 1957
Gilbert, Kevin *Because a White Man'll Never Do It*, Angus & Robertson, 1973
Hughes, Robert *The Fatal Shore*, Pan Books, London, 1988
Keesing, Nancy (Ed) *History of the Australian Gold Rushes*, Angus & Robertson, Australian Classics Edition, 1971.
Krauth, Nigel *Matilda my Darling* Allen & Unwin, Sydney, 1983
McNamara, Ian *Australia All Over*, ABC Enterprises, Sydney, 1992
Maris, Hyllus and Borg, Sonia *Women of the Sun*, Penguin Books Australia Ltd, 1985
Neidje, Bill *Story about Feeling*, Magabala Books, Broome, WA, 1989
Readers Digest *Book of Australian Facts*, Latest Edition

RAIL TRAVEL

Berry, Scyld *Train to Julia Creek, A Journey to the Heart of Australia*, Hodder & Stoughton, London, 1985
Bromby, Robin (Ed) *Australian Rail Companion*, Sherbrooke Sutherland, Sydney, 1989
Clow, Margaret *The Mecca of Our Desires: Kuranda and the Famous Barron Falls* (reprint of original edition of 1914), Ray Langford, Atherton, Queensland, 2003
Dennis, Anthony and Rayner, Michael *Ticket to Ride: A Rail Journey Around Australia* Simon & Schuster, Australia, 1989

Kennedy, Ludovic *A Book of Railway Journeys, An Anthology*, Great Britain, Fontana/Collins, 1981
Taylor, Colin *Great Rail Non-Journeys of Australia*, University of Queensland Press, Brisbane, 1986
Taylor, Colin *Traincatcher* IPL Books, Wellington, NZ, 1996
Whitelock, Derek *Gone on The Ghan (and other great railway journeys of Australia)* Savvas Publishing, Adelaide, 1986

AUSTRALIAN RAILWAY HISTORY AND SPECIALIST BOOKS

Adam Smith, Patsy *When we Rode the Rails*, J M Dent, Melbourne, 1983
Belbin, Phil and Burke, David *Changing Trains*, North Ryde, Methuen, Australia, 1982
Bromby, Robin *The Country Railway in Australia* Cromarty Press, Sydney, 1983
Bromby, Robin *Rails to the Top End*, Cromarty Press, Sydney, 1987
Churchman, Geoffrey B *Railway Electrification in Australia and New Zealand*, IPL Books, Sydney & Wellington, 1995
Daddow, Viv *The Puffing Pioneers and Queensland's Railway Builders*, University of Queensland Press, Brisbane, 1975
Ellis, R F *Rails to the Tableland*, ARHS, Brisbane, 1976
Fischer, Tim, *Transcontinental Train Odyssey: The Ghan, The Khyber, The Globe*, Allen & Unwin, Crows Nest, NSW, 2004
Gunn, John *Along Parallel lines, A History of the Railways of New South Wales 1850-1986*, Melbourne University Press, 1989
Kerr, John *Triumph of Narrow Gauge, A History of Queensland Railways* Boolarong Publications, Brisbane, 1990

APPENDIX C: AUSTRALIAN ENGLISH

Some expressions which are common in Strine (Australian English) may be unfamiliar to the visitor. More commonly-used examples are:

arvo	afternoon
barbie	barbecue
bathers	swimming costume (especially in Victoria and Tasmania)
bewdy	excellent! well done!
black stump	fabled remains of a tree marking the farthest outback
blue	fierce argument, fight, bad mistake
bushranger	highwayman, bandit
chips (bag of)	packet of potato crisps
chunder	vomit
coldie	can or stubbie of cold beer
counter lunch	pub meal served at the bar
crook	sick, ill, off-colour
daks	trousers
doona	duvet
dunny	toilet (originally outside as in bush dwellings)
esky	portable ice-box
go bush	leave civilization
hoon	dangerously foolish young person
lollies	sweets, candies
Pom	English person
road house	outback transport café-cum-pub, sometimes with accommodation
sanger	sandwich
see ya (later)	goodbye
she'll be right	don't worry
snags	sausages
strides	trousers
stubbie	375ml bottle of beer

stubbies shorts (trouser)
sunnies sunglasses
the bush outback, woodland, remote country and by extension the population of such areas
thongs sandals held loosely on feet usually by rubber strips between the second and the big toe and over the sides, as with English flip-flops
tinnie aluminium fishing boat; also a can or stubbie of cold beer
togs see bathers
troppo foolish, affected by the heat
tucker food
ute small motor truck, a car with an open tray back
witchetty grub an edible wood-boring caterpillar
Woop Woop any unnamed remote outback town (derogatory)
wowser person who disapproves of drink, dancing, fun
wowserism having a wowser attitude
yakka manual work

APPENDIX D: GLOSSARY OF RAILWAY TERMS

12-chain curve a curve of 241m radius. Railway people still use chains when describing curve radii just as nautical people use knots for wind and vessel speeds rather than km/h.
broad gauge rail line of greater than standard gauge (qv)
catenaries the wires carrying power on an electrified railway
combined gauge rail line of three or more rails combining two or more different gauges
consist (as a noun) the composition or make-up of a train
DMU (diesel multiple unit) trainset of diesel-powered carriages which may be coupled to others of the same kind
eight-coupled (steam locomotives) locomotive with eight driving wheels (four axles)
EMU (electric multiple unit) similar to DMU (qv) but electric-powered
HST High Speed Train (British Rail)
Irish gauge 1600mm (5ft 3in) between rails
mixed train train consisting of passenger coaches and goods vans or wagons
motive power depot glorified large-scale engine shed
narrow gauge railway line of less than standard gauge (qv)
rake a string of carriages or other vehicles forming the trailing part of a train (ie other than the locomotive or power unit)
reverse curve compound left/right curve in the track
roundhouse large engine shed with a turntable in the middle
standard gauge railway line 1435mm (4ft 8½in) between rails
TGV Train à grande Vitesse – the French high-speed trains
through train a train which goes from an origin or to a destination which is beyond or off the normal route of services on a particular line; similarly 'through carriage' and 'through service'.
Tilt train a train with bodywork designed to lean right or left when going round curves
token small container enclosing authority to proceed on single-track section
trainset a train (usually passenger) of fixed consist (qv)
triple gauge rail track consisting of four rails combining three different gauges ie 1067mm, 1435mm and 1600mm
XPT the express passenger train of New South Wales based on the British InterCity 125 high-speed train

APPENDIX E: BUS/RAIL CONNECTIONS

IN NEW SOUTH WALES (operated for Countrylink unless otherwise stated)

- Narrandera and Griffith from **Wagga Wagga** (C 9112)
- Gundagai and Tumut from **Cootamundra** (C 9111 and local)
- Griffith, Hay and Mildura (Vic) from **Cootamundra** (C 9111)
- Tocumwal and Echuca (Vic) from **Albury** (C 9394)
- Cooma and Bombola from **Canberra** (C 9120 and local)
- Thredbo (for Mt Blue Cow) from **Canberra – private bus service** (C 9099)
- Mudgee from **Lithgow** (C 9088)
- Nyngan, Cobar, and Bourke from **Dubbo** (C 9097 and local)
- Cowra from **Bathurst, Blayney and Cootamundra** (C 9109)
- Forbes from **Parkes** (C 9109)
- Oberon from **Mount Victoria** (local)
- Cooma, Bega and Eden from **Canberra** (local)
- Glen Innes and Tenterfield from **Armidale** (local)

In addition, railway buses provide potentially useful cross-country links between some of the railway routes, as follows:

- Cootamundra (Main South line) to Condobolin (Western mainline) (C 9111)
- Cootamundra to Orange and Bathurst (Western mainline) (C 9109)
- Dubbo (Central west line) to Parkes and Broken Hill (Western main line) (C 9109, 9020)
- Cootamundra to Canberra (local)
- Wagga Wagga (Main South line) to Griffith (C 9112)
- Grafton City (North Coast mainline) to Moree (North-west) (C 9094)

IN VICTORIA (operated by V/Line passenger unless otherwise stated)

- Echuca from **Bendigo** (C 9076)
- Lakes Entrance and Orbost from **Bairnsdale** (Gippsland line) (C 9412)
- Robinvale and Euston (NSW), and Mildura from **Swan Hill** (C 9110 & local)
- Maryborough from **Castlemaine** (V/Line local timetable)
- Daylesford from **Woodend** (Bendigo line) and **Ballarat** (V/Line local timetable)
- Korrumburra and Leongatha from **Dandenong** (C 9098)
- Stawell, Horsham and Dimboola from **Ararat** (C 9401, 9413)
- Hamilton from **Ballarat** and **Warrnambool** (V/Line local)
- Port Fairy, Portland and Mount Gambier (South Australia) from **Warrnambool** (C 9415)

V/Line rail-operated coaches provide useful links between some rail routes:

- Bairnsdale to Canberra (C 9412) **Not available for V/Line Victoria pass**
- Echuca to Murchison East (Goulburn Valley) (C 9421 and local)
- Benalla (NE interstate line) to Shepparton (Goulburn Valley) (C 9421)
- Echuca to Murchison East (Goulburn Valley) (V/Line local timetable)
- Ballarat (Western line) to Camperdown and Warrnambool (V/Line local timetable)
- Ballarat to Geelong (C 9119)
- Ballarat to Castlemaine (Bendigo line) (C 9411)
- Bendigo (Northern line) to Shepparton (Goulburn Valley) (C 9395)

IN QUEENSLAND

The buses are private, but mostly operated by McCafferty's, a Toowoomba-based company with an office in Roma St Transit Centre, Brisbane.

- A bus runs daily between Barcaldine (Midland line) and Mitchell (Western line) via Blackall (Yaraka branch) at 17.20 to reach Mitchell at 00.15, returning at 02.00 to arrive in Barcaldine at 09.00 (C 9073).

- Buses leave Cloncurry (Mount Isa line) daily for Winton and Longreach (Midland line) at 08.35, Winton 14.00 and arriving in Longreach at 16.00. The return service from Longreach is at 10.15, Winton 12.55, arriving in Cloncurry at 17.35 (C 9073).
- There are indirect coach links between Mount Isa (Queensland) and Alice Springs and Tennant Creek (route of The Ghan) by McCafferty's services. The timetables are as follows (C 9075, 9428):

McCafferty coach service 480 leaves from Mount Isa at 19.45, arriving at Tennant Creek at 03.00, connecting with service 883 at 03.35, reaching Alice Springs at 09.30.

Returning, McCafferty coach 881 departs Alice Springs daily at 15.30 with a quick connection in Tennant Creek, arr 22.25, dep 22.30 on service 483 to reach Mount Isa at 06.15 the next day. On Mondays and Thursdays the Inlander arrives at Mount Isa in good time for the coach departure, and the coach arriving at Mount Isa on Monday or Friday allows a train connection for Townsville that day. Rail departures from Alice Springs to Adelaide are at 12.45 on Thursday and 14.00 on Saturday, and from Tennant Creek there is a Darwin departure at 23.21 on a Monday. Twenty hours in Tennant Creek from 03.00 to nearly midnight might understandably not appeal to the average traveller, but that's the way it is!

- Previous editions of this book have given details of bus/rail connections in Queensland's Gulf Country. Coral Coaches and other private services in this area are no more (except north from Cairns to Mossman and Cape York). Until some other operator moves in, there are no coach connections between Cloncurry and Normanton, Croydon and Forsayth, or Mount Surprise and Atherton.

INDEX

mus = museum
rlwy = railway